Contents

Swindon College

Foreword

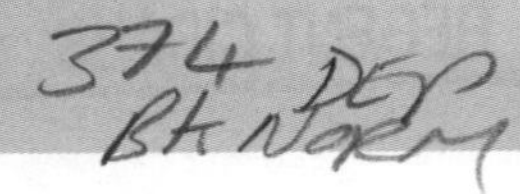

Learning to succeed

In June 1999 the Government published the White Paper *Learning to Succeed – a new framework for post-16 learning*. This built on the Green Paper *The Learning Age*, which set out how lifelong learning can enable people to develop their potential, so providing a workforce equipped with the skills and knowledge that our economy needs as we enter the next millennium. *Learning to Succeed* only applies to England – the implications for the rest of the UK are outlined at the end of this foreword.

Learning to Succeed proposes changes which aim to streamline the way education and training is delivered throughout England. Some of these changes, which are planned for implementation over the coming two years, will directly affect the education and training opportunities described in *Second Chances*.

The main proposals which are relevant to users of *Second Chances*

A national Learning and Skills Council

A **national Learning and Skills Council** is to be established from April 2001, to take responsibility for the planning and provision of post-16 education and training in England (excluding higher education).

The responsibilities the Council will take over include the following which are of particular relevance to users of *Second Chances*:

- the funding of further education colleges (from the FEFC)
- the funding of Modern Apprenticeships and other Government-funded training and workforce development (from the TECs)
- the funding of and, in partnership with LEAs, the development of arrangements for adult and community learning
- funding and providing information, advice and guidance to adults
- advising the Government on National Learning Targets, including those for adults.

Local Learning and Skills Councils

The national Learning and Skills Council will work through a network of between 40 and 50 **local Learning and Skills Councils**, which will plan and co-ordinate local post-16 education and training provision. They will work closely with local Learning Partnerships.

The responsibilities of the local Learning and Skills Councils will include:

- raising the standards and ensuring the quality of local post-16 education and training provision
- ensuring that provision matches local learning and skills needs
- focusing local provision more closely on customers' needs, eg by opening up colleges or training centres in the evenings and all year round, if this meets a local demand
- providing fair and accurate information on the range of opportunities in their area
- providing objective assessments of the quality of provision.

It is proposed that the boundaries of the new local Learning and Skills Councils should coincide with those of other key organisations, such as local authorities, Government Offices etc, and contain a resident population of at least half a million. The areas covered will not necessarily be identical to those covered by the present local TECs. Decisions about boundaries will be made in Autumn 1999.

Key date: April 2001

From April 2001, the proposed changes may particularly affect the provision of education and training for adults described in the following chapters.

Chapter 5 *Sources of information, advice and guidance* – responsibility for planning and funding adult information, advice and guidance will transfer to the Learning and Skills Council.

Chapter 6 *A brief introduction to education and training* – the Learning and Skills Council will take over many funding responsibilities from TECs and the FEFC. Provision of Work-based Learning for Adults will become the responsibility of the Employment Service.

Chapter 9 *Further and adult education* – funding for further education will be taken over by the Learning and Skills Council, and responsibility for the provision of local adult and community education will also be taken over by the local Learning and Skills Councils, working together with LEAs.

Chapter 19 *Work-based Learning for Adults and other government-funded training* – responsibility for Work-based Learning for Adults will transfer from TECs to the Employment Service.

Chapter 23 *Training for self-employment* – will no longer be the responsibility of the TECs.

While responsibility for funding, and overall responsibility for planning, co-ordination and ensuring quality standards, of adult education and training is to be transferred from existing organisations by April 2001, there may not be a sudden dramatic change in local provision. Therefore, this edition of *Second Chances* remains a useful guide to available provision, even for those adults now considering learning opportunities immediately beyond 2000. However, as the new organisations assume their new functions and implement their own plans, these will start to be reflected in changes to local provision at grass-roots level.

The Gazetteer – some information will no longer be relevant, eg TECs will no longer exist.

It is important that advisers keep themselves informed of local developments as they arise, in order to supplement the information provided in *Second Chances*, as necessary.

Learning to Succeed – the implications for Scotland, Wales and Northern Ireland

Scotland: as highlighted in *Second Chances*, the education and training system in Scotland is very different from England. In February 1998, the Government accepted the Garrick Committee's recommendation that there should be two separate funding councils in Scotland, one for further education and one for higher education, and The Scottish Further Education Funding Council (SFEFC) was established on 1 January 1999. A Consultation Paper *Opportunities and Choices* was published in March 1999, to stimulate ideas and encourage debate about post-school provision for 16-18 year olds in Scotland.

Wales: the arrangements for post-16 education and training are currently similar to those in England. In March 1999, the Education and Training Group for Wales (ETAG) published its report *An Education and Training Action Plan for Wales*. This will be submitted for consideration to the National Assembly for Wales.

Northern Ireland: arrangements are very different from England: The Training and Employment Agency is responsible for vocational training, and further education is funded directly through the Department of Education Northern Ireland. Northern Ireland ministers have recently announced the outcome of a strategy review, *Strategy 2010*, following earlier proposals for taking forward lifelong learning in Northern Ireland. Consequently, a Northern Ireland Skills Task Force has been established and a Consultation Paper on further and higher education has been published.

In time, the future shape of post-16 learning in Scotland, Wales and Northern Ireland will become clearer, as the various governing authorities further develop their ideas and arrangements. Until specific proposals are made and pass into law, you can assume that the information in *Second Chances* relating to these areas of the UK is still valid.

Section 1 General information

1. Introduction

***Second Chances* is a reference source for:**

- staff working with agencies or organisations involved in providing information, advice and guidance to adults about education and training opportunities
- adults wishing to research for themselves information about education and training opportunities.

Main features of *Second Chances*

- The information covers the whole range of learning opportunities, from basic skills through to postgraduate-level opportunities.
- It covers information relevant to adults aged 19 and over, whatever their background or employment status, including those considering returning to learning or employment, retired people, adults with special needs, or those who have recently arrived from overseas.
- It is designed as a useful reference both for less experienced front-line information staff as well as for more experienced adult guidance advisers.
- Sources of further information and advice are provided throughout.

***Second Chances* is divided into four sections:**

- **Starting points** – sets the scene: introducing the concept of lifelong learning, and providing pointers for those assisting potential new learners. It also summarises sources of information, advice and guidance for adult clients.
- **General information** – provides the background information that most learners need to know, including a detailed look at finance for education and training, and information about the qualifications available across the UK.
- **How and where to learn** – information on the range of learning opportunities.
- **Specialist information for particular groups** – includes organisations set up to offer specialist support, information, advice etc.

The Gazetteer lists, by geographical area, organisations involved in providing information, advice and learning opportunities for adults, including local careers services, TECs/LECs, and further and higher education institutions.

Publishers' addresses – full contact details of the publishers most frequently listed at the end of each chapter are provided after The Gazetteer (addresses of other publishers are given alongside the title of the publication).

Accuracy: the information provided in *Second Chances* was accurate at the time of publication. However, information changes quickly, so you should always check with the contact sources provided. An updated version of *Second Chances* is available on the DfEE's website: www.dfee.gov.uk

Using *Second Chances* – routefinder

As a supplement to the contents list and indexes, the brief guide below offers one approach to finding the most appropriate chapters in Section 3.

While the routefinder provides some starting points, it may not be suitable for every query. For particular clients, other chapters are also likely to be relevant. Clients who fall into one of the groups listed in Section 4 should also consult the relevant chapter in that section.

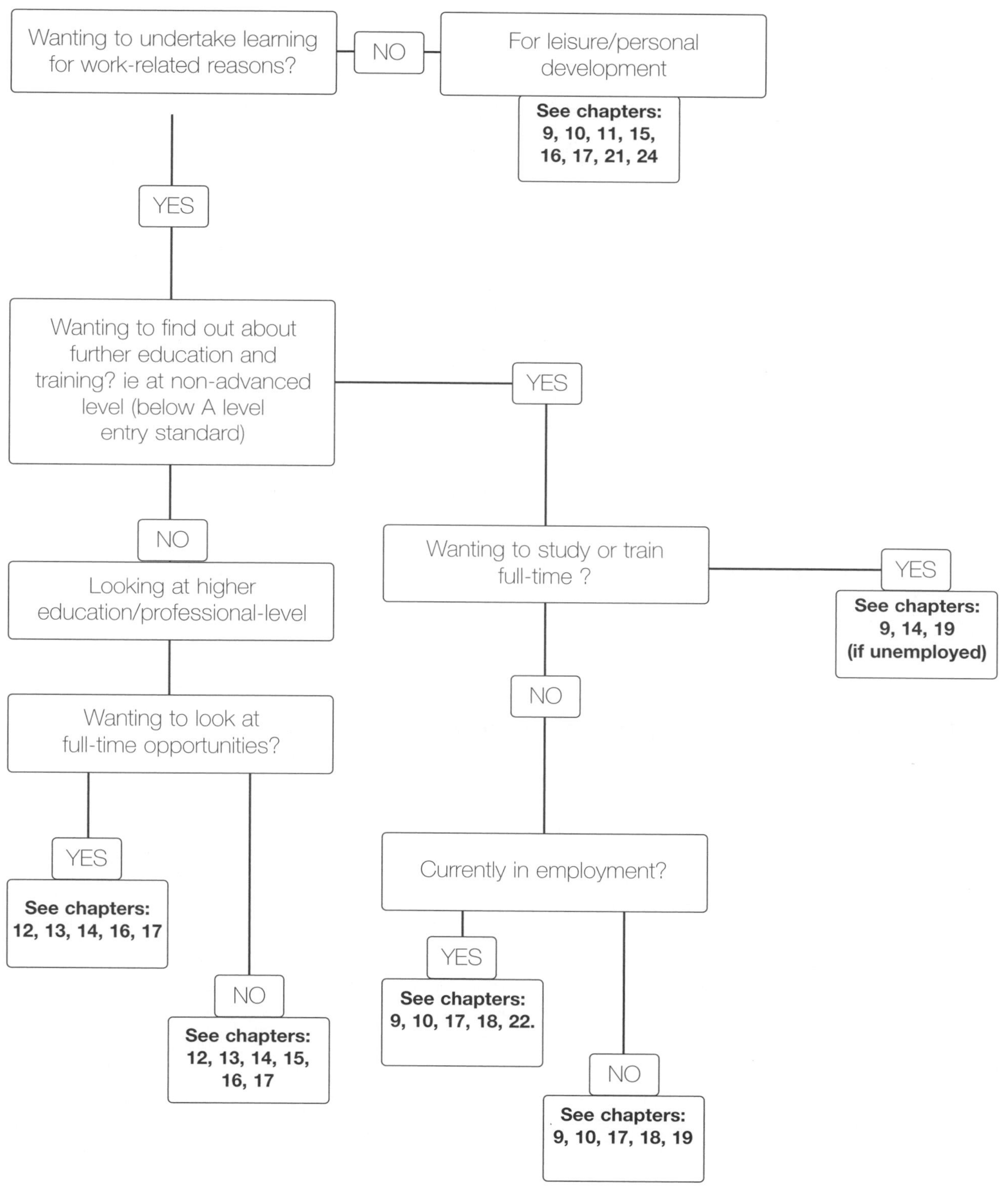

2. Lifelong learning

This chapter covers:

- the importance of lifelong learning
- national initiatives to encourage participation in learning
- checkpoints for advising potential learners.

'Lifelong learning can enable people to play a full part in developing their talent, the potential of their family and the capacity of the community in which they live and work.'
The Secretary of State, in the foreword to the Government White Paper, *Learning to Succeed*, published in June 1999.

The Government, through various initiatives, is committed to the concept of 'lifelong learning' – that it is important for everyone, regardless of their age or employment status, to continue with learning throughout their lives.

Some of the reasons that make lifelong learning important:

- 'Jobs for life' are a thing of the past. People are likely to change jobs many times during their working lives. They will therefore continually need to learn new skills and new ways of working.
- Skills and qualifications are increasingly in demand. The proportion of unskilled and semi-skilled jobs is decreasing, a trend set to continue well into the new millennium. Those who have not kept their skills up to date will be disadvantaged.
- The ever-increasing pace of change in information and communications technology is having a huge impact on the way organisations operate, and on the skills that individual employees need.
- Employees with the right skills will be valued by employers. Skilled employees help to improve productivity and profitability – crucial to the success of our economy.

Initiatives to encourage participation in learning

A range of initiatives are being brought in to help adults to access appropriate learning opportunities, and to help ensure that the skill and qualification levels of the population are raised. These include:

- **Learning Direct** – the national telephone helpline which provides callers, free of charge, with information about appropriate learning opportunities. It can also provide information about funding, childcare provision, and local guidance provision. Tel: 0800 100 900 – lines are open from 9am to 9pm Monday to Friday, and 9am to 12 noon on Saturdays.
- **Ufl – University for Industry concept** – opening for business in 2000, the Ufl will provide access to suitable learning opportunities, so that people both in and out of the workplace can update their skills and learn new ones. The Ufl will endorse opportunities that offer high quality learning programmes, and commission new learning programmes to fill the gaps. There will be an emphasis on developing basic skills and learning opportunities that make use of information and communication technologies. The first sectors to be covered will be automotive components, multimedia, environmental technology and retailing. The Ufl will be accessed through the Learning Direct helpline.

- **Local Adult Information and Advice Services** – the aim is to ensure that a local information and advice service of reliable quality is available to adult learners and potential learners throughout England. Delivery of these services is the responsibility of local Learning Partnerships, which draw together a wide range of local organisations including local authorities, careers services, employers and voluntary and community organisations. These services are being pioneered, in 1999/2000, by six pathfinder partnerships: Kent and Medway; North West London; Manchester; Salford, Tameside and Trafford; North Nottinghamshire; Sandwell; York and North Yorkshire. The programme will be extended nationwide in 2000/2001.

- **Individual learning accounts** – an initiative to encourage people to plan for and invest in their own learning. For the first million accounts opened, the government will contribute £150 (through TECs), and account holders have to contribute an initial £25. The contact point for information is the local TEC. More information can be found in leaflets, and on the DfEE website: ntweb1/ukll/ukll/ila/index.htm.

- **National Learning Targets** have been set by the government, for 2002. This includes the Learning Participation Target: a 7% reduction of non-learners among the adult population aged 16-69 (for England; other areas have their own targets).

- **Lifelong Learning Partnerships** are being established throughout England to improve the planning and coherence of local post-16 learning. They will include further education colleges, careers services, local authorities and schools. As part of their remit, Lifelong Learning Partnerships will develop local targets linked to the National Learning Targets, and establish frameworks for new student support arrangements in further education. A Partnership Fund of £25 million is available over the next three years to help development of the Partnerships.

Learners should also look out for:

Adult Learners' week – each year there is a special national focus on opportunities to learn, with local input, called Adult Learners' Week. It is usually in May. For information about the week and local events, contact: NIACE – The National Organisation for Adult Learning, 21 De Montfort Street, Leicester LE1 7GE. Tel: 0116 255 1451.

Media initiatives – eg through the BBC, who periodically run programmes to encourage adults to consider learning opportunities such as learning IT, with helpline backup, providing information and other resources.

Checkpoints for advisers

You can encourage individual clients to enter learning, by helping them to realise the potential benefits and by helping them to overcome any perceived barriers and difficulties. Here are a few of the ways advisers can help ensure a successful outcome.

Helping clients to overcome perceived barriers to learning

'It's so long since I've learnt anything....I don't think I could return to it now...'

Many clients have been away from a classroom for a long time, and are apprehensive about returning to learning. They do not always recognise that, in fact, they have never stopped learning, albeit in a different way from formal schooling. Clients can be encouraged to identify all that they have learnt to do, and the knowledge they have acquired, since leaving school. This could be through informal and formal training at work, evening classes, taking positions of responsibility in local clubs or organisations, voluntary or community activities of all kinds, organising social events, managing a home and family budget, their own reading etc.

'I've always been hopeless at exams, so there's no point in doing a course'

People who have not undertaken learning for some time may be unaware that a range of assessment methods are now used besides traditional exams, and that many qualifications can be gained through types of assessment which do not involve exams at all.

Helping clients to be clear about their aims

If clients are clear about their own aims and objectives for learning, it will help them to select an appropriate learning opportunity, therefore reducing their chances of dropping out. Clients' learning objectives may include:

- updating their skills in their existing field of employment
- gaining qualifications for the first time in their existing field of employment, or for a new field
- improving their chances of changing jobs
- improving their chances of gaining promotion
- proving something to themselves, or others
- learning for the personal challenge.

Raising issues about time

Successful learners are realistic about the time commitment necessary, and make good use of their available time. Clients need to research courses carefully, making sure they have accurate information about how much time will be needed, both in formal taught sessions (where applicable) and the time required for their own independent learning. Some people find it useful to work out a personal time management plan.

Allaying fears about study skills and techniques

Fear of failing – because of lack of confidence in the ability to write essays, present assignments etc – may prevent some people from even considering returning to learning. New learners may be unaware of how much help is available for study skills: some courses have study skills incorporated into the course; free-standing study skills courses or workshops may be available; there may be learning support units that the student can take advantage of. The course tutor will be able to provide advice and guidance on this. The publications listed at the end of this chapter also provide useful information.

Helping clients to get started successfully

It may be worth encouraging clients who have been away from study for some time, and are planning a lengthy period of learning, to consider doing some kind of short course beforehand. It could be an evening class, a weekend study course, or an Open University module. This will help to increase the client's confidence as a learner, give them some learning skills, and demonstrate their capabilities to admissions staff for further courses.

Further information

Further information on the topics, initiatives and agencies mentioned in this chapter may be found in local careers centre libraries and public libraries.

There are many resources on studying and learning available, but the following are some that clients may find useful.

The Good Study Guide – by Andrew Northedge, available from the Open University Worldwide, The Berrill Building, Walton Hall, Milton Keynes MK7 6AA. Tel: 01908 858785. Price £8.99. ISBN 0 74920 044 8.

How to Study Effectively and *How to Write Essays*, priced £12 each, as Open Learning Resources from the National Extension College (NEC), 18 Brooklands Avenue, Cambridge CB2 2NH. Tel: 01223 316644.

How to Write Essays – by John Clanchy and Brigid Ballard, published by Addison Wesley Longman, Edinburgh Gate, Harlow CM20 2JE. Tel: 01279 623928. Price £11.99. ISBN 0 73390 3940.

How to Study and Learn – available from bookshops or How To Books. Price £9.99. ISBN 1 85703 435 X.

How to Study – ISBN 0 7494 2351 X, and *How to Win as a Part-time Student* – ISBN 0 7494 1672 6, price £8.99 each. Available from bookshops or Kogan Page.

Lifelong Learning and Higher Education – published by Kogan Page. Price £19.99. ISBN 0 7494 2794 9.

NIACE – The National Organisation for Lifelong Learning – publishes a range of publications on topics related to lifelong learning. Contact NIACE, 21 De Montfort Street, Leicester LE1 7GE, tel: 0116 204 4200, for a copy of their publications catalogue.

National Learning Targets for 2002 – information can be obtained from PO Box 5050, Sherwood Park, Annesley, Nottingham NG15 0DJ. Tel: 0845 60 222 60. E-mail: dfee@prologistics.co.uk
The information is also available on the DfEE website: www.dfee.gov.uk/nlt/targets.htm

3. The labour market

This chapter covers:

- factors that affect the labour market: global factors, new technology and social factors
- future trends and opportunities
- who provides local labour market information
- flexible working practices.

The labour market is the supply and demand of labour, that is, how many jobs are available compared with how many people there are qualified and able to do the work.

To help ensure that the country has a workforce equipped with the skills that industry requires, the Government has set up the Skills Task Force. The Task Force has been asked to help create a National Skills Agenda, with the specific role of advising on the main skills gaps and shortages, current and anticipated, in the labour force in England, and how they can be addressed. To date, the Task Force has produced two reports (listed at the end of this chapter); the final report is due to be published in Spring 2000.

The match of jobs to workers depends upon a number of factors, such as how well the economy is doing nationally, advances in technology, and social trends.

The global economy and political factors

- A large proportion of world trade is carried out by multinational companies. Because of their size they can establish or relocate factories, research and development facilities or head offices wherever the economic climate is favourable.
- Events in the economies of other parts of the world, such as the recent economic difficulties in the Far East, can have an impact in the UK, especially on particular parts of the economy.
- Some companies find that using overseas rather than UK companies for certain operations – perhaps printing services or data processing – can be more economic.
- The way the European single market operates and the single European currency have an effect on the UK economy.

The impact of new technology

Perhaps the largest cause of change at work has been the impact of the new information and communication technologies.

- The scale and speed of developments in information and communication technology have created whole new industries, and new opportunities for people who have developed the necessary skills and knowledge.
- In some sectors of industry and business, new technology has de-skilled jobs or changed them significantly, or has replaced them completely.

- The internet is already having a significant impact on the way that many companies do business. Its effect is expected to continue, as more businesses use it to reach customers and carry out their business operations.

- Jobs at all levels increasingly demand information technology skills; IT skills are designated as one of the 'Key Skills' required by employers in all sectors.

Social trends

The make-up of the workforce, such as the number of people available to work, their age, gender and other relevant social factors, has an effect on the labour market. There have been a number of significant changes over recent years.

- The increased participation of women in the labour market, encouraged by flexible working hours, part-time employment and an increase in jobs in the service sector. The increasing provision of childcare and more employers adopting 'family friendly' working practices are also having an effect.

- More young people are staying on in full-time education, so delaying their entry into the world of work and gaining higher levels of qualifications.

- The workforce is ageing. By 2002, the number of people aged over 35 is expected to increase by 1.4 million, an increase of over 8%. In contrast, the number of 25-34 year olds is predicted to fall by 12% – there will be almost one million fewer 25-34 year olds in 2002 than in 1997.

National trends

All the above factors of change are reflected in the following national trends.

- The decline in employment in the manufacturing industries, mining, the utilities and agriculture is expected to continue – for example, it is predicted that employment in the engineering sector will reduce by nearly 25% between 1997 and 2007, as companies aim for greater efficiency and productivity.

- The growth of the service sector is predicted to continue: it is expected that the fastest growing employment areas will be those concerned with the public services like health and education, in personal and protective services and in business services, which include advertising, consultancy, accountancy and law.

- An increasing proportion of available jobs are part-time, and this trend is set to continue, rising from 29% in 1997 to 31% by 2007. Part-time employment is most common in the service industries, and most of the new jobs are expected to be taken by women.

- Self-employment increased rapidly through the 1980s, and, after a small fall in the early 1990s, is expected to continue to rise more gradually, to account for 15% of total employment by 2007. Most self-employed people are male, although the proportion of females is rising.

- Employment opportunities for women are increasing more rapidly than for men – over the last fifteen years almost all of the employment increase has been accounted for by women. By 2007, women are expected to account for 48% of total employment.

- There is a trend towards contracting out services as businesses cut costs, improve efficiency and compete. This can lead to an increase in the number of small firms.

What opportunities will there be?

People without skills and qualifications will become increasingly disadvantaged in the workplace. The Government has set a range of **National Learning Targets** to help ensure a well qualified workforce. This includes the target for England that by 2002, 50% of adults who are in employment, or actively seeking employment, should have a qualification at level 3 (ie NVQ level 3/Advanced GNVQ/2 A levels or the equivalent).

- There has been a shift away from manual and low-skilled occupations towards higher level occupations, particularly to jobs at a managerial, professional and technical level. This trend will continue during the first few years of the new millennium.
- Employees of the future will need to be increasingly adaptable and flexible, and should expect to change career at least once during their working lives – which could include periods of temporary employment or self-employment.
- Traditional career progression routes will become rarer – people will need to take more responsibility for their own skills development and career planning.
- More jobs will be on temporary or fixed-term contracts – such as for a specific project.
- Employers will increasingly require their workforce to be flexible and adaptable, so they will expect employees to have wide-ranging skills and abilities.
- Employees will need not only job-specific skills, but also the following key skills, which are increasingly sought by employers for jobs at all levels: application of number, communication, problem solving, information technology, the ability to work with others, and the ability to improve one's own learning and performance.
- Current areas of skill shortage include information technology specialists and health care workers, including nursing staff. There are particular shortages in the teaching profession. The construction industry is also presently experiencing skill shortages. Some areas of the engineering industry are experiencing difficulties recruiting staff, particularly at skilled technician and craft level.
- There is expected to be future demand for people with childcare qualifications, and for those with skills to work in service areas like sales, tourism and leisure (including hospitality and catering), personal and protective services.

Information sources include Labour Market and Skill Trends 1998/99.

Local labour markets

Information on the labour market in a particular area can be gained from a variety of sources:

- Training and Enterprise Councils (TECs) and Local Enterprise Companies (LECs)
- Chambers of Commerce
- careers services
- local authorities
- local newspapers
- local television and radio.

All TECs/LECs produce labour market assessments of their local area. This includes information on attainment of qualifications, employment and unemployment figures, the skill shortages experienced by local employers and details of any employers or businesses who are investing in the area.

Economic development units or departments of local councils work very closely with TECs and LECs. The information they publish may include:

- the employment structure in the local area
- details of sites and premises available to employers
- available funding support
- local business directories.

Flexibility

There is a trend towards flexible working arrangements, away from the traditional full-time permanent contract. Flexible working arrangements can include the following patterns:

- **flexible working hours or flexitime** – allows employees to work an agreed number of hours over the week or month as they choose (although being at work during a core time each day is usually required). A variation of this could be annualised hours, where a set number of hours are worked over the year.
- **part-time work**
- **job sharing**
- **term-time only working**
- **working from home** – developments in communications technology, in particular, enable people to work effectively from home
- **temporary work** – short-term contracts, seasonal work and agency work
- **freelancing** – many people with professional skills work on a self-employed basis, selling their services to employers as they are required
- **career break schemes** – planned, negotiated time away from work, which could be for several years, with a guaranteed job at the end of the break.

Advantages of flexible working practices

- Flexible arrangements can help employees who need to balance their working lives with other responsibilities and commitments, such as childcare or education.
- Flexible arrangements can help to open up opportunities to people with disabilities if full-time work presents difficulties.
- Working flexibly can enable people who are developing their own business to earn an income whilst doing so.
- Flexibility helps employers by allowing them to adjust their staffing levels to their requirements, and by attracting staff who may not otherwise have considered opportunities within their organisation.

About 70% of organisations have been found to offer some form of flexible working arrangements to employees with care responsibilities.

It is possible that the future will see more people generating their incomes through a 'portfolio' of different arrangements – for example, combining freelancing with periods of short-term contract employment, or part-time employment.

Further information

The Department for Education and Employment's Skills and Enterprise Network issues a number of useful publications, including the following:

Labour Market and Skill Trends – published annually.
Labour Market Quarterly Report.

These are both free, and available from DfEE Publications, PO Box 5050, Sudbury, Suffolk CO10 6YJ. Tel: 0845 60 222 60. E-mail: dfee@prologistics.co.uk

Labour Market Trends incorporating Employment Gazette – published monthly by the Office for National Statistics. Available through subscription from The Stationery Office Publications Centre, PO Box 276, London SW8 5DT. Tel: 020 7873 8499. Also available from Stationery Office bookshops. Annual subscription price £85, single copies £9.

Towards a National Skills Agenda – First Report of the National Skills Task Force, 1998 (ref SKT1), and *Delivering Skills for All* – the Second Report of the National Skills Task Force, 1999, available as a full report (ref SKT5) or as an Executive Summary (ref SKT5ex). The reports are published by the DfEE, and are available from DfEE Publications, PO Box 5050, Sudbury, Suffolk CO10 6YJ.
Tel: 0845 60 222 60. E-mail: dfee@prologistics.co.uk

The reports are also available on the DfEE website: www.dfee.gov.uk/skillsforce

New Ways to Work – 309 Upper Street, London N1 2TY. Tel: 020 7226 4026.
E-mail: nww@dircon.co.uk

The Freelance Centre – Suite 2, 170 Kennington Park Road, London SE11 4BT.
Tel: 020 7820 8511. Website: www.freelancecentre.com
Send an SAE for a copy of *The Freelance Report*, which helps people to avoid some of the pitfalls of freelancing.

Industrial Common Ownership Movement – Vassalli House, 20 Central Road, Leeds LS1 6DE.
Tel: 0113 246 1738. Information about workers' co-operatives, which are active in all business sectors. E-mail: icom@icom.org.uk

4. Career development

This chapter covers:

- reasons for a career change
- skills needed in the workplace today
- assistance available for learning while in work
- developing skills outside the workplace.

A career, or 'pathway through life', is usually taken to mean the series of jobs or steps which make up a working lifetime. Each job involves a number of tasks and entails certain skills and responsibilities. During a career, individuals need to be able to transfer their developing skills to new projects and new work, demonstrating a flexible approach to challenges and problem solving.

Changes within the world of work mean that people today have less job security, and the concept of career development has become increasingly relevant. 'Development' can be a lateral or sideways move, undertaken to broaden an individual's skills and interests. People entering the workforce can now expect to make a number of career moves – trends in employment would suggest that up to seven direction changes may be made during a working lifetime.

Aims underlying career progression

Individuals have different underlying aims steering their career progression. They may seek:

- more varied and interesting work, achieved through upward promotion to gain additional responsibilities, or by lateral moves into more specialised areas
- a complete change of job
- a change of environment – a new employer, new location
- greater control over their expenditure of time and energy, considering self-employment, job sharing, flexible working arrangements or promotion
- to fulfil ambitions for status, aiming to reach a position of influence
- more money, to meet growing personal and family financial responsibilities, or to support an expensive hobby, for example.

Ways forward in work

Meeting the demand for flexible key skills

In an age of rapid technological advancement, survey work has shown that, rather than knowledge and job-specific skills which can quickly date, recruiters, potential clients, financial backers and others consider the developmental level of an individual's skills. People with a solid grounding in key skills – and the ability to update them throughout life – will have a head start in the workplace and beyond.

While regarding these personal qualities as important:

- cheerfulness and a sense of humour
- flexibility
- adaptability,

recruiters are interested in an applicant's level of key skills in:

- communication
- numeracy
- information technology

and their ability in:

- working with others
- improving their own learning and performance
- problem solving.

These key skills can be developed both within and away from the workplace, and individuals can gather evidence demonstrating a progression in skill levels from 1 to 4. New key skill qualifications will be available from September 2000 for communication, application of number, and information technology.

Assistance through networking

Recent surveys have shown that up to 80% of job vacancies are never advertised. Many of these posts are filled by people previously known to the employer. For those in work and seeking to develop their career, it is necessary to be known to people making decisions. This may involve volunteering for extra activities, such as being involved in quality assessment and development groups, consultative/focus groups or other circles. It may necessitate getting known by others outside the present work setting, for example through joining professional groups, chambers of commerce, Business Link, or whatever is most relevant. Leisure activities which establish contacts across a broad cross section of people may also be useful.

Personal development plans

In the new Learning Age – promoted by the government in office – individuals are encouraged to draw up personal development plans to identify a general – or even specific – progression pathway for their working life, clarifying personal skills, key and job-specific skills, together with the underpinning knowledge that they need to develop in order to progress. Most people do plan at least a few steps ahead, developing a number of alternative ideas, establishing a wide network of contacts and gaining diverse experience in order to be prepared for possible changes in circumstances, in the workplace or at home.

Skills development in the workplace

Lifelong learning

During the last decade, there has been a drive to introduce the concept and practice of lifelong learning – promoting a continuous acquisition of skills through an individual's lifetime. With a low rate of unemployment – less than 4.5% across Britain as a whole – and most of the nation's labour force in work, the major focus of lifelong learning is in the workplace. An increase in short-term contracts and little prospect of entering a 'career for life' has meant that it is important for employed individuals to work towards accreditation of their current skills in the workplace, gaining National Vocational Qualification (NVQs) or Scottish Vocational Qualifications (SVQs) – qualifications specifically designed by industry lead bodies for the particular industry. NVQs/SVQs have now been established to accredit work-based skills across all occupations.

 **Consult:** *Chapter 5 on Qualifications for detail on NVQs/SVQs.*

Some workers can provide sufficient evidence of their ability to work to a required standard from jobs undertaken up to two years previously, through the accreditation of prior learning system, or APL. This can reduce the time necessary to achieve NVQs/SVQs. Local colleges, TECs or LECs can help with APL.

Employers may:

- organise in-company training so that several employees can update their skills at the same time – more economical for the company
- allow time off for participation in short or part-time courses at a local learning centre, or for a residential study block of an open learning course
- agree to pay part or all of the course fees
- already run an 'employee development scheme'.

Learning job-specific skills

It has always been recognised that an employer has responsibility for training staff in the skills of the job they are employed to do. Often, this means 'on-the-job' training, perhaps with day release to college to gain additional qualifications. For more support with learning job-specific skills:

 **Contact:** *Professional bodies or associations, local TECs or LECs (see The Gazetteer) to check if specific courses are available.*

With advances in technology, diversification of companies and new markets, employees need to follow programmes of training to update their knowledge and skills in order to perform their jobs effectively. Employers may fund their training in the use of new software, the acquisition of specific marketing techniques for new products, attendance at cultural briefings for the new overseas outlets – whatever is appropriate in the circumstances.

Learning additional skills and knowledge at work

If training in job-specific skills is considered largely the responsibility of the employer, learning such things as competence or understanding in additional areas may not be. Depending on the particular job, the employing organisation and the proposed mode of learning, employees may be able to present a business case to their employer for supporting them, at least partially.

For example, for employees in the sales section of a company with European customers, it may be useful to speak another language. The employer might contribute to course fees for modern language evening classes. However, if customers speak good English, an employer may see no obvious advantage to the company in offering this assistance.

Help for employers

There are a number of initiatives designed to encourage employers to support their staff in pursuing additional or add-on learning, besides essential training to develop job-specific skills.

The Spring 1999 budget brought in tax incentives to encourage employers to contribute to their employees' **individual learning accounts** – a saving initiative through which individuals will be able to fund their own learning. It is due to start up in 2000.

National Learning Targets

Mentioned above in the introductory section, the overall aim of these targets is:

'To improve the UK's international competitiveness by raising standards and attainment levels in education and training to world class levels.'

Some of the specific Learning Targets for the year 2002 are:

- 85% of 19 year olds to gain a level 2 qualification
- 60% of 21 year olds (50% of all adults) to be qualified to level 3
- 28% of adults to reach level 4
- 45% of medium-sized or large organisations to be recognised as Investors in People
- 10,000 small organisations (below 50 employees) to be recognised as Investors in People.

People who have personal development plans formulated around the standard of lifelong learning, and who are keen to learn in work, might investigate whether their employer, or a prospective employer, is committed to contributing to the National Learning Targets. Employers may well give serious consideration to an employee's proposals for training – to involve him or herself and colleagues.

 **Consult:**

Learning and Working Together for the Future: a strategic framework to 2002 – published by DfEE, obtainable free of charge from DfEE Publications – ref LWT2.

Developing a Learning Organisation: an introductory guide to improving an organisation's potential for learning – by Peter Lassey, published by Kogan Page, price £18.99. ISBN 0 7494 2413 4

Learning Targets website for more information about National Learning Targets at: www.dfee.gov.uk/nlt/targets.htm

DfEE Employment News *– published monthly by the DfEE, free from Employment News, CENTRAL DESPATCH, DfEE, Room W125, Moorfoot, Sheffield S1 4PQ.*

Some areas have developed special programmes in connection with the National Targets. An example of this is:

The City Workers' Study Voucher Scheme

The City Workers' Study Voucher Scheme is operated by the Corporation of London. It aims to encourage individual development, helping to maintain a qualified and dynamic workforce in the City of London. The scheme is a partnership between the Corporation of London, City employers and City workers. Each partner pays one third towards the cost of a course of study for a City worker. Anyone working in the City of London ('the Square Mile') is eligible. Already, the scheme has helped hundreds of workers pay for a very wide range of courses, including modern languages, marketing, human resources and development, the internet, diving, field archaeology and IT packages. Free careers guidance and counselling is available to participating workers.

 **Contact:**

City Workers' Study Voucher Scheme *–
Corporation of London Education Department,
PO Box 270, Guildhall, London EC2P 2EJ.
Tel: 020 7332 3542. E-mail: dep.education@ms.corpoflondon.gov.uk*

Investors in People (IiP)

This award is given to organisations who can demonstrate that they meet certain quality standards, including the training and development of their staff. If a company is interested in working towards the Investors in People standard, evidence of actively supporting staff in learning is essential. Once a company has achieved the award, it will have to prove, every three years, that it maintains the quality standards, so support for identified development needs can still be a useful addition to the IiP portfolio. For more information about IiP:

 **Contact:** *The local TEC or LEC Investors in People contact.*

Employee development schemes

There are many variations, but all aim to develop the workforce. Some, such as Ford's EDAP (Employee Development and Assistance Programme), urge participants to undertake learning that is not related to their job, encouraging staff to appreciate the wider benefits of learning. Other company programmes have a close bearing on their area of work. More and more employers are beginning to see that there are clear advantages in developing their workforce. Many companies report that supporting learning leads to increased staff motivation and loyalty, which in turn can result in increased productivity. For more information:

Contact: *Workplace Learning Division, Department for Education and Employment – Room E8e, Moorfoot, Sheffield SI 4PQ. Tel: 0114 259 3036.*

TECs or LECs (details in The Gazetteer) may be able to provide information about local enterprises which operate employment development schemes.

Professional/industrial organisations

If your employer is part of a network of similar companies, there may be support available for training, for example accountancy firms along the M4 corridor.

National Training Organisations (NTOs)

NTOs are influential, independent, employer-led sector organisations recognised by the DfEE to work strategically with their employment sectors and with government across education and training throughout the whole of Great Britain. They will help government extend and improve its dialogue with employers to ensure that the needs of business are taken into account when developing policy.

NTOs draw together wider employment interests including professional bodies, education, trade unions and trade associations. They work closely with the Qualifications and Curriculum Authority (QCA) and the Scottish Qualifications Authority (SQA) which have responsibility for developing the work-based vocational qualifications – NVQs and SVQs respectively. NTOs outputs include the National Occupational Standards and Modern Apprenticeship frameworks.

By Spring 1999, over 65 NTOs had been recognised, covering the interests of 83% of the national workforce. The NTO National Council can help with giving leads to relevant sector NTOs.

Contact: ***National Training Organisation Division, DfEE** – Room E4a, Sheffield S1 4PQ. Tel: 0114 259 3525.
E-mail: mike.ward@dfee.gov.uk Website: www.open.gov.uk/*

***NTO National Council** – 10 Meadowcourt, Amos Road, Sheffield S9 1DX. Tel: 0114 261 9926.
E-mail: admin@nto-nc.org Website: www.nto-nc.org*

***Qualifications and Curriculum Authority (QCA)** – 29 Bolton Street, London W1Y 7PD. Tel: 020 7509 5555.
E-mail customerservices@qca.org.uk Website: www.qca.org.uk/*

***Scottish Qualifications Authority (SQA)** – Hanover House, 24 Douglas Street, Glasgow G2 7NQ. Tel: 0141 248 7900.
E-mail: mail@sqa.org.uk Website: www.sqa.org.uk*

The National Training Federation (NTF)

NTF is the major national association for training providers, and represents the interests of its members at local, regional and national levels. NTF member organisations provide a range of training and educational opportunities covering all vocational areas, all leading to an NVQ or SVQ. Training is available both for unemployed individuals wishing to enter a certain area of work (which may be supported by government-funded training initiatives), and for employees already working in a particular industrial sector.

Training is normally undertaken on employers' premises, and is specifically job-related. Normally, four days a week are spent in the workplace, with one day a week devoted to off-the-job training. Many people who are unemployed at the start of their training gain full-time jobs when they complete the course .
For further information:

 **Contact:** *National Training Federation – Seymour House, 30-34 Muspole Street, Norwich, Norfolk NR3 1DJ. Tel: 01603 623262. E-mail: billwood@trainingfed.co.uk*

Chambers of commerce

Individual UK chambers of commerce run thousands of short courses throughout the year. Local chambers offer courses which are directly related to the needs of local enterprise organisations. Seminars and workshops, lasting from half a day to around three days, deal with changes in legislation – VAT, sick pay, health and safety issues, national minimum wage, working time directives – as well as covering specific skills such as word processing, producing spreadsheets and supervising.

 **Contact:** *Local public libraries hold details of the nearest chambers of commerce.*

Business Link

Business Links are agencies set up to advise new small and medium-sized businesses. They are run by partnerships of various bodies such as TECs, larger commercial enterprises and chambers of commerce. They can advise employers on issues such as developing their workforce's skills.

 **Contact:** *TECs and LECs can provide contact details for local Business Link operations.*

Business support networks

In many local areas, small businesses have established their own support networks, particularly to offer help to each other in becoming established, or to pool resources.

 **Contact:** *A local library, TEC or LEC (details in The Gazetteer) may be able to provide details of district and regional networks.*

The Industrial Society

The Industrial Society is an independent, not-for-profit campaigning body with over 10,000 member organisations from every part of the economy. Everything that the Society is engaged with, from training to consultancy, from publishing to advocacy, is driven by a commitment to improve working life.

The Industrial Society campaigns through learning:

- running training courses at their School of Coaching
- acting as consultants, helping firms to tackle workplace problems and access best practice
- as a publisher, producing books, reports and award-winning video training packages
- providing Best Practice Direct services to members.

Member organisations benefit from access to the Society's Employment Law Helpline, networking and information services, discounts on courses, conferences and publications, and access to the Industrial Society Partnership Charter.

☞ **Contact:** ***The Industrial Society*** *– Robert Hyde House,*
48 Bryanston Square, London W1H 7LN.
Tel: 020 7262 2401. E-mail: customercentre@indsoc.co.uk
Website: www.indsoc.co.uk

Keeping skills up to date

Updating skills to keep pace with technical change and development is a necessary part of work these days. There are many short courses on offer from a range of providers such as professional bodies, colleges and commercial training firms. Many of these courses are now embedded in the further education sector learning provision.

A government initiative known as PICKUP sought to promote professional, industrial and commercial updating. There is no longer a central body for this, but Guildford Educational Services produces a Windows version of PICKUP, which is a national training directory providing details of over 30,900 training courses offered by a wide range of training organisations. Many of the course entries are for short, part-time training sessions through which individuals can update or upgrade their qualifications. The directory is updated continuously. New CD-Roms are issued to subscribers four times a year.

☞ **Contact:** ***Guildford Educational Services*** *– 32 Castle Street,*
Guildford GU1 3UW. Tel: 01483 579454.
E-mail: info@gesvt.com Website: www.gesvt.com

Local FE colleges can supply further information on suitable short courses for updating skills (details in The Gazetteer).

Further help

Besides encouraging their employers to become involved in lifelong learning for all their workforce, individuals may be able to obtain their own support.

Members of trade unions can ask their local representative about training or learning support initiatives that may be available.

Those who have identified a specific vocational learning route may be able to obtain funding through a Career Development Loan (CDL).

Contact: ***Career Development Loans*** *free helpline, available between 8am and 10pm, Monday to Sunday: 0800 585 505 to obtain a free information pack and application form.*

Although much of the initiative and enthusiasm for learning may arise from employees in the first instance, increasing numbers of employers are seeing the economic benefits of a keen workforce who are motivated through learning at work.

Skills development outside the workplace

Additional training or study

Some individuals are given encouragement or assistance by their employer to train or study whilst in work. Other employees are expected to study in their own time. Those wanting to acquire new knowledge may have to stop work for a while to study full or part-time on a college or university course, or by following an open or distance learning course. This latter mode is well suited to career development because studies can be fitted around time in work, and formal qualifications are not normally needed to get started.

Finding help and support

Employers may be able to advise on which qualifications are 'essential' and which ones are 'desirable'. Personnel or human resources and development managers in larger companies can be a useful source of advice to their employees.

Quality newspapers and professional journals or magazines regularly publish profiles of individuals working in different occupational categories or specialisms within a particular industrial sector, describing their progression routes. Advertisements in the recruitment sections of newspapers and in vacancy bulletins are a useful lead to the skills and qualification levels which employers seek from applicants to particular posts.

Careers advisers can be a great source of help and advice on progression routes. Guidance interviews can help individuals to determine the best way forward, but are usually costed for adults in employment. Those not in work can seek advice and help from the Employment Service's team of personal advisers in Jobcentres. People over 25 who have claimed jobseeker's allowance for two years can elect to follow a period of study through the education option of the New Deal programme.

Contact: *Local careers company centres and local Jobcentres: details in the phone directory.*

Courses and qualifications

For many careers, there are specific qualifications to aim for at entry level and for progression within the profession. Courses not directly related to a particular line of work may also improve an individual's prospects by developing and upgrading the person's key skill levels.

For help on available qualifications in specific occupations:

 **Consult:** *British Qualifications – see 'Further information' at the end of this chapter.*

Some training schemes which may seem designed primarily for young people are also open to adults. For example, the National Trust Careership scheme, which is a Modern Apprenticeship leading to a National Vocational Qualification at level 3 in either horticulture or countryside management, accepts applicants at any age.

 **Contact:** ***The National Trust** – Careership Office, Lanhydrock Park, Bodmin, Cornwall PL30 4DE. Tel: 01208 265245. E-mail: crojmk@smtp.ntrust.org.uk*

Alternatives

Career development need not be viewed only in traditional terms. For many individuals, job sharing, self-employment or working freelance can be the right direction for developing their career. Some people may wish to develop a hobby, interest or voluntary activity into paid employment, eventually building a career.

In 1998, the DfEE set up an **Adult and Community Learning Fund** to help organisations and groups of individuals to fund unusual opportunities for learning within the local community. Grants of between £300 and £6400 from a £2.3 million sum can be awarded to assist programmes which will include learners who are wary of education or are in other ways excluded from mainstream learning programmes.

Further information

Build your own Rainbow (99 ed) – a workbook for career and life-management, price £15.00 plus £1.30 p&p. Published by Management Books 2000 – Cowcombe House, Cowcombe Hill, Chalford GL6 8HP. Tel: 01285 760722. E-mail: m.b.2000@virgin.net. Or order from the website: www.mb2000.com ISBN 185252 300 X.

Directory of Guidance Provision for Adults in the UK, 1999 – published by ADSET, price £27.50 (plus £2.75 p&p for non-members). Obtainable from Chancery House, Dalkeith Place, Kettering, Northants NN16 OBS. Tel: 01536 410500. E-mail: info@adst-plus.co.uk

British Qualifications (99 ed) – published by Kogan Page, price £33.50 plus £3.00 p&p. ISBN 0 74941817 6.

British Vocational Qualifications (3rd ed) – published by Kogan Page, price £32.50 plus £3.00 p&p. ISBN 0 7494 2548 2.

International Dictionary of Adult and Continuing Education – by Peter Jarvis, published by Kogan Page, price £35.00 plus £3.00 p&p. ISBN 0 7494 2671 3.

Keynotes or Keynotes Plus! – a series of careers guidance notes for adults, plus a computerised version, published by Lifetime Careers Publishing, price £125 for the set. ISBN 1 873408 62 5.

Some of these resources may be available in public reference libraries.

5. Sources of information, advice and guidance

This chapter covers:

- the main providers of information, advice and guidance
- computer-based information and guidance systems
- using the internet
- ensuring a successful outcome to learning.

There are a variety of agencies involved in providing information, advice and guidance to adults about education and training opportunities. This ranges from agencies providing factual information about learning opportunities through to those providing in-depth personal careers and educational guidance, where clients are helped to assess themselves, clarify their goals, and work out possible suitable future options. Many agencies hold local and national databases of education and training opportunities which clients may use independently. Providers of information, advice and guidance include, of course, the providers of learning opportunities. Fees may be charged for some in-depth guidance services.

To reinforce and strengthen existing provision, Local Adult Information and Advice Networks will be developed over the next three years, which will help ensure that advice and information is more comprehensively available.

The main providers

Learning Direct

Learning Direct, launched in February 1998, is a telephone helpline which helps callers with learning and career enquiries. Callers may be anyone over 18 (whatever their employment status), employers and staff from institutions. Learning Direct can provide information about the range of learning opportunities across the UK. It can also provide information about costs and childcare provision, and can direct enquirers to their local guidance service. More information can be found on the Learning Direct website at www.learningdirect.org.uk

The Learning Direct telephone number is 0800 100 900.
Lines are open from 9am to 9pm Monday to Friday, and to 12 noon on Saturdays. People with hearing impairments can contact Learning Direct through a minicom on the same number. Information for people who are visually impaired can be sent in Braille.

Careers services

Careers services offer information, advice and guidance to anyone in full-time education (except universities) and to young people for about two years after they leave. Careers services contract with the DfEE to provide the service in a particular area. The providers of careers services are listed in The Gazetteer, by geographical area, at the end of this book.

Many careers services offer a range of options to adults (some priced). These can include one-to-one interviews, psychometric testing, computer-aided guidance, help with CVs and jobsearch skills, and use of careers information libraries. Some careers services also offer services to businesses, such as redundancy counselling, employee development, help with recruitment and selection.

Adult clients may need to make an appointment to talk through their education and training needs, but most services allow adults to browse freely in their careers information library, and make use of computer databases.

Professional careers advisers hold a Diploma in Careers Guidance or NVQ level 4 in Guidance. Other staff who support the work of careers advisers, including providing information, may also hold relevant NVQ qualifications.

The professional bodies which are concerned with guidance provision for adults are:

The Institute of Careers Guidance – 27a Lower High Street, Stourbridge DY8 ITA. Tel: 01384 376464. Website: www.icg-org.uk E-mail: hq@icg-uk.org

The National Association for Educational Guidance for Adults (NAEGA) – contact NAEGA at PO Box 869, Cambridge CB3 7GR. Tel: 01223 263178.
Website: homepage.virgin.net/naega.guidance E-mail: naega.guidance@virgin.net

TECs and LECs

Training and Enterprise Councils (TECs) and Local Enterprise Companies (LECs) are independent bodies led by local business people in partnership with the public and voluntary sectors. Their main aim is to support economic growth and prosperity. There are 78 TECs in England and Wales, and 22 LECs in Scotland.

In Northern Ireland, responsibility for training and enterprise lies with the Training and Employment Agency. Their headquarters is Adelaide House, 39-49 Adelaide Street, Belfast BT2 8FD.
Tel: 028 9025 7777. Website: www.tea-ni.org/

The responsibilities of TECs and LECs include offering training and enterprise services, through many different organisations and employers in their local areas. This includes the government-funded training programmes for people who are unemployed or who want to return to work after a break.

Amongst the training programmes they offer for adults are Work-based Learning (Training for Work in Scotland), Modern Apprenticeships (aimed at young people – training must be completed by the age of 25) and business start-up. Many TECs also provide services for adults who want information and advice about careers, education, training or employment.

Higher education careers services

Higher education institutions usually have a careers advisory service offering help to their graduates and undergraduates. Some universities participate in the 'mutual aid' scheme, whereby recent graduates can receive help from a higher education careers service other than the one at which they studied, for example in their home town, for up to three years after graduation. However, not all institutions offer this service, and priority is given to an institution's own students. Possibly, only a limited service may be offered, such as use of an information room, and a charge may be made for this.

Graduate Careerline is a national telephone advisory service for people within three years of graduating. Enquirers pay for the telephone call but the advice is free. It is staffed by experienced graduate careers advisers.

☞ **Contact:** *Tel: 020 7554 4515 on Tuesdays from 3pm to 8pm.*
Tel: 01415 534177 on Wednesdays from 3pm to 8pm.
Or tel: 0117 928 8149 on Thursdays from 3pm to 8pm.

The CSU Prospects website is a guide to graduate jobs, careers and postgraduate study in the UK, and contains an electronic version of the Prospects careers information leaflet series: www.prospects.csu.ac.uk

CSU provides products and services to higher education institutions, including working with AgCAS, the Association of Graduate Careers Advisory Services, in the production of joint careers information publications.

Further education colleges

All further education colleges offer information and advice to prospective students, and to students on college courses. Some colleges offer advice about benefits. Many colleges operate information and advice services to prospective students through a central admissions service. Prospective students may find it useful to talk to teaching staff involved in the course they are considering. Most colleges offer open days and evenings when staff are available to provide information and advice.

Guidance shops

In many areas there are shop front-style centres, providing information and advice on education and training opportunities. The range of services available varies considerably; not all provide in-depth careers guidance. Some provide help with CVs and jobsearch techniques. Some areas have mobile centres for outreach work.

Commercial providers

There are many organisations providing careers advice and counselling as profit-making companies. Many offer a range of psychometric tests and assessments. Fees vary enormously, so potential enquirers should make several enquiries before committing themselves. Companies are usually listed in local business telephone directories.

Jobcentres

Jobcentre staff can advise, particularly on government-funded training opportunities. Some Jobcentres hold a small collection of careers information and books, and relevant databases of information on local opportunities.

Libraries

Local public libraries may provide some or all of the following:

- local further and adult education information – some may hold course databases
- general careers and educational reference books
- open learning materials
- access to the internet
- access to specialist journals and newspapers.

College/university libraries are obviously essential facilities to learners, and students who are attending courses at institutions will be introduced to the facilities available. These libraries are likely to hold databases of learning opportunities and allow students access to the internet.

Citizens Advice Bureaux (CAB)

Like the library, they are not experts in the subject but can provide some information. They should be able to advise students who are having difficulty obtaining information on benefit entitlements.

Computer-based information and guidance systems

There are many useful computer software programs related to education, training, careers, CVs and other careers topics.

They include:

- **information databases** – providing information about education and training courses, or about occupations
- **guidance systems** – self-evaluation programs which suggest possible suitable career options on the basis of responses made by the client, often linked to an occupational information database.

Adults may access computer-based information and guidance systems through careers services and other adult advisory and guidance agencies. Educational institutions usually subscribe to various computer-based systems for the benefit of their students. Information databases may also be available through libraries and Jobcentres.

A few of the available software systems which are the most relevant to the adult user are described below.

Training Access Points (TAPs)

Training Access Points are databases of information on education and training opportunities in a particular geographical area. TAP databases cover the whole range of learning providers, including public, private and voluntary sectors. There is now a national network of TAP databases, which collectively hold information on over half a million learning opportunities across the UK.

Local TAP databases can be found in guidance shops, libraries, careers centres and Jobcentres. The service may also be available by phone or post. TAPs are designed to be very easy to use. The speciality of a TAP database is its comprehensiveness and local focus. A number of TAPs now have a presence on the internet, some with on-line searchable databases.

Local careers and guidance services should be able to provide information about local TAP databases. Information about TAPs can be found on the website of the National Training Information Central Support Unit (NTICS) at www.ntics.clara.net

UK Course Discover

UK Course Discover is a national database of further and higher education opportunities, produced by ECCTIS 2000. It is available by subscription. It provides information on over 100,000 courses at over 1000 universities and colleges of higher and further education throughout the UK. UK Course Discover can be found in careers centres and other guidance agencies, educational institutions and libraries.

Teachers and advisers can obtain information about subscribing from:

ECCTIS 2000 Ltd, Oriel House, Oriel Road, Cheltenham GL50 1XP. Tel: 01242 252627.
Website: www.ecctis.co.uk E-mail: 101472.2254@compuserve.com

The PICKUP National Training Directory

The PICKUP database, produced by Guildford Educational Services, contains information on over 30,000 vocational short courses and training opportunities.

☞ **Contact:** *Guildford Educational Services, 32 Castle Street, Guildford GU1 3UW. Tel: 01483 579454. Website: www.gesvt.com E-mail: info@gesvt.com*

Adult Directions

A career-matching program and occupational database designed for use by all adults. As well as generating job suggestions based on the user's likes and dislikes, Adult Directions provides information on many issues which adults face in relation to careers, education and training. The job suggestions are described with direct reference to the responses made by the user in the matching program. In this way the client gets a picture of how job ideas fit their perceived interests, skills, experience and abilities.

☞ **Contact:** *CASCAiD Ltd, Holywell Building, Holywell Way, Loughborough LE11 3UZ. Tel: 01509 283390. Website: www.cascaid.co.uk E-mail: enquiry@cascaid.co.uk*

The following three software programs are published by **Progressions Limited** – Sutton House, Weyside Park, Catteshall Lane, Godalming, Surrey GU7 1XJ. Tel: 01483 413200. Website: www.progressions.co.uk E-mail: info@progressions.co.uk

Odyssey

This is an occupational database with job information supplied by the DfEE. It contains over 1400 job titles with various searches to get the user to the job profile. The latest version has salary information and links to the internet from many of the job and general information articles.

Pathfinder for Windows

Pathfinder takes the user through a series of questions, based on the JIIG-CAL Occupational Interest Profile and Job Suggestions program. The user is presented with an interest profile and job suggestions based on their responses. Users can see the pros and cons of each job suggestion, and detailed information about each job. Pathfinder is designed for use both with young people and with adults.

Explorer

An occupational database, suitable for users of all ages, including adults. Information may be accessed through one of four different search routes – job title, career area, qualification level and keyword search.

The following two software programs are published by **Lifetime Careers Publishing** – 7 Ascot Court, White Horse Business Park, Trowbridge BA14 0XA. Tel: 01225 716023. E-mail: sales@wiltshire.lifetime-careers.co.uk

Keynotes Plus!

Keynotes Plus! is a computerised version of Keynotes, a series of careers guidance leaflets for adults covering general topics in relation to career choice and change, education, training, jobhunting and employment. Keynotes Plus! allows clients to choose, view and print the information leaflets by selecting particular topic areas, or through a keyword search.

KeyCLIPS

KeyCLIPS is a computer package which allows users to explore the occupational information contained in the CLIPS careers information leaflet series. Users enter search factors such as qualification level, subjects and work skills, to generate a list of relevant CLIPS leaflets which users may view or print off.

Computer-based learning

Many learning opportunities are available through computer packages, particularly in the field of open learning. This allows the learner to work through the package at a time and pace to suit themselves. This could either be from home, or through an open learning centre.

Using the internet

More and more homes now have access to the internet, and educational institutions usually provide access to the internet for their students. The Internet obviously enables learners to access a wealth of information worldwide. E-mail facilities can provide a useful way of communicating between student and tutor, especially on open and distance learning courses.

The internet is, of course, a useful source of information about education, training, careers and job opportunities, but users should check how up-to-date information is, and that it has been provided by an authoritative source. The following sites may be of interest:

www.dfee.gov.uk
The DfEE website, which includes information on a wide range of government initiatives and policies. It includes lists of careers services (and links where possible) and TECs.

www.qca.org.uk
The site of the Qualifications and Curriculum Authority, containing information about academic and vocational qualifications for England, Wales and Northern Ireland. For information about Scottish qualifications, look at the Scottish Qualifications Authority website: **www.sqa.org.uk**

www.newdeal.gov.uk
For information about the New Deal.

www.prospects.csu.ac.uk
For information about graduate careers, jobs and postgraduate opportunities.

www.ucas.ac.uk
Includes information on higher education courses and institutions, with links to institutions' websites, and a database of Access courses.

www.careersoft.co.uk
This site includes links to sites of higher education establishments, and to industry professional bodies.

www.datalake.co.uk
Contains, amongst other items, a worldwide directory of higher education establishments.

www.ceg.org.uk
The PlanIT website contains information about opportunities in Scotland, including a database of Access courses and further and higher education. It also contains occupational information.

Ensuring a successful outcome to learning

Besides access to information about learning opportunities, there are other issues that new learners need to consider. Learners need to organise and plan their time, and to develop the necessary study skills.

Checklist for successful learning:

- well-managed time
- effective study skills
- the ability to organise yourself and resources
- finding the necessary space.

Time management skills

This is the key to successful study, especially if you are fitting learning around full-time work or family commitments. Potential learners should:

- make sure they know how much time will be required for the course they are undertaking **in addition to** any scheduled classes, eg time for reading, researching, writing up notes, doing assignments etc
- look at how they currently spend their time, and if time is tight, try to re-organise their time more efficiently – re-prioritising daily activities etc, to create sufficient study time
- make sure they use their learning time effectively – it is helpful to devise a regular timetable of study periods, at a time of day when they can learn effectively, and then stick to it!

Effective study skills

Most course providers offer opportunities for students to develop their study skills. This could be as an integral part of the course itself, through short workshops or courses, or through more informal 'drop-in' learning centres.

Study skills include:

- note-taking – from oral presentations and from texts
- reading – how to read effectively when researching or reading set texts
- producing written work – essays, project reports and other assignments.

Organising resources

During most courses of learning, students will generate and accumulate a wealth of notes, handouts, leaflets and books, perhaps also tapes and videos etc, and computer disks containing their work. Learners will need to access this information for reference, revision and other reasons. Therefore, planning an efficient and secure storage and retrieval system is vital. Losing the final draft of an essay on disk, or some essential handouts, can turn into a crisis!

Space to learn

Most learners need to spend some time studying at home, besides using libraries and other learning facilities. Space has to be found at home that is free from distractions and interruptions, and suitable for working – not always easy in a busy household. Ground rules may need to be negotiated with other family members.

Word processing skills

Students undertaking courses which require written essays, reports etc will find that having basic word processing skills will be a huge asset, if not essential. If students do not have access to word processing facilities at home, the institution offering the course is likely to have facilities that they can use.

Giving some consideration to the above issues will help ensure that the learner is well prepared, and has a positive outcome to their learning experience.

Further information

There are many reference publications on careers, education and training. Below are listed a few examples to provide a general starting point. Many of these will be available for reference in careers centres and some in local libraries. Most bookshops can order copies to purchase.

Occupations – published annually by COIC. Price £30.00 for 1999 edition. ISBN 0 86110 749 7. A comprehensive and substantial guide to careers, including information on the work, skills and interests, the pay and conditions, opportunities, prospects, entry requirements, training available and late entry to the profession.

Returning to Work – 8th edition, published 1996 by Sage Publications, 6 Bonhill Street, London EC2A 4PU. Tel: 020 7374 0645. Price £16.99. ISBN 1 85396 337 2.

CRAC Directory of Further Education (DOFE) – published annually by Hobsons, price £76.50 for 1999/2000 edition. ISBN 1 860176208. Information on over 75,000 further education courses in the UK – through full-time, part-time and distance or open learning.

The Penguin Careers Guide – published by Penguin Books, Bath Road, Harmondsworth, Middlesex UB7 0DA. Price £9.99. ISBN 0 140 46964 8. Information on job opportunities. The book covers areas such as management and working for oneself. Provides information on part-time and job sharing opportunities.

The Which? Guide to Changing Careers – a Which? consumer guide, available through Trotman, or from Which Ltd. Tel: 0800 252 100. Price £10.99. ISBN 0 85202 704 4.

Career Skills – published by Cassell and Co, Stanley House, 3 Fleet's Lane, Poole, Dorset BH5 3AJ. Tel: 01202 665432, and available through Trotman. Price £12.99. ISBN 0 304 714172. Helps the reader to create and follow a successful career plan.

The 1999 What Color is Your Parachute – A Practical Manual for Job Hunters and Career Changers – price £13.99. ISBN 1 58008 008 1.

Making Career Transitions – published by Kogan Page, price £9.99. ISBN 0 7494 2662 4.

Managing Your Career in a Changing Workplace – published by Kogan Page, price £9.99. ISBN 0 7494 2664 0.

Net that Job – Using the World Wide Web to develop your career and find work – published by Kogan Page, price £8.99. ISBN 0 7494 2574 1.

Independent Colleges – published by ISCO, 12a Princess Way, Camberley, Surrey GU15 3SP. Price £6.99. ISBN 0 90193 648 0. A directory of courses at over 600 institutions in the independent sector.

University and College Entrance: The Official UCAS Guide – published by UCAS, available through Trotman. Price £19.95. ISBN 0 948241 69 1. Published annually, it provides information about all UK degree and HND courses at publicly-funded institutions.

Choosing Your Degree Course and University – published by Trotman, price £14.99. ISBN 0 85660 376 8.

Section 2 How and where to learn

6. A brief guide to education and training

This chapter sets the scene for the more detailed information on education and training opportunities given in the rest of this section of *Second Chances*.

The education system in the UK can be split into the following broad categories:

- academic study
- vocational education
- vocational training.

Academic study

This leads to the more traditional qualifications, originally based on the theoretical study of academic subjects. They include A and AS levels, General Certificate of Secondary Education (GCSE), Scottish standard and higher grades, International Baccalaureate, degrees and Diplomas of Higher Education.

Vocational education

This covers qualifications relevant to the world of work and relating to broad occupational areas, with more practical work than most academic courses. These 'bridge' courses lead to the General National Vocational Qualifications (GNVQs) and, currently, General Scottish Vocational Qualifications (GSVQs).

Vocational training

Qualifications in this category are about work and the ability to do a particular job. They are available at a number of different levels. They include: National Vocational Qualifications (NVQs) and Scottish Vocational Qualifications (SVQs), BTEC first, national and higher national qualifications, and Scottish National Certificates. Other bodies which administer vocational awards include City and Guilds, and OCR, which offers RSA and other vocational qualifications.

Qualifications offered by professional bodies also fit into this category.

Who offers education and training for adults?

Opportunities for adults are offered through the following channels:

- **public sector providers of education** – this includes adult/community education services, further education colleges, specialist colleges for areas such as art and design, agriculture, music etc, tertiary colleges or sixth form colleges, universities, colleges and institutes of higher education, and the adult residential colleges
- **independent training providers or colleges** – operating on a commercial basis
- **employers** – who offer training to their staff, and financial (and other) support for staff following courses at colleges, or through professional bodies
- **providers of government-funded training programmes** – these could include independent training organisations, further education colleges or voluntary organisations, which contract to provide training for unemployed people
- **voluntary organisations** – which often provide training, sometimes certificated, for their volunteers

- organisations offering **open or distance learning** courses – these could be public or private sector organisations
- **community-based training or education providers** – which may be supported by funding from public, private or voluntary agencies, but operate separately from mainstream educational establishments.

Some definitions

Further education and tertiary colleges

These have traditionally offered work-related (vocational) courses. In 1993, the colleges became autonomous from local authority control.

Most colleges offer a mixture of full and part-time courses with qualifications at the equivalent of craft and technician levels, and many also offer courses up to professional or degree level. They cover general educational and recreational subjects as well as those relevant to employment.

Some offer short courses geared specifically to the needs of people coming back into education after a number of years, often called Return to Learn, Fresh Start or something similar.

Adult education/community education services

These offer a range of courses for adults in a particular local education authority area. Courses are mostly part-time, with some courses in the evening. Usually these courses are non-advanced. Subjects can be work-related, educational, leisure activities or hobbies.

Community schools

Some schools call themselves 'community schools' and integrate mature students into their classes with regular pupils, usually studying academic subjects (for example mathematics GCSE).

Higher education

Higher education is advanced level education (entry standard equivalent to A level or above), offered mainly through universities and colleges or institutes of higher education. Higher education includes degrees, Higher National Certificates or Diplomas (HNCs/HNDs) and Diplomas of Higher Education.

Most courses are full-time, but many courses are part-time.

Some universities run courses for adults through their Continuing Education, or Extra Mural departments or Short Course Units – the name varies. These courses do not have the breadth of the degree programmes.

Some institutions 'franchise' one, two or more years of a degree or HND course to another. So you may be able to take the first year of a course at your local further education college, and then go on to a university, or take a complete course at one college which is validated and awarded by a different college or university.

Independent providers

There are a number of independent providers of education and training, offering courses at all levels and in mostly specialist subjects – from management training to beauty therapy. One example is the University of Buckingham, an independent university offering intensive two-year degree courses.

Distance and open learning

Distance and open learning is the term used where the learner learns independently, using a variety of resources and ways of learning and keeping in touch with the tutor, other than attending scheduled classes. Open and distance learning includes correspondence learning, where students can now use electronic means, as well as the post, to liaise with their tutors.

Contact with tutors on open learning courses may include occasional face-to-face meetings, to discuss progress. Open learning can involve the use of computer-based learning packages, which students may use at home, or through an open learning centre offering the necessary computer facilities, perhaps with tutor back-up.

There are often no entrance qualifications to distance and open learning courses, and a vast range of subjects are offered including degrees and postgraduate professional level courses (through the Open University). There is a lot of emphasis on self-discipline as the courses are so flexible.

The main providers

The Further Education Funding Council (FEFC) is the body through which UK public sector further education colleges receive their money. Each college is autonomous and manages its own affairs, applying to the FEFC for a large portion of its finance.

See also the foreword for changes proposed in the government White Paper, *Learning to Succeed*.

The Higher Education Funding Council (HEFC) operates in a similar way to the FEFC. Separate funding arrangements apply in Wales, Scotland and Northern Ireland.

Local Education Authorities (LEAs), Regional or Islands Councils, and Education and Library Boards

The LEAs are part of the local council which holds certain responsibilities in the education field. They fund most adult and community education services, community colleges and tertiary colleges, as well as schools in their area.

Training and Enterprise Councils (TECs) and Local Enterprise Companies (LECs)

There is a network of TECs (in England and Wales) and LECs (in Scotland) set up by the government's Department for Education and Employment, to organise, fund and monitor assistance to the local economy through work-related training and other measures.

They contract with local training providers such as colleges, training companies or voluntary organisations to deliver training programmes, which include, Work-based Learning for Adults (in England). They are also a source of information and advice about training and enterprise matters.

See also the foreword for changes proposed in the government White Paper, *Learning to Succeed*.

In Northern Ireland the Training and Employment Agency (T&EA) administers Jobskills – the training programme for 16-24 year olds. They contract with training organisations to deliver Jobskills, which leads to NVQs.

Business and industry

The government, through the TECs, LECs, and the T&EA are encouraging organisations to carry out more training, with a range of measures and assistance on offer. National Learning Targets have been set to help ensure improvement of the skills and qualifications of the workforce.

Some larger employers have their own training and study centres, and employ their own trainers. Others buy in assistance from local colleges and consultants. National Vocational Qualifications (NVQs) have been structured to allow people to be accredited for competencies in the workplace.

The voluntary sector

This sector is a major provider of training and education which can often be transferred to professional paid work. Examples might be training for volunteers working with adult literacy groups, second language providers, counselling organisations, probation and social workers.

Further information

There are many reference directories of further and higher education; relevant publications are listed in the other chapters of this section. Here are a few examples to provide a general starting point. Databases of education and training opportunities, held at careers centres, can also provide useful information.

Directory of Further Education – published annually by Hobsons. 1999/2000 edition priced £76.50. ISBN 1 860176208. Covers over 75,000 further education courses in the UK.

University and College Entrance: The Official Guide – published annually by UCAS, available from Trotman. For entry 2000 edition, price £19.95. ISBN 0 948241 69 1.

Mature Students' Guide – available from Trotman, price £7.99. ISBN 0 85660 162 4. Guide to getting into higher education for those aged 21 plus.

Independent Colleges – available from Trotman, price £6.99. ISBN 0 90193 648 0. A directory of courses at over 600 independent institutions.

7. Qualifications

This chapter covers:

- general points – what qualifications are, what they are used for, how they can be achieved, who needs them and who awards qualifications?
- the national qualifications framework
- summaries of qualifications in England, Wales and Northern Ireland, and in Scotland
- England, Wales and Northern Ireland: general academic and vocational qualifications
- Scotland: general academic and vocational qualifications
- Credit Accumulation and Transfer Schemes (CATS)
- APL and APEL
- overseas qualifications.

What are qualifications?

A formal recognition of skills and knowledge, awarded by a recognised body. They range from general academic qualifications, through to highly vocational qualifications.

What are qualifications used for?

They are used as evidence of achievement:

- they may be required for admission to further and higher education courses
- they are usually asked for by employers when recruiting
- they allow access to membership of professional bodies.

How can qualifications be achieved?

- Through full or part-time study on a formal taught course.
- Through open or distance learning – where students study independently using various resources, with access to back-up support from a tutor.
- Certain qualifications can be gained through accreditation of prior learning, or assessment in the workplace.
- Some qualifications are structured so that learners can undertake units or modules (which are each independently assessed) over a period of time, at a pace to suit themselves, so gradually building up to the full qualification.

Who needs qualifications?

Essential

There are some jobs for which specific qualifications are essential – for example professional jobs such as nursing, law, medicine, architecture or teaching.

Desirable

To enter most professions and trades it is helpful either to have a general qualification or the relevant specific one. However, there are no hard and fast rules; some employers prefer applicants to have relevant, practical experience and others will require the exact qualification.

Useful

Although experience is often enough for employment in smaller firms, or for self-employment, it is becoming increasingly important to have some formal recognition and proof of skills and knowledge, in particular for employment with larger employers.

Who awards qualifications?

There are many different awarding bodies. They include the various bodies who award GCSEs and A levels, and bodies such as Edexcel and City and Guilds who are involved in awarding a wide range of vocational qualifications. Universities award their own qualifications.

The national qualifications framework

The table below shows the national framework of qualifications for England, Wales and Northern Ireland, indicating the approximate equivalence between general and vocational qualifications. However, as academic and vocational qualifications are very different, it is not meaningful to equate them directly. Therefore, the information below should only be taken as a rough indication of equivalence.

Level 1/ Foundation	**Level 2/ Intermediate**	**Level 3/ Advanced**	**Levels 4-5 Higher level**
4 GCSEs at grades D–G	4/5 GCSEs at grades A*–C	2 A levels or equivalent	First degree, BA, BSc, BEd etc
Foundation GNVQ	Intermediate GNVQ	Advanced GNVQ	Some professional qualifications
	First diploma	National diploma or certificate	Higher national diploma or certificate
NVQ level 1	NVQ level 2	NVQ level 3	NVQ level 4/5

Summary of qualifications in England, Wales and Northern Ireland

The Qualifications and Curriculum Authority (QCA) has overall responsibility for academic and vocational qualifications in England. ACCAC is the Qualifications, Curriculum and Assessment Authority for Wales, and the body for Northern Ireland is the CCEA.

General academic qualifications

The main ones are:

- **General Certificate of Secondary Education (GCSE)**
- **A levels** and, from Autumn 2000, **Advanced Subsidiary (AS) levels**
- **Degrees** – such as Bachelor of Arts (BA), Bachelor of Science (BSc), Bachelor of Education (BEd).

Vocational education qualifications

General National Vocational Qualifications (GNVQ) – these cover broad occupational areas, and act as a 'bridge' between academic and very specific vocational qualifications. GNVQs are offered at Foundation, Intermediate and Advanced levels.

Vocational qualifications

These are used to prove competence in a job or activity. They include:

- **National Vocational Qualifications (NVQs)**, which are available in a wide range of occupations, at all levels
- qualifications set by **professional bodies** for entry to that profession, for example in accountancy, architecture or surveying
- other vocational qualifications.

Summary of qualifications in Scotland

Academic and vocational qualifications in Scotland are the responsibility of the Scottish Qualifications Authority (SQA). The educational system is different in Scotland from the rest of the UK, and changes in some of the qualifications offered are being implemented over the next few years.

- **General academic qualifications** currently available are Scottish standard and higher grades, and the Certificate of Sixth Year Studies (CSYS).
- **Vocational** qualifications available currently include national certificates, General Scottish Vocational Qualifications (GSVQs) and Scottish Vocational Qualifications (SVQs).

The new reforms involve a new structure for National Qualifications. As part of these reforms, the existing CSYS and GSVQs are being phased out. Scottish qualifications and these reforms are described in more detail later in this chapter.

The next section of this chapter describes the main available qualifications more fully.

General academic qualifications (England, Wales and Northern Ireland)

General Certificate of Secondary Education (GCSE)

GCSEs are the standard way of recognising achievement at the age of 16 in England, Wales and Northern Ireland. GCSEs are also available to adults.

There is an extremely wide range of subjects: from English, maths, biology and French, to Gujarati, Japanese, health studies, photography, and art amongst many others.

GCSEs are awarded by the following bodies: AQA, Edexcel, OCR and the Welsh Joint Education Committee, and overseen by the Qualifications and Curriculum Authority (QCA).

Each subject has a syllabus which describes what will be assessed and which methods (coursework and external examinations) will be used. Achievements are assessed by a combination of coursework (marked by teachers) and terminal, end-of-course examination (marked by external examiners for the examining board responsible for that particular GCSE).

GCSE certificates show achievements which must meet recognised national standards. Grades are awarded on a scale from A* to G.

Students who are aiming to use their GCSEs to help gain employment should note that many companies look for grade C or above in maths and English.

Ways of preparing for GCSE

- **Rules, syllabuses and exam timetables** can be obtained from examination boards.
- **Past examination papers** are useful for seeing the types of questions that are asked.
- **Examiners' reports** are published by exam boards, describing how questions were answered and what the examiner was looking for.

Where to study

You can study for GCSEs by attending a day or evening, full or part-time course at a further education college or adult education centre, community college or through open or distance learning.

It is possible to take a GCSE without studying on a regular basis at a school or college, by registering as an external candidate. Candidates wishing to take a GCSE in this way will need to find out what the regulations are for the particular subject by contacting the relevant examining board, an FE college or adult education centre.

Other general qualifications below GCSE standard

A large number of different awarding bodies offer qualifications which can lead on to further study or provide evidence of your skills and knowledge in a particular subject. These are described in Chapter 10.

Advanced level (A level)

A levels can be used as a route into some careers; in particular they are the route for school leavers to get into higher education institutions.

A levels are widely offered in further education colleges and school sixth forms. A levels can also be studied for through distance learning. They provide academic and study skills in a wide range of subjects. Anybody, of any age, may study for A levels. In some subjects, for example chemistry or French, prior knowledge of the subject (such as that gained at GCSE level) is needed before proceeding to A level.

From Autumn 2000, each A level will be divided into six units. Each unit will be separately assessed. Three AS (Advanced Subsidiary) units will be taken in the first half of an A level course, followed by three A2 units in the second half of the course, to complete the A level course.

A levels are currently offered by the following awarding bodies: AQA, Edexcel, OCR, Welsh Joint Education Committee and the CCEA in Northern Ireland.

Advanced Subsidiary (AS level)

Advanced Subsidiary (AS) qualifications will be offered from Autumn 2000, to replace the old Advanced Supplementary (AS) levels.

To achieve a new Advanced Subsidiary qualification, you must successfully complete three AS units, which form the first half of an A level course. The new AS level will be worth half an A level, and will count towards entry to higher education courses.

Access to higher education courses or return to study

There are many courses which cater for adults returning to formal education or study. Most of these are accredited through individual higher education institutions or authorised validating agencies such as the National Open College Network. Many such courses are run at local further education colleges.

Degrees

A higher education degree is a qualification which can provide an entry route to a wide range of higher-level jobs. Some degrees are more vocationally oriented than others; a Bachelor of Education prepares you for teaching, a law degree is a basis for further specialisation in the legal profession, engineering degrees for further training in engineering and so on.

A first degree (as opposed to a higher degree – described later) usually takes three or four years of full-time study (or longer if you study part-time). At the end of the course, students may be awarded an honours degree which is classified as first, second or third class. If this standard is not reached, the student is awarded a pass degree. Examples are BA (Bachelor of Arts), BSc (Bachelor of Science), LLB (Bachelor of Law) and BEd (Bachelor of Education). An honorary degree is something quite different – see below.

A number of degrees are offered through a franchise arrangement between a further education college and a higher education institution. The first year of a degree offered in this way can be carried out at a local FE college and students then usually move to the higher education institution for the rest of the course. In some parts of the country, these arrangements enable students to do the whole degree in their local FE college.

Many institutions operate Credit Accumulation and Transfer Schemes (CATS). This means that it can be possible to accumulate credit through successfully completing modules of a degree course, and also to transfer that credit to a different learning programme. This is particularly useful for students who are not able to complete the whole course, as they can gain credits for the study they have completed successfully. CAT schemes are described in more detail later in this chapter.

Diploma of Higher Education (DipHE)

This is offered by many higher education institutions as a qualification in its own right. It can be gained from a specific DipHE course, which is normally two years full-time, but it can also be equivalent in standard to the first two years of a degree. Many higher education institutions offer credit accumulation and transfer schemes, so that students can gain credit points towards completing the degree at a later stage, as well as gaining the DipHE.

Higher degrees

Masters degrees

These are awarded after following a full-time programme, usually for a year, or part-time programmes for about two years. These are taught courses which generally include some research. A Master of Philosophy (MPhil) is usually taken by doing research for one or two years. Some people do a higher degree to enhance their professional knowledge and therefore fit it in around a job; others follow a first degree immediately with a masters degree, undertaken on a full-time basis.

Examples are MA (Master of Arts), MEd (Master of Education), MSc (Master of Science) and MBA (Master of Business Administration). Note that some universities (such as those in Scotland) call some of their first degrees MA.

Doctorate degrees
A PhD (Doctor of Philosophy) is awarded after doing several years' research in any subject – at least three years full-time, more if you study part-time.

Honorary degrees
Some universities award honorary degrees to famous or distinguished people who do not have to do anything by way of study but are simply – distinguished!

Vocational education qualifications (in England, Wales and Northern Ireland)

General National Vocational Qualifications (GNVQs)
GNVQs cover broad occupational areas, including health and social care, business, manufacturing, art and design, hospitality and catering, and engineering.

- They are aimed mainly at full-time students, aged 16-19, but can also be studied by adults.
- All GNVQ courses include the key skills of communication, application of number and information technology.
- GNVQs are made up of a series of separately assessed units, which build up towards the qualification.
- GNVQs are available at foundation, intermediate and advanced levels.
- From Autumn 2000, Advanced GNVQ will be available both as a full 12-unit award, and as a new single award (six-unit) qualification.
- GNVQs are currently awarded by three bodies – Edexcel, City and Guilds and OCR (Oxford, Cambridge and RSA Examinations).
- Advanced GNVQs can provide entry to a degree or Higher National Diploma (HND) course, or can lead to employment.

Vocational qualifications

The following are available in England, Wales and Northern Ireland.

National Vocational Qualifications (NVQs)
NVQs are designed to reflect the skills, knowledge and understanding needed to do a job to the standards of competence set by industry, commerce or the professions. These standards are developed in collaboration with employers, employees' representatives and professional bodies.

The most important feature of NVQs is that it is not necessary to have attended a taught course in order to get the qualification, although further education colleges provide courses leading to NVQs.

NVQs are offered in units of competence which you can build up over a period of time. Candidates have to provide evidence, which is assessed, to demonstrate their competence in the various aspects of the work. This can be done at the workplace, at college or through Accreditation of Prior Learning (APL) (see below). Providing the evidence is authentic, relevant and current, it can come from previous work and life experience as well as from formal learning.

NVQs are available in a huge range of work areas, and are awarded at five levels, covering basic to professional-level skills.

BTEC first and national diplomas/certificates

BTEC qualifications are awarded by the Edexcel Foundation. They are related to particular fields of employment, such as agriculture, construction or art and design; some BTEC qualifications are in specific job areas, such as interior design or polymer technology. BTEC Firsts are at introductory level, while the diplomas and certificates are roughly equivalent to A level standard and can lead on to higher education – degrees, HNDs or other higher-level vocational courses. Diplomas are awarded following full-time study; certificates after part-time study.

BTEC higher national diplomas/certificates (HND/C)

These are advanced-level qualifications, awarded by the Edexcel Foundation, which relate to a particular occupational field. The courses combine theory and practice, and prepare students for roles at technician, supervisory or management level. Higher national full-time courses lead to diplomas, and the part-time courses lead to certificates. It can be possible to continue with a further year's study to top up to a degree.

Other vocational qualifications

There are a range of other available vocational qualifications, besides those leading to the award of NVQ, GNVQ or BTEC qualifications, as previously described. Some of the main providers of other vocational qualifications are described below.

City and Guilds

City and Guilds are involved in awarding over 500 qualifications, related to all areas of business and industry. Besides NVQs and GNVQs, City and Guilds offers a number of other qualifications, including qualifications in basic skills. The City and Guilds Group also includes Pitman Qualifications, well known for their commercial qualifications, and NEBS Management, who offer a range of management and supervisory qualifications.

OCR

OCR (Oxford, Cambridge and RSA Examinations) is the result of an alliance between the University of Cambridge Local Examinations Syndicate and the RSA Examinations Board. OCR therefore offers a wide range of academic and vocational qualifications, including NVQs and GNVQs, key skills, specialist teaching qualifications and all the well known RSA office and business qualifications.

London Chamber of Commerce and Industry Examinations Board

The LCCIEB is a major examining and assessment body for business-related qualifications. Areas covered include administration, secretarial, accounting, management, marketing, foreign languages, and information technology. A Vocational Access Certificate and qualifications in Wordpower and Numberpower are available. It is also involved in awarding NVQs.

Professional bodies

Almost every professional organisation, such as the Royal Institution of Chartered Surveyors, or the Chartered Institute of Marketing, has its own examination structures. Achieving their qualifications leads to membership of that particular organisation. The relevant professional body can provide information – contact addresses can be found through reference libraries and careers centres.

Scottish qualifications

The educational system is different in Scotland from the rest of the UK, and the next two or three years will see the implementation of some changes to the qualifications available in Scotland.

Academic and vocational qualifications in Scotland are the responsibility of the Scottish Qualifications Authority (SQA).

Qualifications currently available

Standard grade

These are the Scottish counterpart to GCSE.

The standard grade awards are made on a scale of 1 to 7, where 1 is the highest. Grade 3 is broadly equivalent to a grade C at GCSE.

Each course has three or four separate elements; two or three are taken by a formal examination and are marked externally by examiners. In most subjects, one element is marked internally by school or college staff. The amount of assessed coursework varies from course to course.

Adults may take standard grades through further education colleges.

Standard grades will not be affected by the forthcoming reforms.

Scottish higher grades and Certificate of Sixth Year Studies (CSYS)

Higher grades are normally taken in the fifth year of secondary education, one year after standard grade; candidates in full-time education usually take five subjects. A wide range of academic subjects are available. Possession of an appropriate number of higher and standard awards enables applicants to enter all the Scottish universities. Higher awards can also be used for exemption from the preliminary examinations of most professional bodies.

The Certificate of Sixth Year Studies is taken in the sixth year of secondary schooling.
Scottish highers and the CSYS will be affected by the reforms described below.

National Certificate modules, clusters and group awards

- Over 3,000 **National Certificate modules** are available, covering most occupational areas. These are offered at schools, as well as in colleges.
- **National Certificate clusters** – these are packages of modules.
- National Certificate group awards – known as **GSVQs** (General Scottish Vocational Qualifications) – which are broad-based qualifications, designed mainly for 16-19 year olds in schools and colleges, and may be taken by adults returning to education.

These National qualifications are being reformed (see below).

Scottish Vocational Qualifications (SVQs)

SVQs are nationally recognised awards, offered by the SQA, and are the Scottish counterparts to NVQs. SVQs demonstrate the candidate's competence to perform in particular work areas to the standards required by business and industry.

Scottish Progression Awards, which have been recently introduced, are a way of showing that candidates have completed a programme of personal development to national standards. They are stepping stones to full SVQs, and are currently available in six occupational areas.

Higher national diploma (HND) or certificate (HNC)
These are intended for students who have completed the National Certificate programme, or who have an appropriate group of higher and standard grades, A levels or GCSEs. Some students may qualify, at the discretion of a college, on grounds of maturity and experience. The length of the programme varies, and whether you are awarded a certificate or diploma depends on the level of study. Higher National qualifications are increasingly being offered on a part-time basis.

More than 1,000 courses are on offer, in areas such as business administration, travel and tourism, engineering and agriculture.

HNCs/HNDs are run at further education colleges and higher education institutions. They are recognised by many professional and technical bodies.

Degrees
Degrees in Scotland generally last four years ; many first degrees in Scotland lead to the award of 'MA' rather than BA.

Awards offered by professional bodies – these are often the same as for the rest of the UK, although there are some differences in professional qualifications, notably for the legal profession.

Reforms to qualifications 1999-2002

The main difference is that new National Units, and National Courses (which are made up of units) will be introduced. There will also be Scottish Group Awards (SGAs) which are recognised groupings of these units and courses. The new National Units and National Courses will be at five levels:

- Access
- Intermediate 1
- Intermediate 2
- Higher
- Advanced Higher.

Standard grade courses (on which the new Intermediate Courses are benchmarked) will not be affected by the reforms.

The current highers will be available for the last time in 2000. They will be replaced by **National Qualifications at Higher Level**. The 'old' highers and 'new' highers will be of similar value.

The Certificate of Sixth Year Studies will be phased out and replaced by **National Qualifications at Advanced Higher level** by 2002.

Most National Certificate modules and short courses will be retained as National Units, together with new National Units.

GSVQs are being phased out.

For more information

The Scottish Qualifications Authority (SQA) – based at two sites:

Ironmills Road, Dalkeith, Midlothian EH22 1LE. Tel: 0131 663 6601 – for information about Scottish standard grades and highers.

Hanover House, 24 Douglas Street, Glasgow G2 7NQ. Tel: 0141 248 7900 – for information about vocational qualifications.

For general enquiries contact the SQA helpline: 0141 242 2214.

The SQA website contains useful information: www.sqa.org.uk

Credit Accumulation and Transfer Schemes (CATS)

Many further and higher education institutions offer credit-based programmes, in which units or modules of study are assigned a number of credit points at a particular level. CAT schemes allow learners to accumulate credit towards qualifications within an institution, and to transfer credit from one institution to another. Full-time, part-time, distance and open learning courses can all form part of a CAT scheme.

At higher education level, most institutions give credit values to their degree programmes of study. In England, Wales and Northern Ireland, there are a number of credit frameworks in operation, which are mostly similar, but do show some variations. In Scotland, there is a single Credit Accumulation and Transfer Scheme (SCOTCAT).

When assigning credit, account is normally taken of the total time that a typical learner would take to complete the study, and of the level of the particular programme of learning, eg whether first, second or third year undergraduate, or at masters degree level.

In many cases, credit can be assessed and awarded for prior learning, which can then count towards a further qualification. For example, credit may be given for:

- previous higher education programmes
- higher education short courses
- awards of professional bodies
- employer's in-house education and training programmes
- learning from experience, often, but not only, at work.

An increasing number of professional qualifications and in-company education and training programmes are credit rated by higher education institutions towards their certificates, diplomas and degrees.

Institutions may charge a fee for assessing previous study for credit.

Accreditation of Prior Learning (APL) and Experiential Learning (APEL)

The process of gaining credit for existing qualifications is known as Accreditation of Prior Learning (APL). If prospective students want their experience taken into account and can demonstrate skills and knowledge, this is called Accreditation of Prior Experiential Learning (APEL).

Applicants have to prepare evidence of relevant prior learning by compiling a portfolio of their achievements. This has to be related to the learning outcomes of the units, or entry requirements for which they are seeking exemption. The portfolio can therefore give them credits for the formal entry requirements or for part of the course itself. Applicants apply for APL or APEL to the individual institution which offers the service, and they will advise whether it is worthwhile gaining credit in this way, and of any fees chargeable. Some institutions offer APEL/APL support to help applicants to compile a portfolio.

Overseas qualifications

UK NARIC provides information on the equivalence of overseas qualifications to institutions and organisations through a subscription service, and individual students are able to use its enquiry service free of charge. UK NARIC publishes an advisers' guide to comparability of UK and international qualifications – *International Comparisons* – available on CD-Rom or on the internet, which is updated three times a year.

Overseas teaching qualifications
To teach in England, people with overseas teaching qualifications should contact the organisations below.

For teaching in England and Wales contact:
The Department for Education and Employment Teachers' Qualifications Team – Mowden Hall, Staindrop Road, Darlington DL3 9DG. Tel: 01325 392 123. Qualified Teacher Status (QTS) is normally granted automatically to teachers trained in the European Union, but they still need to contact the DfEE for verification.

For teaching in Scotland, contact:
The General Teaching Council for Scotland – Clerwood House, 96 Clermiston Road, Edinburgh EH12 6UT. Tel: 0131 314 6000.
Website: www.gtcs.org.uk E-mail: gtcs@gtcs.freeserve.co.uk

For teaching in Northern Ireland, contact:
Department for Education Northern Ireland, Teachers' Salaries, Waterside House, 75 Duke Street, Londonderry BT47 1FP. Tel: 01504 319000.

Further information

The Qualifications and Curriculum Authority (QCA) – 29 Bolton Street, London W1Y 7PD. Tel: 020 7509 5555. Information about academic and vocational qualifications (for England, Wales and Northern Ireland) can be found on their website: www.qca.org.uk

The Scottish Qualifications Authority (SQA) – based at two sites:
Ironmills Road, Dalkeith, Midlothian EH22 1LE. Tel: 0131 663 6601 –
for information about Scottish standard grades and highers.

Hanover House, 24 Douglas Street, Glasgow G2 7NQ. Tel: 0141 248 7900 –
for information about vocational qualifications.

For general enquiries contact the SQA helpline: 0141 242 2214.
The SQA website contains useful information about the available qualifications: www.sqa.org.uk

The National Academic Recognition Information Centre (UK NARIC) – ECCTIS 2000 Ltd, Oriel House, Oriel Road, Cheltenham, Gloucestershire GL50 1XP. Tel: 01242 260010.
E-mail: naric@ecctis2000.co.uk Website: www.naric.org.uk (section open to non-subscribers under development)

ACCAC – Qualifications, Curriculum and Assessment Authority for Wales, Castle Buildings, Womanby Street, Cardiff CF1 9SX. Tel: 029 2037 5400.
Website: www.accac.org.uk E-mail: info@accac.org.uk

AQA – Devas Street, Manchester M15 6EX. Tel: 0161 953 1180. Website: www.aqa.org.uk

City and Guilds – 1 Giltspur Street, London EC1A 9DD. Tel: 020 7294 2468. Customer Services Enquiry Unit: 020 7294 2800. Website: www.city-and-guilds.co.uk
E-mail: enquiry@city-and-guilds.co.uk

CCEA – Clarendon Docks, 29 Clarendon Road, Belfast BT1 3BG. Tel: 028 9026 1200.
Website: www.ccea.org.uk E-mail: info@ccea.org.uk

Edexcel Foundation – Customer Response Centre, Stewart House, 32 Russell Square, London WC1B 5DN. Tel: 020 7393 4500. Website: www.edexcel.org.uk E-mail: enquiries@edexcel.org.uk

LCCIEB Customer Service – Athena House, 112 Station Road, Sidcup DA15 7W.
Tel: 020 8302 0261. Website: www.lccieb.org.uk E-mail: custo.serv@lccieb.org.uk

OCR – Head Office, 1 Regent Street, Cambridge CB2 1GG. Tel: 01223 552552.
Website: www.ocr.org.uk E-mail: helpdesk@ocr.org.uk

SCOTCAT – HEQC, Scottish Office, Albert Chambers, 13 Bath Street, Glasgow G2 1HY.
Tel: 0141 353 3445.

Welsh Joint Education Committee – 245 Western Avenue, Cardiff CF5 2YX Tel: 029 2026 5000.
Website: www.wjec.co.uk E-mail: info@wjec.co.uk

Many of the resources listed below are available for reference in careers libraries in careers centres, educational institutions and public reference libraries.

British Qualifications – published by Kogan Page, price £33.50 paperback. ISBN 0 7494 2866 X.

British Vocational Qualifications – published by Kogan Page, price £32.50. ISBN 0 7494 2548 2. This gives greater detail about NVQs than *British Qualifications*.

International Guide to Qualifications in Education (4th edition 1995) – published by Cassell plc, Stanley House, 3 Fleet Lane, Poole BH15 3AJ Tel: 01202 665432. Price £100.
ISBN 0 72012 217 1. Available at main libraries.

NVQs and How to Get Them – published by Kogan Page, price £8.99. ISBN 0 7494 2812 0.

Directory of Further Education – published annually by Hobsons. 1999/2000 edition priced £76.50. ISBN 1 860176208. Covers over 75,000 further education courses in the UK.

How to Choose Your GCSEs – published by Trotman, price £8.99. ISBN 0 85660 362 7.

Which A levels? – published by Lifetime Careers Publishing, price £10.99. ISBN 1873408 88 9.

University and College Entrance: The Official Guide – published annually by UCAS, available from Trotman. For entry 2000 edition, price £19.95. ISBN 0 948241 69 1.

8. Money

This chapter covers the main sources of financial assistance for education and training.

There will always be some financial outlay or pressure on existing finances when undertaking training, especially if you embark on a full-time course. This involves not just personal commitment, but often changes in the family lifestyle too.

Potential learners need to:

- **plan ahead** – investigate as many sources of funding as possible, and make sure that they are clear about **all** the costs involved besides the course fees: eg books, materials and equipment, registration and examination fees, travel costs etc
- **consider their liabilities** – eg mortgage, rent, household bills, any outstanding loans etc, and scale down their financial commitments as much as possible
- **review their assets and income** – eg house, car, savings, interest from savings and shares, partner's income.

Sources of financial assistance

This is a complex area. Most people who are studying or training are supported by help from several sources. Any financial assistance available from public funds, which could be in the form of a loan or a non-repayable grant or bursary, depends on:

- the course or training opportunity being taken
- the student's/trainee's personal circumstances.

A **summary indication** of possible sources of assistance is given below, for use as a preliminary reference to the rest of the chapter.

As eligibility rules and regulations are often complex, you should not assume you are eligible for the funding sources mentioned before consulting additional more detailed information from the relevant bodies, and getting an application approved by the organisation concerned.

Summary of sources of financial assistance

Please note that the information below provides only a general outline indication of the usual sources of funding/financial assistance available, to use as a starting point. For more information on each, see later in this chapter.

General

- **Individual learning accounts**: special personal bank accounts, to encourage people to plan for and invest in their own learning. Account holders who are in work will be eligible for various financial incentives.
- **Career Development Loans**: available for vocational courses. From high street banks, in conjunction with the DfEE.

- **Vocational Training Relief (VTR)**: tax relief for people paying for some types of training, including working towards NVQs and SVQs. VTR will be abolished in 2000-01, when the national framework is in place for the government's new individual learning accounts. Discounts will be available on these accounts.

- **Employers**: many employers pay towards course fees, or allow paid time off work to employees who are studying courses relevant to their job. Employers may also contribute to employees' individual learning accounts.

- **Studying while on benefits**: people who have been getting Jobseeker's Allowance for, normally, three months, are eligible to study on a part-time course of further education of up to, and including, a maximum of 16 hours a week, provided they continue to actively seek work. Part-time study on other courses may be allowed at the discretion of the Employment Service.

Financial support related to particular types and levels of courses

- **Work-based Learning for Adults** – the training programme for unemployed adults: a training allowance equivalent to the trainee's benefits plus approximately £10 a week is provided. There is also some help with travelling costs. (Training for Work is the counterpart programme in Scotland).

- **The New Deal** provides opportunities for full-time study or training, during which participants continue to receive their benefit level of income.

- **Full-time further education courses**: tuition fees are normally payable for students aged 19 and over (18 and over in Scotland) when they start the course. From Autumn 1999, new arrangements for financial assistance for new students is replacing LEA discretionary grants in England and Wales. Assistance will include help from Access Funds, administered by colleges, and some other forms of assistance. Scotland has a separate system of bursaries.

- **Part-time further education courses**: colleges may reduce or waive course fees to students in financial hardship, usually defined as those who receive benefits. Basic education is normally free.

- **Full-time higher education courses**: tuition fees, of up to £1,025 a year (for 1999/2000), are payable; contributions are means-tested. Students under 50, and those aged 50-54 who plan to return to work after studying, may apply for a student loan to finance their living costs. Hardship loans and Access Funds can provide some additional help for students in particular difficulty.

- **Part-time higher education courses**: tuition fee waivers are being introduced for students on benefits. Loans will be available to students on a low income from Autumn 2000. Support from Access Funds is also available.

- **Adult education bursaries** are available for students studying at the adult residential colleges.

- **Postgraduate courses**: fees are payable by students (apart from postgraduate initial teacher training courses). Some financial assistance is available through bodies such as the research councils and Arts and Humanities Research Board.

- **Sponsorships and scholarships**: some employers **sponsor** students on particular higher education courses, such as engineering or business. **Scholarships** are sometimes offered for places on particular courses – applicants compete for these places.

- **Charities and trusts** offer limited financial assistance. Usually the terms and conditions of the trusts restrict the range of people who are eligible.

Help for students studying certain subjects

- **Dance and drama**: from Autumn 1999, a Dance and Drama Awards scholarship scheme will offer help to many students on dance, drama and stage management courses.
- **NHS bursaries**: NHS-funded places are available on a range of pre-registration courses in professions related to medicine, including physiotherapy, speech and language therapy and nursing.
- **Teacher training for shortage subjects**: extra financial assistance is available for students studying in England and Wales.

Each of the funding arrangements outlined above is explained in more detail later in this chapter.

Students with disabilities
Some extra help is available. This includes:

- assistance for specialist equipment
- assistance with transport
- the Disabled Students' Allowance, for people on higher education courses (described in the higher education section of this chapter).

Some state benefits, such as income support and housing benefit, that are not generally available to full-time students, may be available for students with disabilities on full-time courses.

People with disabilities should always seek information and advice about possible extra financial support from course providers and Employment Service or Benefits Agency staff.

For further information

SKILL – National Bureau for Students with Disabilities – The Chapter House, 18-20 Crucifix Lane, London SE1 3JW. Information line tel: 0800 328 5050.
Website (which contains much useful information about funding): www.skill.org.uk
E-mail: info@skill.org.uk

SKILL publish useful information sheets, and the following two booklets:

Financial Assistance for Students with Disabilities – one booklet on further education and training, and the other on higher education – price £2 each to individual students, and £6.50 to advisers and other professionals.

Individual learning accounts

Individual learning accounts aim to encourage people to plan for and invest in their own learning. As well as the contributions made by the individual account holders to their own accounts, employers will also be encouraged to contribute to their employees' accounts.

A limited number of individual learning accounts are now becoming available through Training and Enterprise Councils (TECs) and Chambers of Commerce, Training and Enterprise (CCTEs).

During 2000, a national framework of learning accounts will be launched. Whilst anyone will be able to open an account, they are particularly aimed at those in full or part-time work (and not in full-time education). These account holders qualify for certain financial incentives:

- up to the first million people* to open an account qualify for a contribution of £150 to their account from their local TEC or CCTE, as long as they contribute of at least £25 of their own money

- during 2000, a system of discounts for certain courses will become available:

  - a 20% discount off the cost of eligible courses, capped at £500 in each year (but only available from the second and subsequent years for those with a starter account)

  - an 80% discount off the cost of certain courses, including computer literacy.

In addition, employees will not be subject to tax or National Insurance contributions on an employer's contribution to a learning account (subject to certain conditions). The employer's contributions to learning accounts will be tax deductible, providing the employer extends the offer to the lowest paid employees on a similar basis.

Note: Until it is replaced by the new system of discounts in 2000, Vocational Training Relief is currently available for fees for vocational training courses, and individual learning account holders may qualify (see section on VTR later in this chapter).

Whilst individual learning accounts are in their development phase, the bodies administering them – TECs/CCTEs in England and Wales – may decide to give priority for their contribution to certain groups, or for certain types of course.

Information can be found on the website: www.lifelonglearning.co.uk/ila

Career Development Loans

Career Development Loans (CDLs) help people to pay for vocational education or training by offering a deferred repayment bank loan.

Those in learning already funded by the state (eg full-time students, participants in the New Deal for 18-24 year olds, and those receiving Jobseeker's Allowance), will not qualify for the £150 contribution from TECs, although those in the New Deal for 25+, people with disabilities and lone parents may qualify. You can get more information from the local TEC.

CDLs can be used for any course, whether it is full-time, part-time, open or distance learning, as long as it:

- is vocational
- lasts no longer than two years, plus up to one year's practical work experience, if it is part of the course. CDLs can also support 24 months of a longer course.

Eligibility criteria include that applicants:

- are 18 or over on the date of application
- live, or intend to train, in Great Britain (Northern Ireland residents may apply for CDLs, but not for courses based within Northern Ireland)
- intend to use the education or training for work in the UK or elsewhere in the EU, or within the European Economic Area.

Applicants cannot use a CDL to pay for anything that is being funded by another source. Therefore, you are not entitled to a CDL if you are eligible for financial assistance through a Local Education Authority for a course at a publicly-funded institution, or if you are employed and your employer receives a grant for your training.

Applicants may be employed, unemployed or self-employed.

CDLs are available through a partnership arrangement between the Department for Education and Employment and four major banks – Barclays, The Co-operative, Clydesdale and The Royal Bank of Scotland.

You can apply to borrow between £300 and £8000 to pay for up to 80% of your course fees, plus the full cost of books, materials and other related expenses.

Applicants who have been out of work for three months or longer may be able to borrow 100% of their course fees. In this case the application must be endorsed by the local Training and Enterprise Council (TEC), Chamber of Commerce Training and Enterprise (CCTE), or Local Enterprise Company (LEC) in Scotland.

In certain circumstances, people on full-time courses may be able to borrow money to help cover their living expenses.

No repayments are made on the loan during the period of study or training and for up to a month afterwards. The Department for Education and Employment pays the interest during this period. At the end of the interest-free period, repayments of the loan are payable over a period agreed with the bank.

If, one month after completing the training, the CDL recipient is still unemployed and claiming related benefits, or is employed and receiving one of certain benefits, such as family credit, they may apply to the bank to postpone the start of the repayments for up to 17 months.

 **Contact:** *Career Development Loans, Freepost, Newcastle Upon Tyne NE85 IBR. Tel: (freephone) 0800 585505 (for a free information pack and application form); from 8am to 10pm Monday to Sunday.*

Vocational Training Relief (VTR)

At present, people paying for training which can count towards National Vocational Qualifications (NVQs) or Scottish Vocational Qualifications (SVQs), General National Vocational Qualifications (GNVQs) or General Scottish Vocational Qualifications (GSVQs) can claim basic rate tax relief on the cost of the course.

In addition, those aged 30 or over can also claim VTR for any full-time course lasting between four weeks and a year which does not lead to NVQs/SVQs, so long as it provides skills or knowledge relevant to, and intended to be used in, employment or self-employment.

Costs that qualify include tuition fees, examination and registration fees, payments for awards and certificates, assessment fees (including accreditation of prior learning) and essential course materials provided by the training organisation (but not textbooks, equipment or travel). There are various conditions which must be fulfilled, including a residency requirement. The individual must make the payments personally, and must not be receiving, or entitled to receive, financial assistance from other government-funded sources (although relief can be claimed if funding is through a CDL or if they get access funds). Individuals qualify for VTR even if they themselves do not pay tax.

In practice, the way the individual student or trainee gets the VTR is by deducting tax relief at the basic rate from their course fees before paying them, and the course provider then claims this back from the Inland Revenue.

However, the VTR arrangements currently operating **will be abolished sometime after April 2000**, when the national framework for individual learning accounts is launched, bringing with it a new system of discounts (as described in the section in this chapter describing individual learning accounts).

For more information about the scheme running up to April 2000, see Inland Revenue leaflet **1R 119 – Tax Relief for Vocational Training**, available from any tax office.

Employers

Employers may financially assist their employees' learning in various ways:

- contributing to course fees and other costs, such as examination fees
- allowing paid time off to study
- contributing to their employees' individual learning accounts.

In general, financial assistance is only considered for courses relevant to the employee's work, although some large employers have established employee development programmes which may include providing support towards learning across a wide range of fields.

It is always worthwhile approaching your employer for assistance.

Some employers, such as the armed forces, may allow employees to undertake full-time study while retaining their salary.

Some employers offer assistance in the form of sponsorships for higher education courses – see the *Sponsorships and scholarships* section later in this chapter.

Studying on benefits

The rules are in this area are complex. Claimants should always check with their local Benefits Agency on the most up-to-date rulings about studying whilst on benefit.

Full-time students cannot normally receive benefits (there are some exceptions – see below) but it can be possible to study part-time as an unemployed person and still receive benefits.

Jobseeker's allowance claimants

People getting jobseeker's allowance (JSA) may, as a concession within the benefits system, follow **part-time** courses of education or training.

Further education

In England, courses which are funded by the Further Education Funding Council, with up to 16 'guided learning hours' a week are regarded as part-time. Guided learning hours are all times when staff are present to give guidance towards the qualification. It also includes time when staff assess a student's achievements.

In Scotland, courses that are funded by the Scottish Office count as part-time if they consist of 16 hours or less of classroom or workshop-based learning under the direct guidance of teaching staff, or if they are 21 hours or less a week, made up of 16 hours or less of classroom or workshop-based learning under the direct guidance of teaching staff (and additional hours using learning packages with the support of teachers).

Higher education and other courses

For courses that do not fall into the further education category, the regulations currently do not specify a set number of maximum hours a week. The most important factor is that the course must not be described as full-time. Each case will be assessed individually.

Whatever the level of the course they are following, JSA claimants must prove that they are continuing to actively seek work, and must be prepared to give up the course to take up a suitable job offer. Claimants must normally have been in receipt of benefit for the three months before the start of the course, although there are exceptions to this. Claimants are asked by the Employment Service to complete a student questionnaire to show that they fulfil the conditions.

Full-time students are not normally eligible for Jobseeker's Allowance. Exceptions to this are:

- students who are undertaking a full-time course under the New Deal
- students who have a partner and dependant child, where both adults are students – they can only claim JSA during the summer vacation
- prisoners on temporary release
- women getting maternity allowance or statutory maternity pay.

People following a full-time Work-based Learning for Adults training programme through their local TEC/LEC receive a training allowance equivalent to their benefits plus £10, plus possible help with other expenses.

People with disabilities on full-time courses may be entitled to income support.

For further information

Local Jobcentres.

Unemployment and Training Rights Handbook 1999 – published by the Unemployment Unit/Youthaid, 322 St John Street, London EC1V 4NU. Tel: 020 7833 1111.

SKILL (The National Bureau for Students with Disabilities) – 4th Floor, Chapter House, Crucifix Lane, London SE1 3JW. Telephone information line: 0800 328 5050. Website: www.skill.org.uk

Work-based Learning for Adults

Work-based Learning for Adults is a training programme for unemployed people; eligibility for the programme, and what it offers, is described in more detail in Chapter 27 *Unemployment*. Those who undertake Work-based Learning for Adults receive a training allowance equivalent to their benefits plus an additional £10 a week. Help with travel costs and childcare costs may also be available. There are no fees for the training itself.

The New Deal

Within the **New Deal for those aged 18-24**, full-time education and training is one of the four options available, if a job cannot be found by the participant. In this case, the participant is guaranteed the equivalent of jobseeker's allowance.

Under the **New Deal for those aged 25+**, participants may undertake full-time education or training, during which they are still entitled to jobseeker's allowance.

For further details of full-time education and training under the New Deal, see Chapter 24, and for information on the New Deal in general, see Chapter 27.

Full-time further education

Further education courses are non-advanced courses (up to level 3 standard, eg A level, Advanced GNVQ, NVQ 3 or the equivalent in Scotland). They are offered mainly at further education colleges.

Students aged 19 and over when they start the course (18 and over in Scotland) are normally liable for paying course fees. There are some circumstances where this may not apply, such as if the course is concerned with basic education.

New arrangements for financial assistance for new students are being brought in from September 1999 in England. These replace the former system of Local Education Authority discretionary grants.

Under the new arrangements, there are a number of ways that students may be able to get help:

- Through **Access Funds**, administered by the further education colleges for their own students. The Access Funds are intended to help students who are on low incomes and in the most need. Money from Access Funds can be used towards any of the costs related to the student's course. Students should ask their FE college for a copy of their policy for allocating their Access Funds.
- Help towards **childcare** may be available. Colleges get funding so they can provide free or subsidised childcare places for students on benefit or low incomes.
- Students on low incomes who are studying at a specialist agriculture and horticulture college or at an art and design college and need to be **residential** may get help through the college towards their residential costs.
- Some colleges have hardship funds or bursaries which may provide some additional funding to students in particular difficulties.

Wales
New arrangements are also being introduced which will be broadly similar to the above.

Scotland
Scotland operates a system of bursaries for students in further education. Young people and adults may apply for bursaries through the college where they will be studying. Funding available for bursaries is limited, and whether students are granted bursary funding, and how much they may get, depends on a variety of factors.

Northern Ireland
For the academic year 1999/2000, students may apply through their regional Education and Library Boards for discretionary grants for further education courses. Budgets are limited. This is the last year that discretionary awards will be available. Student support for further education in Northern Ireland is currently under review, and new arrangements should be put into place from Autumn 2000. At the time of publication, no information is yet available about any new arrangements.

For further information
Financial Help in Further Education – free booklet published by the Department for Education and Employment. Copies should be available in colleges and careers centres, from the DfEE publications centre, tel: 0845 6022260. It is available on the DfEE website: www.dfee.gov.uk
E-mail: dfee@prologistics.co.uk (quoting reference FHFE).

Financial Assistance for Students with disabilities – for students in further education, published by SKILL, 4th Floor, Chapter House, Crucifix Lane, London SE1 3JW. Cost to students £2.00. Telephone information line: 0800 328 5050. Website: www.skill.org.uk

Part-time further education

Course fees may be reduced or waived for people in financial hardship, usually defined as those receiving certain state benefits. Concessionary fees may apply only to courses leading to recognised qualifications – this should be checked with the college or adult education service offering the courses. There are generally no fees for basic education courses.

Students should also enquire from their college about any other financial assistance which might be available to them.

When considering course costs, applicants should make sure they are aware of any additional costs, such as registration and examination fees, and costs of any materials.

Note: Other possible sources of assistance which may apply to particular further education students (those on particular full or part-time further education courses) are described elsewhere in this chapter under the following headings:

- Individual learning accounts
- Career Development Loans
- Vocational Training Relief
- Studying on benefits
- Sponsorships and scholarships
- Charities and trusts
- Dance and drama courses.

Full-time higher education

The information provided below applies particularly to students whose homes are in England and Wales, who are new entrants to higher education.

Support for students living in Scotland and Northern Ireland is, however, currently broadly similar **except that** Scottish students studying in Scotland on a course which is one year longer than the comparable course in England and Wales are **not** asked to make a contribution to tuition fees in their final year.

In Scotland, the **Scottish Awards Agency for Scotland** administers financial support to higher education students, and in Northern Ireland, the five regional **Education and Library Boards** fulfil this function. Information booklets for students living in Scotland and Northern Ireland are listed at the end of this higher education section.

Higher education courses which the information in this section applies to are courses leading to:

- first degrees, such as a BA, BSc, BEng or BEd
- Diplomas of Higher Education

- higher national diploma (HND)
- other designated courses.

Most people on full-time higher education courses in publicly-funded colleges or universities are financed by the following sources:

- means-tested assistance towards the cost of tuition fees
- a student loan – to help with living expenses
- support from partners or parents
- earnings and savings
- Access and Hardship funds – administered by colleges.

Eligibility

To qualify for assistance towards fees and loans, there are personal eligibility criteria, which includes a **residence requirement**. The main stipulations are that students must have been 'ordinarily resident' in the British Isles for the three years immediately before the start of the academic year in which the course begins, and must be ordinarily resident in England, Wales, Scotland or Northern Ireland on the first day of the academic year in which the course starts.

Previous study at higher education level which included help from UK or EU public funds, or if the college where the course was taken was publicly funded, may exclude students from entitlement to further financial support. **It is important that these students seek information and advice from their LEA, as the rules relating to previous study are complex**.

Tuition fees

A student's annual contribution to their course fees is means-tested. The maximum contribution for the academic year 1999/2000 is £1,025. The amount payable by the student will depend on their own income for that year, and that of their family, if applicable. If the student qualifies as an 'independent student' and is married, this means the husband's or wife's income.

To qualify for independent status, the student must meet one of the following conditions:

- be aged 25 or over before the start of the academic year for which they are applying
- have been married for at least two years before the start of the academic year for which they are applying for support
- to have supported themselves for at least three years before the start of the academic year of the course (this includes any time when unemployed or on a government training scheme).

For 'independent' students who are married, the husband or wife is expected to make some contribution to tuition fees, and possibly also living costs, if their residual income (ie the income remaining after certain allowances from gross income) is £14,700 or more a year. For students who do not qualify as independent (and therefore the parents' income is taken into account) the student or their parents will be expected to make a contribution if the parents' residual income is more than £17,370 a year.

Under these arrangements, it is estimated that about a third of students are not required to make any contribution to their fees.

- All students must apply to their local education authority for assessment for tuition fee support, the student loan and supplementary grants.

- Tuition fees are paid directly to the university or college.

Living costs

From Autumn 1999, the main source of funding is through a **student loan**. These are government-funded loans administered by the Student Loans Company. Around three quarters of the maximum loan will be available to all students under the age of 50, and to those aged 50-54 who are planning to return to work after studying. Entitlement to the remaining quarter of the loan is means-tested by the LEA. Students then decide how much loan they want, and inform the Student Loans Company.

The maximum loan available for 1999/2000 for a student living away from home, and not studying in London, will be £3,635, or if they live at home, £2,875.

The loan will have an interest rate linked to inflation, so that in real terms no one repays more than was borrowed.

Students are required to start to pay back the loan after the course, once their income rises above a certain threshold (£10,000 a year for those starting to repay in 2000). If their income falls below this level, repayments will be suspended. There is no fixed time limit for repayment.

Note: **Medical students** – for the first four years of a medicine or dentistry course, the above arrangements will apply, and from year five, non-repayable bursaries will apply.

Supplementary grants

Some students are entitled to extra help towards living costs.

- **Students with dependants** – means-tested grants are available for students with dependants. Dependants can include children, husband or wife, and other financially dependent adults. For dependent children, the allowances range from: under 11 years – £435 through to £1,660 for a dependent child of 18 or over.

- **Single Parent's Allowance** – students may be able to receive an extra allowance of up to £1,025. The LEA can give more information on this.

- **Maintaining a home** – some extra help is available for students who have to maintain a home for themselves and a dependant, other than the home they live in when attending the course.

- **Students with disabilities** – Disabled Student Allowances (DSAs) are available to help to pay for extra costs or expenses that students may have that arise because of their disability, and are available to students of all ages. This includes a specialist equipment allowance, non-medical helpers allowance and a general allowance, which may cover other items. DSAs are not means-tested. LEAs may provide help towards extra travel expenses. A DfEE leaflet, *Bridging the Gap* is available from LEAs or from the Student Support Information Line – listed at the end of this section.

Access Funds and Hardship Loans

Access Funds – available through institutions to provide selective help to students with particular financial difficulties. The size of the funds is limited, and students must meet certain eligibility rules and show that they have explored other ways of supporting themselves. Applicants should already have taken out a student loan and applied for a Hardship Loan.

Hardship Loans – usually meant for students who have already enrolled and begun studying. Up to £250 a year is available for students in difficulty. Students must have received the first instalment of their student loan before applying.

Other possible sources of assistance which may apply to particular higher education students, or those on particular full-time higher education courses, are described elsewhere in this chapter under the following headings:

- Sponsorships and scholarships
- Charities and trusts
- NHS bursaries – for professions allied to medicine
- Teacher shortage subjects (England and Wales).

Further information

Student Support Information Line – telephone 0800 731 9133. Provides information about student support in higher education in England and Wales, and copies of the free booklet *Financial Support for Students in 1999/2000* – published by the DfEE, which gives detailed information on tuition fee support, loans etc. Copies should be available at careers centres, and information is also available on the DfEE website: www.dfee.gov.uk

Bridging the gap – DfEE leaflet on Disabled Students' Allowances – available from LEAs or through the Student Support Information Line.

Financial Assistance for Students with Disabilities – for students in higher education – published by SKILL (The National Bureau for Students with Disabilities) – 4th Floor, Chapter House, Crucifix Lane, London SE1 3JW. Cost to students £2.00. Telephone information line: 0800 328 5050. Website: www.skill.org.uk

Student Loans Company – 100 Bothwell Street, Glasgow G2 7JD. Tel: 0800 405 010. Website: www.slc.co.uk

For students in Scotland – *Student Support in Scotland* is a guide published by the Student Awards Agency for Scotland, Gyleview House, 3 Redheughs Rigg, South Gyle, Edinburgh EH12 9HH. Tel:0131 476 8212. Website: www.student-support-saas.gov.uk

For students in Northern Ireland – *Financial Support for Students in Higher Education in 1999/2000* is a guide published by the Student Support Branch, Department of Education for Northern Ireland, Rathgael House, Balloo Road, Bangor, Co Down BT19 7BR. Tel: 028 9127 9279. Available from Education and Library Boards or from the Student Support Branch.

Part-time higher education

Tuition fee waivers

From September 1999, part-time higher education students will be able to have their fees waived if they meet certain conditions. The criteria which must be met include the following:

- students have to be getting income support, JSA, housing benefit or council tax benefit, or they should be able to show that the sole income of their family is DSS benefits, or that the family's income is below the threshold for receiving income support
- the part-time course must be a first degree, HNC, HND or similar undergraduate course funded by the HEFCE (the fee waiver does not apply to postgraduate studies)
- the part-time course must be at least 50% of full-time study.

All students, no matter how far they are into the course, will be eligible. The universities or colleges will be responsible for assessing eligibility when deciding if fees can be waived. Students who feel they might be eligible for fee waivers should contact the institution concerned for the full details.

Note: The information applies, at the date of publication, particularly in England; students in other areas of the UK should check with their institutions.

Individual institutions may apply fee waiver policies that are broader than the above; prospective students on low incomes who wish to follow a part-time course should always contact the institution for information and advice.

Loans for part-time students

From Autumn 2000, part-time higher education students on a low income will be entitled to loans of at least £500, to help with the costs of the course.

Access Funds

Part-time students are eligible to apply for help from the institution's Access Fund, as described in the section on full-time higher education.

Adult education bursaries

Adult education bursaries are available for students attending full-time courses of liberal adult education at one of the eight UK adult long-term residential colleges in England, Scotland and Wales.

The bursaries for English and Welsh residents are paid by the Further Education Funding Council, and administered by the residential colleges through their awards office.

The bursary includes:

- payment of tuition fees
- a maintenance grant, for living expenses, plus certain additional allowances
- in some cases, travelling costs if they are over £70 a year.

To be eligible, applicants must be recommended by the college for a bursary, be 20 years old or over before the start of the academic year in which the course begins, and satisfy residency criteria.

The personal maintenance grant is means-tested. The maintenance grant covers college term-time and the vacations at Christmas and Easter. The rates of grant for full-time attendance of 30 weeks plus Christmas and Easter vacations for the academic year 1998/99 are:

- students living in college in the London area – £3,658
- students living in college elsewhere – £2,886
- students living in the parental home – £2,180.

Each of the above includes £70 towards travelling expenses.

Other grants may be payable, including the dependants grant, two homes grant and the Disabled Students' Allowance.

For further information

For residents of England and Wales, contact: The Awards Officer, Adult Education Bursaries, c/o Ruskin College, Oxford OX I 2HE. They provide copies of the booklet *Adult Education Bursaries* – annually published by the Residential Colleges Committee, which provides information for English or Welsh residents wishing to study at the English long-term residential colleges.

For English and Welsh residents wishing to study at Coleg Harlech in Wales, contact: Ms A Thomas, The Further Education Funding Council for Wales, Lambourne House, Cardiff Business Park, Llanishen, Cardiff CF4 5GL.

For Scottish residents, contact: Student Awards Agency for Scotland, Gyleview House, 3 Redheughs Rigg, South Gyle, Edinburgh EH12 9HH.

For residents of Northern Ireland, contact: Ms A Thompson, Student Support Branch, Department of Education for Northern Ireland, Rathgael House, Balloo Road, Bangor BT19 7PR. **Please note however, that, for the academic year 1999/2000 no adult education bursaries are available for residents of Northern Ireland**.

There are no specific bursary schemes for residents of the Channel Islands or the Isle of Man wishing to study at the long-term residential colleges. Applicants from these areas should consult their local education authorities about the possibility of financial assistance.

Postgraduate courses

Unlike first degree students, intending postgraduate students must initiate their own search to raise finances. The only exception for this is for postgraduate initial teacher training courses, such as the Postgraduate Certificate in Education (PGCE), where no tuition fees are payable by the student, whatever the family's income.

The limited number of grants are available on a competitive basis, often based on the class and type of your degree.

The following bodies offer funding for particular subject areas, which are strongly competed for:

- **Arts and Humanities Research Board** (established by the British Academy, Department for Education for Northern Ireland and the Higher Education Funding Council for England): administers two schemes of postgraduate awards – *Postgraduate Professional and Vocational Awards* which covers art and design, librarianship, information science, media studies, drama, archive administration, archaeology, theology, interpreting and translating, and *Postgraduate Studentships in the Humanities*, which includes English language and literature, media and communication studies, modern languages and literature, linguistics, music and performing arts, history of art and architecture, film and design, history, classics, archaeology, philosophy, religious studies and law.
- **Biotechnology and Biological Sciences Research Council** (BBSRC): non-medical biology and biotechnology
- **Engineering and Physical Sciences Research Council** (EPSRC): physical sciences, technology and engineering
- **Economic and Social Research Council** (ESRC): economics and social sciences
- **Medical Research Council** (MRC): biomedical subjects
- **Natural Environment Research Council** (NERC): life, environmental and geological sciences
- **Particle Physics and Astronomy Research Council** (PPARC): particle physics and astronomy.

Other possible sources

- Many employers fund postgraduate study as part of their employees' career development (generally undertaken on a part-time basis).
- There are a number of scholarships and bursaries available, offered by various charities and other organisations.
- Career Development Loans offer a way to finance certain postgraduate courses. CDLs are described in more detail earlier in this chapter.
- The Association of MBAs offers a Business School Loan Scheme, through NatWest Bank.
- Certain banks run loan schemes for postgraduate students on particular courses, such as law.
- Some Training and Enterprise Councils offer some assistance.
- Full and part-time postgraduate students may apply to the institution for help from Access Funds.
- Until 2000-01, Vocational Training Relief is available for any full-time vocational course lasting between four weeks and one year, for students or trainees aged 30 or over.

Further information

Course providers and higher education institutions' careers services may be able to advise.

Guide to Postgraduate Studentships in the Humanities and *Guide to Postgraduate Professional and Vocational Awards* – both published by Arts and Humanities Research Board, 10 Carlton House Terrace, London SW1Y 5AH. Tel: 020 7969 5256. Information on the schemes can be found on their website: www.ahrb.ac.uk

The Directory of Graduate Studies and the condensed version, *Postgrad: The Students' Guide* – annually published by Hobsons. These and similar postgraduate directories include some information about funding, and should be available for reference at careers centres.

The Grants Register – published by Macmillan – and the *Directory of Grant Making Trusts* – published by the Charities Aid Foundation – should be available in reference libraries, and list possible funding sources.

Postgraduate Study & Research – an AgCAS booklet, from CSU, Despatch Department, Prospects House, Booth Street East, Manchester M13 9EP, price £2.65.

Student Support in Scotland: A guide for Postgraduate Students 1999-2000 – available from the Student Awards Agency for Scotland, Gyleview House, 3 Redheughs Rigg, South Gyle, Edinburgh EH12 9HH. Tel: 0131 476 8212. Website: www.student-support-saas.gov.uk

Sponsorships and scholarships

Sponsorships for students on full-time courses (usually a degree) are offered by a number of employers and related organisations. Sponsorships vary considerably, but typically could include:

- a bursary (which would be additional to the normal financial support)
- guaranteed vacation work
- spending work experience placements at the company, for students on sandwich courses

Students rarely enter into a formal agreement to work for the sponsor on graduation, but the intention is that sponsorship allows employers to introduce prospective graduates into the company, and that this will lead into a job offer when they graduate.

Most sponsorships are in vocational subjects, such as engineering, construction and business-related fields. Competition is strong for sponsorships.

Scholarships

There are some scholarships and bursaries for students, awarded by individual universities and colleges. These are awarded on a competitive basis, and competition is strong. Some scholarships are open to undergraduates of any subject. Others are for particular subject areas. Scholarships are likely to provide no more than a small financial supplement to funding from other sources.

For further information

Sponsorship for Students – published annually by CRAC/Hobsons, price £8.99 for the 2000 edition. ISBN 1 8601 7627 5. Lists sponsorships for HND/degree courses.

University Scholarships and Awards 2000 – published by Trotman, price £10.99. ISBN 0 85660 440 2.

Also, consult course prospectuses and course providers.

Charities and trusts

There are some charities and trust funds which make payments to students. Any grant is usually small. Support may be aimed at a particular age group, often under 25, is sometimes restricted to people living in a particular locality, or is aimed at those studying a particular subject area – but such assistance is worth looking into. Assistance may be available for students experiencing financial hardship during a course, but funding for a whole course is rare. Sometimes the help is in the form of a loan. Any financial assistance available is in demand and not easy to get.

It is extremely difficult for undergraduate students who are already benefiting from statutory funding (through assistance with tuition fees, loans etc) to find additional funding through charitable bodies. Funding for postgraduate students is also limited.

Educational Grants Advisory Service (EGAS)

The Educational Grants and Advisory Service offers guidance and advice to students who are over 16. EGAS is primarily concerned with helping disadvantaged students, giving priority to lone parents, people with disabilities, refugees, asylum seekers and people from low-income backgrounds. Student Advisers can provide information on grants, loans, benefits and bursaries, to make sure that students are getting all the statutory grants and benefits for which they are eligible, before recommending possible charitable sources of funding.

EGAS itself is not a grant-giving body, but is part of the Family Welfare Association, which is trustee to various educational trusts.

 **Contact** *EGAS, 501/5 Kingsland Road, London E8 4AU.
Tel: 020 7254 6251. Send a stamped addressed envelope, and a student enquiry form will be sent by return post.*

Trade unions

Trade unions may offer some assistance; anyone in a trade union should enquire.

The General Federation of Trades Unions Educational Trust makes small grants for full-time and Open University students. However, there are limiting criteria. People must be studying subjects within economic theory and history, industrial law, history and principles of industrial relations. Individual trade unions may have other schemes.

 **Contact:** *The General Federation of Trades Unions Educational Trust,
Central House, Upper Woburn Place, London WC1H 0HY.
Tel: 020 7387 2578. Website: www.gftu.org.uk E-mail:gftuhq@gftu.org.uk*

For further information

Course providers may be aware of possible charities or trusts.

Some **LEA awards departments** keep lists of local educational charities and trusts.

Local **adult careers guidance services** may hold relevant information.

The Educational Grants Directory – published by Trotman, price £18.95. ISBN 1 900360 31 4. This and other similar directories are usually available in public reference libraries.

Help for students studying certain subjects

Dance and drama courses

From September 1999, a Dance and Drama Awards scholarship scheme offers financial assistance to students on approved dance, drama and stage management courses at 29 independent colleges. There will be awards for up to 820 students to enter training each year. These new awards can provide:

- fee support of over £6,000 a year
- special help for people from low income families, to help make sure they can complete the training.

Students must audition for funded places. Successful students will not be required to contribute more than the prevailing maximum contribution to undergraduate fees (£1,025 for 1999/2000) towards the cost of their fees. Students on higher education courses will be able to apply for means-tested support for student fees and loans, through their local education authority (or in Scotland the Student Awards Agency; in Northern Ireland, the Student Support Branch). Students on further education courses will have access to a Hardship Fund, administered through the college, to help those from low income families with tuition fees, and eligible students with other expenses.

There is no upper age limit of eligibility for the scheme. Awards are open to students living in all parts of the UK and other EU countries. Eligibility includes a residence requirement.

National Health Service bursaries

The NHS funds places on courses leading to registration for nursing and midwifery and many professions allied to medicine. The arrangements cover diploma, degree and postgraduate level courses, so long as they lead to professional registration in the following:

- nursing and midwifery (there are different arrangements for degree and diploma students)
- occupational therapy
- physiotherapy
- speech and language therapy
- radiography
- orthoptics
- chiropody
- dietetics

- prosthetics and orthotics
- dental hygiene
- dental therapy.

The arrangements

- Course fees are paid for by the NHS.
- No student contribution to fees is required.
- Means-tested bursaries (or non means-tested bursaries for students on nursing and midwifery **diploma** courses).
- Access to student loans for the balance of the student's maintenance (living) costs (except for students on postgraduate courses).

The means-tested bursary is made up of an allowance towards day-to-day living costs, and there are allowances for particular circumstances, including for dependants, single parents and older students. The basic rate of support (at 1998/99 levels) is between approximately £3,300 and £5,200 (including loans) for full-time students.

Applying

Once the applicant has been offered a place, the institution will notify the NHS Student Grants Unit (in England – see below for contacts elsewhere in the UK), who will contact the applicant. For nursing diploma students, training institutions will contact students direct.

Please note: while the majority of places on courses in the professions listed above will be NHS-funded, course providers may offer additional places on these courses which are not NHS-funded. For students recruited on non NHS-funded places, the financial arrangements will be the same as for undergraduates of all other subjects in full-time higher education.

Students on nursing and midwifery diploma courses

Basic rates of non means-tested bursaries for full-time students on NHS-funded diploma places range between approximately £4,600 and £6,000 (1998/9 rates) depending on the age of the student and whether they are studying in London or elsewhere. Allowances available include the older students' allowance and dependants allowances.

Medicine and dentistry courses

The arrangements for students entering undergraduate medical and dental courses will be the same as those for undergraduates on other higher education courses for the first four years of training. In year five and beyond, students will not have to pay tuition fees, and NHS non-repayable bursaries, assessed against family income, will be available towards maintenance.

For more information

For study in England:

The NHS Student Grants Unit, Room 212c Government Buildings, Norcross, Blackpool FY5 3TA. Tel: 01253 856123.

For study in Wales:

The Welsh Health Common Services Agency, Education Purchasing Unit, Ground Floor CP2, Welsh Office, Cathays Park, Cardiff CF1 3NQ. Tel: 029 2082 5111.

For study in Scotland:
The Students Awards Agency for Scotland, 3 Redheughs Rigg, South Gyle, Edinburgh EH12 9HH. Tel: 0131 556 8400.

For study in Northern Ireland:
The Department of Education for Northern Ireland, Rathgael House, Balloo Road, Bangor BT19 7PR. Tel: 028 9127 9418.

Teacher training (shortage subjects)

Financial incentives are available for intending secondary **maths and science teachers** in England and Wales on PGCE courses: a £5000 incentive is payable, half paid on entry to the course, and half on appointment as a teacher.

In addition, the **Secondary Shortage Subject Scheme** (England) and the **Priority Subject Recruitment Initiative** (Wales) provide additional financial support for some intending teachers.

Assistance through the Secondary Shortage Subject Scheme is open to students undertaking initial teacher training courses, at either undergraduate or postgraduate level, in one of the secondary shortage subjects. These are mathematics, science, modern foreign languages, design and technology, information technology, music, religious education and geography. Applications are made to the teacher training provider, and assessment is based on need. The maximum amount available in any one year is £5000.

The Priority Subject Recruitment Initiative in Wales is similar. (There is no similar scheme operating in Scotland.)

For more information on these initiatives contact:

The Teacher Training Agency's Teaching Information Line, tel: 01242 545 4454.

Further information

Learning Direct on 0800 100 900 can provide information on financing a wide range of learning.

9. Further and adult education

This chapter covers:

- the position of adults in further education today
- further education provision in colleges and elsewhere
- adult education centres and colleges
- useful organisations and publications.

Further education (FE)

Further education colleges are expected to attract an extra 700,000 students by 2002. Many of these will be adults – who are already the majority of FE students – so adults need not feel out of place in an FE college. Colleges are involved in the delivery of the New Deal, the University for Industry (UfI) and meeting the needs of individual learning account holders. Funding and inspection of further education will be done differently from April 2001, following the White Paper, *Learning to Succeed* (see the foreword of this book). These changes will not concern students directly, but adult learners should find that information, guidance and education become more widely accessible and provision more evenly distributed throughout the country as a result.

Adult clients may have little knowledge or experience of further education. For instance, they may not know that:

- full-time further education courses still mostly start in September and last 36-38 weeks, until June or July – despite the beginnings of a move away from the traditional academic year, with some colleges offering courses all year round
- colleges also offer day release, block release and sandwich courses to fit in with the needs of local employers and employees
- course provision has become more flexible, with many courses taught in modules or through independent study; therefore courses can be tailored to meet the needs of individual students
- most further education courses lead to qualifications: GCSEs, standard grades, highers and advanced highers, A and AS levels, GNVQs, Access courses and a range of vocational courses leading to NVQs, City and Guilds and National and Higher National qualifications
- qualifications offered by various professional bodies, such as in accountancy and banking, may be gained through study at a local FE college
- the range of subjects is enormous, and increasingly further education colleges are offering degree courses in partnership with universities and colleges of HE – possibly just the first year of the course with the following two or three years at the partner institution.

To find out what is available, adult clients should:

- consult directories, databases or Learning Direct (telephone 0800 100 900) about the availability of courses
- obtain a prospectus, which should give details of courses and describe the resources and expertise of the college
- ask for information leaflets which give more detail about the individual courses – they should cover course subjects and teaching and assessment methods, hours of attendance at college and anticipated study time required at home
- investigate timetabling of possible subject combinations and availability of additional courses in basic maths, foreign languages, IT skills etc – or 'return to study' courses – if needed
- request information on the success rates and destinations (into employment and higher education) of previous students
- find out about fees and any financial help available
- ask for information about help with childcare, transport etc
- having decided on a course, obtain an application form.

Increasingly, colleges have marketing, student services or admissions officers whose job is to provide information to prospective students.

Adult education

Adult education provision by local education authorities varies considerably; some LEAs may only subsidise a few courses offered by local colleges or voluntary groups, while others still maintain active and well resourced adult education centres. Whoever adult education is provided by, it offers mainly part-time courses, often for two to three hours a week. Subjects include study skills, assertiveness and time management as well as recreational and leisure subjects. Some handcrafts and office skill courses may be a useful introduction to possible career areas. Courses may be offered through a variety of means: traditional evening classes, daytime classes and, increasingly, summer schools, distance learning and weekend schools. There are a number of adult residential colleges.

Classes tend to be more flexible if there is no examination syllabus to follow, and may be student-led. Practical courses such as woodwork and upholstery may allow students to suggest a project of their own and get tuition and help to complete it. Often people attend the same class for a number of years as they enjoy the hobby and want tuition as they go along. Beginners as well as more experienced people are welcome at all these classes.

Providers of adult education include:

- colleges of further education which offer full-time further education courses as well as part-time courses
- adult or community education centres run by some LEAs, which usually offer part-time courses running for a few hours a week

- community colleges or community schools – schools which also offer a range of community facilities such as adult education, youth work, use of school premises and equipment by community groups; adult education courses are usually part-time
- secondary schools which may offer adults access to classes to study for GCSEs, A and AS levels etc
- voluntary organisations – Workers' Educational Association, The University of the Third Age (U3A), for example
- extra-mural departments of universities which aim to provide education accessible to the community, which is not part of longer degree courses.

Money

Fees for further and adult education courses do vary tremendously. Some courses will be offered for a token amount – or even free – but, on the whole, adult education courses need to cover all their costs and therefore a realistic charge is made, based on gaining a viable number of students. However, there may be concessions for different categories of people such as pensioners and those receiving means-tested benefits.

Clients should talk to an adviser at the college or centre where they wish to study before enrolling to see what concessions are available. See also Chapter 8.

Useful organisations

Community Education Association

An association of practitioners and others interested in lifelong learning. It organises training and support on a regional basis in England and Wales.

Contact: *General Secretary, Community Education Association – Ernulf, Barford Road, St Neots PE19 2SH. Tel: 01480 216803. E-mail: comedas@btinternet.com Website: www.cosmic.org.uk/cea*

Community Education Development Centre (CEDC)

CEDC publishes a regular journal, *Network*, and various handbooks and reports relating to community education, runs conferences, and carries out research and development work. CEDC is a voice for community education.

Contact: *CEDC – Woodway Park School, Wigston Road, Coventry CV2 2RH. Tel: 024 7665 5700. E-mail: info@cedc.org.uk*

Educational Centres Association (ECA)

ECA is a voluntary body which aims to promote adult education, and works as a partnership between organisers, teachers and students. Over 150 centres are affiliated. They organise national and regional conferences, and publish a magazine, *Centre Line*, highlighting issues in adult education, as well as useful leaflets.

 **Contact:** *ECA – Berkhamsted Centre, 179 High Street, Berkhamsted, Hertfordshire HP4 3HB. Tel: 01442 875086.*

National Institute of Adult Continuing Education (NIACE)

The main membership organisation for professionals in adult education. It provides an information service to local education authorities and other organisations concerned with adult learning. It undertakes research and development in all aspects of education for adults and publishes handbooks, guides and project reports. NIACE co-ordinates Adult Learners' Week in England and Wales.

 **Contact:** *NIACE – 21 De Montfort Street, Leicester LEI 7GE. Tel: 0116 255 1451. Website: www.niace.org.uk E-mail: enquiries@niace.org.uk*

National Open College Network

This network accredits many courses, largely vocational, from entry level to Access to higher education courses. The word 'open' in the name refers to the fact that the courses and programmes are open to all, not that it is anything to do with open learning. For addresses of local members of the national network, see Chapter 15.

 **Contact:** *National Open College Network Office – University of Derby, Kedleston Road, Derby DE22 1GB. Tel: 01332 622712. Website: www.nocn.ac.uk E-mail: nocn@derby.ac.uk*

Northern Ireland Association for Adult Education (NIAAE)

An interest group formed to raise the profile of adult education and highlight the needs and concerns of adults in education.

 **Contact:** *Hon Secretary, NIAAE – 42 Northland Road, Londonderry BT48 7ND. Tel: 028 7126 5007.*

Community Learning Scotland

This organisation aims to support and promote the development of community education throughout Scotland. It offers training, materials, information and programme development advice for those involved in working with adults, and co-ordinates Adult Learners' Week in Scotland. A full list of publications and services is available on request.

 **Contact:** *Community Learning Scotland – 9 Haymarket Terrace, Edinburgh. EH12 5EZ. Tel: 0131 313 2488. E-mail: cls@cls.dircon.co.uk*

Further information

Call the Learning Direct helpline – 0800 100 900.

Directory of Further Education 1999/2000 – published by Hobsons, price £76.50. ISBN 1 86017 620 8.

Independent Colleges: directory of courses – published by ISCO, price £6.99. ISBN 0 90193 648 0. Includes vocational and academic courses in the private sector.

Directory of Vocational and Further Education 1999/2000 – published annually by Financial Times Management, Slaidburn Crescent, Southport PR9 9YS. Tel: 01704 224331. Price £82 plus £3 p&p.

International Directory of Adult and Continuing Education 1999 – by Peter Jarvis. Published by Kogan Page. Price £35. ISBN 0 7494 2671 3.

The following titles available from Publications Sales, NIACE, 21 De Montfort Street, Leicester LE1 7GE. Tel: 0116 255 1451.

Time to Learn – price £4.95. ISBN 1 86201 065 X.

Adults Learning – a monthly journal.

The Yearbook of Adult Continuing Education – price £14.95. ISBN 1 86201 063 3. Gives details of key contacts and organisations.

Through the Joy of Learning: Diary of 1000 Adult Learners – price £14.99. ISBN 1 86201 001. A variety of experiences in the learners' own words.

10. Basic skills

This chapter covers:

- the necessity of acquiring basic skills
- a description of adult basic education courses and qualifications
- information about the providers of adult basic education
- availability of classes in English for speakers of other languages.

There has been, and will continue to be, an increase in the demand for good basic skills. Everyday life is becoming more complex, and most jobs now need good communication skills. Basic skills – reading, writing, speaking, listening and basic maths – underpin all education and training. Mastery of these essential skills is crucial for progress in our changing world. By basic skills we mean:

'the ability to read, write, and speak in English and use mathematics at a level necessary to function and progress at work and in society in general.'

The Basic Skills Agency

In Wales, basic skills include the ability to read and write Welsh for people whose first language or mother tongue is Welsh.

Basic skills courses

Basic skills courses aim to build up skills and confidence in a friendly and informal way. Tuition takes place in colleges of further education, adult education and community centres, libraries and other centres.

Adult literacy and basic skills programmes were first established on a significant scale in the mid-1970s. These programmes have since expanded considerably. For example, while in 1976 just over 50,000 people were getting help through adult literacy and basic skills programmes organised by LEAs, colleges and voluntary organisations, in 1999 this had risen to almost 350,000 people. Similarly, the number of people receiving help in English for speakers of other languages (ESOL) has been rising steadily.

As well as basic literacy and numeracy, some centres offer courses in English and maths for improvers, and pre-GCSE courses for those not quite ready to be launched straight into a GCSE in English or maths.

Further education colleges

Most colleges now provide learning support, whether in a class, a small group, or individually. Tuition may be a couple of hours a week or it could be more. It's partly up to the individual student, but it also depends on what's available. It's usually free, or at least much cheaper than most other courses.

Open learning

With the increase of open learning, it is now possible to do basic maths and English at home with support from a tutor at a college or open learning centre.

The National Extension College (NEC) has courses suitable for anyone wanting to acquire and develop their basic skills. See 'Open learning courses' and 'Further information' at the end of this chapter.

Drop-in centres

In drop-in centres, clients can just turn up to ask for help with virtually anything from filling in forms to advice on how to help their children at school.

Government-funded training

Programmes for unemployed people, such as Work-based Learning and the New Deal, often provide help to improve literacy and other basic skills. Details are available at Jobcentres. Most TECs (Training and Enterprise Councils) and LECs (Local Enterprise Companies) are playing a key role in encouraging local employers to provide basic skills training for employees. However, although there has been an increase in workplace basic skills training in recent years, the scale of provision is still modest.

Prisons also offer extensive basic skills training, and many probation services provide help with basic education for offenders and ex-offenders in the community. Libraries are an important source of information, and often provide valuable support for local programmes.

Voluntary services

As well as local authority provision in local colleges there are many voluntary literacy schemes. Libraries, volunteer centres, citizens advice bureaux or Educational Guidance Services for Adults (EGSA) should have details.

Family literacy and numeracy

In the last few years a new preventive programme – family literacy and numeracy – has been established throughout England and Wales. The scheme is targeted at parents who have difficulties with basic skills, and works with both the parents and their children. The Basic Skills Agency monitors the programmes, which are funded by the government and delivered through local education authorities.

Getting what the client needs

With basic education readily available in nearly all areas, there is a wide variety in the type and quality of provision. It is important to have an idea of what the basic education is needed for. Someone who wants a job which needs measuring or estimating skills will require different training to someone who wants to learn how to read. It is necessary to shop around to find the scheme that offers the most appropriate tuition.

Clients should ask the course provider:

- if they offer guidance on what's the best course for them
- what it costs
- how progress is reviewed
- if the teaching is one-to-one, in a group or through open and distance learning
- if it's possible to be taught at home
- if they have the Basic Skills Agency Quality Mark for Basic Skills Programmes.

As with all studying it may be very hard work, and the client may not be as successful as they hope – not necessarily through their own fault. Success at this level can sometimes depend on how the student gets on with the tutor. So if there are problems at first, it may just be a question of changing tutor or class.

Qualifications

There are some qualifications for basic education students.

City and Guilds certificates

City and Guilds Wordpower Certificate

There are four levels to this certificate: entry level and levels one, two and three. For each level there are only three requirements to meet:

- read and respond to textual and graphical material
- communicate in writing
- talk to one other person.

City and Guilds Numberpower Certificate

There are four levels, as above. The three requirements are to:

- handle data
- apply number skills
- measure.

 **Contact:** *Customer Services Enquiry Unit, City and Guilds – 1 Giltspur Street, London EC1A 9DD. Tel: 020 7294 2800.*
E-mail: enquiry@city-and-guilds.co.uk Website: www.city-and-guilds.co.uk

OCR qualifications

OCR Key Skills

These are a collection of competence-based units, open to people of any age. The units allow for the assessment and accreditation of the following skills:

- communication
- application of number
- information technology
- personal skills – working with others
- personal skills – improving own learning and performance
- problem solving.

Each of the six areas can be certificated at five different levels of complexity. Each unit is made up of different skill areas, for example:

Communication
- taking part in discussions
- producing materials
- using images to illustrate points
- reading and responding to written materials and images.

Application of number
- collecting and recording data
- representing and tackling problems
- interpreting and presenting data.

These key skills units are offered (perhaps alongside other qualifications including GNVQs and NVQs) by many course centres such as adult education centres and further education colleges.

OCR National Skills Profile

This is designed to create a bridge into mainstream national qualifications, or as an achievement in its own right, especially for people who are experiencing barriers to learning. It certificates key skills and personal and practical work skills at entry level, linked to 13 vocational areas.

 **Contact:** *OCR – Westwood Way, Coventry CV4 8JQ. Tel: 024 7647 0033. Website: www.ocr.org.uk*

Clients with a disability

Most basic education schemes will do their best to help. For example, they may be able to arrange for a tutor to visit the client at home or will suggest a centre where access is easy. See Chapter 29.

Spoken English at work

For clients who need help with spoken English at work:

 **Contact:** *- their trade union representative or employer direct to see if they can provide courses*

- one of the national referral points – eg the Basic Skills Agency.

Useful organisations

The Basic Skills Agency

The Basic Skills Agency is an independent organisation which is funded mainly by the government. It is a registered charity and a company limited by guarantee, which:

- promotes the importance of basic skills and the work of the Agency
- initiates and supports development
- improves the effectiveness of basic skills programmes
- disseminates good practice.

There is a Basic Skills Agency Resource Centre for teachers, based at the Institute of Education Library in central London and a **free Helpline** for people who want to find out about improving their basic skills (Tel: 0800 700987).

 **Contact:** *The Basic Skills Agency – Commonwealth House, 1-19 New Oxford Street, London WC1A 1NU. Tel: 020 7405 4017. E-mail: enquiries@basic-skills.co.uk Website: www.basic-skills.co.uk*

Campaign for Learning

This DfEE-instigated campaign includes suggestions for family learning activities which may be helpful for people whose learning needs are at a basic level, among others.

 **Contact:** *Campaign for Learning – 19 Buckingham Street, London WC2N 6EF. Tel: 020 7930 1111. Website: www.campaign-for-learning.org.uk*

Referral services

You or your client can contact one of the national referral points. They will put you in touch with someone locally, probably the LEA, Regional or Islands Council, or Education and Library Board, or possibly a voluntary scheme.

England and Wales

 **Contact:** *The Basic Skills Agency National Referral Service. Tel: 0800 700 987.*

Scotland

There is no equivalent to the Basic Skills Agency in Scotland at present; contact individual local authorities.

Northern Ireland

 **Contact:** *Adult Basic Education Support Service (Northern Ireland), 2nd Floor, Glendinning House, 6 Murray Street, Belfast BT I 6DN. Tel: 028 9032 2488. E-mail: abess@egsa.dnet.co.uk*

English for speakers of other languages

Classes or one-to-one tuition in English for speakers of other languages (ESOL) or English as a second language (ESL) are available for residents of the UK whose first language is not English, if they need English for work, education and training or for health and social reasons.

ESOL and ESL courses are provided by:

- Local authorities in adult education centres or community centres.
- Local colleges, which may have specific classes in areas where demand is high. In other areas they may offer general adult literacy courses but will take into account the needs of ESOL students.
- Training providers, who may offer ESOL programmes alongside other government-funded adult training programmes which are primarily to train people for employment.

Most LEAs, Regional and Islands Councils, and Education and Library Boards will provide free basic ESOL tuition, although some will make a charge for courses at a higher level.

Radio and television

From time to time there will be programmes aimed at teaching English to speakers of other languages.

Open learning courses

There are courses available for those whose first language is not English and who wish to improve their reading and writing skills.

The National Extension College offers:

Help Yourself to English: a course for those whose first language is not English and who wish to improve their reading and writing skills. There are three levels: Living and Working, which deals with improving everyday English; Working and Studying, aimed at people planning to take a vocational course; and Studying and Beyond, which is for those aiming at GCSE English and higher education. Cost £105 for each level.

 **Contact:** *Student Advisers, National Extension College – 18 Brooklands Avenue, Cambridge CB2 2HN. Tel: 01223 450500. Website: www.nec.ac.uk E-mail: info@nec.ac.uk*

Further information

The Basic Skills Agency produces a publications catalogue listing the many materials useful to course centres and individuals, such as graded reader books on subjects of interest for adults. The material can be viewed at the Basic Skills Agency Resource Centre – Institute of Education, University of London, 20 Bedford Square, London WC1H 0AL. All the publications are available from their distributors: The Basic Skills Agency – Admail 524, London WC1A 1BR. Tel: 0870 600 2400 or fax: 0870 600 2401.

For an up-to-date list of the resources and courses they offer in basic skills and English for speakers of other languages, contact the National Extension College – 18 Brooklands Avenue, Cambridge CB2 2HN. Tel: 01223 450300.

Clients can also call the Learning Direct helpline (0800 100 900).

11. Leisure classes

This chapter covers:

- a definition of leisure classes, for the purposes of this chapter
- who provides leisure classes and where they may be held
- ideas for learning topics – from alternative technology to sport
- useful organisations and publications.

Leisure learning can include just about anything that is not for immediate vocational purposes. There is an enormous choice of leisure activities and classes for anyone who wishes to devote more time to an existing interest, or try their hand at something new. As well as for its own sake, for recreation or enjoyment, this type of education has a number of practical uses:

- as an introduction to study on a part-time basis, or a return to study after a break
- as evidence of being able to study, which is often an entry requirement for higher education
- as a way of keeping mind and body active, in times of enforced leisure, such as unemployment
- as a way of learning skills (for example car maintenance, French, weaving) and possibly earning money
- to explore a new subject before making a commitment to undertake a more advanced course
- to gain qualifications, if the course leads to certification by a recognised awarding body.

Classes are held in:

- colleges
- adult education centres
- evening institutes
- community centres and village halls
- sports and leisure centres
- schools
- pubs and other places.

Classes are provided by a range of bodies, such as:

some local education authorities, Regional or Islands Councils, Education and Library Boards, university extra-mural departments, the Workers' Educational Association (see also Chapter 12).

Local authority courses

Many local education authorities, Regional or Islands Councils, or Education and Library Boards provide part-time adult education classes, sometimes called community education. Enrolment arrangements vary; some courses have to be booked well in advance, others may only enrol at the first class. Details can be checked with the course centre, local library, LEA or educational guidance centre.

Fees vary from area to area; adults may be entitled to reduced fees if they are retired or receiving benefit. Published course information should give details, or contact the organiser. Many courses have to be self-financing, so students have to pay enough in fees to cover all the costs. Clubs and associations may organise their own classes and get special rates.

How to find out more

Information about local courses may be held at:

- local libraries
- the adult or community education department of the local authority (if there is one)
- adult education centres
- the Workers' Educational Association regional office
- the local press during August and September
- the nearest Training Access Point (TAP) database (see Chapter 3).

The Learning Direct helpline on 0800 100 900 can also offer information on all kinds of leisure learning.

Extra-mural classes

Aimed at taking higher education to the people, a number of universities and other higher education establishments have extra-mural departments, or departments of adult education or centres of continuing education, offering courses to the general public. They are usually concerned with the arts and sciences in general and with local interests, so there are many courses on local history, geography and industry. However, they do not restrict themselves to this sort of work; increasingly they are offering courses relevant to local needs.

Courses may be held at the university or college itself, or elsewhere – sometimes over quite a wide area. Some universities have a separate college or base for their extra-mural work. The departments offer evening classes, part-time classes, short courses, summer schools and public lectures. They are often at a high academic level, and taught by higher education lecturers. They're open to absolutely everyone – no previous academic knowledge or experience is expected.

You can get details of what is on offer by writing to or telephoning the department concerned. Courses will probably also be advertised at the public library. Prospectuses are usually published every year in August or September, or every term. Some also have short course information, mainly for the summer.

Voluntary organisations

Some adult education centres are run by voluntary organisations. They may be linked to the local authority, and be more flexible and open to ideas from the public.

How to find out more

These centres advertise their courses in the same way as other adult education providers, through libraries, the local press and so on.

National Adult School Organisation (NASO)

A national voluntary adult education movement which has existed for 200 years. NASO 'friendship through study' groups meet throughout the country, to discuss a wide range of topics based on the NASO handbook. Regional activities include residential weekends, studying a particular subject in some depth and social outings to visit places of interest.

The national office publishes discussion leaflets and the annual study handbook to help groups with their discussion programme, and publishes a monthly magazine, *One and All.*

The national office also organises study tours abroad, a 'See Britain Summer School' (once a year) and activity weekends to complement studies in the handbook. Groups vary from 5 to 25 people and each group finds its own meeting place, for example a community centre, church hall or a member's home.

There is a small national membership fee.

 **Contact:** *NASO, Riverton, 370 Humberstone Road, Leicester LE5 0SA.*
Tel: 0116 253 8333.

Residential courses

Many places offer weekend, half-week or longer residential courses in a wide range of activities and subjects. Some are run by local authorities at their own residential centres or colleges, some by universities and some by bodies such as the YMCA/YWCA or the Youth Hostels Association. Summer schools are offered by universities, making use of their student accommodation during the vacations. There are also hotels which offer study weekends.

Organisations like the British Trust for Conservation Volunteers and the Field Studies Council offer opportunities to learn conservation techniques and rural crafts. Many of these are courses for the whole family and make ideal short holidays for people who like studying for relaxation. You will find more about these and other organisations in Chapter 24, volunteering.

Costs of all these courses vary enormously, depending on the sort of accommodation and level of catering.

How to find out more

Many of these courses are advertised in the press or in local libraries, and a few directories and lists of residential courses are available. Some course providers are members of the Adult Residential Colleges Association (ARCA). Further information is given at the end of this chapter.

Overseas courses

There are many courses and other learning opportunities abroad – language courses at foreign universities, discovery and adventure holidays and lots more. The WEA, ARCA member colleges and many higher education institutions offer study tours abroad. These are often advertised in the press and are included in some of the publications listed at the end of this chapter.

Sport

Much part-time and recreational education involves sport. Sport and keep fit classes are always among the most popular in adult education. This is one type of provision where there is even more going on in workplaces, leisure centres, and sports clubs.

Sports Councils

The national bodies for sport have information about all sports as well as who to contact for details of the various coaching, refereeing and instructing courses available. The Sports Councils can give out governing body contacts for courses, but do not hold specific details.

Contact:

Sport England *– 16 Upper Woburn Place, London WC1H 0QP. Tel: 020 7273 1500. Website: www.english.sports.gov.uk*

Scottish Sports Council *– Caledonia House, South Gyle, Edinburgh. EH12 9DQ Tel: 0131 317 7200. Website: www.ssc.org.uk E-mail: general.info@ssc.org.uk*

Sports Council for Northern Ireland *– The House of Sport, 2a Upper Malone Road, Belfast BT9 5LA. Tel: 028 9038 1222. Website: www. sportscouncil-ni.org.uk E-mail: library@sportscouncil-ni.org.uk*

Sports Council for Wales *– Sophia Gardens, Cardiff CF1 9SW. Tel: 029 2030 0500. E-mail: stilianos.vidalis@scw.co.uk*

The arts

A huge variety of classes and courses are held in:

- residential colleges
- university extra-mural departments
- adult education classes
- art colleges
- art centres
- museums
- galleries
- community centres.

The Arts Councils (the national bodies for the arts) aim to encourage popular access to the arts. For example, they may operate 'artist in residence' schemes – artists, dancers, photographers, writers, storytellers, actors, film makers or musicians who work with, and give support to, community or education groups.

Contact: *Regional Arts Boards or the relevant regional unit at the Arts Councils.*

***The Arts Council of England** – 14 Great Peter Street, London SW1P 3NQ. Tel: 020 7333 0100. Website: www.artscouncil.org.uk*

***The Arts Council of Northern Ireland** – MacNeice House, 77 Malone Road, Belfast BT9 6AQ. Tel: 028 9038 5200.*

***The Arts Council of Wales** – 9 Museum Place, Cardiff CF1 3NX. Tel: 029 2037 6500. Website: www.ccc.acw.org.uk*

***The Scottish Arts Council** – 12 Manor Place, Edinburgh EH3 7DD. Tel: 0131 226 6051. Website: www.sac.org.uk*

You can usually find details of short courses in particular arts and crafts in special interest magazines, or the weekend supplements of broadsheet newspapers.

The National Extension College offers a number of distance learning materials for leisure courses.

Contact: *Student Advisers, National Extension College, 18 Brooklands Avenue, Cambridge CB2 2HN. Tel: 01223 316644.*

Personal development

The last 20 years have seen a rapid expansion of activities in holistic education: for example assertiveness training, counselling, life planning, stress management and a host of others. All deal with the whole person – spiritual, physical, emotional, social and intellectual. There are many courses to help people to develop self-confidence, as well as new skills and insights. Many of these are run by local adult education centres; there are also private practitioners who may advertise locally or nationally.

The Human Potential Research Group (HPRG)

The largest established humanistic education centre in Europe. It offers workshops dealing with both professional and personal development and a two-year part-time MSc in Change-agent, Skills and Strategy.

Contact: *Course Secretary, HPRG, Department of Educational Studies, University of Surrey, Guildford GU2 5XH. Tel: 01483 259760. Website: www.surrey.ac.uk/education E-mail: j.gregory@surrey.ac.uk*

Alternative lifestyles

Some people experiment with a wide variety of alternative ways of living. Alternative community living often means sharing, playing and working together, sometimes pooling personal resources, sometimes not. Some communities offer educational programmes and invite people to participate in them. Some of the books in 'Further information' at the end of this chapter tell you more.

Environmental issues

Some environmental organisations which offer education and training courses or materials are listed in Chapter 24 – Volunteering. The following also provide learning opportunities.

Centre for Alternative Technology

The centre is open to the public most days of the year and has a wide range of displays and information on renewable energy, organic growing, healthy buildings and all aspects of sustainable living. It also runs short residential courses for adults (usually at weekends) on solar energy, windpower, waterpower, organic growing, blacksmithing, building techniques for energy conservation and other topics. The centre also arranges tailor-made courses for groups, as well as long-term volunteering opportunities which include education and training. Some of its courses are accredited by the University of Bristol or lead to National Vocational Qualifications. The centre also produces some distance learning materials.

 **Contact:** *Centre for Alternative Technology – Machynlleth SY20 9AZ. Tel: 01654 703743. Website: www.cat.org.uk E-mail: courses@cateducation.demon.co.uk*

The Soil Association

The Soil Association is a charity which promotes organic food and farming. It has a network of local groups throughout the country. Members receive a quarterly magazine called *Living Earth*.

 **Contact:** *The Soil Association – Bristol House, 40-56 Victoria Street, Bristol BS1 6BY. Tel: 0117 929 0661. Website: www.soilassociation.org E-mail: info@soilassociation.org*

Henry Doubleday Research Association

The Association has over 25,000 members and carries out research into ecologically sustainable methods of organic growing. There is a ten-acre area of demonstration organic gardens and a thriving shop and restaurant selling organic produce. Open all year round.

 **Contact:** *Henry Doubleday Research Association – Ryton Organic Garden, Ryton on Dunsmore, Coventry CV8 3LG. Tel: 024 7630 3517. Website: www.hdra.org.uk E-mail: enquiry@hdra.org.uk*

Politics

Participation in politics provides an opportunity to learn about different topics. Organisations hold meetings, discussions, day schools or workshops on issues as diverse as agriculture, transport, economics, the media, defence and the prison system. These events can be a chance to learn and share ideas with influential people from politics and education.

Some adult education institutes and university extra-mural departments run courses about politics.

Political parties

 **Contact**

Conservative Central Office – 32 Smith Square, Westminster, London SW1P 3HH. Tel: 020 7222 9000.
Website: www.tory.org.uk
E-mail: ccoffice@conservative-party.org.uk

The Labour Party Headquarters – Millbank Tower, Millbank, London SW1P 4GT. Tel: 020 7802 1000.
Website: www.labour.org.uk
E-mail: labour-party@go2.poptel.org.uk

The Liberal Democrats – Party Headquarters – 4 Cowley Street, London SW1P 3NB. Tel: 020 7222 7999.
Website: www.libdems.org.uk
E-mail: libdems@cix.co.uk (cix in roman numerals)

 **For clients interested in trade union activities:**

Trades Union Congress – Congress House, Great Russell Street, London WC1B 3LS. Tel: 020 7636 4030.
Website: www.tuc.org.uk E-mail: info@tuc.org.uk

Further information

Adult Residential Colleges Association (ARCA) – PO Box 31, Washbrook, Ipswich IP8 3HF. For information about member colleges – some of which are historic houses in countryside settings – which specialise in short-stay residential adult education courses. Many of the colleges also offer study tours in the UK and overseas. Website: www.aredu.org.uk

National Coaching Foundation – 114 Cardigan Road, Headingley, Leeds LS6 3BJ. Tel: 0113 274 4802. Send stamped addressed envelope (£1 worth of stamps please) for information on sports governing bodies, training, sport and disability etc. Website: www.ncf.org.uk
E-mail: coaching@ncf.org.uk

Time to Learn – published annually by the National Institute of Adult Continuing Education, 21 De Montfort Street, Leicester LE1 7GE. Tel: 0116 255 1451. Price £4.95. ISBN 1 86201 065 X. Lists residential courses in the UK and overseas.

Courses for All – published annually. Free from the Field Studies Council, Head Office, Preston Montford, Montford Bridge, Shrewsbury SY4 1HW. Tel: 01743 850674/850164.
Website: www.field-studies-council.org E-mail: fsc.headoffice@ukonline.co.uk

Natural Break Holidays and Developing Skills Training Programmes – brochures available free from British Trust for Conservation Volunteers (BTCV) – 36 St Mary's Street, Wallingford, Oxfordshire OX10 0EU. Tel: 01491 839766. Website: www.btcv.org.uk E-mail: natural-break@btcv.org.uk

Residential Courses Programme – available free (A5 sae preferred) from Centre for Alternative Technology, Machynlleth, Powys SY20 9AZ. Tel: 01654 702400. Website: www.cat.org.uk

A Year Off ... A Year On? – published by Lifetime Careers Wiltshire. Price £8.99. ISBN 1 873 408 64 1. Contains information about some unusual ways of studying abroad, as well as other ways of spending a career break.

Good Non-Retirement Guide 1999 – by Rosemary Brown. Published by Kogan Page. Price £14.99. ISBN 0 7494 2868 6. Whilst this guide is primarily aimed at older people, it incorporates a useful directory of organisations offering leisure activities and holidays.

Adult Continuing Education Yearbook – published annually by NIACE. Includes lists of short-term residential colleges and adult and community education centres.

The Governing Bodies of Sport Address Book and Training and Education Courses Guide – available for £1.50 postage and packing charge, from Sport England Publications, PO Box 255, Wetherby LS23 7LZ. Tel: 0990 210255.

Kindred Spirit – Articles on personal and spiritual development, earth mysteries. Resources directory advertises a wide range of courses, centres, retreats, places to go, things to do. Annual subscription £12, four issues per year, or £3 per issue including p&p. Three years' subscription costs £28.50. Available from specialist shops for £3.00 or from Kindred Spirit, Foxhole, Dartington, Totnes TQ9 6EB. Tel: 01803 866686. Website: www.kindredspirit.co.uk E-mail: editors@kindredspirit.co.uk

Diggers and Dreamers 2000/2001 – the guide to communal living. £10 from bookshops, or £11 including p&p from Edge of Time Ltd, BCM Edge, London WC1N 3XX. Tel: 0800 083 0451.

12. Higher education – first degrees

This chapter covers:

- the choice of courses and qualifications in higher education
- entry requirements for mature students
- choosing and applying for a course
- credit accumulation and transfer
- different ways of studying for a degree.

Higher education is traditionally associated with study after A level or equivalent at the age of 18 upwards. However, with the recent expansion in the number of places, universities now recruit a high proportion of mature students. They are being encouraged to widen access to higher education for previously under-represented groups through financial incentives and rewards (unfortunately awarded to the institution and not the student – although the student should also benefit through improved services).

Adults considering higher education should be aware of:

- the choice of courses on offer – degrees such as BA, BSc, BEd etc (some are called MSci or MA in Scotland), HNC/HND, DipHE etc
- the variation in lengths of courses (two years for HND; three to four years for most degrees or longer for medicine etc)
- availability of part-time and sandwich courses as well as standard full-time courses
- the fact you can sometimes do one or more years of a higher education course at a further education college
- the need for self-discipline; clients may not be aware of the amount of private research and background reading involved.

Entry requirements for mature students

The entry requirements for each course vary enormously. Although the minimum requirements are generally accepted as five GCSE passes and two at A level (or equivalent), popular courses at popular universities will be more demanding. But most of the information published applies to 18 year old school leavers; mature applicants are often treated very differently. They may not be asked for such specific qualifications. Access courses designed especially for mature students, or even evidence of recent advanced level study, are often accepted for entry. Most institutions will interview their mature applicants to find out:

- at what level they have studied recently, and how successfully
- what success they achieved at school (if appropriate)

- what employment they have had, whether paid or voluntary, and the level of responsibility they have held – as supervisor or manager, for example
- any professional or vocational qualifications they have or are studying for
- key skills gained during their career
- any hobbies and interests which may be relevant to the course.

In most cases, universities will look favourably on mature applicants, provided that they can satisfy the admissions tutor that they have:

- the ability to complete the course
- the self-discipline required to cope with degree-level study
- sufficient interest in and understanding of the subject.

Mature students are advised to contact the department of the university or college they wish to apply to direct, to discuss their qualifications and experience.

See Chapter 14 for details of Access courses, and Chapter 8 for information on student finance.

Choosing a course of study

Choosing course of study from the hundreds which are on offer can be difficult. There are 92 publicly-funded universities (and one private one), and the range of subjects is enormous.

To assist in this search, clients can:

- use some of the computer programs widely available, such as ECCTIS, or the handbooks and general guides to higher education, some of which are listed at the end of the chapter
- use prospectuses, video prospectuses and the institution's website (given in the *UCAS Official Guide to University and College Entrance*) to find out more about the course, the methods of course delivery and assessment and the university or college itself
- visit the institution, either individually or on publicised open days.

In choosing a course subject, clients should consider:

- whether the subject is one they really want to devote three or four years of their lives to
- whether they want to study a specific subject, or to take a course that will qualify them for a job – such as a physiotherapy degree or a degree offering qualified teacher status
- if they prefer to take a single subject or to make up a degree from a number of major and minor subjects
- whether they would value a year's work experience in industry, which may be available on some vocational courses

- if they want to study a foreign language, is it practical for them to spend a term or a year abroad as part of the course?

There is no right or wrong choice. It is simply a matter of individual preference.

Applying for higher education

Applicants for full-time and sandwich first degrees – including teaching, medicine and art and design courses – DipHE and HND courses at all UK universities and most colleges of higher education, will go through the Universities and Colleges Admissions Service (UCAS) system. UCAS acts as a central clearing house for all applications. Art and design students should be aware of the two different application routes. Application forms – and instructions for filling them in – are available direct from UCAS, from your local college or from your local careers centre. Electronic application is also available.

 **Contact:** *UCAS, Rosehill, New Barn Lane, Cheltenham GL52 3LZ. Tel: 01242 227788. Website: www.ucas.ac.uk*

Some useful questions

- Is there a mature entry exam? Some universities will allow applicants with no qualifications to sit their entrance exam to determine whether they have the ability to do the course. What help do they offer students wishing to take this route, and what format does it take?
- Does the university have any linked Access courses, and what success level do they require?
- Will they accept students with other qualifications?
- Are there any taster courses? Is there the opportunity to sit in on some lectures beforehand?
- Do they have any special mature accommodation, for example for people with children?

Some colleges of higher education and specialist colleges operate outside the UCAS system. Applicants need to contact these colleges direct.

Part-time study

Some mature applicants find full-time study is impossible because of financial constraints. Giving up a job in order to study is not always an option. Many educational institutions are introducing an increasing number of part-time courses. Birkbeck College in London specialises in part-time courses for adults.

Some part-time degree courses are offered largely as distance learning packages, such as those offered by the Open University. Others will offer a mix of Saturday, weekday and evening lectures. Some courses assume some limited attendance during the day alongside full-time students. Clients should contact the institutions of their choice for further information.

Open University

The Open University was created specifically for mature students – although since the introduction of tuition fees it now also attracts more young people. It allows students to work from home with only the minimum amount of attendance at seminars and, for some courses, summer schools. There are no formal entry requirements. For further information, see Chapter 16.

Credit Accumulation and Transfer Schemes (CATS)

The increase of modular courses and a variety of government and European Union initiatives have led to much greater flexibility in the provision of higher education. Many universities and colleges subscribe to Credit Accumulation and Transfer Schemes which means that students can collect credits from a number of different courses and use them towards their final qualification. Scotland has one centralised SCOTCAT scheme; England, Wales and Northern Ireland operate a number of schemes.

CATS enable students to:

- transfer across subject boundaries within one institution
- transfer within a subject but across different institutions in both the UK and abroad
- accumulate credits for previous experience or skills acquired so that those with non-traditional backgrounds may be able to enter courses – known as accreditation of prior learning (APL) or accreditation of prior experiential learning (APEL)
- gain part exemption from examinations of professional bodies – or use professional body qualifications as credit towards an academic course
- combine periods of full-time and part-time study
- continue studying after a break.

Further information

Degree Course Offers 2000 – by Brian Heap. Published by Trotman. Price £18.99. ISBN 0 85660 435 6. Lists all the different courses available at universities and other higher education institutions, and the qualifications likely to be needed for entry.

Choosing your Degree Course and University – by Brian Heap. Published by Trotman. Price £14.99. ISBN 0 85660 367 8. Compares the contents of different degree courses and ranks institutions according to teaching and research.

The Push Guide to Which University '99 – published by McGraw Hill, available through Trotman. Price £11.99. ISBN 0 07709 463 8. All the other information – like the Student Union ambience and the proportion of mature students.

Degree Course Guides – published by CRAC at £5.50 each. There are 35 individual subject guides to all the courses in the particular area.

The Complete Guides Series 2000 – published by UCAS/Trotman. Price £12.99-£14.99 depending on which of the seven subject areas you choose.

The Laser Compendium of Higher Education 2000-2001 – published by Butterworth Heinemann, Linacre House, Jordan Hill, Oxford OX2 8DP. Price £24.99. ISBN 0 75064 370 6. Details of all first degrees and higher national qualifications, including those available at FE colleges.

Springboard Sponsorships for Students 2000 – published by CRAC. Price £8.99. ISBN 186017 627 5.

COSHEP/UCAS Entrance Guide to Higher Education in Scotland 2000 – available from Trotman. Price £8.00. ISBN 0 948241 68 3.

University and College Entrance: The Official Guide for entry in 2000 – available from Trotman. Price £19.95. ISBN 0 948241 69 1.

The Mature Student's Guide to Higher Education – published by UCAS. Free.

The Mature Students' Guide: Getting into higher education for 21 plus – published by Trotman, 1994. Price £7.99. ISBN 0 85660 162 4.

The NATFHE Handbook of Initial Teacher Training – published annually and available from Trotman. 1999 edition price £13.00. ISBN 0 90139 047 X.

Studying for a degree: How to succeed as a mature student in higher education – by Stephen Wade, published by How To Books. Price £9.99. ISBN 1 85703 415 5.

Net that Course – by Irene Krechowiecka, published by Kogan Page. Price £8.99. ISBN 0 7494 2958 5. How to use the internet to find out about degree courses, including overseas study and 'virtual' visits to institutions.

13. Higher education – higher degrees

This chapter covers:

- reasons for postgraduate study
- qualifications available
- types of postgraduate study (taught courses or degrees by research; part-time, full-time or distance learning etc)
- postgraduate funding, including research councils
- sources of further information.

Why do people study for a higher degree?

- To change career direction.
- To gain specific practical skills, or analytical skills through academic research.
- To improve their employment prospects – postgraduates are less likely to be unemployed than graduates.
- Because they want to study a particular subject at greater depth.
- To update existing skills or knowledge of the subject of their first degree.

Traditionally, graduates studied for a higher degree immediately after a first degree, but increasingly postgraduate opportunities are being used as a form of career development. Many postgraduate courses are open to people who are not graduates.

Types of course available

- Vocational courses leading to qualifications which are required for particular professions – for example Postgraduate Certificate of Education (PGCE) for would-be teachers, Postgraduate Diploma in Law and Legal Practice Course for those wanting to become solicitors or barristers, Diploma in Social Work for social workers.
- Vocational courses which are not compulsory but which may help entry to particular occupations, for example the qualifications of the Institute of Personnel and Development or journalism courses.
- Skills courses which add practical abilities to academic knowledge, such as computer programming, languages or secretarial skills.
- Academic courses leading to certificates, diplomas, masters degrees or doctorates in virtually any subject imaginable.

The number of postgraduate qualifications has increased in recent years, with the major growth being in business administration, computing, environmental studies and media and communication.

Methods of study

Postgraduate qualifications can be gained in a variety of ways:

- taught courses
- degrees by research
- part-time or full-time study
- modular programmes.

Taught courses

These courses usually last a year, which is longer than the normal academic year, or occasionally two years. A masters degree course is made up of lectures and examinations, followed by months of private research for a thesis or dissertation. A certificate or diploma course is shorter and does not usually include the research element. Sometimes there is a system of continuous assessment to measure progress throughout the course. Certificates and diplomas are usually awarded after vocational courses in specific fields, such as teaching. Degrees may be Master of Arts (MA), Master of Education (MEd), Master of Science (MSc) or Master of Business Administration (MBA). There are also some taught doctorates, such as DBA or DEng.

Research degrees

The research begins with the student deciding what he or she wants to study, why, where and under whose supervision. They should look at the record of different institutions and the individual academics they would be working under. Research degrees include a Master of Philosophy (MPhil) which usually takes one or two years, or a doctorate (PhD) which takes at least three years – usually longer – if studied full-time. It is possible to study for a one-year masters degree before converting to a PhD. Some universities offer a one-year Master of Research (MRes) programme of study. This provides research training, with strong links with industry, which will help students who wish to go on to a PhD doctorate.

Students need to check the requirements of individual institutions. If they hope to get research council funding, students should choose and apply for a course as early as possible.

The advantage of a degree by research is that only the topic of study is fixed. How it is studied is up to the student to decide, in consultation with their supervisor. This can be exciting, but it can also be daunting to those used to studying set syllabuses. Self-motivation is vital.

Research degrees are awarded by thesis – an extended written account of the research and its findings. Usually this will be about as long as the average novel.

Part-time courses

Many postgraduate courses are now available on a part-time basis. Arrangements for part-time study vary enormously. Courses by instruction often require one full day's attendance a week at college for two or three years. Degrees by research, when experimental work is not necessary, may be achieved through evening attendance only. It takes about three years for an MPhil, and four or five or more for a PhD. The advantage of studying part-time is that study can be undertaken while you are working. However, students should think carefully about the various demands on their time which might make it difficult to follow a part-time course. Once again, motivation is vital.

Modular courses

More and more taught courses are being offered on a modular basis – the mix and match method of study. Courses are divided into a number of units, some compulsory and some optional. A degree will be awarded when a particular number of credits or units have been obtained. The main benefit of this type of study is that the student can concentrate on areas that they enjoy, but should be careful not to exclude the fundamentals which employers may be interested in.

Open learning

The Open University and other open learning colleges offer a range of higher degrees or equivalents, which may be a more flexible way to study. See Chapters 16 and 17. Many universities also now offer their courses by open or distance learning.

Who awards higher degrees?

Like first degrees, higher degrees are awarded by universities. All universities in the United Kingdom, including the Open University, award higher degrees of some kind; the exact kinds of degree vary with the institution.

Where to study

Most universities offer research degrees. Some specialise in taught programmes, others have expertise or facilities for particular research topics. Many have highly specialised facilities for research into scientific or medical subjects; competition is very fierce for places at these universities. As the degrees are awarded by the universities themselves, it is usually possible for the scheme of research to change and develop as it progresses.

Colleges and institutes of higher education may offer higher degrees. There are also business schools, which may be independent or attached to higher education institutions. Higher degrees from these bodies may be awarded by a nearby university.

Entry requirements

Most institutions expect a good academic background for entry to a postgraduate course. Exact requirements vary according to the popularity of the course. Higher qualifications are likely to be demanded for a research degree than for a taught course.

Many institutions will accept qualifications other than the usual first degree, if they think the applicant will add something to the study group or if they can fund themselves through the course. For some courses, such as Masters in Business Administration (MBA) and Diploma in Social Work (DipSW), you need relevant work experience as well.

Applicants should contact the admissions tutor for the course they are considering to check entry requirements.

Credit accumulation and transfer schemes (CATS)

You can accumulate credit for previous study and experience, and use it towards gaining a postgraduate qualification. See Chapter 12 for more details.

How to apply

There is no central application scheme, like that for first degrees. Applicants should:

- use directories and databases such as those listed at the end of this chapter to discover which institutions offer programmes in their areas of interest
- obtain and read prospectuses or view video prospectuses

- visit the institution's website
- find out who the admissions tutor is for the course, and if possible arrange to see them in person; alternatively write or telephone
- apply direct to the individual institution.

A covering letter and/or CV may help to persuade admissions tutors of the student's enthusiasm and suitability. Applicants for research degrees will have to submit a fairly detailed scheme, outlining what they intend to study and how they intend to approach it. They should be prepared for some searching questions on this and will almost certainly be interviewed before being offered a place.

Overseas study

British university graduates are held in high regard abroad and consequently postgraduate work is available, especially in the USA and Canada, where scholarships may be available.

Postgraduate funding

Fees and living costs have to be budgeted for. Postgraduate courses may have an academic year of 44 weeks and require expensive equipment and books. Printing and binding a thesis alone can cost about £200. This is why so many students study for postgraduate qualifications part-time whilst in paid employment.

Getting any finance for postgraduate study, particularly for non-vocational subjects, is not easy. Student loans on a par with those for first degree students are only available for Postgraduate Certificate in Education (PGCE) initial teacher training courses. PGCE students' fees are also paid by the DfEE.

Other funding depends on a variety of factors:

- the class of degree; a research studentship usually requires a 2.1 honours degree
- the course subject
- where you live
- reasons for wanting to do the course.

Research councils

There are six government-funded research councils which offer awards covering tuition fees and a contribution towards maintenance and expenses, plus the British Academy which funds humanities research. Competition for this funding is very fierce, and there are nothing like enough awards to go round.

Types of research council funding are:

- Advanced Course Studentships – for taught masters degrees
- Research Masters training awards and Standard Research Studentships – for PhD and MPhil students
- Co-operative Awards in Science and Engineering (CASE) – similar to Standard Research Studentships but involving work with industry or other research outside higher education.

Clients should note that:

- research councils do not fund MBAs
- additional allowances may be available for dependants, mature students and registered disabled students
- funding is largely allocated to specific institutions and courses, approved by the research councils, so students are offered funding when they are offered a place on the course; otherwise, applicants for competition funding apply direct to the research councils.

See Chapter 8 for more information on student finance.

Local government opportunities – The Improvement and Development Agency

Provides a small number of training awards for careers guidance qualifications, on behalf of the DfEE. Applicants (usually graduates, but not always) must be over 25 and have been out of full-time education for two years.

 **Contact:** *The Improvement and Development Agency – Layden House, 76-86 Turmill Street, Farringdon, London EC1M 5LG. Tel: 020 7296 6600. Website: www.idea.gov.uk*

Other means of funding

- Higher education institutions have Access funds that students can apply for.
- NHS bursaries are available to graduates on courses which lead to professional registration related to medicine.
- Some charitable grants are available, but these are not likely to cover your full costs.
- Government departments and professional bodies may fund certain courses.
- Some Training and Enterprise Councils (TECs) and Local Enterprise Councils (LECs) may provide training allowances for unemployed people wishing to attend certain vocational courses.
- Employers may offer sponsorship, and in rare cases study leave.
- Students can study part-time and support themselves through paid employment.
- Career Development Loans (see Chapter 8), or other bank loans, can be used to fund education and training. There are specific loan schemes for law students and for MBAs.
- Paid research or teaching assistant posts in higher education offer opportunities for postgraduate study.
- Students can use their own savings, or receive financial support from partners or family, and regard it as an investment in their future which may pay dividends in the long term.
- Individual learning accounts can be used as saving accounts to raise funds for study; the advantages are being able to use the account to raise a loan or to gain tax relief on expenditure on education.

- Some local education authorities may channel limited funds into postgraduate study.
- European funding is available, usually allocated to the higher education institutions rather than to individual students.

Further information

Broadsheet newspapers, specialist journals and the educational press, such as the Times Higher Education Supplement, carry details of postgraduate opportunities.

Residents of Northern Ireland seeking advice on finance should contact the Department of Education for Northern Ireland – Rathgael House, Balloo Road, Bangor BT19 2PR. Tel: 028 9127 0077.

Student Support in Scotland: A Guide for Postgraduate Students 1999-2000 – available from Student Awards Agency for Scotland – Room 113, Gyleview House, 3 Redheughs Rigg, Edinburgh EH12 9HH. Website: www.student-support-saas.gov.uk/pgrad.htm

How to Choose Your Postgraduate Course – published by Trotman. Price £11.99. ISBN 0 85660 432 1. Includes information about funding and overseas opportunities.

Business Schools Directory 1999/2000 – available from Trotman. Price £29.99. ISBN 0 7506 3956 3. Describes all postgraduate and post-experience business courses in the UK.

How to Choose Your MBA – published by Trotman. Price £8.99. ISBN 085660 321 X.

Postgrad: The Students' Guide 2000 – published by CRAC/Hobsons. Price £6.50 per volume. Set of four volumes covering different subject areas. Brief listings only.

Postgrad: The Directory of Graduate Studies 1999/2000 – published by CRAC/Hobsons. Price £109.99. Comprehensive directory. Information is also available on their website: www.postgrad.hobsons.com

Casebook 2000 series – published by CRAC/Hobsons. Price £9.99 each. As well as describing graduate employment opportunities, most titles in the series also feature postgraduate study.

Prospects Postgraduate Directory – published by CSU. Price £95 for a set of three volumes.

Prospects Postgraduate Funding Guide – published by CSU. Free on request.

Prospects Postgrad – published by CSU. Price £9 for a year's subscription; three issues per year. Course and research vacancy information. See also the website: www.prospects.csu.ac.uk

GET: Graduate Employment and Training 2000 – published by CRAC/Hobsons. Price £20.99. Information is also available on the website: www.get.hobsons.com

Postgraduate Study and Research – published by AgCAS/CSU. Price £2.65.

Gaining a Master's Degree: How to invest in your own future – by Allen Brown, published by How To Books. Price £9.99. ISBN 1 85703 450 3.

14. Access courses and other adult routes

This chapter covers:

- different ways of returning to education at various levels
- courses which are specifically Access to higher education courses
- providers of Access and equivalent courses
- information on accreditation of prior learning and credit accumulation and transfer.

There are many courses designed to encourage adults to re-enter the education system and to take part in lifelong learning. The government is keen to widen access to further and higher education and is actively encouraging institutions to recruit students from social and ethnic groups which have been under-represented in the past.

Adults thinking of returning to learning after a break could consider:

- Starting with a short part-time course, such as an evening class, perhaps in a leisure or recreation subject. As their interest in the subject grows, they may consider working towards qualifications, or changing to study something 'more serious'.
- Attending a full- or part-time course at a further education college, perhaps studying alongside young people. Many schools, especially those which call themselves community colleges, accept mature people in to study alongside their younger pupils, usually for GCSEs, A levels or other traditional academic qualifications.
- Using open or distance learning to gain A level or equivalent qualifications quickly, if already of a sufficient educational standard.

Adult routes

The traditional routes are not for everyone, particularly if their first experience of learning was not positive. Courses geared specifically to give adults a 'second chance' work to build up the individual's confidence. They are designed to take into account the fact that most people need a lot of encouragement to start learning after a break.

Skills updating

There are professional updating courses for people who have been away from the workplace for a number of years and had skills qualifications before. Many of these courses are for those who have been raising a family. For example, there are courses for returning to teaching or nursing, re-entry to General Practice (medicine), and updating in information technology and office skills.

Starting afresh

There are many courses for people who have no qualifications or who want to start afresh. They include:

- pre-Access courses
- Access to higher education courses

- short 'taster' courses at universities – such as 'Uniprep' at the University of Hertfordshire (one day a week for 12 weeks) or 'Beginner's Guide to University' at the University of Sunderland (15 weeks full-time)
- foundation courses
- women returners' courses (see also chapter 27)
- local study skills and refresher courses with a variety of names.

The rest of this chapter will consider these types of courses.

What are these courses like?

- These courses are usually structured, with as much support as possible. Tutors are there not only to teach but also to counsel. They can give advice on any type of problem in doing the course – whether it's difficulties with the actual studying or financial or childcare matters. Educational guidance is an essential part of the course. Tutors will analyse what the student has done before the course and, by going through available options, advise on the next move.
- The courses are student-centred; this means they are designed and adjusted in response to what people want.
- The aim of these courses is to give students the study skills and the confidence they need to make the most of the education system. Students have the opportunity to investigate different higher education subject options.
- For some students, these courses provide a faster route to qualifications and higher education than GCSEs/Standard grades and A level/Highers and Advanced Highers.
- Some classes start and finish so that children can be dropped off and picked up from school; many courses are part-time and available in the evenings or during the day.
- Courses can often be adapted to help people with any special requirements they may have due to age, gender, race or disability.
- Some are specifically designed for women and people from minority ethnic groups
- Extra English language support may be available.

What is available?

Provision varies from one place to another. In areas with long-established courses a wide variety of subjects are available, particularly for learning to use new technology. In other areas there may be less choice and only general courses on offer.

Although all the courses are for adults coming back into education they are not all at the same academic level. They range from basic literacy and numeracy courses to higher education preparation courses . No formal entry qualifications are needed; it's up to the individual student and tutor to decide which are appropriate. Students and their advisers should always check the level of the course, as names can be misleading. For example, 'access' is sometimes used for courses other than those preparing students for higher education.

Access to higher education courses

Access courses have been around for over 20 years. They are designed to meet local needs and are targeted at specific groups within communities. Students on the courses may have difficulties returning to education, but will have shown that they have the potential to succeed in higher education. Access courses have been called the third route into higher education – alongside A levels/Highers and Advanced GNVQs.

Access courses are designed to provide the skills and understanding needed to succeed on a degree course. They are open to 'mature' people, that is over 21; but in reality the average age tends to be 25 to 35. There are no formal entry requirements, but students should check individual course details. Competence in English and maths may need to be assessed, and many Access courses have these subjects built into their programme.

Typical subject areas are: an introduction to arts, humanities, or social sciences, health studies, science, business studies, performing and related arts, information technology, art and design. Access programmes, as distinct from courses, are likely to be more customised, modular, covering more subjects and incorporating accreditation of prior learning.

Access courses and programmes are validated on behalf of the Quality Assurance Agency by 34 Authorised Validating Agencies, most of which are members of the National Open College Network. There are about 40,000 Access students in England, Wales and Northern Ireland. About three-quarters of Access students stay in their own area to study.

Most courses last one or two years. They may be gained by full- or part-time college attendance or through distance learning. Some are directly linked to a particular degree course, so that success on the Access course gives automatic entrance to that degree course. With others, entry to a degree course is not always guaranteed but admissions tutors usually welcome students from Access courses because of their motivation and their good grounding in study skills.

The Scottish Wider Access Programme (SWAP)

This programme is creating new ways into higher education through the design of Access courses and of individual programmes guaranteeing entry to higher education, as well as through credit transfer and flexible study plans. It has three regional consortia established to develop and co-ordinate access to higher education in Scotland. Many of the access programmes are offered in further education colleges; most are full-time, but some are part-time or through open learning. Individual colleges are allocated funds which they can use to help support students on the programmes.

 **Contact:** *North of Scotland – NORSWAP, PO Box 11763, Peterhead AB42 4ZA. Tel: 01771 622924. E-mail: norswap@ifb.co.uk*

South East of Scotland – SWAP East, 57 George Square, Edinburgh EH8 9JU. Tel: 0131 650 6861. Website: www.stevenson.ac.uk/swapeast E-mail: swapeast@ed.ac.uk

West of Scotland – SWAP West, Charles Oakley Building, Central College of Commerce, 300 Cathedral Street, Glasgow G1 2TA. Tel: 0141 553 2471. Website: www.swap.demon.co.uk E-mail: swap_west@swap.demon.co.uk

Open College Networks

Open College Networks (OCNs) are local accreditation bodies. Although OCNs have always been involved in validating access to HE courses, they also accredit a comprehensive range of other programmes at levels up to and including Access courses. The membership of Open College Networks (OCNs) includes over 2900 provider organisations of education and training, further and higher education institutions, sixth-form colleges, adult and community education centres, TECs, voluntary organisations, private and public employers. Open College Networks offer credits for learning which you might have done on a formal course, or informally through work, a training scheme or voluntary work.

OCNs are linked nationally through the National Open College Network (NOCN) which actively supports the National Credit Framework. This framework is a system of levels and credits for accrediting learning which allows for comparisons of breadth and depth, as OCN courses do not have a common syllabus or examination.

- There are four levels of achievement, from entry level to level three. Level three is the equivalent of A level and NVQ level 3. Level two is the equivalent of GCSE.
- Each credit represents 30 hours of learning, which may be done in the classroom or during private study.
- Credits achieved on an accredited learning programme can be recognised by other networks in the National Open College Network through a credit accumulation and transfer system.
- Access course students must achieve a minimum of 16 credits (the majority at level three) in order to gain the Access Certificate.

The National Credit Framework

OCN Entry level	No equivalent	No equivalent	No equivalent
OCN Level one	NVQ1	GNVQ (F)	GCSE D-G
OCN Level two	NVQ2	GNVQ (I)	GCSE A-C
OCN Level three	NVQ3	GNVQ (A)	A level

Contact: *The Administrative Officer, National Open College Network – University of Derby, Kedleston Road, Derby. DE22 1GB Tel: 01332 622712. Website: www.nocn.ac.uk E-mail: nocn@derby.ac.uk*

The National Open College Network

Members of the network can help with queries or information about the National Credit Framework, and the achievement or transfer of credits within the system. Many networks publish directories of all Access courses in their areas.

Accreditation Consortium for South Anglia (ACSA),
University of Essex, Wivenhoe Park, Colchester CO4 3SQ
Tel: 01206 873023. Website: www.essex.ac.uk/acsa
E-mail: acsa@essex.ac.uk

Chiltern Region Open College Network (CROCN),
Winslow Centre, Park Road, Winslow MK18 3DN.
Tel: 01296 715479. E-mail: crocn@buckscc.gov.uk

Gloucestershire Open College Network (GOCN),
Conway House, 33-35 Worcester Street, Gloucester GL1 3AJ.
Tel: 01452 509714. Website: www.gocn.org.uk
E-mail: gocn@glos.tec.org.uk

Greater Manchester Open College Federation (GMOCF),
Paul Building, Denison Road, Victoria Park, Manchester M14 5RX.
Tel: 0161 248 5429. Website: www.users.globalnet.co.uk/~gmocf
E-mail: gmocf@globalnet.co.uk

Hertfordshire Access Consortium (HAC), University of Hertfordshire,
College Lane, Hatfield, Hertfordshire AL10 9AB.
Tel: 01707 285213. Website: www.herts.ac.uk/hac/
E-mail: a.herbert@herts.ac.uk

London Open College Network (LOCN), 15 Angel Gate,
City Road, London EC1V 2SF. Tel: 020 7833 8289.
Website: www.locn.org.uk
E-mail: locn@locn.org.uk

Merseyside Open College Network (MOCN), Suite 304-306,
The Cotton Exchange Building, Old Hall Street, Liverpool L3 9LQ.
Tel: 0151 2550515. Website: www.mocn.co.uk
E-mail: ocn@mocn.co.uk

North Anglia Open College Network (NAOCN), Wensum Lodge,
169 King Street, Norwich NR1 1QW. Tel: 01603 674337.
E-mail: naocn@argonet.co.uk

North and East London Accreditation Federation (NELAF),
NELAF Coordinating Centre, 707 Forest Road, London E17 4JB.
Tel: 020 8527 7064. E-mail: NELAF@nelafocn.demon.co.uk

North East Midlands Open College Network (NEMOCN),
South East Derbyshire College, Parklands Centre, Stanhope Road,
Long Eaton NG10 4QN. Tel: 0115 946 1118.
Website: www. burton-college.ac.uk/~nemap/
E-mail: nemocn@nemocn.demon.co.uk

North Wales Access and Credit Consortium (NWACC), University of Wales Bangor, College Road, Bangor, Gwynedd LL57 2DG. Tel: 01248 371529. E-mail: croeso@nwacc.demon.co.uk

Northern Ireland Open College Network (NIOCN), Room 80B06, University of Ulster, Art and Design, 1-51 York Street, Belfast BT15 1ED. Tel: 028 9032 0511. E-mail: nocninfo@niocn.co.uk

Open College Network for Central England (OCNCE), Westwood Site, University of Warwick, Coventry CV4 7AL Tel: 024 7652 4728. E-mail: cesam@frost.warwick.ac.uk

Open College Network of Cumbria and South West Scotland (OCNCSWS), Chatsworth House, 1 Chatsworth Square, Carlisle CA1 1HB. Tel: 01228 514770. E-mail: ocncs@carlisle.ac.uk

Open College Network: Kent and Medway (OCNKM), Rooms Hg1-3, Keynes College, University of Kent, Canterbury CT2 7NP. Tel: 01227 827823. E-mail: d.c.gittins@ukc.ac.uk

Open College Network North West Midlands (OCNNWM), c/o Staffordshire University, College Road, Stoke-on-Trent ST4 2DE. Tel: 01782 292712. E-mail: g.y.evans@staffs.ac.uk

Open College Network Northumberland (OCNN) and the Borders, Open Learning Centre, Cottingwood Lane, Morpeth, Northumberland NE61 1DX. Tel: 01670 503605. E-mail: ocnnet@aol.com

Open College Network – South Central (OCNSC), Eastpoint Centre, Burgoyne Road, Thornhill, Southampton SO19 6PB. Tel: 023 8036 3413. E-mail: admin@hocn.co.uk

Open College Network South East Midlands (OCNSEM), Stonehill School, Stonehill Avenue, Birstall, Leicestershire LE4 4JG. Tel: 0116 267 1148. E-mail: ocnsem@sem.u-net.com

Open College Network of the South West (OCNSW), Academic Partnerships, University of Plymouth, Drake Circus, Plymouth, Devon PL4 8AA. Tel: 01752 232381. E-mail: ocnsw@plymouth.ac.uk

Open College Network (South Yorkshire and Humber Region) (OCNSYH), Sheffield Hallam University, 37 Broomgrove Road, Sheffield S10 2BP. Tel: 0114 225 2585. Website: www.shu.ac.uk/ocn E-mail: ocn@shu.ac.uk

Open College Network West (OCNW), 53 Oxford Street, Weston-super-Mare, Somerset BS23 1TR. Tel: 01934 612727. Website: www.dspce.dial.pipex.com/ocnwest E-mail: ocnwest@dial.pipex.com

Open College Network of the West Midlands (OCNWM), University of Wolverhampton, Gorway Road, Walsall, West Midlands WS1 3BD. Tel: 01902 322958. Website: ocnwm.wlv.ac.uk:8000 E-mail: in5713@wlv.ac.uk

Oxfordshire Open College Network (OxOCN), Cricket Road Centre, Cricket Road, Cowley, Oxford OX4 3DW. Tel: 01865 775746. E-mail: oxocn@patrol.i-way.co.uk

South East Wales Access Consortium (SEWAC), University of Wales Cardiff, 2 North Road, Cardiff CF1 3DY. Tel: 029 2037 8378. Website: www.dspce.dial.pipex.com/sewac/ E-mail: sewac@dial.pipex.com

South of England Open College Network (SEOCN), University of Brighton, A Block, Lewes Road, Brighton BN2 4GJ. Tel: 01273 642930. Website: www.brighton.ac.uk/seocn/ E-mail: seocn@bton.ac.uk

South West Wales Open College and Access Consortium (SWWOCAC), Hendrefoilan (Study Block), Hendrefoilan Avenue, Swansea SA2 7NB. Tel: 01792 297300. E-mail: swwocac@aol.com

Surrey Open College Federation (SOCF), Runnymede Centre, Chertsey Road, Addlestone, Surrey KT15 2EP. Tel: 01932 569894. E-mail: socf@surreycc.gov.uk

The Regional Open College Network for the North (TROCN), University of Teesside, Borough Road, Middlesbrough, TS1 3BA. Tel: 01642 384212. Website: www.trocn.co.uk E-mail: trocn@tees.ac.uk

Thames Region Accrediting Consortium (TRAC), Thames Valley University, University House, Ealing Green, London W5 5ED. Tel: 020 8567 6678. E-mail: trac@tvu.ac.uk

Tyneside Open College Network (TOCN), 1 Heaton Road, Byker, Newcastle-upon-Tyne NE6 1SA. Tel: 0191 224 3434. E-mail: toc@onyxnet.co.uk

West and North Yorkshire Open College Network (WNYOCN), Leeds Metropolitan University, No 4 College Close, Beckett Park Campus, Leeds LS6 3QS. Tel: 0113 283 7460. Website: www.lmu.ac.uk/ocn E-mail: open.college.network@lmu.ac.uk

Alternatives to Access courses

If there are no specific Access courses running locally, there may be a similar course available designed by the college itself with a special arrangement with a higher education institution.

For example, in Scotland, there are currently over 3000 National Certificate Modules to choose from (to be known as National Units under qualification reforms being implemented). These can provide a basis from which to build up to higher-level qualifications.

Some higher education institutions accept a completed Open University foundation course for entry to certain degree courses. Individual institutions can provide information.

National Vocational Qualification (NVQ) level 3, which may be gained in the workplace, at college or by a combination of both, may be accepted for entry to some vocational degree or Higher National Diploma or Certificate courses. NVQs can include an element of Accreditation of Prior Learning (see below), so may be particularly relevant to adults wishing to use their knowledge and experience to return to education.

Foundation courses

A number of higher education courses incorporate a foundation year, mainly intended for students leaving school with the 'wrong' A level subjects – eg arts A levels for entry to an engineering or science degree course. These courses may also be appropriate for mature students without the usual entry qualifications. There are also some free standing foundation courses.

Accreditation of prior and experiential learning (APL) (APEL)

This is the process which enables people to gain certification for their past achievements, often outside the formal education system – for example in work, leisure or community activities. Identified learning can be matched against nationally recognised qualifications at various levels.

Many universities and colleges of higher education now subscribe to Credit Accumulation and Transfer Schemes (CATS). These allow accumulation of academic credits towards awards (undergraduate or postgraduate degrees) through the process of APL (or APEL).

Summer schools at Scottish universities

There are a number of summer schools aimed to encourage non-traditional entrants to higher education, including mature students. Students should enquire at individual universities.

Further Information

List of Access Courses Preparing Students for Entry to Courses of Higher Education – available free of charge by phoning 0845 602 2260. Published annually by the DfEE.

To search for information about Access courses, starting from a keyword, a subject, a region etc, see: Website: www.ucas.ac.uk/access/

Pickup National Training Directory – see chapter 4 for details – includes short courses at universities for people thinking of taking a degree course.

UCAS Complete Guides Series 2000 – published by Trotman. Price £12.99 – £14.99 depending on the subject. Includes degrees which incorporate a foundation year.

15. Adult residential colleges

This chapter covers:

- details of the eight adult residential colleges at which students receive adult education bursaries
- courses offered by these colleges
- student eligibility
- where to find out about other adult residential education provision.

What are they?

There are eight colleges offering long-term residential adult education in the UK. They provide educational opportunities for adults whose full-time studies stopped when they left school. The colleges are designated for support by the Further Education Funding Council (FEFC), which means that nearly all the students attending are funded for up to one year full-time by a special bursary. The education they offer is mainly academic.

How they work

The colleges have a number of things in common.

- Though often vocationally orientated, they offer academic education, not training
- They are mainly residential (with non-residential courses at some)
- None of them demands formal entry requirements
- Selection is normally by interview: applicants may also have to write an essay and usually have to give the names of referees
- Most of them offer an Access to higher education qualification, which may also be suitable for entry to some professions
- The courses offered are mainly in humanities and social sciences, with many including computing skills: some of the colleges are also concerned with industrial relations and trade union studies
- The teaching is geared to the learning needs of each student; there are regular individual or small group tutorials with lectures and seminars and a lot of individual study – essay-writing is an important element
- Terms are usually September to December, January to Easter, Easter to June.

Money

Adult education bursaries are available for one-year full-time diploma and certificate courses – provided the applicant has not previously received a bursary or state funding for higher education. Bursaries cover maintenance, fees and some travelling expenses. They are not available for courses leading to professional qualifications. See chapter 8 on student finance for details of how to apply for a bursary.

Applications

There is no central admissions system. Applicants can get prospectuses and application forms from the colleges.

A limited number of overseas students is accepted by all colleges. Some have specific charitable trusts for this purpose. However, fees are normally higher than for UK students. Application is normally through the British Council.

The colleges and the courses they offer

Coleg Harlech

Courses

The course leads to the University of Wales Diploma in General Studies, which satisfies university entry requirements. Full or part-time study options.

Subjects

Social sciences, performing arts, literature, history and idea, information technology, and Welsh.

There is also an Access to nursing and health care programme. Short residential courses are also offered.

Entry requirements

Minimum age 20. Entry is by interview alone, with no written work required. One referee is needed.

Notes

The college has about 140 students – both men and women. It has its own audio-visual centre, theatre and squash courts with study bedrooms in halls of residence. A number of special bursaries and scholarships are available.

 **Contact:** *The College Secretary, Coleg Harlech, Harlech LL46 2PU. Tel: 01766 780363. Website: www.harlech.ac.uk/ E-mail: harlech.ac.uk*

Co-operative College

Courses

The college offers a 21-week residential programme leading to Open College Network nationally-recognised Access certificate for higher education (Certificate in Policy Studies). Students can also achieve the RSA CLAIT (Computer Literacy and Information Technology) certificate during their studies. The programme runs twice yearly, beginning in July and January.

Subjects

All students do mathematics, computing, key skills and communication skills, case studies and a personal/business project. They also do five additional optional units from sociology, psychology, economics, politics, history, geography, credit unions, business finance, and business skills.

Entry requirements
The programme is targeted at adults who do not have formal learning qualifications. Enquiries and applications are welcome throughout the year, and entry is dependent on interview. Eligible students get a bursary.

Notes
Other courses are for co-operative managers from developing countries, trainee managers, directors and employees of co-operatives. Eight study bedrooms can accommodate students with disabilities. Weekend residential courses are held for the co-operative members programmes. The college is an accredited centre to run NVQ programmes, and offers an extensive range of programmes at NVQ levels 3 and 4.

 **Contact:** *Education Services Manager, Co-operative College, Stanford Hall, Loughborough LE12 5QR. Tel: 01509 857204/218.*
E-mail: mervyn.wilson@co-opcollege.zee-web.co.uk

Fircroft College

Courses
The college offers a one-year full-time residential or non-residential programme resulting in an Access qualification, making students eligible for higher education. Short residential courses are also available.

Subjects
Community organisation, study skills, economics, politics, sociology, African Caribbean history, race and ethnicity, literature, mathematics, ecology and information technology.

Entry requirements
Minimum age 20, but no upper age limit.

Entry to Access course by application form and interview. Apply at any time, preferably before the end of May for the following September.

Entry to short courses by application form.

Notes
20 residential places for Access courses each year. Facilities for people with sensory impairment and for people in wheelchairs. Part of Selly Oak Colleges (800 students, 50 nationalities) with many recreational and sporting facilities.

 **Contact:** *The Registrar, Fircroft College of Adult Education, 1018 Bristol Road, Selly Oak, Birmingham B29 6LH.*
Tel: 0121 472 0116. E-mail: j.wilcox.fircroft@sellyoak.ac.uk

Hillcroft College (a residential college for women)

Courses

A one-year modular course leads to the Certificate of Higher Education in Combined Studies and Social Studies (validated by the Open University). It is recognised as equivalent to a first year degree course at some universities, and for entry to professional courses.

Subjects

Computing, social work, women, health and the community, mathematics for the social sciences, research methods, women's history, women's studies, developmental studies, modernism, social and political studies, psychology, human biology, sociology of education, art and design issues.

The college also offers the Diploma in Higher Education (an extension of the Certificate in HE), as well as a number of other full-time and part-time courses in IT/computing, English for Speakers of Other Languages (ESOL) and introductory management studies.

Entry requirements

Minimum age 21. Two referees and an interview.

Notes

Women only. Mainly residential (single study bedrooms) but some day students. About 75 full-time students a year.

Contact: *The Secretary (AE), Hillcroft College, South Bank, Surbiton KT6 6DF. Tel: 020 8399 2688. E-mail: enquiry@hillcroft.ac.uk*

Newbattle Abbey College

Courses

33-week courses are offered leading to a Diploma in European Studies or a Diploma in Scottish Studies, both of which are recognised as Access qualifications for entry to universities and colleges all over the UK. The college also offers a variety of short courses throughout the year.

Subjects

Mandatory modules for the Diploma in European Studies are: The Making of the European Union, Social Policy in Europe and Europe and the Wider World. Study of French is also obligatory. Optional modules include: Europe's Cultural Renaissance, Religion and Secularisation, and courses in sociology, psychology and philosophy. Scottish Studies includes three mandatory modules in Scottish history, plus options from Scottish nationalism, literature, art or drama as well as economics and philosophy and the Gaelic language. It is possible to mix and match modules from the two diploma courses.

Entry requirements

Minimum age is 20. Entry is based on interview and the only requirements are enthusiasm and aptitude as the course is quite intensive. Two referees are requested.

Notes

The college building dates back to the 12th century, and is in extensive grounds seven miles south of Edinburgh. There are 80 study bedrooms available to the 50 full-time students plus those on short courses, a 17th century drawing room and a computing suite.

Contact: *The Director of Studies, Newbattle Abbey College, Dalkeith, Midlothian EH22 3LL. Tel: 0131 663 1921. E-mail: office@nac.sol.co.uk*

Northern College

Courses

A full-time, nine-month diploma course is offered, which is recognised as a valid university entrance qualification. Part-time places are available. The college also offers the first year of the Sheffield Hallam University BA(Hons) Combined Studies degree course. Many short courses are available, some lasting three days, others six weeks.

Subjects

These courses cover a number of basic disciplines and study skills. Optional subjects include: psychology, sociology, history, European studies, information and communications technology, women's studies, popular culture and literature.

Entry requirements

Admission to the diploma and degree courses is by interview. Minimum age usually 21.

Notes

Residential accommodation in single and double study bedrooms. Non-residential places available. Children's centre provided on campus for children aged two and a half to 14 years – limited places available. Support from a personal tutor and student services. Access to e-mail and the internet is provided in the library and learning resource centre.

Contact: *The Courses Office, Northern College, Wentworth Castle, Stainborough, Barnsley S75 3ET. Tel: 01226 776010. Minicom: 01226 776026. Website: www.northern.ac.uk E-mail: info@northern-college.shu.ac.uk*

Plater College

Courses

One year courses leading to the Certificate in Higher Education following one of five Pathway options: politics and economics, legal studies, social administration, pastoral studies, theology. The certificate provides access to UK and most overseas universities.

All students study the social teaching of the Catholic Church, and there are optional courses in English language and in mathematics to GCSE standard and IT to CLAIT.

Entry requirements

Minimum age 21. Essay and interview. As well as two referees, reference will be asked from a parish priest. Although this a Catholic college, applications are welcomed from other practising faiths and from anybody interested in understanding and alleviating social problems. Reference will be asked from someone able to vouch for your moral standing. Candidates should also have some record of service to the community.

Notes
A Catholic college with mass said every day. 80 students of both sexes. Students can use the University of Oxford library and take part in general undergraduate activities.

 **Contact:** *The Tutor for Admissions, Plater College, Pullens Lane, Oxford OX3 0DT. Tel: 01865 740500. Website: www.plater.ac.uk E-mail: reception@plater.ac.uk*

Ruskin College

Courses
One-year courses leading to the Certificate of Higher Education.

Subjects
History, English studies, women's studies, sociology, employment studies, economics, politics, community and youth work and computing. Two year full-time Diploma in Social Work. Two year part-time MA in Women's Studies, MA in Popular Memory and Public History. The Ruskin learning project also runs part-time courses in a wide variety of subjects.

Entry requirements for Certificate of Higher Education
No formal academic qualifications required, but an interest in learning and life experience are important. Minimum age 20. Entrance by a piece of writing about yourself and personal or telephone interview.

Notes
Approximately 180 full-time students. Approximately 40 non-resident 'external' students. Limited family accommodation. Small nursery.

 **Contact:** *The General Secretary, Ruskin College, Walton Street, Oxford OXI 2HE. Tel: 01865 310713. Website: www.ruskin.ac.uk E-mail: enquiries@ruskin.ac.uk*

Other Residential Colleges

There are many other residential colleges, which offer mostly short-term leisure courses (see chapter 11) but also some which may lead to qualifications. Some specialise in music, art or creative writing for example, while others offer a wide range of studies. There is even a college especially for WI members. All these are listed in:

Adult Continuing Education Year Book – published by NIACE. Price £14.95. ISBN 1 86201 063 3.

16. The Open University (OU)

This chapter covers:

- the range and level of courses offered by the Open University
- the learning resources and tutorial support provided
- provision for students with disabilities or living in remote areas etc
- addresses of regional centres
- the costs involved.

The Open University (OU) is the only university that caters particularly for mature students, including people without any qualifications. Its approach takes into account the problems adults have in returning to study (although an increasing number of school-leavers are turning to the OU as an alternative to full-time university study). As well as taking students who want to study for degrees, it has developed a wide range of non-degree courses to cater for the education of the community. Listed below are some of the ways the OU differs from other universities.

- All the students are adults (that is 18 years or older).
- The majority of students are part-time.
- Most of the work is done by distance learning – correspondence and audio visual materials, home kits, supported by personal contact with tutors.
- Some courses include residential schools.
- Some courses have radio and TV programmes associated with them.
- It has no minimum entry requirements; any EU resident can apply but non-UK residents may find their choice of courses restricted for operational reasons.
- Degree level courses run from February to November, not October to June (although some business and education courses have two intakes a year).
- Short courses usually take five or six months and may have more than one starting date.
- Courses can be spread over many years, with breaks in between if required.
- Students can start at any level suitable for them, and take as many or as few courses as they like.

Courses available

First degrees

These are modular, combining different courses. Each course completed successfully earns points towards a general or honours degree. Whether the degree is a BA or BSc will depend on the balance of courses taken.

People who have not studied at degree level before should start at level 1. The courses to choose from cover the arts, social sciences, maths, science or technology. After that, students can pick from over 170 second-, third-, and fourth- level courses (including educational studies), until they acquire the points needed. It is not necessary to specialise in one subject; a degree can be made up from a very wide spectrum. However, specialist degree profiles may also be studied to gain recognition by most professional institutes.

Each course takes about nine months with 12 to 15 hours of work a week (sometimes longer). Although each course has to be completed within a set time, there is no limit on the time taken to gain a degree.

Exemptions

Students may be awarded credit for other HE qualifications (for example HNC).

Higher degrees

It is possible to study for a BPhil, MPhil or PhD full- or part-time internally (at Milton Keynes or Oxford) or externally part-time. These are all research degrees. Places are limited, and demand is greater than supply.

The OU also offers a programme of taught higher degrees. With these, students get structured input, and are not required to achieve the degree on the basis of independent research alone. The following are currently available:

- MA in Humanities
- MA in Education
- MA and MSc in Social Sciences
- Doctorate in Education
- Postgraduate Certificate in Education
- MA in Open and Distance Learning
- MSc in Mathematics
- MBA
- MBA (Technology Management)
- MSc in Computing for Commerce and Industry
- MSc in Manufacturing Management Technology
- MSc in Development Management (proposed)
- MSc in Science (proposed)
- MSc and Postgraduate Diploma in Environmental Decision Making.

Non-degree courses

For students who don't want a degree, there are single courses or packs of self-standing materials. There are several kinds:

- A programme of scientific and technical updating courses, including two programmes of courses at MSc level on *Computing for Commerce and Industry, and Manufacturing: Management and Technology.*
- Training and in-service education for teachers, for example the PGCE and the Advanced Diploma in Educational Management; and packs, such as *Cross-phase and Curriculum; Science Education.*
- Health and social welfare, courses in the Health and Social Welfare Diploma Programme; and packs; *Mental Handicap: patterns for living; and Child Abuse and Neglect.*
- Management education – courses for managers run through the Open Business School. Courses like *The Effective Manager* are aimed at people in work; students can get a professional diploma in management, a professional certificate in management or progress to an MBA (to which there is fast-track entry for graduates).
- Personal and cultural education; study packs in the arts and the history of ideas; *Looking at Paintings; and The Changing Countryside.*
- Most courses from the undergraduate programme.
- Return to study packs, for example *Living Arts, Into Science.*

Courses start at different times through the year. Packs are available at any time.

Preparing for degree-level study

Since 1985, the OU has provided its own preparatory packages for new undergraduate students. For advice about preparation and the courses available:

 **Contact:** *The Regional Enquiry Service at the relevant OU regional centre; the address is at the end of the chapter.*

Preparation is worthwhile as an OU degree is hard work. Most students need at least 15 hours a week for study – some find it is nearer 20.

How it's done

There are usually four elements in any course.

The correspondence material

Students are sent their materials by post. They include specially written textbooks (called course units), some notes, perhaps CD-Roms, or some experiments (with kits for science and technology courses), exercises and self-assessment tests. There are also assignments which are sent back to be marked. Some are questionnaires marked by computer, others are essays, exercises or projects marked by tutors. There may also be audio tapes, records, computer software, slides or videos.

Broadcasts

Some courses include radio and television programmes on the national BBC network. These make the course more immediate or help to reinforce some of the more difficult ideas in the correspondence texts. For students outside the UK these programmes may be sent on video or cassette.

Support from tutors and student services

Course tutors hold regular tutorial meetings of students for discussions and lectures at local study centres. Tutorials are a valuable chance to talk to fellow students. As there are many level 1 students, tutorials at this level are made widely accessible. For higher-level courses there are fewer students, so the tutor may be some way away and it may be more difficult to attend tutorials. In some remote areas, such as some parts of Scotland, extra telephone and E-mail tuition is available for students who are far away from a study centre.

Support will also be provided by tutor feedback on assignments, and by contact with the tutor by phone, E-mail or correspondence. Student Services staff in each regional centre provide additional support.

Residential schools

Some courses include a one-week residential course, usually in the summer. These are held at a university. They provide a chance for students to experience the traditional university atmosphere, use equipment (laboratories, university libraries) and meet fellow students and staff. Most students agree that summer schools succeed completely in these things. Most first degree students will go to quite a few, as about half the courses have summer schools – especially those in science and technology. It is possible to be excused from summer schools (for a single parent, for example); it is also possible to choose courses without summer schools. Some, mainly Open University Business School courses, have shorter residential schools, usually held at weekends.

How it's assessed

Continuously

The degree is not achieved purely on the strength of passing an exam. Students are assessed continuously. Computer-marked and tutor-marked assignment results are recorded and assessments are combined with the final exam result to produce an overall grade for the course.

By exam

At the end of most courses there is a three-hour exam at a local centre which contributes to the total marks.

Transferability

Previous qualifications may enable students to qualify for a degree without taking as many courses, through credit exemptions (maximum of 180 credit points).

The OU also has a scheme which allows students to study for a time at another institution and count that study towards their OU degree.

For enquiries about credit transfer and directly transferred credits:

Contact: *Credit Transfer Centre, The Open University, PO Box 80, Milton Keynes MK7 6AS. Tel: 01908 653077 (24 hour answering service).*

Students with disabilities

The OU has an office for students with disabilities and can arrange, for example, taped material for people with visual impairment and transcripts for people with hearing impairment.

 **Contact:** *The Office for Students with Disabilities, The Open University, PO Box 79, Milton Keynes MK7 6AS. Tel: 01908 653745.*

Studying in remote areas

Students who live in an area of Scotland too far away from a study centre to attend regularly, if at all, will be supported by the regional centre. They will also be allocated a course tutor who will be able to provide support by post, telephone, E-mail or occasional meetings.

Contact: *Regional Centre, 10 Drumsheugh Gardens, Edinburgh EH3 7QJ. Tel: 0131 225 2889.*

What it costs

The cost of a 60 point course is generally £390 (it costs half as much for a 30 point course) or around £660 if the course includes a week's residential school.

Students may pay course fees by low-interest instalments by charging the fees to an Open University student budget account.

Some courses require access to a computer. There is a computer hire scheme for level 1 courses. Funds are available from the OU to help students who are on income support or on low incomes; details are available on request when applying for a course. Local authority financial help is very patchy.

Some employers are generous and sponsor employees who are OU students. Students should apply to their employers' personnel or training department. The OU has a special booklet to help employers decide whether to back its students.

How to Apply

First degree courses

The OU year starts in February, and applications should be in by October of the previous year. It's first come, first served, so students are advised to apply as early as possible.

See *Courses, Diplomas and Degrees* brochure from The Central Enquiry Service, The Open University, PO Box 724, Milton Keynes MK7 6ZS. Tel: 01908 653231 – or from any regional centre.

Postgraduate courses

See *Research Degree Prospectus or the Higher Degrees Prospectus*, from The Central Enquiry Service, The Open University, PO Box 724, Milton Keynes MK7 6ZS. Tel: 01908 653231 – or from any regional centre.

Other courses

The university also offers a wide range of self-contained study packs for people who are interested in a particular field but do not wish to enrol on a course.

Contact: *Open University Worldwide, The Berrill Building, Walton Hall, Milton Keynes MK7 6AA. Tel: 01908 858785.*

Is it worth it?

Are OU degrees as good as others?

The OU type of modular degree is getting more common. Employers and others are getting more familiar with the idea of a degree that shows students have worked hard for some years at several subjects rather than studying one or two subjects in greater depth. Indeed, 40,000 employers have paid for their staff to enrol on OU courses. Most British universities accept OU credits for entry to later years of their own courses and also accept OU degrees for postgraduate study. Most professional institutes and bodies recognise OU degree profiles.

Students

'They give a good indication of its worth. When they've done an OU degree they're often hooked, and keep on doing other OU courses for years.'

Open University Students' Association (OUSA)

Membership of the Students' Association includes all currently registered students of the OU and does not carry a subscription.

The Association provides the support services necessary to effectively represent students' views, both within the OU and outside. It also offers help with educational and welfare problems, sponsors weekend schools, organises self-help study groups, encourages the formation of societies for special interest groups, operates a marketing service, and provides a range of social activities for members and their families through its branches.

The governing body is the annual National Conference attended by representatives from all study centres and affiliated societies. A National Executive Committee has responsibility for implementing the policies determined by National Conference.

The Association's offices are on the University's main campus.

Contact: *Open University Students' Association, PO Box 397, Walton Hall, Milton Keynes MK7 6BE. Tel: 01908 654093.*

More information

To buy OU publications:

 **Contact:** *Open University Worldwide, The Berrill Building, Walton Hall, Milton Keynes MK7 6AA. Tel: 01908 858785.*

For other information:

Contact: *The Regional Enquiry Service at any OU regional centre – the addresses are listed below.*

OU Regional Centres

Region 01 – London
The Open University, London Region, Parsifal College, 527 Finchley Road, London NW3 7BG. Tel: 020 7431 1048.
Area covered: Greater London.

Region 02 – South
The Open University, Southern Region, Foxcombe Hall, Boars Hill, Oxford OXI 5HR. Tel: 01865 735140.
Area covered: Berkshire, Buckinghamshire, Channel Islands, Dorset, Hampshire, Isle of Wight, Oxfordshire, part of Wiltshire.

Region 03 – South West
The Open University, South West Region, 4 Portwall Lane, Bristol BSI 6ND. Tel: 0117 925 6523.
Area covered: Avon, Cornwall, Devon, Gloucestershire, Somerset, Scilly Isles, most of Wiltshire.

Region 04 – West Midlands
The Open University, West Midlands Region, 66-68 High Street, Harborne, Birmingham B17 9NB. Tel: 0121 428 1550.
Area covered: Hereford and Worcester, Shropshire, most of Staffordshire, Warwickshire, West Midlands.

Region 05 – East Midlands
The Open University, East Midlands Region, Clarendon Park, Clumber Avenue, Sherwood Rise, Nottingham NG5 1AH.
Tel: 0115 962 5451.
Area covered: Derbyshire, Leicestershire, Lincolnshire, Northamptonshire, Nottinghamshire, South Humberside, part of Staffordshire (Burton on Trent area).

Region 06 – East Anglia
The Open University, East Anglia Region, Cintra House, 12 Hills Road, Cambridge CB2 IPF. Tel: 01223 361650.
Area covered: Bedfordshire, Cambridgeshire, Essex, Hertfordshire, Norfolk, Suffolk.

Region 07 – Yorkshire
The Open University, Yorkshire Region, 2 Trevelyan Square, Boar Lane, Leeds LS1 6ED. Tel: 0113 245 1466.
Area covered: North Humberside, North Yorkshire, South Yorkshire, West Yorkshire.

Region 08 – North West
The Open University, North West Region, Chorlton House, 70 Manchester Road, Chorlton-cum-Hardy, Manchester M21 9UN. Tel: 0161 861 9823.
Area covered: Cheshire, part of Derbyshire, Isle of Man, Lancashire, Greater Manchester, Merseyside.

Region 09 – North
The Open University, North Region, Eldon House, Regent Centre, Gosforth, Newcastle upon Tyne NE3 3PW. Tel: 0191 284 1611.
Area covered: Cleveland, Cumbria, Durham, Northumberland, Tyne and Wear.

Region 10 – Wales
The Open University in Wales, 24 Cathedral Road, Cardiff CF1 9SA. Tel: 029 2066 5636.
Area covered: Wales.

Region 11 – Scotland
The Open University in Scotland, 10 Drumsheugh Gardens, Edinburgh EH3 7QJ. Tel: 0131 225 2889.
Area covered: Scotland.

Region 12 – Northern Ireland
The Open University in Northern Ireland, 40 University Road, Belfast BT7 1SU. Tel: 028 9024 5025.
Area covered: Northern Ireland, Republic of Ireland.

Region 13 – South East
The Open University, South East Region, St James' House, 150 London Road, East Grinstead RH19 1ES. Tel: 01342 410545.
Area covered: Kent, Surrey, East Sussex, West Sussex.

General enquiries
Central Enquiry Service, PO Box 724, The Open University, Walton Hall, Milton Keynes MK7 6ZS. Tel: 01908 653231.

17. Open/distance and other independent learning

This chapter covers:

- a description of open and distance learning
- how to choose a course
- information about providers of open and distance learning
- other resources for independent learning, such as books, audiotapes, computer programs, TV and radio broadcasts, the internet etc.

What is open or distance learning?

Open learning is a broad definition of flexible learning which can include using a resource centre, some face-to-face tuition as well as studying at home from prepared materials. The student has control of the learning situation. Distance learning is literally learning at a distance from the provider, where any personal tuition which accompanies the course materials is likely to be by post, telephone or computer link.

- Individuals can learn at a
  - time
  - place
  - and pace

  to suit themselves.
- Student-centred learning methods and appropriate media, such as video, text, audio and computer packages are used.
- Typically an open learning course comprises:
  - a pack of learning materials
  - arrangements for tutorial support as and when required.
- Many producers of open and distance learning materials are now aligning their materials with National (or Scottish) Vocational Qualifications.
- Few courses have entrance qualifications.
- As a method of learning, open or distance learning can be lonely and hard, requiring a great deal of self-discipline.
- Open and distance learning courses are usually a way of getting qualifications, whereas learning packages are usually designed for retraining or updating skills.

How much do the courses cost?

Prices vary greatly, depending on whether for a package or a course, and therefore how much tutorial support is included. Students can send for several prospectuses and compare prices.

Accreditation

Open and Distance Learning Quality Council (ODLQC)

As most open colleges are private enterprises outside government control, the Open and Distance Learning Quality Council (ODLQC) was formed to develop a system of accreditation approved by the Department for Education and Employment (DfEE). ODLQC is an independent body, and has been operating since 1968. Its independent assessors, drawn from the professions and universities, inspect every aspect of a college and give approval if the Council criteria are being met. Most approved colleges show their accreditation certificate in their prospectus.

If you want information about where to find a particular course at an accredited college, or you want to check whether a college is accredited (and if not, whether your course is available at one which is) ODLQC has an advisory service. Colleges accredited by the ODLQC are listed towards the end of this chapter.

 **Contact:** *The Secretary, ODLQC – 27 Marylebone Road, London NW1 5JS.*
Tel: 020 7935 5391. Website: www.odlqc.org.uk/odlqc
E-mail: odlqc@dial.pipex.com

Non-accredited colleges

There are many colleges that are not accredited. They offer courses in anything you can think of – photography, languages, drawing, piano playing, aromatherapy, PCV or LGV driving, religion, to name a few. Some offer value for money, but there is no easy way of knowing. Prospective students can try to contact people who have done the course to find out whether they found it satisfactory.

Choosing a college

There are a few big colleges which offer a range of courses – professional subjects, for example banking and accountancy, or GCSE courses. The others tend to be more specialist.

It's very hard to judge in advance how good the colleges really are. Accreditation helps, but not with choosing between two accredited colleges, or if a college which offers an apparently tailor-made course is not accredited.

Students can ask the colleges the following questions, which reflect just some of the issues which concern the ODLQC when its inspectors assess a college.

- Has the course material been written or adapted especially for the purpose of open or distance learning?
- When was the last time the course was thoroughly revised?
- Is the course already written?
- Is there a refunds policy? If so, for what?
- Will they send a specimen of the course material?

Association of British Correspondence Colleges (ABCC)

ABCC is a trade association representing 17 of the colleges. It produces a free broadsheet and will offer advice to potential students. Its members also have an agreed code of ethics designed to maintain standards.

 **Contact:** *The Secretary, Association of British Correspondence Colleges – PO Box 17926, London SW19 3WB Tel: 020 8544 9559. Website: nationline.co.uk/abcc E-mail: abcc@msn.com*

Complaints

Dissatisfied students can:

- contact ODLQC (see above) – they will take it up with the college
- contact ABCC (see above) if the complaint is about one of their member colleges.

Open College of the Arts (OCA)

The OCA has the slogan 'Adventure in the Arts'. It was set up in 1985 as an educational trust, on the premise that everyone has an artist inside them, if given the skills they need to achieve their creative potential. Structured home-study courses are offered in a wide range of subject areas, supported by tutors who are themselves practising artists. There are over 30 courses, most of which are university-accredited, which have attracted some 40,000 students. Subjects available are: art and design, painting, sculpture, understanding art, drawing, singing, textiles, interior design, calligraphy, video production, photography, creative writing, creative reading, garden design, dance and music.

Course costs range from £249 to £399. Students can start at any time of the year. You do not need previous experience and can study at your own pace. You can gain credits towards higher education qualifications.

 **Contact:** *Open College of the Arts – Hound Hill, Worsbrough, Barnsley S70 6TU Tel: 01226 730495 or Freephone: 0800 731 2116. Website: www.oca-uk.com E-mail: open.arts.@ukonline.co.uk*

National Extension College (NEC)

The National Extension College (NEC) is a registered educational charity established in 1963 for distance learning below degree level, enrolling over 10,000 learners each year.

NEC provides over 140 courses designed to appeal to learners from all walks of life, whether they are looking to develop learning skills, wanting to gain a recognisable qualification, seeking to extend expertise in a chosen field or studying purely for pleasure.

Gaining a qualification is optional, but you can achieve a wide range of GCSEs and A levels, as well as professional and vocational qualifications including Association of Accounting Technicians (AAT), Chartered Institute of Marketing (CIM) and Pre-school Learning Alliance (PLA). NEC also offers Open University preparatory courses and provides tuition for several University of London degrees, Institute of Linguists qualifications, and The Engineering Council Part 1 & 2 examinations.

NEC students set the pace of their own study, enrolling at any time and working as many or as few hours as they choose. All tutoring is by phone and post and there is no need to attend a college or any other institution except for sitting examinations. Advice and feedback is available from expert personal tutors assigned to each student on enrolment. NEC's Student Advisers welcome telephone calls from prospective and existing students seeking guidance and help in their choice of studies.

A free full-colour Guide to Courses is available on request.

 **Contact:** *Student Advisers, National Extension College – 18 Brooklands Avenue, Cambridge CB2 2HN. Tel: 01223 450500. Website: www.nec.ac.uk E-mail: info@nec.ac.uk*

Colleges accredited by the ODLQC (1999)

*Airline Recruitment and Training Company – Ashley House, 86-94 High Street, Hounslow TW3 1NH. Tel: 020 8814 1222.
Website: www.artc.co.uk E-mail: julie@artc.co.uk*

*Business Training Ltd, Sevendale House – 7 Dale Street, Manchester M1 1JB. Tel: 0161 228 6735/6.
Website: www.writersbureau.com E-mail: writersbureau@zen.co.uk*

*Cambridge Tutorial College – College House, Leoville, St Ouen, PO Box 530, Jersey JE3 2DB. Tel: 01534 485052.
Website: www.cambridgetraining.com
E-mail: learn@cambridgetraining.com*

*The Chartered Institute of Transport – 80 Portland Place, London W1N 4DP. Tel: 020 7467 9400.
Website: www.citrans.org.uk E-mail: gen@citrans.org.uk*

*Cheltenham Tutorial College – 292 High Street Cheltenham, GL50 3HQ. Tel: 01242 241279.
Website: www.cheltenhamtc.org.uk/cheltenham
E-mail: tutor@chelt.win-uk.net*

The Civil Service Correspondence School – Ware, Hertfordshire SG12 9DZ. Tel: 01920 465926.

*The College of Sales & Marketing Management – Romeland House, Romeland Hill, St Albans AL3 4ET. Tel: 01727 812500.
E-mail: ismuknet@nildram.co.uk*

Epping Forest College – Flexible Learning Unit, Borders Lane, Loughton, IG10 3SA. Tel: 020 8508 8311.

*Greenwich School of Theology – 29 Howbeck Lane, Clarborough, Near Retford, Nottinghamshire DN22 9LW.
Tel: 01777 703058.*

Henley College Homestudy Unit – Henley College, Henley Road, Bell Green, Coventry CV2 1ED. Tel: 024 7661 1021. Website: www.henley-cov.ac.uk

Hornsby International Dyslexia Centre – Glenshee Lodge, 261 Trinity Road, London, SW18 3SN Tel: 020 8877 3539. E-mail: dyslexia@hornsby.demon.co.uk

Horticultural Correspondence College – Little Notton Farmhouse, 16 Notton, Lacock, Chippenham SN15 2NF. Tel: 01249 730326. Website: www.btinternet.com/~hc.college E-mail: hc.college@btinternet.com

Institute of Chartered Shipbrokers – TutorShip, 3 St Helen's Place, London EC3A 6EJ. Tel: 020 7374 4411. Website: www.ics.org.uk E-mail:icslon@dial.pipex.com

Institute of Chiropodists and Podiatrists – 27 Wright Street, Southport, Merseyside PR9 0TL. Tel: 01704 546141.

Institute of Counselling Tutorial Service – 6 Dixon Street Glasgow G1 4AX. Tel: 0141 204 2230.

Institute of Heraldic & Genealogical Studies – Northgate, Canterbury CT1 1BA. Tel: 01227 768664. E-mail: ihgs@dial.pipex.com

International Graphology Association – Stonedge, Dunkerton, Bath BA2 8AS. Tel: 01761 437809. E-mail: educ@graphology.org.uk

International Institute of Reflexology – 32 Priory Road, Portbury, Bristol BS20 7TH. Tel: 01225 865899. E-mail: reflexology_uk@hotmail.com

International School of Navigation – 53 High Street, Amble, Northumberland NE65 0LE. Tel: 01665 713437. Website: www.isn.nu E-mail: steve@isn.nu

JEB Distance Learning – 30A Dyer Street, Cirencester GL7 2PF. Tel: 01285 641747.

Kevala Centre (International Yoga School) – Hunsdon Road, Torquay TQ1 1QB. Tel: 01803 215678. Website: www.kevala.co.uk E-mail: theiys@kevala.co.uk

KLC School of Interior Design – KLC House, Springvale Terrace, London W14 0AE. Tel: 020 7602 8592.

London Montessori Centre – 18 Balderton Street, London W1Y 1TG. Tel: 020 7493 0165. Website: www.montessori.ac.uk

London School of Classical Homoeopathy – 94 Green Dragon Lane, Winchmore Hill, London N21 2NJ. Tel: 020 8360 8757.

The London School of Journalism – 22 Upbrook Mews, London W2 3HG. Tel: 020 7706 3790. Website: www.home-study.com E-mail: info@lsjournalism.com

Manchester College of Arts and Technology – City Centre Campus, Lower Hardman Street, Manchester M3 3ER. Tel: 0161 953 5995. Website: www.mancat.ac.uk

Mercers College – Ware, Hertfordshire SG12 9DZ. Tel: 01920 465927.

Montessori St Nicholas Centre – 18 Balderton Street, London W1Y 1TG. Tel: 020 7493 0165.

National Council for the Training of Journalists – Latton Bush Centre, Southern Way, Harlow CM18 7BL. Tel: 01279 430009. Website: www.itecharlow.co.uk/nctj E-mail: nctj@itecharlow.co.uk

National Extension College – 18 Brooklands Avenue, Cambridge CB2 2HN. Tel: 01223 450500. Website: www.nec.ac.uk E-mail: info@nec.ac.uk

National School of Salesmanship Ltd – Sevendale House, 7 Dale Street, Manchester M1 IJB. Tel: 0161 228 6733/4. E-mail: writersbureau@zen.co.uk

Northern Institute of Massage – 100 Waterloo Road, Blackpool FY4 1AW. Tel: 01253 403548.

Open Learning Centre International – 24 King Street, Carmarthen SA31 1BS. Tel: 01267 235268. Website: www.olc.ccta.ac.uk E-mail: po@olc.ccta.ac.uk

Projects Group plc – 1 Mulgrave Chambers, 26 Mulgrave Road, Sutton, Surrey SM2 6LE. Tel: 020 8770 9393. Website: www.theprojectsgroup.plc.uk E-mail: courses@theprojectsgroup.plc.uk

RRC Business Training – 27/37 St George's Road, London SW19 4DS. Tel: 020 8947 7272. E-mail: rrc@solo.pipex.com

Rhodec International College of Interior Design – 35 East Street, Brighton BN1 1HL. Tel: 01273 327476. Website: www.rhodec.com E-mail: contact@rhodec.com

*Solutions Open Learning, Swindon College – North Star Avenue,
Swindon SN2 1DE. Tel: 01793 498404.
Website: www.swindon-college.ac.uk
E-mail: sol@msxchg.swindon-college.ac.uk*

*Tactics for Exam Success – Garrard House, 2 Homesdale Road,
Bromley BR2 9LZ. Tel: 020 8313 9317.
Website: www.tacticsforexamsuccess.co.uk
E-mail: enquiries@tactics.demon.co.uk*

*Tiller School of Navigation and Seamanship – 30 Wilmot Way,
Banstead, Surrey SM7 2PY. Tel: 01737 211466.
Website: yacht-club.net/tiller
E-mail: andy_d_thomson@compuserve.com*

*Unison Education & Training – 20 Grand Depot Road,
London SE18 6SF. Tel: 020 8854 2244.
Website: www.unison-education.org.uk
E-mail: open.college@unison.co.uk*

*West Thames College – London Road, Isleworth,
Middlesex TW7 4HS. Tel: 020 8568 0244 ext 517.
Website: www.west-thames.ac.uk E-mail: annh@west-thames.ac.uk*

*Writers Bureau – Sevendale House, 7 Dale Street,
Manchester M1 IJB. Tel: 0161 228 2362.
Website: www.writersbureau.com E-mail:writersbureau@zen.co.uk*

The Open College

The Open College works mainly with employers providing them with corporate training packages. However, it may be able to offer some information to individuals, or employees could ask their employer if they use such packages.

 **Contact:** *The Open College – Portland Tower, Portland Street, Mancester M1 3LD. Tel: 0161 245 3300. Website www.ftmanagement.com*

Open learning in Scotland

Public libraries in Scotland have continued to expand their open learning provision. Further financial commitments from the government through the New Opportunities Fund will allow libraries to develop these services into Lifelong Learning centres, in cooperation with a range of partners. A key element of the centres will be access to electronic resources, the internet and distance learning packages. Public libraries have been described as 'street corner universities', reaching the heart of the community and supporting independent learners. They will now offer opportunities to follow more formal education routes in a trusting and welcoming environment.

 **Contact:** *Local library headquarters, local library, or the Scottish Library and Information Council, Scottish Centre for Information and Library Services, 1 John Street, Hamilton ML3 7EU. Tel: 01698 458888. Website: www. slainte.org.uk E-mail: slic@amlibs.co.uk*

Other independent learning

These are the hundreds of books, tapes, videos and computer programs that enable people to study many subjects. They are different to distance and open learning courses primarily because they offer no tutorial support. Like open learning methods, these systems are useful for those who cannot travel to a course centre or have limited time available for study.

Books

Teach-Yourself and How To books are well known. Similar to these, there are also cheaper, shorter learning guides, as well as DIY books, car manuals, computer handbooks and others. The subject range is wide – anything from aromatherapy to writing science fiction.

Advantages

- They can be an introduction to a subject, before deciding whether to study it further.
- There is a wide subject range available from libraries and bookshops – especially those who specialise in educational books. Sometimes books are advertised in magazines or in connection with a television series. Specialist magazines sometimes advertise self-tuition books on their subject.
- The books are very accessible, and students can dip into them as and when they choose to.
- Many manuals are useful as a source of updating on subjects the student may already be familiar with.

Disadvantages

- It can be difficult to learn a subject from scratch using a book, especially if it is a practical skill, with no assistance.
- It requires patience to find the information needed for a specific purpose.
- Reference books can be quite expensive.

Tapes and CDs

These usually teach languages, as students benefit from listening to the spoken word. They are also popular for management techniques and self-development as they are aimed at busy people who perhaps find listening in the car convenient. They may be expensive, as a large number of tapes are sometimes needed to cover the course, but this may compare favourably with the cost of evening classes and related transport.

Computers

Computers can be used at home in two ways:

- to learn about a wide range of subjects using educational programs and the internet
- to learn IT skills and how to use various software packages.

Educational programs

Most educational software is written for schools, and often the learning can be achieved as easily through more traditional methods. However, with lifelong learning initiatives and more sophisticated technology, more programs for adults are likely to become available. Specialist software designed to teach people with disabilities has been used successfully with, for example, people who are visually impaired, autistic, dyslexic or who have other learning difficulties. Most packages are for IBM-compatible computers. It may be possible to sample materials before buying them.

The internet is a major source of information. If students do not have access on their home computers, there are an increasing number of sites where the internet can be used, such as in further education colleges, internet- or cyber-cafes or some public libraries and community centres. Some educational websites are for subscribers only, but a lot of information is open to anyone. internet novices can take short courses to acquire the necessary 'surfing' skills.

To find out what is available, students can:

- browse through computer magazines available from newsagents and in libraries
- ask at local further education colleges, community schools or adult education centres as they often use educational packages.

Learning computing skills and how to use software packages

It's possible to gain IT skills using magazines and books with a home computer. Software usually comes with a manual and an on-screen 'tutorial' facility. Even those attending a computing class will benefit from also working at home. The quality of user manuals and books teaching programming can vary widely in standard, so examine the products before buying them.

The British Computer Society offers distance learning packages leading to their own professional degree-equivalent qualification and to the internationally recognised European Computer Driving Licence (ECDL).

☞ **Contact:** *British Computer Society – 1 Sanford Street, Swindon SN1 1HG.*
Tel: 01793 417417. Website: www.bcs.org.uk
E-mail: marketing@bcs.org.uk

Ufl

The government, through development of its 'University for Industry' concept (Ufl), is creating a nationwide open and distance learning network which will be capable of meeting a wide variety of learning needs. See chapter 18 for more details.

BBC TV, radio and on-line

BBC Education offers an integrated multi-media approach to adult learning, using broadcast media, on-line and off-screen support. Areas of special focus include learning about the modern workplace, work and life skills (including IT), health and parenting education, language courses and programmes that encourage a hands-on interest in history and science.

Major recent and continuing initiatives include *Computers don't Bite* and *Webwise, History 2000 and Fighting Fat, Fighting Fit.*

The overnight service – *The Learning Zone* – on BBC 2, is provided throughout the year in partnership with the Open University. Programmes cover a wide range of topics, aimed at varying levels of learning need – from supporting accredited learning through to degree-level, training for work from retail to nursing, through to basic skills like getting started with computers. Language learning is one of the most popular offerings for business, travel and leisure learning.

There is a growing range of long-term learning resources available, such as the *Computers don't Bite and Webwise* CD-Rom. Sector-based *Key Skills* CD-Roms are being developed with the support of the European Union. Also, pioneering work incorporating on-demand video and multimedia applications through broadband networks is being progressed as fast as the technology allows.

The *Alert On-line* and personalised E-mail service links learners directly with the whole range of BBC educational resources and with events and publications of specific interest to the individual. Visit websites: www.bbc.co.uk/education and www.bbc.co.uk/alert

BBC Knowledge is both a website and a digital TV channel, providing educational material for young people and adults. Website: bbc.co.uk/knowledge

The BBC has a team of education officers who welcome comments or suggestions about BBC Education's programming. They can be contacted at the following offices:

England: 020 8752 5650

Northern Ireland: 028 9033 8435

Scotland: 0131 469 4278

Wales: 029 2057 288.

Most BBC local radio stations have a producer responsible for education who can give information and advice about programmes. Local radio addresses and programmes are listed in local editions of Radio Times. The BBC also publishes information centrally about local radio.

For other enquiries:

Contact: *BBC Information – PO Box 1116, Belfast BT2 7AJ.*
Tel: 08700 100 222. Website: www.bbc.co.uk/education

Independent Television

The Independent Television Commission (ITC) is the public body responsible for licensing and regulating commercially-funded television services in and from the UK. These include Channel 3 (ITV), Channel 4, Channel 5, public teletext and a range of cable, local delivery and satellite services. A free booklet – *Factfile* – is published annually listing the companies involved. It's available from the ITC address below.

The ITC's Education Department monitors the education and social action output of the ITC's licensees, and the schools' service of Channel 4.

Although education ceased to be a mandatory requirement for Channel 3 licensees, all licensees have committed themselves to providing some local education and social action programming.

A separate fourth channel, S4C, provides a Welsh language service. At other times it screens Channel 4's network programmes in English.

Some cable and satellite programme services also have an educational purpose or component.

Contact: *Head of Education, ITC – 33 Foley Street, London W1P 7LB. Tel: 020 7306 7844. Website: www.itc.co.uk*

Commissioning Editor (Education), Channel 4 Television – 124 Horseferry Road, London SW1P 2TX. Tel: 020 7396 4444. E-mail: viewer_enqs@channel4.co.uk Website: www.channel4.com

Head of Public Relations, S4C – Parc Ty Glas, Llanishen, Cardiff CF14 5DU. Tel: 029 2074 7444. Website: www.S4C.co.uk

Languages

There are many programmes on TV and radio to help teach yourself foreign languages and introduce you to the culture. All have related packs containing books and cassettes or CDs to support the series, but they can be used as courses in themselves.

Local and regional radio

Local radio sometimes publicises adult education opportunities. If not, they may be open to suggestions for future programmes. Scotland, Wales and Northern Ireland have radio services which include programmes in Welsh and Gaelic.

Commercial radio

Commercial radio is licensed and regulated by the Radio Authority. It is not required by legislation to provide educational programmes, although many such programmes are produced. In 1999, there are 237 commercial stations producing a variety of formats.

Contact: *The Radio Authority – Holbrook House, 14 Great Queen Street, Holborn, London WC2B 5DG. Tel: 020 7430 2724. Website: www.radioauthority.org.uk* E-mail: reception@radioauthority.org.uk

Broadcasting Support Services

Provide back-up support such as advice, helplines, websites and publications to specific radio and TV programmes on both BBC and independent stations, usually for programmes that have just been broadcast.

☞ **Contact:** *Broadcasting Support Services – PO Box 7, London W12 8UA. Tel: 020 8735 5000. E-mail: felicity.ford@bss.org Website: www.bss.org*

Further information

Distance & Supported Open Learning UK and Worldwide 2000 – published by CRAC/Hobsons. Price £36.99. ISBN 1 86017 641 0. A complete directory of the programmes on the Open University's International Centre of Distance Learning database.

On Course – a free booklet from the BBC Education Information Unit, Room RG420, White City, London W12 7TS. Tel: Hotline 020 8746 1111.

Improving your Written English, Managing your Business Accounts, Starting a Business from Home, Creating a Web Site and Managing your Time are just a few of the titles available from How to Books (address in chapter 5), mostly priced £9.99.

The *Teach Yourself* series of titles includes *Photography, Business Writing, Intranet, Classical Music* and a range of modern languages. All available from Bookpoint Ltd – 39 Milton Park, Abingdon, Oxfordshire OX14 4TD. Tel: 01235 400414. Books are mostly priced between £6.99-£8.99. Language cassettes are also available at around £11.99, and packs of books and cassettes cost about £18.

Kogan Page (address in chapter 5) publishes a number of 'self-help' titles relating to acquiring business and communication skills.

Most of these materials can be ordered through local bookshops, and there are also on-line bookshops at websites such as:

bookshop.blackwell.co.uk

www.waterstones.co.uk

www.amazon.com

18. The University for Industry concept – UfI

This chapter covers:

- aims and objectives contained within the UfI concept
- the partners who are developing learning centre hubs
- focus of the initial learning programmes
- accessing UfI learning programmes.

The vision

'The more effective people are at their jobs – the more likely it is that Britain will have jobs' – Lord Dearing speaking at a UfI roadshow in June 1999.

17 million adults in Britain lack any formal qualification and, perhaps more importantly, around 8 million people have been identified as having low basic skill levels.

If high-quality learning programmes are made accessible to everyone, at times and in locations to fit their lifestyles, lifelong learning can become an acceptable and familiar part of everyday life – whether taking place in work, at home, at a leisure centre, library, college or shopping mall. Professional support of this learning can help people who were untouched by education the first time round to advance in their learning.

Education will boost the skills base of this country's workforce, allowing business and industry to move into highly-skilled knowledge-based work, rather than trying to compete with the productivity of vast numbers of low-waged workers in India and the Far East. British companies will only remain a competitive force by staying ten years ahead on the learning curve.

So grew Chancellor Brown's concept of a 'University for Industry' – to play a leading role in the learning revolution by 2004. It will attract up to a million new recruits to access educational and training programmes in 1000 learning centres sited in 'lifestyle' locations right across the country.

Although UfI is now in common usage, it is expected that a new, customer-focused brand name will be used in the future.

The aims of UfI

Since its conception in 1998, aims and objectives, strategies and procedures have been steadily put in place in order to launch UfI in October 2000.

Steered by the Department for Education and Employment (DfEE), the UfI has a broad agenda – to help both people and organisations to identify and meet their learning needs – so that individuals can raise their skill levels and employability, and business and industry gain a workforce with the knowledge and creativity to harness new technologies – raising the productivity and competitiveness of individual firms and collectively, of the nation's industries.

The principal aim of UfI is to activate the concept of lifelong learning, central to the government's ideology of a Learning Age. There are new National Targets for Learning to meet before the year 2002, and a National Skills Task Force is working to identify skill gaps across all sectors of industry, gaps which arise in different age bands of the labour force.

 **Consult** *Chapter 2 for more information on lifelong learning*

UFI's objectives

Working with new levels of partnership between the public and private sectors, and by using the latest technology, UfI will help individuals, commercial, industrial and voluntary organisations, to identify and achieve learning targets. This will build on the national Lifelong Learning Partnerships created in 1998, to form broad new Learning & Skills Partnerships to make supported learning a possibility for all. Learning is to be accessible to everyone over the age of 16 – to those both inside and outside the active workforce.

UFI's first task

The UfI is set up to help identify solutions to some of the old problems which have prevented large numbers of Britain's present and potential workforce accessing learning and acquiring new skills. Problems such as:

- lack of learning and personal development time
- the high costs of training
- difficulties with identifying appropriate courses and training programmes to meet individual need
- access and mode of delivery
- fear of failure
- rejection of former learning modes.

UFI's solution

Through the guidance of UfI advisers, suitable high quality learning will be able to be accessed at a time and in a place to suit every individual – whether at home, in the workplace or at an approved centre for learning. It will be delivered by a flexible partnership network linking the public and private sector, making use of broadcasts on TV and radio, the telephone, internet, CD-Roms and paper resources.

Who are the UfI partners?

The DfEE is making a concerted effort to extend franchised partnership networks across academic and business interests in order to keep learning standards keen and the quality of resources high. UfI roadshows staged in nine cities across the country have brought together representatives from all the following organisations, many of whom are now working in partnership to set up pilot learning centres for October '99:

- Schools, colleges, further and higher education institutions
- Training & Enterprise Councils (TECs) and Local Enterprise Councils (LECs)
- LEAs

- Careers service companies
- Adult guidance networks
- Chambers of commerce
- National Training Organisations (NTOs)
- Business Links and Business Connect
- Trade associations
- Professional associations
- Employer organisations
- Trade unions
- TV and radio broadcasters
- Investors in People UK.
- Qualifications & Curriculum Association (QCA), Scottish Qualifications Authority (SQA) and the Qualifications Curriculum and Assessment Authority for Wales (ACCA)
- Libraries
- British Educational Communications and Technology Agency

What has Ufl achieved so far?

Although it will not be up and running until Autumn 2000, considerable progress has already been made on the development of the Ufl. The Ufl transition board and team have now made way for a permanent board and executive management team, and have now established Ufl Ltd as an independent company in its own right.

Development work has included research and analysis of the needs of the market and potential customers. In particular, skills gaps, trends in employment, attitudes towards learning and the quality of existing learning programmes. This work has been carried out in conjunction with other organisations such as industry lead bodies, professional bodies, trade unions and government departments.

Ufl Ltd have taken its first steps towards setting up Ufl learning centres by issuing a call for outline proposals from consortia interested in running Ufl Learning Centre hubs. Ufl called on education providers, employers, trade unions and voluntary groups to form consortia to set up around 1000 learning centres by March 2000. The first of these should be operational by November 1999. An earlier call for expressions of interest in becoming a qualified supplier of Ufl products produced a very good response. Appraisals of all submissions are now underway.

Ufl Ltd are also working on comprehensive promotion and communication plans, which will cover a wide range of activities designed to promote and develop the Ufl brand and to publicise its services. This is a very important role – not only encouraging lifelong learning but ensuring possible customers are aware of how to access the potential of the Ufl.

The government has allocated £44 million in 1999-2000 to provide a firm foundation for the Ufl to take forward its development and implementation plans, leading to national launch in Autumn 2000.

The first four years

To start the learning programmes from a broad base, Ufl will be focusing on four priority learning areas:

- Basic skills – literacy and numeracy – to more than double the present help available for over 500,000 adults by 2002. It is estimated that around eight million people have low basic skills levels at present.
- ICT skills for the workplace.
- Business services and management skills for small and medium-sized businesses.
- Four initial special sectors where there are skills needs now, and where demand will be increasing in the future, or where sectors presently have low levels of training. Initially :
  - automotive component production (there are 70,000 companies nationally)
  - multimedia
  - environmental technology (5000 firms)
  - distributive and retail trades.

Access to the Ufl

One point of entry to the Ufl will be through the existing national learning information helpline – Learning Direct. You can use the free phone line: 0800 100 900 to speak to on-line advisers between the hours of 9am and 9pm, Monday to Friday, and from 9am to 12 noon on Saturdays. Learning Direct has been up and running since February 1998. Adults can use the service to get information on:

- local learning opportunities
- funding for learning
- local childcare provision
- availability of Ufl-approved local guidance agencies.

Qualified advisers are employed to offer advice and information drawn from a range of information databases, while the caller remains on-line. Information can be posted to callers on request. With Learning Direct being promoted as the first port of call for any learning enquiry, and specifically for callers to access information about programmes approved for the Ufl, the number of enquiries is set to rise. All Learning Direct advisers have achieved NVQ level 3 in Guidance.

Contact: *Learning Direct free phoneline : 0800 100 900*
Learning Direct website : www.learningdirect.org

Other access routes to Ufl

Individuals calling in to a local Ufl learning centre will be able to meet a Ufl adviser and become a member of Ufl. You will receive a Ufl passport number which will access your personal record, giving details of any formal qualifications, together with your educational interests. These records are only kept so that Ufl advisers can suggest suitable learning programmes tailored to your specific individual needs.

The Ufl has a website which, after start-up, will allow people to take up membership of the Ufl on-line.

 **Contact:** *Ufl website : www.ufi.co.uk*

Consult: *Ufl – Developing the University for Industry concept – free from Ufl, PO Box 380, Nottingham NG7 3JS. Tel: 0141 300 4924 (Ref UFIDP2)*

The way forward for Ufl

The government believes that within five years from its inception in 1998, the Ufl will be playing a leading role in the learning revolution. By 2002, two and a half million people and businesses will be using the Ufl, and the range of information services will increase year by year. It is believed that, by this date, more than 600,000 individuals will be taking part in Ufl-approved courses by learning each year.

The stimulation of new markets for learning will help to improve the quality of learning resources, and large take-up numbers for Ufl programmes will force down the costs of accessing the learning. Computer software, videos, educational coursework materials, as well as the cost of supported courses will be driven down by competition and the unique position of the Ufl to exploit economies of scale.

- There will be on-line access to enquiry, information and registration systems.
- Websites and bulletin boards will give direct access to providers – including learning delivered on-line and 'taster' opportunities.
- Individuals using multimedia technology access to courses will get personal and technical support.
- Ufl e-mail systems will enable learners to link with and gain support from tutors and other learners, exploiting on-line conferencing.
- Customer feedback systems will help to refine programmes to better suit learners needs.

The DfEE proposes that within five years Ufl should be a part of everyday life – in just the way that the Open University has gained popular acceptance – delivering Ufl services and programmes to 100,000 start-up businesses and 50,000 established small and medium-sized companies every year.

19. Work-based Learning for Adults and other government-funded training

This chapter covers:

- Work-based Learning for Adults in England, and similar programmes in Wales and Scotland
- full-time education and training under the New Deal
- Modern Apprenticeships
- information specifically relevant to Northern Ireland.

Work-based Learning for Adults

Work-based Learning for Adults aims to help people out of work to move into sustained employment, including self-employment. It is delivered locally by Training and Enterprise Councils (TECs) and Chambers of Commerce, Training and Enterprise (CCTEs).

These bodies develop and co-ordinate the programme to match local needs, and carry out marketing and publicity in their local areas. The way in which the programme operates and is delivered therefore varies from area to area, according to the local labour market. Work-based Learning for Adults can be marketed under local brand names.

- TECs and CCTEs contract with approved training providers to deliver the training.
- Training providers can be private training companies, further education colleges, companies offering in-house training, chambers of Commerce, local authorities or any other body deemed suitable.
- Employment Services carry out much of the marketing for the programme, being kept up to date about the training opportunities available. They check eligibility before anyone can enter the programme.

Eligibility

Work-based Learning for Adults is open to people aged 25 to 63 who have been unemployed for six months or more. Certain others who have not been registered unemployed for six months can also be eligible. This can include:

- people with disabilities
- people who need basic skills training in literacy or numeracy or help with spoken English
- returners to the labour market, who have been out of the labour market for two years or more for domestic reasons, such as looking after a child or other relative
- lone parents
- those who have lost their jobs due to a large scale redundancy

- those who are leaving the armed services
- ex-offenders.

Employed status: it is possible to follow Work-based Learning for Adults as an employee. This involves high quality training in addition to that normally provided by the employer.

The length of time spent by trainees on the programme is normally tailored to individual needs.

What the programme offers

Each person joining Work-based Learning has their training needs assessed and an individual training plan is agreed. This could include a mix of elements which may include job-specific training, working towards National Vocational Qualifications (NVQs), help in developing the underlying skills that employers expect (basic employability training) and work experience.

- Most participants in the programme will be training **full-time**, but those whose personal circumstances do not allow them to train full-time may attend **part-time**.
- Training for **self-employment** can include initial support and advice, help to develop business plans, appropriate skills training and ongoing mentoring.
- **Pre-vocational training** is available for people who need extra help before they start job-related training.

Training allowances

Trainees doing Work-based Learning get an allowance which is equivalent to any benefit they are entitled to, plus £10 a week. They may also get help with expenses such as childcare or travel.

People with disabilities

People who need specially adapted equipment or special aids may be provided with this by their training provider.

People with severe disabilities who would have difficulty doing a mainstream Work-based Learning programme can be offered residential training. People with severe disabilities who prefer to train closer to home may be offered Special Local Training. This is customised training, designed by TECs and CCTEs in association with the local Disability Employment Adviser.

In Wales: Work-based Learning for Adults operates along similar lines, under the auspices of Training and Enterprise Councils.

In Scotland: Training for Work is the counterpart to Work-based Learning. It operates along broadly similar lines, and is the responsibility of Local Enterprise Councils (LECs). Participants work towards Scottish Vocational Qualifications (SVQs). Training for young people is delivered through the Skillseekers Initiative, which includes Modern Apprenticeships.

For further information

Contact your local Jobcentre, Employment Service, TEC, CCTE or LEC.

Just the job – an Employment Service booklet which includes information about Work-based Learning/Training for Work.

The New Deal

The New Deal is described in more detail in Chapter 25, Unemployment. This chapter focuses on the opportunities provided by New Deal for full-time education and training.

New Deal for people aged 18-24: full-time education or training is one of the four options available if an unsubsidised job cannot be found during the first few months of New Deal. The education or training must help to provide the skills/qualifications required by the person in order to start work. Those who enter full-time education and training under the New Deal for 18-24 year-olds are guaranteed the equivalent of Jobseeker's Allowance. They can get help towards the cost of books or materials.

New Deal for people aged 25+: full-time education and training may be chosen as the most appropriate programme of help. It provides the chance to retrain in skills, while staying on Jobseeker's Allowance. While most courses are short, it is possible to follow full-time education or training for up to a year. The education and training must be vocational, and must help the person to find work. It could involve a short course to boost existing skills, or training for new skills.

For information on eligibility to New Deal, see chapter 25.

See also:
Booklets available from the Jobcentre.

New Deal telephone information line: 0845 606 0680.

New Deal website: www.newdeal.gov.uk

Modern Apprenticeships

Modern Apprenticeships have been developed by employers and Industry Training Organisations. They are aimed at young people wishing to gain the skills and qualifications needed to become the technicians and managers of the future.

It is possible to start at any stage after leaving full-time education, providing the training is completed by the time the trainee reaches 25 years old. This generally means that, in practice, the upper age for starting is often set at 21. If you are interested, check with your local TEC/LEC, who administer the programme, for advice and information.

Modern Apprenticeships offer structured training leading to NVQ level 3, and include key skills. Trainees are normally employed, and earn a wage set by their employer. Modern Apprenticeships are available in a wide range of occupational areas.

Northern Ireland

The New Deal

The New Deal works the same way in Northern Ireland, but the eligibility criteria are different. Adults aged 25 or more have to be unemployed for **18 months or more** to enter the New Deal for 25+.

Jobskills

Jobskills is a government-funded training programme for young unemployed people in Northern Ireland. It was introduced in 1995 and is concerned with training young people aged 16-24. It is administered in Northern Ireland by The Training and Employment Agency (T&EA).

Entrants to Jobskills must be:

- 16-24 years old following a Modern Apprenticeship framework in employment
- under 22 years old, unemployed and have a disability
- 16 or 17 years old and unemployed or a first time entrant to the labour market.

Entrants receive pre-entry careers guidance from a T&EA careers officer, to help identify the most suitable training options. A Training Credit is then issued detailing the occupational area and level within which the trainee wishes to train. (The Training Credit is a document which commits the T&EA to paying for the training.)

- Non-employed trainees (aged 16 and 17) are paid a fixed-rate weekly training allowance through their recognised training organisation.
- Non-employed trainees aged 18 or over receive a benefit-based allowance made up of an amount equivalent to their benefit.
- Employed status trainees (all ages) receive whatever their employer agrees to pay them.

In certain circumstances travel expenses are paid.

Everyone starting a 'mainstream' Jobskills programme does training towards a Traineeship (NVQ level 2) or Modern Apprenticeship (NVQ level 3).

Jobskills Access is for people who need extra help to prepare them for 'mainstream' training. This can last up to 52 weeks, and could be because they need help with literacy and numeracy, or other similar problems. Entrants with a disability may also enter through Jobskills Access, or direct onto the mainstream programme as appropriate. In either case, extra support/time on the programme may be available.

Further information

Local Training and Employment Agency offices. The T&EA headquarters is Adelaide House, 39-49 Adelaide Street, Belfast BT2 8FD. Tel: 028 9025 7777. Website: www.tea-ni.org/

20. Learners in Europe and beyond

This chapter covers:

- reasons for studying outside the UK
- different ways of studying
- relevant general issues, such as finance
- specific initiatives to assist study in European Union (EU) member states, and the USA.

Why study outside the UK?

Many people are interested in spending a period of time studying or working abroad. Besides the usual primary objective of developing modern language skills, many are intrigued by the possibility of absorbing a different culture and approaching their studies from an alternative social and economic perspective. Others, wanting to work abroad in the future, look forward to gaining awareness of different business culture and of being able to contrast another country's industrial and commercial focus with that of Britain. Before following up ways into studying abroad, there are positive and negative considerations to assess.

- **Advantages are:**

  - learning a new language or improving existing language skills
  - studying subjects not offered in the UK
  - getting useful experience which could help with finding employment abroad (or in the UK)
  - advances in personal maturity, adaptability, open-mindedness
  - the opportunity, perhaps, to study in a 'centre for excellence' in a particular field, for example, study music in Hungary, architecture or history of art in Italy
  - the course of study abroad might be less expensive.

- **Disadvantages are:**

  - qualifications may not be accepted employers or research departments in UK universities
  - the cost can be high. Some EU countries consider EU students as home students and do not charge for tuition, but registration and examination fees have to be paid
  - there may be an exacting language test before starting a course
  - there may prove to be difficulties with the culture change
  - teaching methods differ; there may be difficulties in keeping pace with studies.

Different ways to study abroad

- Doing a full degree course alongside the country's indigenous students.
- Studying for dual (sometimes, triple) qualifications. Some UK universities offer degree courses where study time is split between countries, leading to the award of a foreign degree or diploma, in addition to the British qualification.
- Studying for a UK qualification – for example, on a European studies or modern foreign language course – can involve periods of up to a year spent studying abroad.
- Doing a short-term study programme within a UK course of higher education. ERASMUS – the European-funded student mobility scheme – is part of the SOCRATES European community education programme which operates for both mature students and younger students. Studies done abroad in another European Union (EU) or European Economic Area (EEA) country are recognised as part of higher education courses run by participating UK HE institutions. Applications to the programme must be made through the students' HE institution.

 **Contact:** ***UK SOCRATES-ERASMUS Council –***
Research and Development Building,
The University of Kent, Canterbury CT2 7PD.
Tel: 01227 762712. The UK contact point for information on the SOCRATES-ERASMUS programme and funding.
Website: www.ukc.ac.uk/ERASMUS/erasmus

Issues to consider

Language

Knowledge of the particular country's language is essential for learners to benefit from studying abroad.

Immigration

Each country has different rules. People considering studying overseas should contact the relevant Embassy or High Commission.

Money for studies

Unless a course of study abroad is part of a UK higher education course linked to the SOCRATES-ERASMUS scheme, you will have to fund the course yourself, or seek sponsorship, grants from charitable trusts, or apply to other possible sources of finance. Some employers may finance the cost of taking a course of study abroad. It may be possible to receive assistance through the students' loan company or take out a career development loan.

 **Contact:** *Local education authority's finance department*

***Career Development Loans** on the freephone line:*
0800 585 505 between 9.00am and 9.00pm, Monday to Friday

***The Educational Grants Advisory Service** –*
c/o Family Welfare Association, 501-505
Kingsland Road, London E8 4AU. Tel: 020 7254 6251.
Can offer advice to people who wish to follow a
whole course of study overseas.

 **Consult:** *The European Choice – see chapter booklist*
Finding Funding – a comprehensive guide to grants
for international education published by Central Bureau,
price £9.99 (address below).

There are some schemes which may pay for a period overseas – for example Winston Churchill Travelling Fellowships, usually advertised in the national press.

Also, there are a small number of scholarships available – such as NATO, Fulbright, Commonwealth – for which there is strong competition. Most schemes have an upper age limit of 28.

 **Consult:** *UNESCO Study Abroad – see further information at end of chapter.*

Health and state benefits

Healthcare overseas is expensive. Many countries have reciprocal arrangements with the UK allowing free or reduced-rate healthcare. Check the situation with your national insurance contributions, as going abroad will affect your eligibility for sickness, unemployment and other state benefits when you return to the UK. If you currently receive benefits, retirement or widow's pensions, and are going abroad for more than three months, or you wish to receive benefits while you are away:

 **Contact:** *Local* ***Benefits Agencies***
Inland Revenue, National Insurance Contributions
***Office** – International Services, Longbenton,*
Newcastle-upon-Tyne 2, NE98 I22.
Customer service helpline: 06451 54811.

***Pensions and Overseas Benefits Directorate** –*
Tyneview Park, Newcastle upon Tyne NE98 IBA.
Customer Service Helpline: 0191 218 7878.

***Social Security Office** – Main Exchange,*
Overseas Branch, Castle Building, Stormont Estate,
Belfast BT4 3SG. Tel: 028 9052 2603.

Income tax

If you have dependants, own property or are likely to work in the country you are proposing to study in, the tax position is likely to be complicated. Your liability will largely depend on whether or not you are regarded as a UK resident.

 **Contact:** *The local tax office can provide leaflets and advice.*
You may need to speak to an accountant or contact a Citizens Advice Bureau.

Qualifications

The validity of foreign qualifications in the UK needs to be carefully checked. Some degrees and professional qualifications are not of comparable standing. UK NARIC – the National Academic Recognition Information Centre for the UK – can provide guidelines and comparability statements free of charge to individuals enquiring about formal recognition of particular qualifications. Individuals considering courses of study abroad leading to overseas qualifications might want to establish their relevance for future employment in the UK. Most higher educational institutions in the UK subscribe to the UK NARIC service provided over the internet or on CD-Rom. Publishes *Studying, Training and doing Research in another country of the EU*. For accompanying factsheets, freephone: 0800 581591.

 **Contact:** ***UK-NARIC*** *– ECCTIS 2000 Ltd, Oriel House,*
Oriel Road, Cheltenham, Glos GL50 IXP.
Tel: 01242 252627. E-mail: 100071.444@compuserve.com

Look at: *Chapter 5 – Qualifications*
Chapter 33 – Overseas – students, refugees and asylum seekers

The European Union

Nationals of the following countries are EU citizens:

Spain, Austria, Sweden, Finland, Denmark, Belgium, Germany, the Netherlands, France, Luxembourg, Italy, Greece, Portugal, Ireland and the United Kingdom.

Citizens of these countries, as well as those from Iceland, Norway, Liechtenstein, central and eastern Europe and Cyprus, have 'freedom of movement'. This gives them the opportunity to live, study and be employed in any of the member states of the EU or European Economic Area (EEA) on the same basis as those countries' nationals. Several other countries are presently seeking entry to the EU and have applications outstanding. These include Bulgaria, Cyprus, Czech Republic, Estonia, Hungary, Latvia, Lithuania, Malta, Poland, Romania, Slovak Republic and Slovenia.

European initiatives

The Europe Commission funds several specific initiatives to improve education and training in EU and EEA member states. Organisations such as training bodies, colleges, universities and schools design a project and bid competitively for funds to finance it. Individuals do not receive funds directly but may benefit by participating in a fund-winning project. The European programme initiatives mentioned in this book are the European Social Fund and the Directorate General XXII programmes, 'Leonardo', and 'Socrates'.

You can get more information about current projects in the local area by contacting further education colleges and careers service centres.

Contact: ***UK SOCRATES-ERASMUS Council*** *– see details above*

Socrates Support Unit, Leonardo Support Unit *–*
Central Bureau, 10 Spring Gardens, London SE1A 2BN.
Tel: 020 7389 4004 or e-mail: socrates@centralbureau.org.uk
or leonard@centralbureau.org.uk.
Website: www.britcoun.org/cbeve/

Leonardo Technical Assistance Office *–*
9 Avenue de l'Astronomie, B-1030 Brussels, Belgium.
Tel: 00322 227 0100

European Social Fund Secretariat *–*
Government Office for the South West, Masthouse,
Shepherds Wharf, 24 Sutton Road, Plymouth PL4 OHJ.
Tel: 01752 635034

Socrates

This is an EU programme which covers language training, open and distance learning and exchanges of information and experience at school and higher education levels.

Leonardo

This EU initiative covers vocational training and comprises guidance, placement and exchange programmes for young people, as well as networking and information exchange projects. A strong element is that projects are usually linked to partners elsewhere in the EU.

More information on Europe

Careers Europe

Local careers services have access to the 'Careers Europe' information centre in Bradford. It provides a range of information products and services such as the Eurofacts sheets, Globalfacts and the Exodus database which are information resources covering aspects of studying, living and working in Europe, the USA, Australia, New Zealand and many other countries. Careers Europe can provide help and advice to professional guidance workers. Their Studying in Europe pack is a useful open learning resource for advisers to people wanting to learn outside the UK. The organisation cannot be directly approached by individuals, although their factsheets and Exodus are available for adult callers to careers centres.

Local education authorities

Often these public bodies have a European Liaison Officer. Many further education colleges and universities have a European Officer who may be able to help, although their main task is usually co-ordinating EU-funded programmes.

Central Bureau

The Central Bureau for Educational Visits and Exchanges is the UK national office for information and professional advice on educational exchange, the administration of exchange programmes and support for an international dimension in education and training. The Bureau's principal aim is to improve educational and training provision in the UK through international opportunities for mobility, linking and exchange, partnerships and vocational and in-service training.

The Bureau holds information on such things as:

- Teacher Exchange Schemes within Europe and with the United States.
- International Association for the Exchange of Students for Technical Experience (IAESTE) – students of technical and scientific subjects spend time abroad in course-related work placements.
- Junior Language Assistants Programme – young people aged 18 to 19 who are planning to study German in higher education can spend a year in Germany as an assistant to an English teacher in a school.
- EU programmes such as 'Leonardo' – designed to enable young people to gain vocational experience, sample life and to improve language skills in another EU country.
- International opportunities for work, study and exchanges.
- A range of publications offering information and advice.

 **Contact:** ***Central Bureau*** *– 10 Spring Gardens, London SW1A 2BN.*
Tel: 020 7389 4004 or e-mail: info@centralbureau.org.uk.
Website: www.britcoun.org/cbeve/

eurodesk

This is a regional and national enquiry answering service which disseminates EU information relevant to the education, training and youth fields of over 25 countries. eurodesk information relates mainly to European opportunities for young people and those who work with them.
eurodesk provides internet access to EU programmes information.

 **Contact:** ***eurodesk*** *(UK contact point) – Community Learning Scotland, Rosebery House, 9 Haymarket Terrace, Edinburgh EH12 5EZ.*
Tel: 0131 313 2488. E-mail: eurodesk@cls.dircon.co.uk.
Website: www.eurodesk.org

Other ***eurodesk*** *contact points:*

eurodesk *– Youth Exchange Centre, The British Council, 10 Spring Gardens, London 2BN. Tel: 020 7389 4697*

eurodesk *– Northern Ireland Central Bureau for Educational Visits and Exchanges, 1 Chlorine Gardens, Belfast BT8 5DJ.*
Tel: 028 9066 4418

eurodesk *– Wales Youth Agency, Leslie Court Lon-y-Llyn, Caerphilly, Mid Glamorgan CF83 1BQ. Tel: 029 2088 0088.*

Commonwealth universities

There are opportunities to study for first and higher degrees in the Commonwealth. Contact the Immigration section of the respective High Commission in London, for details of visa requirements for individual countries.

Association of Commonwealth Universities

General enquiries may be made to the Association's library (located in London), which has a full collection of prospectuses, reference books and scholarship information. See also the individual factsheets about study in Australia, New Zealand and Canada.

Look at: *Commonwealth Universities Yearbook, 1999 – a two-volume comprehensive guide to university institutions, price £155 inc. p&p. ISBN 0 85143 164 X.*

Awards for First Degree Study at Commonwealth Universities, 1997-99 – £10.00 surface mail, £12.00 air mail. ISBN 0 85143 159 3.

Awards for Postgraduate Study at Commonwealth Universities, 1997-99 – £24.00 surface mail, £30.00 air mail. ISBN 0 85143 158 5.

Contact: ***Association of Commonwealth Universities*** *– John Foster House, 36 Gordon Square, London WC1H OPF. Tel: 020 7387 8572 Monday to Friday: 9.30am – 1.00pm, 2.00 – 5.30pm. E-mail: ingo@acu.ac.uk. Website: www.acu.ac.uk*

Library opening hours: Tues, Wed, Thurs: 10.00am – 1.00pm; 2.00 – 4.00pm.

American universities

All North American universities are fee-paying and the private universities charge high fees. State universities are cheaper but costs vary widely. The popular areas such as California and the eastern states are up to four times as expensive as a university in the Deep South. State universities charge more for out-of-state students (which includes foreign students).

Unlike Britain, there is no uniformity of approach or entrance requirements to American universities. Only Californian state universities have a unified application procedure – otherwise there is a separate application fee for each one, around $40 to $100.

Bursaries are generally offered only for higher degrees, although some institutions have scholarships for first-degree foreign students. It is worth checking with a particular institution's Dean of Admissions.

The universities in America have a much more flexible course structure than those in the UK.

Permission to work off campus is rarely given to overseas students in the US, and proof must be presented to the immigration authorities that intending students can support themselves and pay their fees. Standardised admission tests are common to both undergraduate and postgraduate programmes. Details are available from the Fulbright Commission.

The Fulbright Commission

This is the first point of contact for people considering studying in the USA. It can provide free information on US universities and application procedures, and has a full collection of reference books, prospectuses and scholarship information. Write, enclosing a stamped self-addressed envelope.

Contact: *The Fulbright Commission – Educational Advisory Service, 62 Doughty Street, London WC1N 2LS. Tel: 020 7404 6994.*

Further information

The European Choice – a Guide to Opportunities for Higher Education in Europe, 1999-2000 – published by the Department for Education and Employment, free from DfEE Publications centre, PO Box 5050, Annesley, Nottingham NG15 ODJ. Tel: 0845 60 222 60. Contains detailed information about financial support, and detailed information on the EU and EEA countries' higher education systems.

A Guide to Higher Education Systems and Qualifications in the European Community – published by Kogan Page (in association with the Commission of the European Communities), price £22.50. ISBN 0 7494 0387 X.

Directory of Higher Education in Institutions in the EFTA States – published by Kogan Page, price £17.99. ISBN 0 7494 1382 4.

Student Handbook: a directory of courses and institutions in higher education for 16 countries not members of the European Community – published by the Council of Europe through The Stationery Office, PO Box 276, London SW8 5DT, price £11.75. ISBN 928 711 96 0 0

UNESCO Study Abroad 2000/2001 – published by UNESCO through The Stationery Office, PO Box 276, London SW8 5DT. Tel: 0870 600 55 22. £17.50 inc. £2.94 p&p. ISBN 0 11 985 2047.

Eurofacts Series, Globalfacts and Exodus, the database of international careers information. Published by Careers Europe, 4th Floor, Midland House, 14 Cheapside, Bradford BD I 4JA. Tel: 01274 829600. Eurofacts are very useful sheets providing information on over 250 topics, including working, studying and training within the EU. Updated annually and held in careers centre libraries. Careers services may also hold Exodus in their career centre libraries. For a full list of products and services, see website: www.careersb.bradtec.co.uk/europe/index.htm

Socrates – Erasmus 2000 – published by the UK Socrates – Erasmus Council in association with ISCO Publications, 12a Princess Way, Camberley GU15 3SP. Tel: 01276 21188. Price, £12.50 plus £1.70 p&p. A UK guide to institutions offering degree and diploma courses associated with the European Communities Socrates programme.

How to Study Abroad – published by How To Books, 3rd edition, price £8.99 plus £1.25 p&p. ISBN 1 85703 169 5. A useful, detailed volume.

The Directory of Work and Study in Developing Countries – published by Vacation Work, price £9.99. ISBN 1 85458 170 8.

Vacation Work also produces resources covering opportunities for study in the USA and Canada, with suggestions for seeking sponsorship.

The website *datalake* carries comprehensive details of worldwide higher education opportunities.www.datalake.co.uk

21. The Workers' Educational Association (WEA)

This chapter covers:

- the background and structure of the WEA
- the type of course available
- addresses of district offices.

The Workers' Educational Association (WEA) is a voluntary body offering classes to adults countrywide. It is an organisation that anyone can join and be involved in planning the local programmes. Its classes and courses are run everywhere – in schools, adult education centres, local halls, members' houses and so on. It uses other organisations' premises, but remains separate and independent, and tries to reach people where they live and work.

How it works

- Despite its name, it is not restricted to any one kind of worker – it is open to all.
- It was established in 1903 to overcome the disadvantages of workers who didn't have access to established channels of education.
- It has about 700 local branches each with its own officers (secretary, treasurer, chairperson), who plan the local programme in consultation with their district office. Anyone can join the WEA and become a member of the local branch. People joining a WEA class promoted by a branch become members automatically.
- The branches make up 13 districts in England, two in Wales and others in Scotland and Northern Ireland, each with a district secretary (listed below). In each district, there are staff who help branches to organise their programme, work with affiliated societies and recruit suitable part-time tutors. Others concentrate on district provision, for example pre-retirement education, trade union and industrial studies.
- Classes may be during the day or evening. There may be crêche facilities attached to daytime classes.
- They run activities in co-operation with local authorities and have a particularly close relationship with some university extra-mural departments.
- WEA classes are designed to develop understanding and some may lead to formal qualifications. Students often take up other work or take further or higher education courses as a result.
- Increasingly, accreditation is available to students who want it.

What it does

The WEA's activities vary from area to area because branches have their own ideas about local needs, and the professional staff who help them have their own interests and expertise. Broadly their work falls into four types of education:

- Education for people in deprived areas, or who suffer from social or educational disadvantage (for example elderly people, people with special needs and unemployed people); in a number of areas the WEA is involved in setting up unemployment centres.
- Trade union education (usually in conjunction with the TUC education service).
- Social and political education (for example courses for school managers, potential councillors, workers in voluntary organisations).
- Liberal education (the traditional WEA class, in subjects like philosophy, art, literature), and also preparation for higher education.

The WEA magazine – *Reportback* – has a circulation of nearly 25,000 and is sent to members and organisations interested in adult education. It is a good way to find out about new developments. For more information contact the WEA at the national office below.

What the courses cost

If it's a trade union course, it's likely to be free. Courses for unemployed people and other disadvantaged groups are often free, but it is up to the local branch. Fees usually have to cover all costs.

How to find out more

The local library should have the names of local branch secretaries; otherwise the district organisers at the addresses below will have details.

District offices

England

Cheshire, Merseyside and West Lancashire: 7-8 Bluecoat Chambers, School Lane, Liverpool L1 3BX. Tel: 0151 709 8023.

Eastern: Botolph House, 17 Botolph Lane, Cambridge CB2 3RE. Tel: 01223 350978.

East Midland: 39 Mapperley Road, Mapperley Park, Nottingham NG3 5AQ. Tel: 0115 962 8400.

London: 4 Luke Street, London EC2A 4XW. Tel: 020 7387 8966/020 7388 7261.

Northern: 51 Grainger Street, Newcastle upon Tyne NE1 5JE. Tel: 0191 232 3957.

North Western: 4th Floor, Crawford House, Precinct Centre, Oxford Road, Manchester M13 9GH. Tel: 0161 273 7652.

South Eastern: 4 Castle Hill, Rochester, Kent ME1 1QQ. Tel: 01634 842140.

South Western: Martin's Gate, Bretonside, Plymouth PL4 0AT. Tel: 01752 664989.

Thames and Solent: 6 Brewer Street, Oxford OX1 1QN. Tel: 01865 246270.

Western: 40 Morse Road, Redfield, Bristol BS5 9LB. Tel: 0117 935 1764.

West Mercia: 78-80 Sherlock Street, Birmingham B5 6LT. Tel: 0121 666 6101.

Yorkshire North: 6 Woodhouse Square, Leeds LS3 1AD. Tel: 0113 245 3304.

Yorkshire South: Chantry Buildings, Corporation Street, Rotherham S60 1NG. Tel: 01709 837001.

Wales

North Wales: 33 College Road, Bangor LL57 2AP. Tel: 01248 353254.

South Wales: 10 Coopers Yard, Trade Street, Cardiff CF1 5DF. Tel: 029 2023 5277.

Scotland

Scottish Association: Riddle's Court, 322 Lawnmarket, Edinburgh EH1 3PG. Tel: 0131 226 3456.

Northern Ireland

1 Fitzwilliam Street, Belfast BT9 6AW. Tel: 028 9032 9718.

National Office

Temple House, 17 Victoria Park Square, London E2 9PB. Tel: 020 8983 1515.
E-mail: info@wea.org.uk Website: www.wea-org.uk

22. Trade union education

TUC Learning Services

TUC Learning Services was set up in 1998 to help unions and their members meet the opportunities and challenges set out in the government's Green Paper *The Learning Age*, and to contribute to realising the vision of creating a learning society.

The unions recognise that they have an important role to play in drawing, in particular, those people with few recognised skills and no formal qualifications into learning and training programmes. Union representatives in the workplace have the potential to reach and encourage these non-traditional learners.

A wide range of approaches and methods have been, and are continuing to be, tested and developed. This reflects the diversity of union membership and often widely differing learning needs – within unions, sectors, cultural backgrounds and geographical locations, for example.

The TUC, through **Bargaining for Skills** projects, has been working with employers, to set up workplace learning centres, taking the learning to the learners, rather than vice-versa.

Union involvement in learning covers a wide range of opportunities, from job specific vocational training to opportunities designed to draw people back into learning for the first time since leaving school. This is typically anything from improving communication and language skills, to an introduction to computers. Specialist and professional unions have an important role in helping their members to keep abreast of new professional and technological developments.

Work is currently underway to support a trained network of **union learning representatives**. In this way, trade unions can help encourage access to and take up of the available learning and training possibilities for many workers who may well have been otherwise excluded. Advice, guidance and support to help learners make sound decisions about learning opportunities is seen as important, as well as ongoing support once learning has begun. The role of union learning reps is important in these respects.

The **Union Learning Fund** has been an important development. The first six months of this initiative, from September 1998 – March 1999, covered over 20 unions and provided assistance to 44 projects. Early results include over 2500 people trained, over 20 learning centres established, over 100 learner representatives trained, at least six new qualifications developed and well over £500,000 raised by unions to extend the scope of their Union Learning Fund work. There are currently over 100 ULF projects, which are testing and trying out innovative partnership approaches. Recent Union Learning Fund successes include assisting those facing barriers because of freelancing, geographical isolation, or their particular work patterns.

The trade unions are keen to promote positive partnership approaches with employers, providers and other organisations, and to encourage the uptake of programmes and initiatives such as the Ufl and individual learning accounts, especially by those employees who would otherwise have been unlikely to have taken advantage of such opportunities.

Trade union representatives

Trade union representatives, including union safety representatives, have a legal right to paid time off from work for education and training connected with their duties as union representatives. The legal rights are embodied in the Employment Protection Consolidation Act and the Health and Safety Commission's regulations.

Each year the TUC offers facilities to between 20,000 and 30,000 members to train for their work as full-time officers, shop stewards or safety representatives. This is done through colleges of further and higher education, the WEA, and at the TUC National Education Centre.

The TUC runs courses in the regions through public educational bodies. It supplies core materials – a basic set of key studies it wants all its approved courses to cover. Courses are usually done by day release and take between two and ten days. The TUC pays the course fees and the employer continues to pay wages. Day-release courses are normally for trade union representatives, shop stewards and health and safety representatives. Participants have to be nominated by their union, who forwards their application to the TUC regional education officer.

Full-time officers or union branch secretaries should be able to provide information. If for any reason they haven't got this information, those interested could contact the TUC regional education officer, who also arranges evening classes and day schools.

TUC Regional Education Offices

East and West Midlands: 24 Livery Street, Birmingham B3 2PA. Tel: 0121 236 4464.

Northern, Yorkshire and Humberside: 30 York Place, Leeds LS1 2ED. Tel: 0113 242 9296.

North West: Transport House, Islington, Liverpool L3 8EQ. Tel: 0151 298 1216.

South East and East Anglia: Congress House, Great Russell Street, London WC1B 3LS.
Tel: 020 7467 1238.

Wales and South West England: Transport House, 1 Cathedral Road, Cardiff CF1 9SD.
Tel: 029 2022 7449.

The Scottish Region: 4th Floor, 145-165 West Regent Street, Glasgow G2 4RZ.
Tel: 0141 221 8545.

Northern Ireland: Northern Ireland Committee (ICTU), 3 Wellington Park, Belfast BT9 6DJ
Tel: 028 9068 1726.

The TUC course programme is accredited through the National Open College Network (NOCN). The structure of accreditation will enable credits earned through the TUC education programme to be transferred to vocational awards or other further and higher education and training opportunities.

Individual unions

All unions are concerned with training their officials (whether full or part-time). Many have their own education service. For example, Unison (the public service union) offers a wide range of courses through UNISON Open College, ranging from basic education through to professional-level qualifications.

In general, courses are only for members of the union concerned. Trade union newspapers or journals provide information about opportunities.

Larger unions may have scholarships or offer financial help to members returning to study – especially those attending adult residential colleges. These awards are usually additional to other grants.

General Federation of Trades Unions (GFTU)

The GFTU is the federation for specialist unions; currently there are 34 affiliated unions. Through their Educational Trust, the GFTU offer a wide range of trade union courses for union members, reps and officers. Many courses are accredited through the Open College Network.

The GFTU Educational Trust also makes small grants for full-time and Open University students. However, there are limiting criteria. People must be studying subjects within economic theory and history, industrial law, history and principles of industrial relations. Individual trade unions may have other schemes.

☞ **Contact:** *The General Federation of Trades Unions Educational Trust,*
Central House, Upper Woburn Place, London WC1H 0HY.
Tel: 020 7387 2578. Website: www.gftu.org.uk
E-mail:gftuhq@gftu.org.uk

Further information

Education Year Book 1999/2000 – published by Pearson Education, 12-14 Sladeburn Crescent, Southport PR9 9YF. Tel: 01704 226881. Price £92. ISBN 0 273 641 581. Contains lists of education officers for most of the major unions.

Adult Continuing Education Year Book 1998/9 – published by NIACE, 21 De Montfort Street, Leicester LE1 7GE. Price £14.95. ISBN 1 886201 063 3. Includes a section on trade union education with a list of many trade union contacts.

23. Training for self-employment

This chapter covers:

- what people thinking about self-employment should consider
- sources of support and advice
- organisations offering training
- possible sources of financial assistance
- course providers
- useful publications.

Many people find the idea of working independently strongly appealing, and, although recent statistics have not shown the predicted expansion in this workstyle, self-employment is still a popular occupational choice. 12% of all workers were self-employed in the first quarter of 1999 – about 3.2 million people, three-quarters of whom work full-time. A quarter of the self-employed workforce are female.

Recent trends in self-employment have moved towards franchised contracts, freelance consultancy, teleworking and working from home, in addition to individuals delivering a service to others – the more traditional type of self-employment.

Checklist for those considering self-employment:

- a business idea – which has the potential to succeed
- trade or job skills in the area planned for trading
- business skills – from market research and publicity, to book-keeping and tax records
- personal skills – enthusiastic approach to problem solving, determination etc.

Support and advice

There are ample sources of business advice and guidance to help people who intend to start their own business. They should be encouraged to do thorough research and preparation, getting as much help as possible before becoming self-employed.

Effective planning before business start-up has been shown to be the key factor in the survival of new business ventures. The self-employed must consider and plan for many contingencies, such as peaks and troughs in demand and variations in cash flow.

Many young people, and some adults, like to talk through their plans at a basic level with careers service staff, before being signed to sources of specific assistance.

Some of the main sources of help are listed below. Other useful information resources are the business sections of public libraries, and local authority environmental services or economic development units, where up-to-date local business and labour market information is gathered to help inward investors and those considering starting a business. Some local unitary authorities may provide additional help with marketing, premises, training and fund raising.

Business Link

Business Link is an organisation of agencies, established by the Department of Trade and Industry (DTI), which aims to offer ready access to a comprehensive range of business support services, principally for new small and medium-sized businesses. Individuals can expect to have their needs met, regardless of the nature of their business enquiry, through either the help of information officers based within local Business Links, or, by referral to partner organisations, such as Training and Enterprise Councils or Local Enterprise Companies or Chambers of Commerce. The aim of Business Link is to offer a single point of contact for every kind of business need.

Contact: *DTI's **Business Link Signpost Line**: 0345 567765 which provides callers with details of their nearest Business Link. The Business Link initiative also has a website carrying useful information: www.businesslink.co.uk*

*In Wales, the initiative is called **Business Connect Wales**. Dialling the main number – 0345 969798 – directs those callers who are potential inward investors to North and South Wales to phone 0345 775577 and, for Mid-Wales, to phone 0800 269 300.*

Organisations offering training and support

Business Link (see above) can give people advice about available training, but individuals interested in becoming self-employed may be put in touch with some of the following:

TECs and LECs

Training and Enterprises Councils (TECs) in England and Wales, and Local Enterprise Companies (LECs) in Scotland, provide a wide range of training and enterprise measures. These include programmes designed to help unemployed people train for self-employment, such as Work-based Learning for Adults (WBLA). The programmes are specifically designed to meet the needs of local businesses, so provision varies from area to area. The kinds of training available can include:

- Initial support and advice.
- Enterprise awareness – events which help people interested in working for themselves to understand the implications of setting up and running a business.
- Business planning – help for managers who want to learn how to develop a business and training plan. There are free planning kits for businesses at various stages of development, backed by professional support at special rates.
- Business training – available through short and part-time courses to help people set up or develop a business. This is supported by open learning facilities, seminars in book-keeping, marketing, management, and other skills for established owner-managers of small firms.

- Low-cost consultancy – helps firms review their strategy for training and development and is available to help established companies develop their management team, develop new training arrangements and work with other businesses to meet future skill needs.
- Ongoing mentoring while on WBLA.

Some TECs and LECs have their own databases of information on business training courses.

 **Contact:** ***Local TEC or LEC*** *for more information (their address is in The Gazetteer).*

Northern Ireland LEDU *– LEDU House, Upper Galwally, Belfast BT8 6TB.*
Tel: 028 9049 1031. E-mail: ledu@ledu-ni.gov.uk.
Website: www.ledu-ni.gov.uk

Learning Direct

Help is available through this free national helpline for people seeking up-to-date information on training courses offered by the full range of education training bodies in their area. This includes programmes designed to support businesses and commercial enterprises, and business start-ups. On-line advisers have links with comprehensive databases of training opportunities which can also be consulted in local careers centres.

 **Contact:** ***Learning Direct*** *free helpline – 0800 100 900*

Shell LiveWIRE

This organisation operates throughout the UK. Shell LiveWIRE co-ordinators can offer advice to young people, aged between 16 and 30, who are considering self-employment. There is an annual competition for new businesses.

 **Contact:** *Phone the Shell LiveWIRE national helpline: 0345 573252 for a free start-up business information pack. Website: www.shell-livewire.org*

Instant Muscle is an organisation with 45 centres across England and Wales providing help to unemployed people setting up their own business. One feature of their help is drawing up a sound business plan which can be submitted to organisations which are possible sources of funding.

 **Contact:** ***Instant Muscle Ltd –*** *Springside House,*
84 Northend Road, London W14 9ES.
Tel: 020 7603 2604. E-mail: head-office@instant-muscle.org.uk

Help in rural areas

The Countryside Agency offers help to established businesses employing between five and 20 people in English rural areas.

Technical advice and training in a wide range of skills is available from experts in subjects like woodworking machinery, upholstery, thatching, saddlery, forgework, wheelwrighting and furniture restoration. For more information:

 **Contact:** ***Countryside Agency*** *– Craft Training Department,*
141 Castle Street, Salisbury SPI 3TP
Tel: 01722 336255. Website: www.countryside.gov.uk

Or, look in the phone book for the number of a local office.
Ask for the business adviser.

The Telework, Telecottage and Telecentre Association (TCA)

Individuals can access up-to-date computer software, and make use of the internet, by working at their nearest telecottage. Training and demonstrations are often available.

Contact: *TCA – WREN Telecottage, Stoneleigh Park, Warwickshire CV8 2RR.*
Tel: 024 7669 698 or e-mail tca@ruralnet.org.uk to get contact information for all the telecottages. Website: www.tca.org.uk

Business start-up

Helping the unemployed through New Deal

People who are unemployed may be eligible for financial support and assistance with starting a new business.

If a young adult has a sound business idea, is aged between 18 and 24, and has been out of work and claiming benefit for six months, they can be helped through the **New Deal** initiative, operating through their local Jobcentre. Arrangements are made for them to meet with a Business Link adviser to see if their business idea is viable and, afterwards, on a weekly basis to analyse their progress. If their business idea appears sound, they are able to sign off Jobseekers' Allowance (JSA) and get a training allowance for six months – this amounts to their former JSA, plus £15.38.

New Deal conditions rule out paying wages from business profits during this initial start-up period. Any profits made must be ploughed back into the enterprise to cover initial outlays and on-going costs. At the end of the six-month period, if the business is successful, it will be regarded as fully-fledged and wages may be drawn from profits. If unsuccessful, the starter may return to signing on and receiving JSA.

Individuals over 25, who have been out of work for more than two years and who have a proposal for self-employment, can apply through their Jobcentre to join a Work-based Learning programme funded by the local TEC and delivered in their area by Business Link (or another enterprise agency). This scheme helps individuals who have presented sound proposals at interview to run a business for an initial period of six months, and get an allowance equal to their benefit, plus £10. During this period they are signed off JSA, to which they may return if their business is unsuccessful.

☞ **Contact:** ***The local Jobcentre or local TEC or LEC*** *(address in The Gazetteer).*

High Street banks

Most major banks offer free advice and a package of special services for people considering starting a business. This includes low interest rate loans of between £5k and £250k – to help with spending on business assets, or to cover the cost of materials, research and development etc – which can be awarded to help people with insufficient security to cover a normal bank loan. This financial help is made available through the Department of Trade and Industry's Small Firms Loan Guarantee Scheme.

The Prince's Trust

This initiative was set up to support people between the ages of 14 and 30 who lack opportunity or the means to make the most of their lives. For those who are unemployed or under-employed, and unable to raise the finance elsewhere, the Prince's Trust can provide soft loans, ongoing advice, sales opportunities and development awards to help fledgling businesses to survive. The Trust's personal development courses can help young people aged 16-25 to build confidence and key skills to increase their employability and career prospects, while other kinds of training, mentoring and support, form other aspects of the Prince's Trust initiative.

 **Contact:**

The Prince's Trust – *18 Park Square, London NWI 4LH.*
Freephone: 0800 842 842. E-mail: printrust@princes-trust.org.uk
Website: www.princes-trust.org.uk

The Prince's Scottish Youth Business Trust –
Mercantile Chambers, 53 Bothwell Street, Glasgow G2 6TA.
Tel: 0141 248 4999.

The Prince's Trust – *Northern Ireland, Midland Building,*
Whital Street, Belfast BT15 1JP. Tel: 028 9074 5454.
E-mail: info@wiredup.net

Local enterprise agencies

There are 150 independent local enterprise agencies in England, and 15 in Wales. In Scotland, there are 42 enterprise trusts.

The National Federation of Enterprise Agencies represents over 120 members in England. Its principal activities are business counselling and follow-up, business training, financial support and help with managed workspace.

Local enterprise agencies and trusts offer free counselling and advice. Their target market is start-ups and microfirms of up to ten employees.

 **Contact:** *the addresses below for details of local enterprise agencies or trusts and the services they offer:*

England and Wales
National Federation of Enterprise Agencies *–*
Trinity Gardens, 9-11 Bromham Road, Bedford MK40 2UQ.
Tel: 01234 354055. E-mail: alan.bretherton@nfea.demon.co.uk.
Website: www.nfea.com

Scotland
Scottish Business in the Community (SBC) *–*
30 Hanover Street, Edinburgh EH2 2DR.
Tel: 0131 220 3001. E-mail:sbc@sbcscot.freeserve.co.uk

Northern Ireland
Northern Ireland LEDU *– LEDU House, Upper Galwally, Belfast BT8 6TB. Tel: 028 9049 1031.*
E-mail: ledu@ledu-ni.gov.uk. Website: www.ledu-ni.gov.uk

Help in areas of deprivation

Under the umbrella organisation of the **Regional Development Agency**, there will be local initiatives supporting all aspects of urban regeneration, including business enterprise. In many areas, multi-agency partnerships have successfully bid for all sorts of regeneration support from the European Union. Projects vary from area to area.

 **Contact:** *the local* ***Regional Development Agency****, TEC or LEC (see The Gazetteer) or* ***Business Link****,* ***Business Connect or LEDU*** *(see above).*

Enterprise support in Scotland

Local Enterprise Companies

The LECs, in addition to delivering local development and training, are responsible for advising and supporting people who want to set up in business and those running existing small businesses. They now work in partnership with the Scottish Business Shop Network (see below) to offer a range of services. These vary from area to area, but may include business counselling and advice, subsidised training and financial assistance through various enterprise schemes. They are accountable to either Scottish Enterprise, or the Highlands and Islands Enterprise, depending on the location. For information on support in your area:

 **Contact:** *the local LEC (addresses and telephone numbers are listed in The Gazetteer).*

Scottish Enterprise

Scottish Enterprise was formed from the merger of the Scottish Development Agency and the Training Agency in Scotland in 1991 and covers Grampian, Tayside, Central, Fife, Strathclyde, Dumfries & Galloway, Borders and Lothian. Scottish Enterprise provides a range of services to individuals and firms through its network of 13 Local Enterprise Companies (LECs). These services include advice, training, financial and property assistance, environmental projects and business development advice. For further information on business start-up, and for business development advice in these areas of Scotland:

Contact: *the local **LEC** (addresses and telephone numbers are listed in The Gazetteer).*

Highland and Islands Enterprise

Highlands and Islands Enterprise (HIE) network came into being as a statutory body in 1991. Its tasks are to design and deliver economic and community development, training, and environmental renewal. The HIE area covers Highland Region, Orkney, Shetland, Western Isles, the Argyll district of Strathclyde Regional and the western part of Moray district in Grampian Region.

The network has substantial powers and resources to achieve its economic and social targets. These include financial assistance to businesses and community and cultural projects, providing factories and offices, providing training programmes, and various measures for environmental renewal.

Ten private-sector led Local Enterprise Companies (LECs) provide the front-line delivery of assistance and advice on behalf of HIE, supported by its strategic core body in the Highlands capital of Inverness.

Contact: ***Highlands and Islands Enterprise (HIE)*** –
Bridge House, 20 Bridge Street, Inverness IV1 1QR.
Tel: 01463 234171 or e-mail hie.general@hient.co.uk.
Website: www.hie.wco.uk

Scottish Business Shop Network

The Scottish Business Shop Network has 38 shops throughout Scotland. They provide a range of integrated business advisory services to small businesses throughout Scotland, in partnership with the Local Enterprise Companies. Services include access to government departments, company information, patents advice, and a franchise desk.

Contact: *Use the freephone number of the **Scottish Business Shop Network**, to get details of area shops: 0800 787878. People calling from outside Scotland should phone the Glasgow Business Shop on 0141 1221 5513 and they will be redirected to local centres.*

Enterprise support in Wales

Welsh Development Agency

Under the Government of Wales Act, 1998, there is now one development body responsible for the whole geographical area, formed by the merger of the Development Board for Rural Wales and the Land Authority for Wales with the Welsh Development Agency or WDA. The WDA was first established in 1975, and its present remit is to help further the regeneration of the economy and improve the environment in Wales.

Its main activities include site assembly, providing premises, encouraging investment by the private sector in property development, grant-aiding land reclamation, stimulating quality urban and rural development, promoting Wales as a location for inward investment, helping boost the growth, profitability and competitiveness of indigenous Welsh companies, and providing investment capital for industry. Its sponsoring department is the National Assembly for Wales.

 **Contact:** ***WDA*** *– Principality House, The Friary, Cardiff CF10 3FE. Tel: 08457 775577 (English) and 08457 775566 (Welsh).*

However, most training for self-employment and business start-up throughout Wales is primarily catered for by TECs.

 **Contact:** *Business Connect on 0345 969798, or the local TEC (see The Gazetteer).*

Enterprise support in Northern Ireland

The Local Enterprise Development Unit (LEDU) is a company sponsored by the Department of Economic Development in Northern Ireland. It is the lead agency responsible for promoting and expanding small businesses in Northern Ireland that, generally, do not employ over 50 people. LEDU offers financial assistance, business advice and counselling on all aspects of business.

 **Contact:** ***Northern Ireland LEDU*** *– LEDU House, Upper Galwally, Belfast BT8 6TB. Tel: 028 9049 1031. E-mail ledu@ledu-ni.gov.uk*

Co-operative business

Workers co-operatives are owned and democratically controlled by their employees, who work together as equals. This can be a way of reducing the solitude of self-employment. There are co-operatives active in all business sectors.

The Industrial Common Ownership Movement (ICOM) is the UK federation for workers' co-operatives. It can provide information to the public and to its members on aspects of setting up and running co-operatives, and can also carry out promotional activities on their behalf.

Contact: ***Industrial Common Ownership Movement (ICOM)*** – *Vassalli House, 20 Central Road, Leeds LS 1 6DE. Tel: 0113 246 1738. E-mail icom@icom.org.uk*

Additional support is available in Scotland:

Contact: ***Employee Ownership Scotland Ltd*** – *Building 1, Unit D9, Templeton Business Centre, Templeton Street, Glasgow G40 1DA. Tel: 0141554 3979. E-mail eos@sol.co.uk*

In Northern Ireland, foundation grants of up to £500 can be made available to help start up community or co-operative businesses or social economy initiatives. Advisers at NICDA can offer help from the earliest stages of development planning.

Contact: ***NICDA Social Economy Agency*** – *23-25 Shipkey Street, Derry BT48 6DL. Tel: 01504 371733. E-mail nicdaderry@compuserv.com*

Business schools

Business schools throughout the UK run short or part-time courses aimed at people about to set up a small business, or who are already running one. Training can cover all aspects of the support that is needed in starting and launching a business – from formulating a business plan and seeking financial backing to product marketing and employment law. Some charge a fee for training, but this is often nominal as financial support is commonly given by the local TEC or LEC, or by the DTI. There is no training allowance.

The Association of Business Schools (ABS), founded in 1992, has almost 100 higher education member institutions of high professional standing. Located throughout the UK, they offer a range of services both to companies and to individuals, which will vary slightly according to regional industrial profiles and with established specialisms.

Full information about the wide range of courses offered by schools of the Association is available in their regularly-updated directory.

 **Consult:** *The ABS Undergraduate Directory of Business Schools 1999/2000, £19.99 plus £3.00 postage and packaging. ISBN 0 75063 955 5. Available from bookshops or the publishers – Heinemann, Direct Mail Department, Halley Court, Oxford OX2 8EJ. Tel: 01865 888180.*

 **Contact:** ***Association of Business Schools (ABS)*** *–*
334-354 Gray's Inn Road, London WC1X 8BP.
Tel: 020 7837 1899. E-mail abs@the-abs.org.uk
Website: www.the-abs.org.uk

Adult education courses

Many adult education centres, colleges, universities and the Workers Education Association (WEA), run short or part-time courses on self-employment and starting a small business. They may also offer courses on topics related to running a business, such as book-keeping, employment law or general management. Some of these courses may involve open learning.

 **Contact:** *Local colleges, universities, WEA or community education centres.*
Learning Direct free helpline – 0800 100 900.

Open learning courses

A variety of distance learning colleges, like the National Extension College, the International Correspondence Schools and RRC Business Training, offer both general courses in business management and specific ones in subjects like marketing or accountancy. The Open University Business School also runs many professional business-related courses.

 **Consult:** *The Open Learning Directory – (see details in Chapter 18).*
Learning Direct free helpline – 0800 100 900.

ICS business course

International Correspondence Schools (ICS) offers the ICS diploma course in Starting Your Own Business. Seven units take participants from the initial business idea through to the business plan, and cover all aspects of basic finance and budgeting. The whole course costs £229, which includes all materials and tutor support.

There is also an ICS diploma course in Business Management, which covers team leadership and decision making, as well as fundamental aspects of human resource management, financial management, and marketing. This course costs £419, including all materials and tutor support, and a diploma is awarded upon successful completion.

Courses can be paid for by instalments. Courses are valid for up to three years from starting, and students need to spend an average of three to four hours a week studying.

 **Contact:** ***International Correspondence Schools*** *– 8 Elliot Place, Glasgow G3 8EP. Tel: 0141 2212926. Website: www.icslearn.com*

NEC business courses

The National Extension College (NEC) offers **Business Start-up**, which covers developing your business idea, legal and financial planning, and practical planning issues; and **Business Growth**, which covers business evaluation, general and financial management, quality, practical planning issues, and European export. Together, the courses comprise activity-based self-study units covering all aspects of setting up and running a business. Both are available, with six tutor-marked assignments, at £150 each or £270 for both.

Essential Book-keeping is a course to develop skills for business or personal finance, and has five tutor-marked assignments covering all key procedures. These can lead to accreditation with either RSA stage 1, LCCI pre-first level practical book-keeping, Pitman level 1 in book-keeping and accounts or the Institute of Certified Book-keepers certificate at level 2, depending upon the final exams taken. The course costs £175.

All course fees can be paid by instalment. Course applicants who are UK residents paying the price of a course in full, and who are not getting government assistance, can claim 23% tax relief.

 **Contact:** ***National Extension College*** *– Student Advisers, 18 Brooklands Avenue, Cambridge CB2 2HN. Tel: 01223 450500. E-mail info@nec.ac.uk Website: www.nec.ac.uk*

Financial Times Management

This company offers a wide range of management and supervisory distance learning courses and resources, covering topics such as finance, strategy, decision making and delegation. The resources available include workbooks, videos and CD-Roms. Course prices can range from £99 to £2000.

 **Contact:** ***Financial Times Management (FTM)*** *– Customer Services, 16th Floor, Portland Tower, Portland Street, Manchester M1 3LD. Tel: 0161 245 3300. General enquiries can be e-mailed to bronagh.doherty@ftmanagement.com Website: www.ftmanagement.com*

The OU small business courses

The Open University's Business School offers a range of courses and materials to support small businesses. There is a set of study packs (ref P788) entitled *Build a Better Business*, which consists of 29 separate modules on a wide range of basic management topics, covering aspects of business planning, marketing, human resource management and organisation. Individual modules are available for £49.99 plus VAT.

The OU also offers a Professional Certificate in Management (NVQ level 4). It comprises three modules – *The Effective Manager* (ref B654), *Accounting for Managers* (ref B655), *Managing Customer and Client Relations* (ref B656) each of which takes six months to complete and costs around £800 with tax relief.

 **Contact:** ***The Open Business School*** *– School of Management, The Open University, Walton Hall, Milton Keynes MK7 6AA. Tel: 01908 655827. E-mail ouwenq@open.ac.uk/ Website: www.open.ac.uk*

RRC Business Training

RRC Business Training provides complete training packages to meet the needs of those seeking to gain professional qualifications or to develop their business and office skills. RRC has over 70 years experience in developing comprehensive, up-to-date and effective open and distance learning courses. RRC also provides a full range of training and consultancy services, including web and multimedia training programmes for companies of all sizes. Areas of expertise include health and safety, environmental management, accountancy, book-keeping, payroll, credit management, marketing, sales management, project management, quality assurance, administration and management.

RRC is accredited by the Open and Distance Learning Quality Council (ODLQC) for its overall distance learning operation, and by awarding bodies for its distance and open learning courses.

 **Contact:** *The Customer Service Team:*

RRC Business Training *– 27-37 St George's Road, London SW19 4DS. Tel: 020 8947 7272. E-mail rrc@dial.pipex.com Website: www.rrc.co.uk*

Further information

There are numerous guides to self-employment on the market, a few of which are excellent – others, less so. Kogan Page publishes many titles in the Business Enterprise Series which offer help with legal and financial issues, taking up a franchise and other aspects of self-employment. Some examples of useful Kogan Page titles are:

Getting Started – How to Set Up Your Own Business by Robson Rhodes, price £8.99; *Buying Your First Franchise* by Greg Clarke, price £7.99 or *Your Business: Making it Work for You* by Mike Shaw, price £14.99.

How To Books publish:

Starting Your Own Business by Jim Green, price £9.99
Starting a Business from Home by Graham Jones, price £9.99
Getting More Business by Sallyann Sheridan, price £9.99
Doing Business on the Internet by Graham Jones, price £12.99.

These books, and other titles, may be held in public or careers centre libraries.

Your Business Start-Up Action Kit – published by Trotman, is a CD-Rom priced at £29.36 plus £3.70 p&p.

Leaflets on tax and national insurance for self-employed people are available through public offices such as the Tax Office, Benefits Agency and the Jobcentre.

24. Volunteering

This chapter covers:

- what to consider before doing voluntary work
- the breadth of opportunities for volunteers
- national and regional voluntary organisations.

The range of voluntary work and the variety of groups who need volunteer helpers is enormous. The tasks undertaken should always be of value to the organisations or to the individuals that volunteers work with, but should also benefit the individual volunteer.

Positive considerations for volunteering

- The breadth of voluntary opportunity means that potential volunteers can always find an activity to match their skills and interests. For the unemployed or retired, voluntary work can help to maintain skills and develop new interests. Often, maturity is an asset in the voluntary field.
- Although most volunteers are not paid, many express satisfaction at being able to help a particular cause. However, some volunteers do get payment to cover reasonable expenses, while a small number of volunteers go on to get a paying job with the organisation.
- Some voluntary bodies – for example, The Samaritans – require volunteers to undergo a thorough training programme. Many organisations help their voluntary workers to gain qualifications on the job.
- The experience of a new area of work is useful to those considering a change of career. Some professions – for example, social work and youth work – require voluntary experience before accepting training entrants.
- Voluntary work keeps people active and in contact with others, often leading to a widening of friendships.
- Volunteers who are unemployed will not stop receiving benefits if they are still available for full-time work and are actively seeking work. Details can be checked with the Benefits Agency.
- Through the government's recent initiative for Millennium Volunteers – expanding volunteer activity across the 16-24 age group within local communities – participants gain formal recognition of their achievements by having MV on their CV and receiving a certificate after 100 hours of volunteer work, and an MV Award of Excellence after 200 hours of voluntary activity. The Department for Education and Employment (DfEE) is funding a large number of proposals for voluntary projects, in areas as wide-ranging as language development for ethnic communities, football training, crime prevention, mentoring and study support.

Voluntary work

Positive aspects	**- training**
	- new skills
	- getting qualifications
	- a job trial
Prospects	**- further training**
	- paid employment
	- other voluntary work
Benefits for the volunteer	**- sense of achievement**
	- meeting other people
	- regular activity
	- positive use of skills and energy
Benefits for the recipient	**- things get done which, perhaps, would not have happened**
	- quality of life is improved

Voluntary opportunities

There is a vast range of possibilities in volunteering, and before opting for one particular area, consider the following points:

- It is highly desirable that a volunteer chooses an organisation which is of interest to them and which they care about – perhaps choosing an activity that they enjoy doing or want to learn to do.
- As a first step, potential volunteers need to get information and advice on all aspects of volunteering from their local volunteer bureau, which will be listed in the telephone directory. Alternatively, they should contact one of the national agencies listed at the end of the chapter.

Among the main areas of voluntary work are:

Counselling

Organisations like Relate or The Samaritans provide a long and thorough training for volunteers. Other counselling organisations may be listed in Yellow Pages.

Education

Volunteers can help with basic skills training – in adult literacy programmes or numeracy tutoring – or help in special schools or sheltered work places, working with people who have learning difficulties. Training is usually given.

Contact: *Local education authority, library, community centre, school or adult education department.*

For those interested in being a volunteer tutor in Northern Ireland:

The Reading and Writing Help Service (Northern Ireland) – *2nd Floor, Glendinning House, 6 Marray Street, Belfast BT1 6DN. Tel: 028 9032 2488.*
E-mail: abess@egsq.dnet.co.uk.
The service can refer callers on, to an appropriate course.

Advice and information

Volunteers work in Citizens Advice Bureaux, independent advice centres, legal aid centres and law surgeries, and for welfare rights projects. Most of these organisations provide training.

Consult: *The phone book or Yellow Pages, under counselling and advice.*

Environmental work

Volunteers help to conserve the countryside – conserving energy, animal and plant life and natural resources, to preserve urban wildlife, conserve buildings and landscapes. Many organisations for the environment offer training in environmental skills. Some offer short, residential working breaks.

Some of the organisations offering voluntary opportunities:

Friends of the Earth (FoE)
Their activities are divided into local and national levels. At national level, campaign areas include energy, pesticides and water, urban transport issues, tropical rainforests, air pollution and countryside issues. At local level, groups are involved in practical projects – these activities may vary from area to area as each group acts independently. The head office has the addresses of active local groups.

Friends of the Earth – 26-28 Underwood Street, London NI 7JQ. Tel: 020 7490 1555.
Website: www.foe.co.uk E-mail: info@foe.co.uk

CPRE (Council for the Protection of Rural England)
Works towards maintaining a living and beautiful countryside through action on conservation issues and planning casework. There is a branch in every county and committees in many district boroughs. It is a registered charity. The national office below has details of local branches and their training programmes.

CPRE – 25 Buckingham Palace Road, London SW11 0PP. Tel: 020 7976 6433
Website address: www.greenchannel E-mail: cpre@gn.apc.org

British Trust for Conservation Volunteers (BTCV)

BTCV is the UK's leading practical conservation charity. Every year it supports over 95,000 volunteers from all sections of the community in activities to promote and improve their environment.

The work involved is diverse – from a few hours a week to full-time, from planting a local community garden to a working holiday repairing footpaths in Iceland. Areas of expertise include sand-dune conservation, drystone walling, fencing, path work, scrub clearance, coppicing and hedge laying.

Training is provided and there are opportunities to manage projects. Work can also lead to nationally recognised qualifications such as NVQs. Many of the volunteers go on to successful careers in environmental and related fields.

BTCV – 36 St Mary's Street, Wallingford OXI0 0EU. Tel: 01491 839766.
Conservation Volunteers Northern Ireland (CVNI) – 159 Ravenhill Road, Belfast BT6 0BP. Tel: 028 9064 5169.

BTCV – Gwarchodwyr Cefn Gwlad, Wales Conservation Centre, Forest Farm Road, Whitchurch, Cardiff CF4 7JH. Tel: 029 2052 0990/2181.

The Scottish Conservation Projects – Balallan House, 24 Allan Park, Stirling FK3 2QG. Tel: 01786 479697.

Website:www.btcv.org.uk E-mail: information@btcv.org.uk

The Tree Council

Promotes tree planting and the care of trees for environmental purposes and promotes and co-ordinates the National Grid Tree Warden Scheme and WPA Trees Love Care Days. There is a free periodical Tree News and a small range of publications. Organises annual Esso National Tree Week in November and December and Esso Walk in the Wood in May.

The Tree Council – 51 Catherine Place, London SWIE 6DY. Tel: 020 7828 9928.
Website: www.treecouncil.org.uk

Greenpeace

Greenpeace is an independent and non-political, international organisation, dedicated to protecting the environment by peaceful means.

Greenpeace – Canonbury Villas, London N1 2PN. Tel: 020 7865 8100.
Website address: greenpeace.org E-mail: info@uk.greenpeace.org

National Trust – Working Holidays, PO Box 84, Cirencester, Gloucestershire GL7 1ZP. Tel: Brochure hotline 0891 517 751 (calls cost 50p a minute)

Marine Conservation Society – 9 Gloucester Road, Ross-on-Wye, Herefordshire HRJ 5BU. Tel: 01989 566017.

Volunteering through New Deal

For those who have been out of work and claiming benefit for at least six months, New Deal provides the opportunity to work for at least 30 hours a week for a six-month period with the Environment Task Force or ETF. This includes the equivalent of one day's training which can lead to qualifications. Workers get an allowance equal to their Jobseeker's Allowance, plus an extra £400 paid in equal installments over the six-month period. On New Deal, the first £4 of weekly travel expenses are also paid. The ETF works on community projects, helping to enhance, conserve and protect features of the local environment.

 **Contact:** ***New Deal personal advisers***, *based at Jobcentres.*

Work with children and young people

Youth work, organised by local education or leisure departments and other organisations – nurseries, crêches and toddler activity clubs, play groups, social clubs, Guides, Scouts, Woodcraft Folk, St John Ambulance, British Red Cross – all requires volunteer helpers. Most groups provide training for their volunteers. Many paid youth workers started out as voluntary helpers. Volunteers working with young people have to agree to screening against police records.

 **Contact:** *The organisations listed above, either at local level or through their national headquarters.*

Working for Childcare

The group campaigns for more positive policies and provision in employer-related childcare, and advises and consults on setting up childcare facilities.

Working for Childcare – 77 Holloway Road, London N7 8JZ. Tel: 020 7700 0281. Website address: www.wfc.org.uk

Social and health services

Thousands of volunteers help in hospitals and with social services departments or the probation service.

 **Contact:** *The Voluntary Service Organiser (VSO) based in hospitals, social services departments or within the probation service.*

Action in the community

Many volunteers have ideas for new projects in their area – such as building an adventure playground, clearing up wasteland, running a campaign for safer roads, helping with crime prevention or setting up a lunch club for elderly people. But they may need advice and support to enable them to make a start.

☞ **Contact:** *the local* ***Council for Voluntary Service (England)****,*
County Voluntary Council (Wales)*,*
Council for Social Service (Scotland)*,*
Council for Voluntary Action (Northern Ireland)
or ***Rural Community Council****. These bodies can give potential volunteers advice about ongoing local initiatives and on how to go about a project, the legal position, how to raise money and so on. They may also run training courses for members of local projects.*

Campaign for Nuclear Disarmament (CND)
Volunteers are wanted for one to two days a week in London.
CND – 162 Holloway Road, London N7 8DQ. Tel: 020 7700 2393.
E-mail: cnd@gn.apc.org Website address: www.cnduk.org

For further information

At the local level:

- Volunteer bureaux in towns and villages
- Council for Voluntary Service (if there is no volunteer bureau)
- Rural Community Council (if there is no volunteer bureau).

Addresses are in the phone book.

At the national level:
The organisations listed below can provide information and advice on most aspects of volunteering. They produce publications and provide training courses, or can steer enquirers to other organisations that help individuals to find suitable voluntary work.

UK

The National Centre for Volunteering – Information Sheets, Regent's Wharf, 8 All Saints Street, London N1 9LR. Tel: 020 7520 8900. Can provide useful free factsheets if you send an A4 stamped addressed envelope. Mark the envelope clearly with the names of the leaflets you want.
The Spirit of Volunteering – a guide to getting into voluntary work (needs a 38p stamp), also, Volunteers working with children; Finding out about volunteering in your area; Residential volunteering in the UK; Volunteers' welfare benefits and taxation; Volunteering overseas; a list of information sources; Accreditation of voluntary work; Volunteer drivers and tax.

Millennium Volunteer helpline: 0800 917 8185 can signpost local organisations which have successfully bid for funds to run volunteer projects.

England

The National Association of Volunteer Bureaux – New Oxford House, 16 Waterloo Street, Birmingham B2 5UG. Tel: 0121 633 4555 or e-mail: navbteam@waverider.co.uk
Contact for information on local volunteer bureaux. Their useful publication: *The Volunteer Bureaux Directory* – £8.00. ISBN 0 952773 360 9, may be held in reference libraries.

Youth for Britain – Higher Orchard, Sandford Orcas, Sherborne, Dorset DT9 4RP. Tel: 01963 220036. A charity which holds a computer database of volunteer opportunities which can be matched to an individual's availability and experience. May be found in local careers centres or public libraries.

British Trust for Conservation Volunteers (BTCV) – 36 St Mary's Street, Wallingford, Oxfordshire OX10 0EU. Tel: 01491 839766. E-mail: natural-break@btcv.org.uk
Website: www.btcv.org.uk

Offers volunteer placements lasting several months, which are suitable for those interested in an environmental career. Publishes the leaflet – *Volunteering for a Better Career*, free to those sending a stamped addressed envelope.

Northern Ireland

Northern Ireland Volunteer Development Agency – 70-74 Ann Street, Belfast BT1 4EH
Tel: 028 9023 6100. E-mail: info.nivda@cinni.org

Their useful publications: *Residential Volunteer Opportunities in Northern Ireland* and *So You want to be a Volunteer? – a guide for those interested in volunteering* are free from the above address, but please enclose an A4 stamped addressed envelope.

Scotland

Volunteer Development Scotland – 72 Murray Place, Stirling FK8 2BX. Tel: 01786 479593.
E-mail vds@vds.org.uk Website: www.vds.org.uk

Learning Link Scotland (LLS) – c/o SCVO, 18-19 Claremont Crescent, Edinburgh EH7 4QD.
Tel: 0131 556 3882. E-mail sarah.morton@scvo.org.uk

Members are voluntary organisations which provide adult education in Scotland. Contact LLS for details of these organisations, training events and meetings.

Wales

Wales Council for Voluntary Action (WCVA) – Information and Research, Llys Ifor, Crescent Road, Caerphilly CF83 1XL. Tel: 029 2085 5100. E-mail enquiries@wcva.org.uk
Website: www.wcva.org.uk

Publishes *A Short Guide to Volunteering Opportunities in Wales* free to enquirers sending a stamped addressed envelope.

Voluntary work away from home

Community Service Volunteers (CSV) – 237 Pentonville Road, London NI 9NJ. Hotline: 0800 374 991. CSV specialises in placing people aged 16-35 in full-time voluntary work away from home, to help people in need, for periods of between four and 12 months. Volunteers receive full board and accommodation, travel costs and pocket money. Regional offices are listed in local phone directories.

Voluntary work overseas

This usually requires a commitment of one or more years. The main overseas voluntary organisations usually ask for professionally trained people to go to a particular country for at least a year. However, it is possible to go for shorter periods. To find out more:

 **Contact:** *The Information Section of the* **National Centre for Volunteering** *(address and telephone above) sending a stamped addressed A4 envelope marked Volunteering Overseas.*

Returned Volunteer Action (RVA) – *1 Amwell Street, London ECIR 1TH. Tel: 020 7278 7019 for the useful publication – Thinking About Volunteering – which provides a full range of information on overseas volunteering opportunities. Price: £3.50. Please enclose a stamped addressed A4 envelope.*

In Scotland

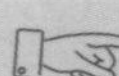 **Contact:** ***Community Learning Scotland*** – *International Services, Rosebery House, 9 Haymarket Terrace, Edinburgh, EH12 5EZ. Tel: 0131 313 2488. E-mail cls@cls.dircon.co.uk Can provide a signposting Eurodesk service for young people aged 15 to 25.*

Further information

The following three publications are available from the Central Bureau for Educational Visits and Exchanges. Postage and packing are free in the UK.

Volunteer Work – £8.99. ISBN 1 898601 04 6
A Year Between – £9.99. ISBN 1 898601 13 5
Working Holidays 1999 – £9.99 ISBN 1898601 26 7

Worldwide Volunteering for Young People – 1999 Directory – £15.95. ISBN 1 85703 397 3
Doing Voluntary Work Abroad – £9.99 ISBN. 185703 132 6. Available from How To Books Ltd.

The International Directory of Voluntary Work – £15.99 plus £1.50 p&p. ISBN 185458 164 3.
Green Volunteers – £10.99. ISBN 88 900167 1 X
Both are available from the publisher Vacation Work.

A Year Off ... A Year On? – £8.99. ISBN 1 873408 64 1. Published by Lifetime Careers Publishing.

Working In The Voluntary Sector – £5.00. ISBN 0 86110 702 0. Published by COIC.

Section 3 Specialist information for particular groups

25. Unemployment

This chapter covers:

- government-funded adult training
- New Deal and other initiatives
- help for ex-service personnel
- adult and community education
- studying while on benefits.

Recent years have seen dramatic changes in employment patterns. Many traditional industries and jobs have disappeared while others have grown. Prospective employers agree that having a positive attitude is vital. There are many ways in which the unemployed can be helped into education and employment.

Training Enterprise Councils and Local Enterprise Councils

There are 78 TECs in England and Wales, and 22 LECs in Scotland, offering training and business enterprise services through organisations and employers in local areas.

 **Contact:** *Local TECs/LECs for information about Work-based Learning for Adults.*

Employment Service

Employment Service advisers at the Jobcentres can advise on employment and training opportunities which are available. Throughout the period of looking for work, the client attends the Jobcentre for regular reviews and Restart Interviews.

 **Contact:** *Jobcentres and Employment Services for details of schemes to help the unemployed, including New Deal. Website: www.employmentservice.gov.uk*

Training Access Points (TAPS)

These are easy-to-use databases found in most local libraries, careers centres and Jobcentres, with information on education and training opportunities in the local area.

Government-funded adult training

There are many government-funded schemes to help the unemployed, organised and administered by the Employment Service. The various schemes come into operation after a set period of unemployment, although they can be accessed earlier by certain groups.

For those who have been jobseeking for 13 weeks or more:

Jobsearch provision

Help is focused on the individual and is available with:

- writing CVs
- applying for jobs
- interview techniques etc.

There are resource areas where jobseekers can use telephones, stationery, stamps, photocopiers etc.

Those who have been on Work-based Learning, returners to work, people who have spent time in prison, and ex-service personnel may access this provision immediately.

Travel to Interview Scheme

This scheme can help towards the cost of travelling to an interview; however, there are certain conditions. To qualify for financial assistance, the job should be:

- beyond daily travelling distance from home
- expected to last at least 12 months, and
- for 30 hours a week or more.

Employment on Trial

This enables someone getting Jobseeker's Allowance to find work and, provided they work more than four weeks and less than 13 weeks, keep their JSA.

For those who have been jobseeking for six months:

Clients will be asked to attend a Restart Interview. This gives a chance to review the situation and access other useful programmes and services, including:

Job Interview Guarantee Scheme

The employer guarantees to interview people with the right skills and experience who have been selected by the Employment Service.

Work Trials

These last up to three weeks, and give jobseekers the opportunity to show employers their skills. As these trials are voluntary, benefits are not affected if you fail to attend or leave early. Extra financial help is available with travel and meal expenses.

Work-based Learning for Adults (WBLA)

WBLA is available through TECs, CCTEs (Chambers of Commerce, Training and Enterprise) and LECs and their training providers. It aims to help adults without work move into sustained employment, including self-employment, through Work-based Learning. It is open to people aged 25 to 63 who have been out of work for more than six months. Similar schemes operate in Wales, through the Welsh TECs, and in Scotland (where it is known as Training for Work) through the Scottish LECs.

Chapter 19 has more details about Work-based Learning for Adults: financial assistance, eligibility, etc.

For those who have been jobseeking for 18 months:

Jobfinder Plus

The jobseeker attends a series of interviews with an adviser, and gets help tailored to their individual needs. If they do not attend Jobfinder Plus interviews, they may lose benefits. Help may involve:

- finding a job
- where to look for vacancies
- sending letters, applying for jobs, writing CVs etc
- updating skills.

New Deal

New Deal is part of the government's Welfare to Work strategy, giving special help to the long-term unemployed. It offers help in getting a job through advice, support, quality training and work experience.

Website: www.newdeal.gov.uk

Telephone: 0845 606 0680

Under New Deal, for those aged between 18 and 24 and claiming Jobseeker's Allowance (JSA) for six months or more:

A personal adviser will aim to find an unsubsidised job for the client. If a job cannot be found during the first few months, there are four options to choose from:

- a subsidised job with an employer for six months (or help in setting up a business)
- work with the Environment Task Force
- voluntary work
- full-time education or training.

At least one day a week is spent training during the New Deal option.

Certain groups of people do not have to observe the six months rule. They include disabled people, returners to work, ex-service personnel, ex-offenders, lone parents, people whose first language is not English, Welsh or Gaelic, people who need special help with basic literacy and numeracy, and people unemployed through large scale redundancy.

Finances

Those who start on New Deal will continue to get JSA while studying the options.

- Those in subsidised employment get the going rate for the job.
- There are grants available to top up JSAs for those who opt for the Environment Task Force or voluntary work.
- Those who go into full-time education and training will get the equivalent of the JSA.

New Deal allowances will not affect entitlement to other benefits such as Housing Benefit, Council Tax benefit etc.

Under New Deal, for those aged 25+ and claiming Jobseeker's Allowance for two years or more (18 months in Northern Ireland):
A personal adviser will organise a series of interviews over six months, and offer practical help with jobsearching, applications and interviews, work-based training, subsidised employment etc. Measures of extra support include:

- Jobplan workshop – a five-day, full-time programme of assessment
- Jobclub – a two-week, part-time course on jobsearch skills, plus practical help at a resource centre for up to 26 weeks – free use of stationery, photocopier etc
- Jobfinders Grant – a one-off payment of £200 if a job offers less than £150 per week
- seeking self-employment.

Certain groups do not have to observe the two years or more rule, and may be eligible after one year. These include disabled people, people who need help with literacy and numeracy, people whose first language is not English, Welsh or Gaelic, ex-offenders and the homeless.

New Deal for lone parents

This is available for anyone looking after at least one school-aged child of their own, who is making a new or repeated claim for Income Support, and all lone parents who are already claiming Income Support. A New Deal personal adviser will have information about job vacancies and training opportunities, childcare, and specialist help for disabled clients, and will also help the client put together a personal development plan.

 **Contact:** *Helpline 0800 868 868*

New Deal for disabled people

This offers a personal adviser service to those who want to get into work or stay in work. In some pilot areas, it is helping people who claim incapacity benefits get into work.

New Deal for jobseekers with disabilities

This offers help to those receiving Jobseeker's Allowance who have a disability or health condition – help and guidance to choose the route into work which best suits the needs of the client.

Chapter 29 has more specific information on education and training for people with disabilities, and has a section on seeking employment.

Finances

There are benefits and programmes through New Deal which may help to overcome financial difficulties.

- ***Childcare costs***

  Extra help is available to pay for childcare costs, through in-work benefits. Up to £60 of costs may be disregarded when benefits are calculated.

- ***Family Credit***

  For people who work 16 hours a week or more and have dependent children.

- ***Back to Work Bonus***

  Available to those who have been entitled to JSA or Income Support for 91 days or more and working part-time while claiming benefit. Built up to a bonus of £1000, it is paid as a tax-free lump sum when the claimant has moved off JSA or Income Support, because of hours worked or amounts earned.

- ***Employers' national insurance contribution holiday***

  Any employer who takes on a person who has been out of work for at least two years can claim back national insurance for up to a year. This may help with employment prospects.

- ***Housing Benefit and Council Tax Benefit***

  Local council offices have the details. Extended payments of Housing Benefit and Council Tax Benefit may be available for an extra four weeks after the end of JSA or Income Support.

- ***Career Development Loans***

  Loans are available to help pay for vocational training. Study can be full-time or part-time, open or distance learning. Loans can cover course fees and materials, and are available from major banks. No repayments are paid during the period of study. Contact 0800 585 505 for an information booklet, or your local TEC/LEC, college or training centre.

Employment Credit

In measures announced in the 1999 Budget, the government is intending to offer a combined package of New Deal for the over 50s and an Employment Credit, to be delivered by the Employment Service. This will include a wages top up to bring those on benefit who find full-time work to the minimum wage level, an enhanced personal adviser service, in-work training grants and a self-employment option.

Other initiatives

Employment Service Direct

A national job hotline for unemployed people looking for work. Callers are connected to an Employment Service recruitment adviser with immediate access to a national database, which holds details of 300,000 vacancies employers are trying to fill.

Tel: 0845 60 60 234: Monday to Friday 9am to 6pm; Saturday 9am to 1pm.

New Deal for partners of unemployed people

Partners of people receiving JSA for six months or more are offered guidance and advice from Employment Service personal advisers.

Employment Zones

This is a new programme. From April 2000, Employment Zones will target resources on unemployed people over 25 in at least 14 areas of the country which suffer from persistently high long-term unemployment. Those in the zones who have been claiming JSA for 12-18 months will agree an action plan with a personal adviser. If they have not found work after three months, they will have access to a Personal Job Account – designed to enable people to set up their own business, improve their skills or gain extra help in finding employment.

Jobskills programme

The Jobskills programme in Northern Ireland is aimed at people seeking to enter or return to work. Trainees include those under 22 who are unemployed and have a disability; and 16-24 year olds following a Modern Apprenticeship.

 **Contact:** *The local Training and Employment Agency Jobcentre.*

Chapter 19 has more information about the Jobskills programme.

Action for Community Employment (ACE)

Only in Northern Ireland, this provides temporary employment of up to one year's duration in a wide range of projects of community benefit. Up to 20% of time is spent on training activities, where possible achieving an NVQ. Those aged between 18 and 64, and unemployed for 12 months, are eligible; those aged 18 to 24 need only have been unemployed for six months. There are special conditions for those registered as disabled.

Community Work programme

A Northern Ireland programme aimed at those unemployed for a year or more, which offers work and training opportunities, on projects of benefit to the community, for up to three years. Participants get a training allowance equivalent to their benefit entitlement, plus an additional training premium. *Action for Community Employment and the Community Work Programme are being phased out.*

Worktrack

A Northern Ireland programme to replace ACE, designed to give advice and guidance to those unemployed for 12-18 months. Its aims are: to develop the skills and competencies of the long-term unemployed; to develop their capacity for seeking, finding and retaining employment; to raise, with employers, the potential of the candidates.

Help for ex-service personnel

Various agencies exist to provide ex-servicemen and women with advice and assistance on employment opportunities and jobseeking. They include:

Regular Forces Employment Association (RFEA)

The RFEA offers service leavers of all ranks a lifelong local job-finding service from 39 branches throughout the UK, provided they have served more than three years, been medically discharged – regardless of length of service – or been made redundant.

 **Contact:** *RFEA – 49 Pall Mall, London SE1Y 5JG. Tel: 020 2321 2011. Website: www.interreach.com.rfea E-mail: rfea@primex.co.uk*

Officers' Association (OA)

The OA has an employment department providing job information and advice for ex-officers. Weekly vacancy lists are circulated.

 **Contact:** *Officers' Association – HQ Royal British Legion, 48 Pall Mall, London SW1Y 5JY. Tel: 020 7930 0125. Website: www.oaed.org.uk/oaed E-mail: postmaster@oaed.org.uk*

The Corps of Commissionaires

The Corps operates as an employment agency and maintains close links with employers. To register:

 **Contact:** *Corps of Commissionaires – Suite 15e, Joseph's Well, Hanover Walk, Westgate, Leeds LS3 1AB. Tel: 0113 245 4293.*

Service Leavers' Support Team (SLST)

The SLST have a number of centres acting as Jobclubs and information centres and obtaining job information from local employers. For addresses of local centres:

 **Contact:** *SLST – HQ Land G1, Erskine Barracks, Wilton, Salisbury SP2 0AG.*

Adult and community education

Many colleges and adult education centres have courses for unemployed people. They may teach new skills, help to get a qualification, or develop ideas about new jobs, as well offering help with the practical problems of unemployment.

 **Contact:** *The local TEC or LEC, educational guidance services for adults, Jobcentre, college, library, or Citizens Advice Bureau.*

Informal learning and self-help

Schools and colleges often have a range of activities, clubs and classes for the local community, and these may include informal learning groups, or the opportunity to set one up. Groups of this kind can give invaluable practical and personal support for the unemployed, and are often available to unwaged people at reduced or nominal rates.

Contact: *Libraries have information about local schools and colleges.*

There are various drop-in and self-help groups operating through the work of voluntary organisations, frequently through local councils for voluntary service. For information about local groups:

Contact: *The Citizens Advice Bureau or library*

Open Learning

As long as the individual is available for work and willing to accept a job, it is possible to study by open learning without losing benefits. There could be a problem with any residential study weeks or periods of full-time tuition. The course organiser needs to be informed, and you can get benefits advice from the Benefits Agency, students' union or college counsellor if necessary.

Studying while on benefits

If you are unemployed and claiming benefit, it is possible to follow a course of study and continue to claim benefits, as long as certain conditions are fulfilled.

Those not entitled to Jobseeker's Allowance

- Full-time students under 19 years of age, attending a full-time course of advanced education.
- Those doing a course which involves more than 16 guided learning hours a week. The number of guided learning hours are in the learning agreement signed by the educational establishment.

- Those attending a full-time course of study which is not funded (in whole or in part) by the Further Education Funding Council (FEFC). In this case there is no definition of full-time and the benefits officer will have to make a decision based on the description of the course given by the educational establishment. If no such description is available, the officer takes account of all the relevant facts, including hours of guided and private study.

The only full-time students who can be entitled to JSA are:

- those with a partner (who is also a student) and a dependent child – this only applies during the summer vacation
- prisoners on temporary release
- those getting maternity allowance or statutory maternity pay.

Others, such as disabled students and lone parent students, will not be able to claim JSA, but will probably be entitled to Income Support.

Learning through New Deal

Full-time students on the full-time education or training option of New Deal receive an allowance equivalent to the JSA, as well as other benefits such as help with rent or paying Council Tax. Course providers will ensure that students have all the books, equipment and materials they need for their studies, and will refund fares to and from home.

Those who opt for vocational training full-time for up to a year can remain on JSA. The training must be vocational and must show that it will be a real help in finding employment.

Part-time students

Clients may be entitled to JSA provided they conform to the requirements of availability and are actively seeking work.

Paying for study

Non-advanced education and training

- There are no fees for studying as part of a government-funded programme which allows people to claim benefits or get a training allowance.
- Fees are payable for full-time courses at further education colleges or adult education centres. Clients need to apply direct to the college for information about access funds.
- Part-time and short courses may have reduced fees for the unemployed, depending on the college's policy.
- Individual learning accounts – a government initiative acting as a saving for learning account to enable people to think about and invest in their own learning.

Advanced education and training

- Adults entering higher education should apply to their LEA for help with fees, loans etc.
- From September 1999, fees will be waived to people in receipt of benefits on certain part-time higher education courses (see Chapter 4 for more details)
- There may be extra help available through access funds and hardship loans – managed by the individual institutions.

- Some open colleges have reduced fees for unemployed people.
- The Open University (OU) has grant funds for those in receipt of benefit. From February 2000, the grants will cover the cost of fees entirely.

Further information

Unemployment and Training Rights Handbook 1999 – published by the Unemployment Unit/Youthaid, 322 St John Street, London EC1V 4NT. Tel: 020 7833 1222.

Available from Trotman & Company Ltd:

Developing your Employment Skills – £8.99. ISBN 0 85660 308 2
Promoting Yourself at Interview – £8.99. ISBN 0 85660 299 X
Applying for a Job – £8.99. ISBN 85703 245 4
The 1999 What Colour is Your Parachute? – £13.99. ISBN 1 58008 008 1
Job-Hunting on the Internet – £9.99. ISBN 1 58008 078 2
Finding a Job on the Internet – £16.99. ISBN 1 84925 310 X
Employability – £12.99. ISBN 0 7494 2408 7.

Available from Kogan Page:

Readymade CVs – £8.99. ISBN 07494 1947 4
Readymade Interview Questions – £8.99. ISBN 07494 1942 3
Readymade Jobsearch Letters – £8.99. ISBN 0 7494 1678 5
Successful Interview Skills – £7.99. ISBN 0 7494 2978 X
Preparing Your Own CV – £6.99. ISBN 0 7494 2852 X
Net That Job! – £8.99. ISBN 0 7494 2574 1
Great Answers to Tough Interview Questions – £8.99. ISBN 0 7494 2656 X

Available from How To Books:

Enhancing Your Employability – £9.99. ISBN 1 85703 371 X
Surviving Redundancy – £9.99. ISBN 1 85703 187 3
Starting Your Own Business – £9.99. ISBN 1 85703 274 8

26. People with children and other dependants

This chapter covers:

- National Childcare Strategy
- carers of children – finances; how and when to study
- childcare provision
- organisations which can help
- help for carers of other dependants.

National Childcare Strategy

The government's National Childcare Strategy was initiated a year ago, linking local authorities, private and voluntary sectors, TECs, employers and FE colleges, to improve and extend childcare provision. It includes:

- **Childcare places** – provision for one million children over the next five years. At present, there is a guarantee of a free nursery place for each child from the beginning of the term in which they are four – for five two-and-a-half hour sessions a week. Increasingly, primary schools are creating nursery units to accommodate four year olds. Plans to increase the number of free nursery places for three year olds will provide 41,500 new places from September 1999. Most of them will be in the private and voluntary sectors. By 2001/2, the proportion of three year olds in free places will be 66%.
- **Early Excellence Centres** – developing models of high quality education and daycare for young children. The aim is to support families so that more people can access adult education and training.
- **Childcare Information Systems Development Project** which will link databases to a national website containing childcare information and details of childcare providers across England.
- **Childcare Information Service**, which is being developed at the same time, will be a freephone service to the public, signposting local services, and offering general information leaflets. ***Both are set to be launched in Autumn 1999.***

The government is also helping parents through **Sure Start**, which is a community-based project to join up services for under-fours and their parents. Some pilot schemes have already been developed and programmes for them will be up and running by the end of the summer. Another round of applications will be made in the Autumn.

Carers of children

Fulfilling the role of parent or carer while taking a course of education or training is very demanding. Childcare should be organised around a suitable course; time to study needs to fit in with the family routine. Forward planning, involving all those who are likely to be affected, is essential. Levels of childcare vary and there is generally a cost.

Financial assistance

- **New Deal for lone parents** – gives financial assistance with suitable childcare, and help with the childcare expenses involved in attending meetings with an adviser. Lone parents can take part in Work-based Learning for Adults without waiting for the six month rule. Childcare expenses may also be available through WBLA.

More details about financial assistance for childcare under New Deal can be found in Chapter 25 – Unemployment.

- **Family Credit** – for people who work 16 hours or more a week and have dependant children. Paid at a fixed rate for 26 weeks. Family Credit helpline: 01253 500 050.
- **Child Maintenance Bonus** – for parents who get child maintenance from an absent partner. Available where one of the partners leaves Income Support or JSA, the bonus will build up in weekly amounts to a possible maximum of £1000.
- **Childcare costs while working** – extra help is available through in-work benefits. Up to £60 of certain childcare costs may be disregarded when Family Credit, Disability Working Allowance, Housing Benefit and Council Tax Benefit awards are calculated.
- The new **Childcare Tax Credit** will pay up to £70 a week for childcare with registered services.

How and when to study
The **Learning Direct** helpline (0800 100 900) can advise on childcare for people returning to education or training. Available from 9am to 9pm Monday to Friday; 9am to 12pm Saturday.

People with children who are under school age can:

- find someone to look after them such as a childminder
- study at home
- find a college or training centre where they have childcare facilities.

People with children of school age can:

- find a course which fits in with the school day
- organise after-school care
- study at home.

As there often isn't a single solution to the problem of childcare, parents usually choose a combination of options.

- Studying at home is a good option, unless the idea is to return to education to meet people.
- More and more colleges are developing courses to fit in with a school day. 9.30am – 3pm is quite common to find, in response to people returning to study.
- Course tutors will discuss childcare concerns with the student – courses are publicised at certain times, but it is amazing how flexible they can be. It may be possible to extend the length of the course and lighten the workload in each year if this is appropriate
- It may not be necessary for mature students to complete all modules of the course. Previous experience may qualify them for accreditation of prior learning. APL gives credit for experience and related qualifications. Students have to prove their previous qualifications and experience with certificates and references, and be ready to have to demonstrate their skills to a tutor. Tutors will know exactly what is required to gain exemption from individual modules.

Open and distance learning

Open learning is a possibility for those who cannot find a place at a local college or training centre. It usually involves the individual studying at home supported by course notes. There are often opportunities for tutorials as well. The Open University has a range of diploma and degree courses, and there are no formal entry requirements. The main entry criterion is the will to study. There is a residential element to OU courses which lasts from two days to one week. Family members are not normally allowed at these summer schools, so care arrangements will have to be made.

Childcare provision

Nurseries

Some colleges have a college crêche or nursery and may offer places to students at subsidised rates.

There are privately-run and workplace nurseries which may accommodate children for part of, or the whole, day, generally opening between 8am and 6pm daily. Local authority or other community-based nurseries are generally more restricted in opening times – usually for the normal school day.

Playgroups

Playgroups usually charge a small fee and take children under school age for two to three hours a day for one to five days a week.

 **Contact:**

Pre-school Learning Alliance – 69 King's Cross Road, London WC1X 9LL. Tel: 020 7833 0991. Helpline number: Tel: 020 7837 5513.

Wales Pre-school Playgroups Association – 2a Chester Street, Wrexham LL13 8BD. Tel: 01978 358195.

Scottish Pre-school Play Association – 14 Elliot Place, Glasgow G3 8EP. Tel: 0141 221 4148. E-mail: pla@pre-school.org.uk

NIPPA – The Early Years Organisation – 6e Wildflower Way, Apollo Road, Belfast BT12 6TA. Tel: 028 9066 2825. E-mail: mail@nippa.org

Playgroup Network

A national voluntary organisation supporting playgroups and parent and toddler groups with training and information to allow them to provide for the needs of their children and families through community groups.

 **Contact:** *Playgroup Network – PO Box 23, Whitley Bay NE26 3DB. Tel: 01642 319030.*

Childminders

Childminders look after other people's children at the childminder's home. Social Services departments keep registers of childminders, who look after children under the age of eight.

The National Childminding Association (NCMA)

Produces a useful information pack for parents and those thinking of becoming a childminder. NCMA may also be able to give you a contact at a local group who may be able to help you. Send a 30p A5 size SAE for details.

 **Contact:** *NCMA – 8 Mason's Hill, Bromley BR2 9EY. Tel: 020 8290 6834. E-mail: natcma@netcomuk.co.uk*

Nannies

Some nannies are trained and have a childcare qualification such as the Diploma in Nursery Nursing. They can be employed on a daily or live-in basis. This option is generally expensive, so more people now consider sharing a nanny to keep the costs down.

Out-of-school schemes

There is an increasing number of after-school facilities for primary age children which also operate in the school holidays.

 **Contact:** *Local school or LEAs for details.*

Other useful organisations

The Parents at Work Association

Over 150 local groups offering mainly informal advice on childcare options in the local area. It produces a pack available from their headquarters in London.

 **Contact:** *Parents at Work Association – 45 Beech Street, Barbican, London EC2Y 8AD. Tel: 020 7628 3565.*

Daycare Trust

A charity which works for quality daycare for children, providing information to parents, and information and advice to employers. Campaigns on behalf of parents and providers of childcare to improve quality and accessibility.

 **Contact:** *Daycare Trust – Shoreditch Town Hall Annexe, 380 Old Street, London EC1V 9LT. Tel: 020 7739 2866. Website: www.daycaretrust.org.uk E-mail: info@daycaretrust.org.uk*

The National Childbirth Trust

Provides education for parents. There are nearly 400 branches throughout the UK, many of which have 'working mothers' groups. The Trust produces a range of leaflets and books including *Working Parents' Companion*, £9.99 plus £1 p&p.

 **Contact:** *The National Childbirth Trust – Alexandra House, Oldham Terrace, Acton, London W3 6NH. Tel: 020 8992 8637.*

National Council for One Parent Families

A training, advisory and information agency and pressure group for lone parents. It provides information on a wide range of subjects and runs regional Return to Work courses for lone parents. These cover issues such as childcare, finance, confidence building and employment and training opportunities. It publishes leaflets and booklets useful to lone parents.

 **Contact:** *National Council for One Parent Families – 255 Kentish Town Road, London NW5 2LX. Tel: 020 7428 5400 from 9.15am to 5.15pm weekdays.*

Gingerbread

A self-help organisation offering support to lone parents. It publishes a series of leaflets available from the London office who can also put you in touch with local groups. Enclose SAE.

Contact: *Gingerbread – 16-17 Clerkenwell Close, London ECIR 0AA. Tel: 020 7336 8183.*

Gingerbread Scotland – Community Central Hall, 304 Maryhill Road, Glasgow G20 7YE. Tel: 0141 353 0953.

Gingerbread Northern Ireland – 169 University Street, Belfast BT7 1HR. Tel: 028 9023 1417. Website: www.gingerbread.org.uk E-mail: office@gingerbread.org.uk

One Parent Families – Scotland

Provides a range of services for lone parents throughout Scotland, including information, guidance and support for lone parents who wish to access education, training or enter employment. Free information leaflets are available to lone parents plus some other publications, eg *Lone Parents' Rights Guide*, price £3, and *Choices Handbook (for Lone Parents Returning to Education or Training)*, price £7.50/free to lone parents.

Contact: *One Parent Families – Scotland – 13 Gayfield Square, Edinburgh EHI 3NX. Tel: 0131 556 3899/4563.*
Website: www.gn.apc.org/opfs
E-mail: opfs@gn.apc.org

Carers of other dependants

There is much less on offer for this group. Much of the help is in the form of support rather than actual care. There are some useful organisations.

Carers' National Association

Can advise on benefits and welfare. They can put people in touch with local support groups offering practical advice.

Contact: *Carers' National Association – 20-25 Glasshouse Yard, London EC1A 4JT. Tel: 020 7490 8818.*

Carersline: freephone 0808 808 7777
10am-12: 2pm-4pm Mondays to Fridays.

Crossroads

Has over 200 local schemes. A carer wishing to attend a course for a few hours a week is the sort of person they like to be able to help.

Contact: *Crossroads – Association Office, 10 Regent Place, Rugby CV21 2PN. Tel: 01788 573653.*

Council for Voluntary Service

Council for Voluntary Service may be able to offer local contacts for organisations which may be able to help.

Contact: *Council for Voluntary Service in local telephone directories.*

The British Red Cross Society

Provides some home caring, but the provision varies according to area.

 **Contact:** *The British Red Cross Society – 9 Grosvenor Crescent, London SW1X 7EJ. Tel: 020 7245 6315.*

Royal Society for Mentally Handicapped Children and Adults (MENCAP)

Aims to promote, in partnership with those concerned, the well-being of people with a mental handicap, and to help the families in supporting them. There are local societies in England, Wales and Northern Ireland. For names of local contacts:

 **Contact:** *Mencap – 123 Golden Lane, London ECIY 0RT. Tel: 020 7454 0454.*
Mencap – 31 Lambourne Crescent, Cardiff Business Park, Llanishen, Cardiff CF4 5GG. Tel: 029 2074 7588.

Mencap – Segal House, 4 Annadale Avenue, Belfast BT7 MH. Tel: 028 9069 1351.

Website: www.mencap.org.uk

Enable

Has over 70 branches providing support. For details of local provision:

 **Contact:** *ENABLE – Information Services, 6th Floor, 7 Buchanan Street, Glasgow G1 3HL. Tel: 0141 226 4541. E-mail: enable@enable.org.uk*

Further information

Choosing a Childminder: A Guide for Parents which covers issues like finding a childminder, questions to ask, settling your child and dealing with problems. £4.00 from National Childminding Association.

Successful Single Parenting: How to combine bringing up children with your other life goals, published by How To Books, £9.99. ISBN 185703 302 7.

27. Women

This chapter covers:

- campaign groups
- general networks
- training providers and development organisations
- professional and vocational organisations.

While women can use all the usual sources of help and information, there are also many special groups focusing on the needs of women in society. Only relevant national groups and networks are featured in this chapter.

Campaign groups

Women's National Commission

The official independent advisory body giving the views of women to government. Membership is drawn from many organisations representing political parties, trade unions, religious groups, professional associations and voluntary bodies. As well as giving advice to government on the views of women's organisations, it produces a *Directory of Women's Organisations in the UK*, various working group and conference reports, and guides for women wishing to gain public appointments.

 **Contact:** *WNC Secretariat – Cabinet Office, Room 56/4, Horse Guards Road, London SW1P 3AL. Tel: 020 7273 0386. Website: www.thewnc.org.uk E-mail: jolawren@cabinet-office.gov.uk*

Fawcett Society

A membership organisation campaigning for women's equality, including equal rights for part-time workers, fair state pensions for women and positive action awards for good practice in education.

 **Contact:** *The Fawcett Society – 5th Floor, 45 Beech Street, London EC2Y 8AD. Tel: 020 7628 4441. Website: www.gn.apc.org/fawcett E-mail: fawcett@gn.apc.org*

Equal Opportunities Commission

Promotes equal opportunities for men and women. Gives advice on discrimination in employment, for employers and employees.

Contact: *Equal Opportunities Commission – Overseas House, Quay Street, Manchester M3 3HN. Tel: 0161 833 9244.* Website: www.eoc.org.uk

General networks

Women Returners' Network

Women Returners' Network helps women return to education, training and employment. Its London office provides a national information service. It publishes a series of free resource sheets, and *Returning to Work, a Directory of Education and Training for Women*.

Contact: *Women Returners' Network – 100 Park Village East, London NW I 3SR. Tel: 020 7279 2900.*

British Federation of Women Graduates

Promotes women's opportunities in education and public life. It works as part of an international organisation to improve the lives of women and girls, and fosters local, national and international friendship. It awards scholarships for postgraduate research for students moving into their final year of study for a PhD.

Contact: *British Federation of Women Graduates – 4 Mandeville Courtyard, 142 Battersea Park Road, London SW11 4NB. Tel: 020 7498 8037. Website: homepages.wyenet.co.uk/bfwg E-mail: bfwg@bfwg.demon.co.uk*

Training providers and development organisations

The Industrial Society

Can help organisations develop and implement equal opportunities and women's development. It offers in-house advice and training and runs short courses throughout the country, some of which are residential. They address the needs of employees at all levels, and include management and personal development, interviewing skills, and career or life planning. For full details:

Contact: *The Industrial Society – Robert Hyde House, 48 Bryanston Square, London W1H 7LN. Tel: 020 7262 2401. Website: www.indsoc.co.uk E-mail: customercentre@indsoc.co.uk*

Young Women's Christian Association of Great Britain (YWCA)

Offers a wide range of formal and informal learning programmes for women aged 13-30 from YWCA projects throughout the country.

 **Contact:** *Youth and Community Department – YWCA HQ, Clarendon House, 52 Cornmarket Street, Oxford OXI 3EJ. Tel: 01865 304214.*

YWCA (Scottish National Council) – 7 Randolph Crescent, Edinburgh EH3 7TH. Tel: 0131 225 7592.

Website: ourworld.compuserve.com/homepages/YWCA/
E-mail: 101607.3174@compuserve.com

Women's Resource and Development Agency (Northern Ireland)

Organises women-only courses in Northern Ireland. Subjects include health, assertiveness and facilitation skills. The project's primary concern is to support women's groups in Northern Ireland. They offer courses in organisation and management skills, tutor training, training materials and back-up support.

 **Contact:** *Women's Resource and Development Agency – 6 Mount Charles, Belfast BT7 1NZ. Tel: 028 9023 0212. E-mail: wrda@iol.ie*

Women's Training Network

A national non-profit making membership organisation. It promotes targeted vocational training to disadvantaged women in areas where women are substantially under-represented, such as electronics, information technology and construction.

 **Contact:** *Women's Training Network – Northway Centre, Maltfield Road, Marston, Oxford OX3 9RF. Tel: 01865 741317. E-mail: owtf@globalnet.co.uk*

Professional and vocational organisations

There are many specialist professional and vocational organisations covering women in all areas of mostly professional work.

Women in Medicine

Provides support and a political voice for women doctors and medical students.

 **Contact:** *Women in Medicine – 21 Wallingford Avenue, London W10 6QA.*

Women into Science and Engineering

Encourages girls and women to consider careers in science and engineering.

 **Contact:** *The Engineering Council – 10 Maltravers Street, London WC2R 3ER. Tel: 020 7240 7891. Website: www.engc.org.uk E-mail: MNBarton@engc.org.uk*

Women's Engineering Society

Promotes the education, training and practice of engineering among women.

 **Contact:** *Women's Engineering Society – 2 Queen Anne's Gate Buildings, Dartmouth Street, London SW1H 9BP. Tel: 020 7233 1974. E-mail: info@wes.org.uk*

Business and Professional Women (UK) Ltd

Offers networking, training and personal development.

Contact: *BPW – 23 Ansdell Street, Kensington, London W8 5BN. Tel: 020 7938 1729.*

Northern Ireland Division – Linda Hutchinson, Divisional Training Coordinator, 217 Scrabo Road, Newtownards, Co. Down BT23 4SJ.

National Federation of Women's Institutes

Offers adult education in local institutes or WI's own Denman College, a residential college for members which has over 500 different courses each year, lasting from two to four days. The college sleeps up to 80 students a night.

Contact: *National Federation of Women's Institutes of England, Wales, the Channel Islands and the Isle of Man – 104 New Kings Road, London SW6 4LY. Tel: 020 7371 9300.*

Denman College – Marcham, Abingdon OX13 6NW. Tel: 01865 391991. Website: www.nfwi.org.uk E-mail: hq@nfwi.org.uk

Contact: *Scottish Women's Rural Institute – 42 Heriot Row, Edinburgh EH3 6ES. Tel: 0131 225 1724.*

Federation of Women's Institutes of Northern Ireland – 209-211 Upper Lisburn Road, Belfast BT10 0LL. Tel: 028 9043 1127.

Co-operative Women's Guilds

Branches throughout the UK to educate women of all ages. They campaign on issues affecting women.

 **Contact:** *Co-operative Women's Guild – 446 Hertford Road, Enfield, Middlesex EN3 5QH. Tel: 020 8804 5905.*

Scottish Co-operative Women's Guild – Robert Owen House, 87 Bath Street, Glasgow G2 2EE. Tel: 0141 304 5551.

Irish Women's Guild – 51 Ava Street, Belfast BT7 3BS. Tel: 028 9069 3824.

National Association of Women's Clubs

Advances education and provides facilities for leisure in order to improve women's lives. Each club is self-governing with its own activity programme.

Contact: *National Association of Women's Clubs – 5 Vernon Rise, King's Cross Road, London WC1X 9EP. Tel: 020 7837 1434.*

Further information

The Penguin Careers Guide – published by Penguin Books, Bath Road, Harmondsworth, Middlesex UB7 0DA. £9.99. ISBN 0 140 46 964 8. Information on job opportunities. The book covers areas such as management and working for oneself. A unique feature is the section under each job category which assesses the current position of, and opportunities for, women.

Career Women 2000 – published by Hobsons, £9.99. ISBN 1 86017648 8.

Women in the Workforce – published by HMSO Publications Centre, Orders Dept, PO Box 276, London SW8 5DT. Tel: 0870 600 5522. Price £19.95. ISBN 0 11495 733 9.

Successful Single Parenting; how to combine bringing up children with your own life and career – published by How To Books, £9.99. ISBN 185703 302 7.

Women Returning to Work – published by How To Books, £12.95. ISBN 1 85703 479 1.

Careers for Women in Medicine: Planning and Pitfalls – available free from the Department of Health, PO Box 410, Wetherby LS23 7LN.

The following two books are available from McGraw-Hill Publishing Company, Shoppenhangers Road, Maidenhead SL6 2QL. Tel: 01628 502500.

Reach for the Top: Women and the Changing Facts of Working Life – £9.99. ISBN 0 87584 739 0.

Reflections for Working Women – £9.99. ISBN 0 07065 5219.

28. Third age

This chapter covers:

- national organisation
- pre-retirement courses
- learning after retirement
- voluntary work
- useful organisations
- older workers
- projects supporting older workers.

The phrase Third Age is popularly used to describe the period in our lives after youth and middle-age.

In the UK, as in Europe as a whole, people are living longer, staying healthier and – quite rightly – expecting a better quality of life. In Europe as a whole, the number of older people as a proportion of total population is predicted to be 25% by 2020. The UK is consistently at the higher end of this demographic trend with about 24% over 60s predicted by 2020.

Older people may wish to study for many reasons.

- Work, full-time or part-time, paid or unpaid
- Citizenship, in order to continue to play a full civic role in their community
- Volunteering, which may require new knowledge or skills
- New technology, in order to keep pace with our changing environment and benefit from it
- Health and welfare support
- Socialising, to combat loneliness
- Fun and personal enrichment
- A desire for self knowledge
- To assimilate or transmit the past, to preserve heritage.

Many of these issues are the same for people of all ages, but older people may find that they are discriminated against because of people's preconceived ideas of what older people should and could do.

NIACE

NIACE is the national membership organisation for adult education and training in England and Wales. It promotes adult continuing education by improving the quality of opportunities available and widening their access.

Contact: *NIACE – 21 De Montfort Street, Leicester LE1 7GE. Tel: 0116 204 4200. Website: www.niace.org.uk E-mail: enquiries@niace.org.uk*

Wales Committee NIACE/NIACE Cymru – Welsh Joint Education Committee, Education Department,245 Wesdtern Avenue, Cardiff CF5 2YX. Tel: 029 2026 5000. E-mail: enquiries@niace.cy.demon.co.uk

Older and Bolder

The National Organisation for Adult Learning, NIACE, started this initiative. It aims to address the absence from education of those over 50 who are, or have been in some way, disadvantaged, and have not been involved in continuing education in any way. It does this through advising and informing all those interested in education and training for older people. NIACE is supported in this by other specialist organisations such as Age Concern, the U3A, and the PRA (see separate entries later in this chapter).

The Older and Bolder initiative:

- has developed a database of existing education and training provision for those aged 50 plus
- encourages positive planning of future provision to meet the unmet needs of older adults, by promoting working partnerships and shaping policy.

The initiative has also:

- published a policy discussion paper *Learning to Grow Older and Bolder*
- created regional and local networks to further the programme aims.

Contact: *Older and Bolder Development Officer, NIACE – 21 De Montfort Street, Leicester LE1 7GE.Tel: 0116 255 1451. Website: www.niace.org.uk E-mail: nicola@niace.org.uk*

Pre-retirement courses

The age at which people retire varies enormously. Pre-retirement courses can help with planning – they usually cover money, activities and leisure, health and relationships.

The Pre-Retirement Association (PRA)

The PRA is an independent national organisation in the fields of mid-career and pre-retirement planning and education. The Association runs a range of courses, catering for mid-life planning, career change, redundancy, early retirement and retirement.

Training for pre-retirement professionals is available through a short course programme, and as a part-time certificate course which offers qualification and accreditation to work as a recognised pre-retirement tutor or organiser. The certificate is validated by Surrey University.

PRA maintains and sells an annual directory of pre-retirement and mid-life courses, surveyed on a national basis, and publishes books and reports for pre-retirement professionals.

 **Contact:** *Rre-Retirement Association – 9 Chesham Road, Guildford GU1 3LS. Tel: 01483 301170. Website: pra.uk.com E-mail: info@pra.org.com*

Scottish Pre-Retirement Council (SRC)

SRC promotes education for retirement, as well as occupational activities for people in retirement throughout Scotland. It provides an information and advice service and organises pre-retirement courses on topics such as money, health, social living and leisure. It also carries out mid-life planning courses for people in their 40s; these are mainly financial planning.

 **Contact:** *The Scottish Pre-Retirement Council – Alexandra House, 204 Bath Street, Glasgow G2 4HL. Tel: 0141 332 9427. Website: www.sprc.org.uk E-mail: amcqown@talkzi.com*

Adult and community education centres

A number of adult education centres now run both day and evening courses.

Workers' Educational Association (WEA)

Many of the 900 branches of the WEA run pre-retirement courses.

 **Contact:** *WEA – Temple House, 17 Victoria Park Square, Bethnal Green, London E2 9PB. Tel: 020 8983 1515. Website: www.wea.org.uk*

A number of financial organisations also offer pre-retirement courses. Be aware that many see these courses as a commercial marketing opportunity.

Learning once retired

Many people take up new activities once retired, and in so doing gain new skills and knowledge without thinking of themselves as formally 'learning'. Many of the opportunities open to others listed in this book will also apply to older people, so the rest of this chapter is aimed at specific provision for older people.

What's available?

- In theory, most adult education and training is open to people of all ages.
- Vocational education, (training for a job), is affected by the availability of work in that field, and acceptance may be limited because of age. Professional bodies will have more information.

Course costs

- Most local authorities make some fee concessions for pensioners attending adult education classes, usually for the non-vocational courses
- For full-time higher education, apply for financial assistance to the LEA. Under 50 year olds can get a student loan; 50-54 year olds are entitled to a loan if they are planning to return to work after completing the course.
- If you need someone to care for you, or are yourself a carer, you may be eligible for special benefits.

Adult, community and further education

In some areas there are separate courses for older people provided by FE colleges, the adult education service, the Workers' Educational Association and others.

The Open University (OU)

Many OU students are retired people studying for pleasure. There are degree and non-degree courses.

 **Contact:** *Open University regional centres.*

The Open College of the Arts

Courses include art and design, drawing, painting, creative writing, music, photography, sculpture, textiles, garden design and history of art.

 **Contact:** *The Open College of the Arts – Hound Hill, Worsbrough, Barnsley S70 6TU. Tel: 01226 730495. Website: oca.uk.com E-mail: open.arts@ukonline.co.uk*

The National Extension College (NEC)

The NEC is a non-profit making body established to provide high quality home study courses for adults, details of which are listed in their free *Guide to Courses* available on request.

 **Contact:** *NEC – 18 Brooklands Avenue, Cambridge CB2 2HN. Tel: 01223 450300 for information about publications; 01223 450500 for student helpline.*

The University of the Third Age (U3A)

U3A is a self-help movement for people no longer in full-time employment, offering a wide range of educational, creative and leisure activities. It operates through a network of 286 local groups, each of which works out its own programme of courses and activities. Resources are available to start new U3As.

Contact: *U3A National Office – 26 Harrison Street, London WC1H 8JG. Tel: 020 7837 8838. or addresses of local groups (send a stamped, addressed envelope). Website: www.u3a.org.uk E-mail: national.office@u3a.org.uk*

Age Concern England – education and leisure

Age Concern England employs a policy officer (education and leisure) with a knowledge of all aspects of education and leisure for older adults. The policy officer co-ordinates an information network open to anyone interested in this field,and publishes the *Education and Leisure Bulletin* three times a year, giving details of initiatives, issues, research, publications and conferences. Factsheet 30 on leisure education, and 45 on fitness for later life, are also available free on receipt of a SAE. They are designed to point individuals with queries in the direction of local and national resources.

Contact: *Policy Officer, Education and Leisure, Age Concern England – Astral House 1268 London Road, London SW16 4ER. Tel: 020 8765 7441. Website: www.ace.org.uk E-mail: nortond@ace.org.uk*

BBC Education

A variety of courses, for leisure and enjoyment as well as for academic study, for all age and ability ranges, are broadcast across BBC's television and national radio networks. The BBC Learning Zone broadcasts throughout weekday nights on BBC 2 and includes courses for those who want to learn purely for pleasure.

Contact: *BBC Education – general information line 020 8746 1111. Website: www.bbc.co.uk/education/ E-mail: edinfo@bbc.co.uk*

Voluntary activities

There are many opportunities for retired people to serve their community. Broadly, voluntary work falls into four main categories:

- clerical and administrative
- committee work
- fund-raising
- direct work with the public.

Many organisations are willing to train volunteer workers either 'on the job' or through special programmes or courses.

 **Contact:** *National Association of Volunteer Bureaux – New Oxford House, 16 Waterloo Street, Birmingham B2 5UG. Tel: 0121 633 4555. E-mail: navbteam@waverider.co.uk*

Local Volunteer Bureaux exist in most towns to match volunteers to local organisations needing help.

Useful organisations

Age Concern

Age Concern has over 1,300 local groups. Some run courses and a range of activities for older people. Local branches should be listed in telephone directories.

 **Contact:** *Policy Officer (Education and Leisure) Age Concern England – Astral House, 1268 London Road, London SW16 4ER. Tel: 020 8765 7200.*

Age Concern Cymru – 4th Floor, 1 Cathedral Road, Cardiff CFI 9SD. Tel: 029 2037 1566.

Age Concern Scotland, 113 Rose Street, Edinburgh EH2 3DT. Tel: 0131 220 3345.

Age Concern Northern Ireland, 3 Lower Crescent, Belfast BT7 1NR. Tel: 028 9024 5729.

Website: www.ace.org.uk E-mail: infodep@ace.org.uk

Age Concern Information Line: 0800 731 4931

Help the Aged

This is the fund-raising and campaigning organisation working for elderly people.

 **Contact:** *Help the Aged – 16-18 St James' Walk, London EC1R 0BE. Tel: 020 7253 0253.*

Help the Aged – Heriot House, Heriothill Terrace, Edinburgh EH7 4DY. Tel: 0131 556 4666.

Senior line for information andadvice: 0808 800 6565
Website: www.hta.org.uk E-mail: info@hta.org.uk

Useful publications

Yours – a monthly magazine written specially for older people. It has a readers' advisory service. Available from newsagents at 95p or on subscription (£13.95 for 12 issues) from Yours, Apex House, Oundle Road, Peterborough PE2 9NP. Tel: 0173 555123.

The Mature Scot Directory – a directory of organisations and opportunities for those over 50, in the Tayside area. Available from Mature Scot (Tayside), 303 Kingsway, Dundee DD3 8LQ. Tel: 01382 827131.

Older workers

Figures for older people in work are predicted to rise.

- 35% of the labour force will be aged 45 or over by the year 2000.
- By 2010 almost 40% will be in that age group, while 16-24 year olds will make up only 17% of the labour force.

As the population ages, we are moving towards an average age of above 40 in the workforce.

Basing job decisions on age can reduce an employer's choice of the most suitable candidates by up to a quarter.

There are various initiatives designed to help older people to start or keep a job.

- **New Deal** – under new measures, the government is about to increase the provision for adults by offering a combination of New Deal for the over 50s and an Employment Credit.
- **Individual learning accounts** – encouraging people of all ages to see the benefits of investing in learning. Nationally available in 2000.
- **A Government Strategy for Older People – The Code of Practice on Age Diversity in Employment**. It calls upon employers to tackle age discrimination. The code will show how organisations and employers can take steps to ensure they choose, retain and develop the best person for the job by eliminating the use of age as an employment criterion. It covers good practice in six main areas: recruitment; selection; promotion; training and development; redundancy; retirement.

You can get a copy of the publication *Age Diversity in Employment* from DfEE Publications, Sherwood Park, Annesley, Nottingham NG15 0DJ. Tel: 0845 60 222 60.

Projects supporting older workers

There are various projects supporting older workers, and new projects are being established all the time; Third Age Challenge Ltd may have details.

Third Age Challenge Ltd (TAC Ltd)

Third Age Challenge Ltd is a not-for-profit organisation aimed at the older (40+) worker. Currently involved in a transnational project, Adapt-Age, TAC Ltd provides job analysis, management and personal and motivation training to SMEs and unemployed individuals.

 **Contact:** *Third Age Challenge Ltd – Temple House, 115 Commercial Road, Swindon SNI 5PL. Tel: 01793 533370. Website: dataday.co.uk/thirdage E-mail: thirdage@dialin.net*

Projects across the country include:

Barnsley

Barnsley Met Training – counselling, training and a placement service for older workers, particularly redundant miners.

 **Contact:** *Barnsley Enterprise Centre – 1 Pontefract Road, Barnsley S71 1AJ. Tel: 01226 774000.*

Bradford

People of Previous Experience (Pope) – an initiative by Bradford TEC. Placing and training older jobseekers.

 **Contact:** *Bradford Training and Enterprise Council – Mercury House, 4 Manchester Road, Bradford BD5 0QL. Tel: 01274 751333.*

Coventry/Warwick

HOST – run by Warwick Business School, funded by Coventry TEC, this well established programme runs three x three-week courses a year, followed by a 16-week assignment with local small businesses. In most cases these turn into a job.

 **Contact:** *CSME – Warwick Business School, University of Warwick, Coventry CV4 7AL. Tel: 024 7652 3741.*

Falkirk
FEAT – a programme developed by Falkirk Enterprise Action Trust, aimed at retraining redundant ship workers.

 **Contact:** *Newhouse Business Park, Newhouse Road, Grangemouth SK3 8LL. Tel: 01324 665500.*

Fenix
A project funded by the EU with partners in Spain and Ireland to develop a model programme for training and support of older workers.

 **Contact:** *Barnsley Enterprise Centre – 1 Pontefract Road, Barnsley S71 1AJ. Tel: 01226 774000.*

Guildford
TAN (Third Age Network) – a self-help group with meetings and a network for jobseeking. Branches also at Crawley, Dartford, Watford and Portsmouth.

 **Contact:** *Tel: 01483 440582 (answerphone).*

Hertfordshire
Herts Careers Service – careers counselling for older people and a register of older jobseekers.

 **Contact:** *Community Development Division – New Barnesfield Centre, Travellers Lane, Hatfield, Hertfordshire AL10 8XG. Tel: 01707 281402.*

Isle of Arran
Arran Textiles – a group of over 50s weavers and knitters have formed a trading company to train young people and market knitwear.

 **Contact:** *Tel: 01770 700654 (answerphone).*

North London
Over 50s Employment Bureau – a well established CAB initiative for jobseekers.

 **Contact:** *Over 50s Bureau – 90 Central Street, London EC1Z 8AQ. Tel: 020 7608 1395.*

North Nottinghamshire, Southwell

Rural Community Council Training of people in isolated rural areas and canvassing of employers for job search.

 **Contact:** *Minster Chambers, Church Street, Southwell NG25 0HD. Tel: 01636 815267.*

West London

Third Age Challenge Ltd – full training programme in life skills, jobseeking and IT skills, in partnership with an FE College and ITEC.

 **Contact:** *Tel: 04325 131434.*

Wiltshire

Workout – part of the Community Council for Wiltshire, runs training programmes for jobseekers.

 **Contact:** *38 Market Place, Chippenham SN15 3HT. Tel: 01793 542532.*

Winchester

EAGER (Executive Action Group for Employment and Recruitment) – run by volunteers, it has regular meetings and jobsearch activity.

 **Contact:** *WOCCS – The Winchester Centre, 68 St George's Street, Winchester SO23 8AH. Tel: 01962 842293.*

York

Third Age Challenge Ltd – a project set up as a community business. All registered members receive some initial training, and then work part-time in running the initiative. Funded by the Employment Service.

 **Contact:** *Merchant House, 11a Piccadilly, York YO1 9WB. Tel: 01904 671171.*

There are some commercial agencies which place older people into different types of job, mainly in the London area.

Contact: *Careers Continued – 14 Trinity Square, London EC3N 4AA. Tel: 020 7680 0033.*

Contact: *Forties People – 11-13 Dowgate Hill, London EC4R 2ST. Tel: 020 7329 4044.*

Further information

Good Non-Retirement Guide 1999 – published by Kogan Page Ltd, £14.99. ISBN 0 7492 2868 6.

Your Retirement – published by Kogan Page Ltd, £9.99. ISBN 0 7494 2905 4.

Mature Students Guide – published by Hobsons, £7.99. ISBN 0 85660 162 4.

Career Guidance for the Third Age: a mapping exercise – published by Hobsons, £9.95.
ISBN 186 017 44 77.

Changing Course – available from Lifeskills, Wharfebank House, Ilkley Road, Otley LS21 3JP.
Tel: 01943 851144. £15.00. ISBN 185252 1619. A practical workbook.

Learning Direct helpline 0800 100 900 – for information and advice on all learning opportunities.

29. People with disabilities

This chapter covers:

- education courses
- learning at home
- training courses
- residential specialist training and further education
- seeking employment
- sources of help and information.

All the other opportunities in this book are not excluded.

People with disabilities remain part of the Careers Service's core client group until settled in their career intention.

They may be looking for:

- education for personal development
- education which leads to a qualification
- education with employment in mind
- training for new skills or an update on existing skills
- training with employment in mind.

Options available include:

- attending a course (general or vocational) at a higher education institution or local college
- studying at home – such as Open College, Open University, correspondence course
- training through Work-based Learning (Training for Work in Scotland)
- attending a course specially designed for people with disabilities at a specialist college of FE or at a residential training college.

Education courses

Higher education institutions and colleges of further education

HE institutions and FE colleges are required under the Disability Discrimination Act to publish disability statements, giving information about their facilities for disabled people. These should include overall policy towards disabled students, admission arrangements, educational facilities and support; physical access to educational and other facilities; names of members of staff with special responsibility for disabled students.

Financial assistance

Generally, students aged 19 and over applying for **further** education courses have to pay their own tuition fees. But they may apply for Access funds direct from the individual college if they are on a low income or in a particular financial difficulty. If they already receive a means-tested benefit, they may not have to pay tuition fees. The college Student Services Officer/Learning Support Manager, or local authority Benefits Adviser, can advise.

Students offered places on **higher** education courses apply to their LEA for financial assistance with tuition fees (means-tested) and student loans. They can also apply for a Disabled Students Allowance (non means-tested) to pay for additional support and equipment. The Disability Co-ordinator at the institution will advise on how to go about this, or, contact SKILL, the National Bureau for Students with Disabilities. Contact freephone 0800 731 9133 for a booklet about DSAs – *Bridging the Gap.*

From September 1999, fees will be waived to people in receipt of benefits on certain part-time HE courses. Chapter 8 has more details.

Educational guidance services for adults

There are national information and guidance services with details of local facilities and opportunities for people with disabilities.

Linking Education and Disability

LEAD is a voluntary organisation in Scotland providing guidance about, and access to, educational opportunities for physically disabled and/or sensory impaired adults in Scotland. Local organisers can visit potential students at home.

☞ **Contact:** *Lead Scotland – Queen Margaret University College,*
36 Clerwood Terrace, Edinburgh EH12 8TS
Tel: 01313 173439. For advice and guidance
phone 0800 100 900 and ask for Lead Scotland.
Website address: www.cali.co.uk/lead
E-mail: lead.scotland@scet.com

Basic education

Basic education tuition may be possible in your home if you are unable to attend classes at a centre or college.

National Federation of Access Centres

Access Centres are based at a number of further and higher education institutions in England, Scotland and Wales. Their purpose is to offer short courses to individual students with physical and sensory disabilities to assess their need for study, writing and communication aids. Students are usually referred by the educational institution they attend or wish to attend. Disabled students' allowances may be used to pay for this. For a list of Access Centres:

 **Contact:** *Access Centre – University of Plymouth, Room 8, The Babbage Building, Drake Circus, Plymouth PL4 8AA. Tel: 01752 232278. Website: www.piym.ac.uk E-mail: swarm@plymouth.ac.uk*

The Learning from Experience Trust

The Learning from Experience Trust publishes a pack to help people with disabilities tackle the barriers they face when seeking employment or training. The pack *Recognising Ability: Make Your Experience Count* contains activities and guidance to help people recognise their abilities and achievements and demonstrate these when applying for a job or a course. Copies of the pack are available for £20 (reduced to £10 for non-profit institutions) plus postage and packing from the Trust.

 **Contact:** *Marie Elgar, Secretary from Experience Trust – Goldsmiths College, Deptford Town Hall, London SE14 6AE. Tel: 020 7919 7739. E-mail: m.edgar@gold.ac.uk*

Learning at home

There are education schemes aimed at mature students learning at home.

- Open learning and correspondence courses.
- Books and other learning approaches – audio-cassettes, videos etc.
- BBC Education.

Open University (OU)

The OU has specialist advisers for students with disabilities. Where possible, they also provide extra support, sometimes including helpers for summer schools.

 **Contact:** *The Office for Students with Disabilities – The Open University, Walton Hall, Milton Keynes MK7 6AA. Tel: 01908 653745.*

The OU Students' Association (OUSA) offers considerable support to members with disabilities.

Contact: *OUSA, Open University, PO Box 397, Walton Hall, Milton Keynes MK7 6BE. Tel: 01908 652026.*

Training courses

Work-based Learning for Adults (Training for Work in Scotland)

Work-based Learning is organised by a network of TECs (Training and Enterprise Councils) in England and Wales or LECs (Local Enterprise Companies) in Scotland. TECs and LECs contract with training organisations locally to provide training to help unemployed people aged 25 to 63 update existing work skills or learn new ones. The aim is to gain skills and qualifications and to take up employment. People with disabilities are eligible for training without waiting for the six-month unemployment rule.

In most areas an integrated programme is provided for able-bodied and disabled people. Particular needs will be considered, and a plan for training will be developed, taking into consideration:

- experience
- employment aims
- the needs of the local labour market
- any support required (including special equipment and adaptations).

More detailed information about Work based Training can be found in chapter 25 – Unemployment.

Money

A training allowance is paid, which is equivalent to any state benefits already received (including Incapacity Benefit and Severe Disablement Allowance), plus a premium of £10 a week. This will not affect any entitlement to benefits linked to social security benefits. Help may also be available with extra expenses such as travel costs and childcare. SKILL or the local Benefits Adviser will advise about resuming benefits if the period of training does not secure employment.

Part-time training

Part-time training may be available if the disability prevents full-time training. There may be a minimum number of hours necessary – the Disability Employment Adviser can advise.

Special help for severely disabled people

Vocational courses are available through Work-based Learning at Residential Training Colleges (RTCs). Local TECs or LECs may be able to arrange special local training if required. The DEA can give more information.

Additional help

Additional help while on Work-based Learning may be available, such as:

- special aids or equipment – providing the tools and equipment needed to overcome the effects of the disability and make full use of the training
- adaptions to premises or equipment – grants for necessary alterations to training locations and/or equipment
- individually-tailored training programmes where existing contracted local provision is not appropriate
- a readership service for the blind – financial help towards a reader for a trainee with visual impairment

- an interpreter service for the deaf – financial help towards an interpreter for a trainee with a hearing impairment.

If a special aid is required in order to take up employment, TECs or LECs should make this possible.

Preparatory courses

Some areas offer introductory courses for people with disabilities who are not sure if they are ready for full-time training or capable of it. The DEA at the local Jobcentre will have details. These courses usually last up to three months and seek to develop self confidence before decisions are made on the suitability of longer-term training.

Work-based Training (WbT)

Work-based Training programmes of training and work experience are organised by the network of TECs (Training and Enterprise Councils) in England and Wales, or LECs (Local Enterprise Councils) in Scotland. The programmes are open to all able-bodied and disabled young people, aged 16 and 17 – eligibility may be extended for some groups, including disabled people, up to age 25. Programmes usually last up to two years. Trainees work towards National Vocational Qualifications. For local information, contact your Careers Service.

Residential specialist training and further education

Residential Training Colleges (RTCs)

For people with all types of disability, vocational training is offered at one of four residential training colleges (see below). RTCs offer specialist facilities, medical and counselling support and expert staff to help people with disabilities gain access to learning and come to terms with lifestyle changes.

Each college differs in the degree of independence it expects. Training is available to men and women aged 19 to 62. Most trainees have been previously employed and have had an illness or accident necessitating a significant change in lifestyle and retraining for employment. Not all RTCs offer all types of training. All colleges accept trainees from around the country. Most training programmes lead to National Vocational Qualifications.

There is no charge to the individual for residential training and benefits are unaffected.

Training courses are available in:

- administrative and clerical appointments
- amenity and commercial horticulture
- audio-visual techniques
- book-keeping and accountancy
- computer-aided draughting and design
- computer servicing
- desktop publishing
- domestic appliance servicing

- electronics manufacture and inspection
- electronics servicing
- engineering manufacture and inspection
- estimating
- food preparation and cookery
- fork-lift truck operating
- gardening and grounds maintenance
- information technology
- joinery and furniture making
- office machine servicing
- secretarial duties
- switchboard and receptionist duties
- travel services
- watch and clock repair
- wholesaling, warehousing and stock control.

Training in basic work skills, number and word power and keyboard skills can also be provided.

Contact: *The Disability Employment Adviser at the Jobcentre, or one of the colleges direct:*

Finchale Training College – Durham DH1 5RX. Tel: 0191 386 2634.

Portland College – Nottingham Road, Mansfield NG 18 4TJ. Tel: 01623 79214 1.

Queen Elizabeth's Training College – Leatherhead Court, Leatherhead KT22 0BN. Tel: 01372 842204.

St Loye's College for Training Disabled People for Employment – Topsham Road, Exeter EX2 6EP. Tel: 01392 255428.

Besides vocational training, some RTCs also offer special foundation courses including basic education, independence skills, communication skills and prevocational studies. Such courses may be funded by the Further Education Funding Council.

Other specialist colleges

There is a large number of specialist colleges, many catering for specific disabilities. Most are residential and take students from any area. Courses are very varied and rapidly changing.

Application may be made directly to the college, but acceptance by the college does not guarantee funding for the placement. Courses may be funded by the Further Education Funding Council (FEFC), jointly funded by FEFC and another agency (for example Social Services Department), or funded wholly by Employment Services or Social Services Department. Employment Services generally fund vocational courses only, particularly those lasting up to 12 months. There is no age restriction. Contact the DEA for information. Both general education and vocational courses may be founded by the FEFC. Strict criteria are set for eligibility for funding.

FEFC produces a guidance booklet *Further Education for Young People With Learning Difficulties and/or Disabilities – The Role of Funding Council*.

☞ **Contact:** *FEFC – Cheylesmore House, Quinton Road, Coventry CV1 2WT. Tel: 024 7686 3265, or from local Careers Services.*

Application to FEFC for funding specialist college placements has to be made through the local education authority or other agency. Often the Careers Service takes the lead role in this. You can get information on specialist colleges from:

NATSPEC (The Association of National Specialist Colleges)
NATSPEC has a membership of over 48 specialist colleges; it publishes a directory containing brief details of member colleges.

☞ **Contact:** *Publicity Officer, NATSPEC – Fair Lea, School Lane, St Martins, Oswestry SY11 3BX Tel: 01691 773210.*

Lifetime Careers Wiltshire

Publishes *COPE* (Compendium of Post-16 Education and Training in Residential Establishments for Young People with Special Needs). Price £24.95. ISBN 1 873408 58 7. Updated every two years. This lists more than 150 establishments, some of which may provide longer term care rather than courses of further education and/or training.

The Admissions Officer at the individual colleges listed in these directories can provide information and a prospectus.

Seeking employment

Disability Discrimination Act

Following an education or training course, people with a disability may need assistance in getting employment. The Disability Discrimination Act makes it unlawful for an employer with 15 or more employees to treat a disabled person less favourably than anyone else because of their disability, unless there is good reason. It also requires employers to make reasonable adjustments to working practices and premises to overcome any substantial disadvantage caused by disability.

Contact: *Telephone: 0345 622 633 Text telephone: 0345 622 644 Faxback: 0345 622 611 Automated line: 0345 622 688.*

Disability Rights Commission

A bill going through Parliament at present will promote equal opportunities for disabled people and work towards an end to discrimination by providing information and advice for disabled people, employers and service providers. It will prepare codes of practice for those involved, and make sure they are complying with anti-discrimination laws.

New Deal

New Deal offers individually-tailored help in finding a job, a chance to show employers what can be done, and the opportunity to gain high-quality training. People with disabilities can access the programme without having to wait for the two-year specified period. New Deal can offer:

- **A personal sdviser** – who might be the Disability Employment Adviser
- **Employment Rehabilitation** – a programme to help people get work by addressing specific employment-related needs arising from the disability
- **Access to Work** – practical help for disabled people at work, for example a communicator, special equipment, adaptations to work premises or help with travel costs.
- **Job Introduction Scheme** – a grant paid to an employer, usually for six weeks, allows the employer to assess a person's ability to do a particular job.

Contact: *The Disability Employment Adviser at the Jobcentre.*

Supported employment

A proportion of people, because of the nature or severity of their disability, are unable to compete for jobs in the open market. Supported employment can offer all kinds of job opportunities, through:

- *supported placements*
  disabled people can work at their own pace beside non-disabled colleagues, and in a way which best suits them

- *employment with Remploy*
  a nationwide organisation, Remploy Interwork, manages placements with employers
- *sheltered workshops*
  may be run by local authorities and voluntary organisations, or factories run by Remploy Limited.

Contact: *The Disability Employment Adviser at the Jobcentre.*

From October 1999, the Disabled Person's Tax Credit (replacing the Disability Working Allowance) will allow wages to be topped-up if earning power is limited by disability.

Sources of help and useful information

SKILL: National Bureau for Students with Disabilities

Promotes opportunities to empower young people and adults with any kind of disability to realise their potential in further and higher education, training and employment throughout the United Kingdom. SKILL provides individual support, promotes good practice and influences policy in partnership with disabled people, service providers and policy makers. They organise national and regional conferences and seminars around the country. They offer an information service with advice on:

- applying to college
- financial assistance while studying
- examination arrangements
- disclosing disability
- looking for work.

Contact: *SKILL – 4th Floor, Chapter House, 18-20 Crucifix Lane, London SE1 3JW. Tel: 0800 328 5050. Website: www.skill.org.uk E-mail: SkillNatBurDis@compuserve.com.uk*

SAIS

SAIS is the umbrella body for voluntary organisations in Scotland, of and for disabled people. It brings together all those interested in integrating people with disabilities into mainstream society, through campaigning and information programmes. Services include:

- disability awareness training
- advice on Access and built environment; education and training opportunities for disabled people
- further education, training and employment directory, also available on CD-Rom
- information on aids and equipment.

 **Contact:** *SAIS – Royal Exchange House, 100 Queen Street, Glasgow G1 3DN. Tel: 0141 226 5261. Website: www.scotconsumer.org.uk E-mail: sharvey@scotconsumer.org.uk*

CanDo

CanDo is a national organisation, based at Lancaster University, which provides employment and careers information to disabled students and graduates on the internet. It includes information on specialist work experience schemes for disabled people, information about sources of financial support, employees' and jobseekers' rights under the Disability Discrimination Act, profiles of over 100 disability organisations, and guidance information on issues such as disclosing disability to a potential employer.

 **Contact:** *Lancaster University CanDo Service – Careers Service, Lancaster LA1 4YW. Tel: 01524 594370. Website: www.cando.lancs.ac.uk E-mail: cando@lancs.ac.uk*

Royal National Institute for the Blind (RNIB)

RNIB Vocational College Loughborough works in partnership with neighbouring Loughborough College of Further Education, offering a wide range of vocational and educational opportunities for visually impaired people from 16 years of age. There is fully supported access to a wide range of courses at Loughborough College allowing students to gain nationally recognised qualifications. The Vocational College offers specialist courses at Foundation level as well as training in Business Administration (including audio-word processing and telephony) and Information Technology at NVQ Level. Access courses also prepare students for mainstream further education.

The External Services Team offers support to students at other colleges in the Midlands, short courses and on-the job training. Employment Assessment and Rehabilitation programmes offer assessment and development of skills, and career choices to be explored.

 **Contact:** *Vice Principal, RNIB Vocational College – Radmoor Road, Loughborough LE11 3BS. Tel: 01509 611077. Website: www.rnib.org.uk E-mail: gjackman@rnib.org.uk*

Visage Project

The RNIB has a helpline and website for employers, as part of their VISAGE Project which runs until the middle of 2000. The helpline on 0800 389 7568 is the first point of contact for advice, guidance, further information and literature. Website address: www.rnib.org.uk

Action for Blind

Action for Blind works with, and for, people who are visually impaired, to open up new opportunities so that they can enjoy equal rights and better facilities to lead the lifestyle they choose. They also run their own services which include accommodation schemes, holidays and specialist hotels, employment and training projects, a cash grant scheme and a national information and advice service.

 **Contact:** *Action for Blind – 14-16 Verney Road, London SE16 3DZ.*
Tel: 020 7732 8771. Website: www.demon.co.uk/afbp
E-mail: info@afbp.org

The Royal National Institute for Deaf People (RNID)

The RNID is the largest charity representing deaf and hard of hearing people in the UK.
The Institute:

- campaigns to change laws and government policies
- provides information and raises awareness of deafness, hearing loss and tinnitus
- offers training courses and consultancy on deafness and disability
- provides communication services including sign language interpreters
- trains interpreters, lip-speakers and speech to text operators
- offers employment programmes to help deaf people at work
- offers *Typetalk*, the national telephone relay service for deaf and hard of hearing people
- provides residential and community services for deaf people with special needs
- supplies equipment and products for deaf and hard of hearing people
- undertakes social, medical and technical research.

 **Contact:** *RNID Helpline – PO Box 16464, London EC1Y 8TT. Tel: 0870 60 50 123.*
Website: www.rnid.org.uk E-mail: helpline@rnid.org.uk

National Association for Tertiary Education for Deaf People

Promotes access to post-16 education of all kinds for deaf and hard of hearing people. Offers communication support through interpreting, note-taking and lip-speaking. Provides an information service and networking for students and professionals in the field. Free publications include an information pack for deaf school leavers and students, a student resource pack, and a tutor's resource pack.

 **Contact:** *SASU – National Association for Tertiary Education for Deaf People,*
Coventry Technical College, The Butts, Coventry CVI 3GD.
Tel: 024 7652 6700. Website: www.covcollege.ac.uk
E-mail: info@covcollege.ac.uk

Royal Society for Mentally Handicapped Children and Adults (Mencap)

Mencap has divisional offices covering England, Wales and Northern Ireland which provide support, advice and information to people with learning difficulties, and also to their families. Mencap's Education, Training and Employment Service Department provides help and advice to parents and professionals on all aspects of special education and training for people with learning difficulties. Mencap runs three colleges for young people, covering social independence and vocational skills training.

Contact: *Mencap – 123 Golden Lane, London ECIY ORT. Tel: 020 7454 0454.*

Pathway Employment Service

Places people with learning difficulties into appropriate employment and provides ongoing support. It does not cover the whole country, but is continuing to expand.

 **Contact:** *Mencap Pathway Employment Service – National Centre, 123 Golden Lane, London ECIY ORT. Tel: 020 7454 0454. Can put enquirers onto their nearest local contacts. Website: www.mencap.org.uk*

ENABLE

Provides information, legal advice, holidays, respite care for children and residential accommodation for people with profound learning disabilities. It also runs a number of training schemes for people with learning disabilities and those wishing to work with people with learning disabilities, as well as a variety of supported employment and job coaching opportunities. ENABLE has over 70 local branches throughout Scotland; each provides mutual support to families in addition to a wide range of social and recreational activities for people with learning disabilities.

Contact: *ENABLE – 6th Floor, 7 Buchanan Street, Glasgow G12 3HL.*
Tel: 0141 226 4541. E-mail: enable@enable.org.uk

Royal Association for Disability and Rehabilitation (RADAR)

A national disability organisation which operates in conjunction with an affiliated network of local and national organisations. It campaigns for disabled people's rights and full integration into society. It runs an information and advisory service, and is active in the fields of employment, mobility, housing, holidays, social service provision, social security, education and civil rights.

 **Contact:** *RADAR – 12 City Forum, 250 City Road, London ECIV 8AF.*
Tel: 020 7250 3222. Website: radar.org.uk E-mail: radar@radar.org.uk

Scope

Scope provides a wide range of services for people with cerebral palsy and their families or carers. These services include schools, an FE college, residential care, information and careers advice, skills development centres, on assessment service and a supported employment programme.

Contact: *Scope – Library and Information Unit, 6 Market Road, London N7 9PW. Tel: 020 7619 7100. Website: www.scope.org.uk*

Cerebral Palsy helpline: 0800 626216 (Monday to Friday 11am to 6pm; Saturday and Sunday 2 to 6pm).

Disabled Living Foundation (DLF)

The Disabled Living Foundation is a national charity providing practical, up-to-date information on many aspects of living with a disability. The DLF's professional advisers respond to written enquiries from healthcare professionals and the general public, relating mainly to special equipment, clothing and footwear. The DLF has a major and permanent exhibition of over 1,000 items of disability equipment. Visitors are welcome by appointment.

 **Contact:** *Disabled Living Foundation – 380-384 Harrow Road, London W9 2HU. Tel: 020 7289 6111. Website: dlf.org.uk E-mail: dlfinfo@dlfinfo.org.uk*

Disability Now

Disability Now is a campaigning newspaper which includes articles, features and links to other organisations and their websites, including those dealing with employment and training issues. Disability Now is sent free to disabled people in the UK who can provide photocopied evidence that they are receiving means tested benefits.

 **Contact:** *Disability Now – 6 Market Road, London N7 9PW. Tel: 020 7619 7332. Minicom 020 7619 7332. Website: www.disabilitynow.org.uk*

Further information

Directory for Disabled People – available from International Book Distributors, Campus 400, Maylands Avenue, Hemel Hempstead HP2 7EZ. Tel: 01442 881900. Price £17.95. ISBN 013 736 489 X.

Disability Rights Handbook 1999-00 – available from Disability Alliance, Universal House, 88-94 Wentworth Street, London E1 7SA. Tel: 020 7247 8776. Price £11.50; £7.50 for individuals on benefits. ISBN 0946 336 946. Information on benefits and services for people with disabilities, including education and training. It is updated every year.

The Educational Grants Directory – available from Trotmans Publishing Ltd. Price £18.95 plus £2.50 p&p. ISBN 1 900360 31 4. Lists educational charities for students in need, including help for students with disabilities.

A Guide to Grants for Individuals in Need 1998/99 – available from the Directory ol Social Change, 24 Stephenson Way, London NWI 2DP. Tel: 020 7209 4949. Price £8.95. ISBN 1 900 360 32 3. Lists charitable funds for the relief of individual distress, including grant-making charities for particular illnesses or disabilities.

Into Work – available from RADAR, 12 City Forum, 250 City Road, London EC I V 8AF. Tel: 020 7250 3222. Price £2.50. Gives advice for jobseekers with disabilities on applying for jobs, legal rights and career choices, and lists sources of help and advice.

Casebook: Equal Opportunities for Disabled Graduates – available from Biblios Publishers' Distribution Services Ltd, Star Road, Partridge Green RH13 8LD. Tel: 01403 710851. Price £9.99.

All things being equal? A practical guide to widening participation for adults with learning difficulties in continuing education – published by NIACE, 21 De Montfort Street, Leicester LE1 7GE. Price to be confirmed. ISBN 1 86201 051 X.

30. Overseas students, refugees and asylum seekers

This chapter covers:

- finances for overseas students and refugees
- the private sector
- useful organisations
- refugees and asylum seekers.

Students

Coming to the UK to study is an option chosen by thousands of overseas students each year. Nearly all the full-time education opportunities outlined in this book are open to overseas students, but there are other considerations relating to studying in a foreign country.

The chosen university or college will send a prospectus on request, with any additional information relating to entry for overseas students, including:

- entry qualifications required
- course fees and examination fees
- accommodation provided by the college and accommodation costs
- an idea of the approximate cost of living in the area
- ability in English language and any entry tests which may be required
- any associations or societies run by the institution or its students, for students of different nationalities – they will often provide support and help.

Costs

The fees at a British university or college are much higher for an overseas student than for a UK or EU resident.

In the UK, overseas students pay the full cost of the course. Two exceptions to this general rule are students from the EU and refugees: both groups qualify for home status along with UK nationals.

Students from EU countries

In order to qualify for financial assistance with tuition fees, on a similar basis to UK students, the following requirements must be met. Students must:

- be a national of an EU country
- have been ordinarily resident in that country for three years immediately before the start of the first academic year of the course
- attend a designated course
- not have studied previously in the UK and received help with fees.

EU students are sent an application form for help with tuition fees by the college offering the place. In England and Wales, applications must be made to the DfEE.

Contact: *DfEE European Team – Student Support Division 1, Mowden Hall, Staindrop Road, Darlington, Co Durham DL3 9BG.*

For applications to Scottish institutions:

Contact: *Student Awards Agency for Scotland (SAAS) – Gyleview House, 3 Redheughs Rigg, South Gyle, Edinburgh EH12 9HH. Students attending a course at a university or college in Scotland may be entitled to free tuition for the fourth year of the course.*

Students planning to study in Northern Ireland should apply to the Education and Libraries Board in the area where their university or college is based.

Non-UK European Union students **cannot** apply for a student loan, supplementary grant, hardship loan or Access funds.

Refugees

People who have been granted refugee status by the government as a result of making an application for asylum, and have remained ordinarily resident in the UK since that time, qualify for home status, and will be eligible for financial assistance with tuition fees.

Qualifications

For information about what an overseas qualification is worth in the UK, the British Council has an office which may be able to help. UK NARIC has information officers who can provide information and advice on the likely recognition of a qualification. They can provide certification of comparability of qualifications, for which a fee is payable. NARIC publishes an *International Guide to Qualifications in Education and Studying, Training and doing Research in Another Country of the EU*.

Contact: *The UK NARIC – ECCTIS 2000 Ltd, Oriel House, Oriel Road, Cheltenham GL50 1XP. Tel: 01242 260010.*

The private sector

There are many private colleges in the UK. Independent colleges cover a wide range of subjects such as advertising, modelling, photography, GCSEs/standard grades, A levels/highers, business studies, computing and secretarial courses to name a few. Some of these have formed into associations in order to guarantee quality standards of teaching and facilities.

British Accreditation Council for Independent Further and Higher Education
BAC was set up in 1984 to inspect and accredit private institutions.

 **Contact:** *BAC – 27 Marylebone Road, London NW1 5JS. Tel: 020 7487 4643. Website: www.the-bac.org E-mail: info@the-bac.org*

The British Association of State Colleges in English Language Teaching
BASCELT offers courses throughout the year for students wishing to learn English. Courses are validated by the British Council and guarantee high standards of teaching, welfare and resources.

 **Contact:** *BASCELT – Cheltenham and Gloucester College of FE, Francis Close Hall, Swindon Road, Cheltenham GL50 4AZ. Tel: 01242 227055. Website: www.bascelt.org.uk E-mail: baselt@chelt.ac.uk*

The Association for Recognised English Language Teaching Establishments in Britain
ARELS is an association of the larger language schools which are recognised as efficient by the British Council. The schools run courses all year and through the summer to suit all ages. They produce a booklet, *Learn English in Britain*, free of charge.

 **Contact:** *ARELS – 56 Buckingham Gate, London SW1E 6AG. Tel: 020 7928 9378. Website: www.arels.org.uk E-mail: enquiries@arels.org.uk*

Independent higher education

The University of Buckingham
The University of Buckingham opened in 1976 as an independent university. Courses start in January each year and generally last two years for degree level study, as they have four ten week terms and fewer holidays.

 **Contact:** *University of Buckingham – Buckingham, MK18 1EG. Tel: 01280 814080.*

Correspondence colleges
It is possible to study through a correspondence college and not come to the UK at all. When choosing a course it is important to check the qualification being offered: the British Council will advise.

Useful organisations

UKCOSA
UKCOSA produces useful free information sheets on various aspects of studying in the UK, and

general advice for students once they are in the UK. They have an advice line for would-be students and their advisers.

☞ **Contact:** *UKCOSA – Council for International Education, 9-17 St Alban's Place, London N1 0NX. Tel: 020 7226 3762. Website: ukcosa.org.uk E-mail: enquiries@ukcosa.org.uk*

The British Council

The British Council promotes Britain abroad. At the London head office there is an education information service for students and would-be students from overseas. Students can enquire about any aspect of the British education system, including funding. Students using this service are recommended to telephone for an appointment first. The British Council is represented in 109 countries – to find out where the nearest office is contact either the London office or the Manchester office, or your nearest British Embassy.

☞ **Contact:** *British Council Information Centre – 10 Spring Gardens, London SWIA 2BN. Tel: 020 7389 4383.*

or *British Council Information Centre – Bridgwater House, 58 Whitworth Street, Manchester M1 6BB. Tel: 0161 957 7000. Website: www.britcoun.org.uk E-mail: enquiries@britcoun.org*

Central Bureau for Educational Visits and Exchanges

This is the office for the provision of information and advice on all forms of educational visits and exchanges. The Central Bureau can also provide some information for overseas students in the UK.

☞ **Contact:** *Central Bureau for Educational Visits and Exchanges (CBEVE) – 10 Spring Gardens, London SWIA 2BN. Tel: 020 7389 4004. Website: www.britcoun.org/cbeve/ E-mail: dmorton@central bureau.org.uk*

or *3 Bruntsfield Crescent, Edinburgh EHI0 4HD. Tel: 0131 447 8024.*

or *1 Chlorine Gardens, Belfast BT9 5DJ. Tel: 028 9066 4418.*

Careers Europe

Information about international career opportunities may be available to careers and guidance staff, where the service subscribes to Careers Europe, the UK Resource Centre for International Careers.

Refugees and asylum seekers

The Refugee Education and Training Advisory Service

RETAS provides direct help to over 2000 refugees and asylum seekers each year to get access to education, training and employment. The Fontana Project is a one-stop shop offering advice, training and mentoring to help refugees return to work.

 **Contact:** *Refugee Education and Training Advisory Service (RETAS) – World University Service (UK), 14 Dufferin Street, London EC1Y 8PD. Tel: 020 7426 5800. E-mail: retas@wusuk.org*

Educational Grants Advisory Service

EGAS is part of the Family Welfare Association, which is trustee to various educational trusts, and is primarily concerned with helping disadvantaged students, including refugees and asylum seekers.

 **Contact:** *EGAS – 501-505 Kingsland Road, London E8 4AU. Tel: 020 7254 6251.*

The Refugee Council

The Refugee Council helps refugees who are seeking information and advice about work or training, including rights to work, jobseeker's allowance etc.

 **Contact:** *Refugee Council – 3-9 Bondway, London SW8 1SJ. Tel: 020 7820 3000. E-mail: info@refugeecouncil.demon.co.uk*

Further information

The following books are available from bookshops or Trotman and Company Ltd:

British Qualifications (29th edition) – price £33.50. ISBN 0 7494 2866 X.

University and College Entrance: The Official Guide 2000 – price £19.95. ISBN 0 948241 69 1.

The Educational Grants Directory – price £18.95. ISBN 190036 031 4.

The International Guide to Qualifications in Education (4th ed) – price £100. ISBN 0 72012 217 1.

Prospects Postgrad UK – postgraduate vacancy information for overseas students wishing to study in the UK. Available free of charge from CSU.

The following books and student information papers are available direct from The Association of Commonwealth Universities – John Foster House, 36 Gordon Square, London WC1H 0PF. Tel: 020 7377 8572.

Awards for First Degree Study at Commonwealth Universities 1997-9 – price £10. ISBN 0 85143 159 3.

Awards for Postgraduate Study at Commonwealth Universities 1997-9 – price £24. ISBN 0 85143 158 5.

ACU Student Information Papers –

Graduate Study at Universities in Britain
Taking a First Degree at a University in Britain.

Single copies are free if you send a foolscap SAE (UK enquiries) or two International Reply coupons (enquiries outside the UK) to the ACU address above.

31. Race/other cultures

This chapter covers:

- race – organisations which can help
- travellers.

All the opportunities outlined in *Second Chances* are open to everyone. There are specialist agencies who can help to promote those opportunities.

Equal Opportunities Commission
Promotes equal opportunities for men and women in employment.

 **Contact:** *Equal Opportunities Commission – Overseas House, Quay Street, Manchester M3 3HN. Tel: 0161 833 9244. Website: www.eoc.org.uk*

RACE

Racial Equality Councils (RECs)
RECs help with any problems caused by a person's race, colour, or ethnic origins. They can provide information on local initiatives and projects.

 **Contact:** *Local RECs through telephone directories or through the Commission for Racial Equality, Elliott House, 10-12 Allington Street, London SWIE 5EH. Tel: 020 7828 7022.*

Commission for Racial Equality (CRE)
The Commission for Racial Equality was set up by the 1976 Race Relations Act to work towards eliminating discrimination, promote equality of opportunity and good relations between people of different racial groups and keep the workings of the Race Relations Act under review.

The CRE publishes numerous leaflets on equal opportunities and people's rights under the Race Relations Act.

 **Contact:** *Commission for Racial Equality – Elliott House, 10-12 Allington Street, London SW1E 5EH. Tel: 020 7828 7022. Website: www.cre.gov.uk E-mail: info@cre.gov.uk*

The CRE also has regional offices around the country:

*3rd Floor, Lancaster House,
67 Newall Street, Birmingham B3 1NA.
Tel: 0121 710 3000.*

*Yorkshire Bank Chambers, 1st Floor,
Infirmary Street, Leeds LS1 2JP.
Tel: 0113 243 4413.*

*Haymarket House, 4th Floor,
Haymarket Shopping Centre,
Leicester LE1 3YG. Tel: 0116 242 3700.*

*Maybrook House, 5th Floor, 40 Blackfriars Street,
Manchester M3 2EG. Tel: 0161 831 7782.*

*Hanover House, 45 Hanover Street,
Edinburgh EH2 2PJ. Tel: 0131 226 5186.*

*Pearl Assurance Building, 14th Floor, Greyfriars Street,
Cardiff CF1 3AG. Tel: 029 2038 8977.*

Race Relations Employment Advisory Service (RREAS)

Employers can contact RREAS for help in putting anti-racial discrimination practices into place. RREAS publishes a leaflet for employers – *Positive Action: Promoting racial equality in employment* – ref PL 957.

 **Contact:** *RREAS – 14th Floor, Cumberland House, 200 Broad Street, Birmingham B15 1TA. Tel: 0121 244 8141/2/3. E-mail: hq.rreas@dfee.gov.uk*

The Windsor Fellowship

The Windsor Fellowship offers personal and management development programmes for undergraduates thinking of a career in commerce and industry. They cover basic management skills, and offer at least six weeks' work experience. They are aimed at black and Asian undergraduates and students from anywhere in the UK. Applications should be made once a place has been offered, but before the start of the course.

 **Contact:** *The Windsor Fellowship – 47 Hackney Road, London E2 7NX. Tel: 020 7613 0373. E-mail: office@windsor-fellow.demon.co.uk*

Travellers

People who don't live in one place continuously are disadvantaged when it comes to education.

Local education authority provision

Provision from local education authorities does vary – some provide special facilities at school whilst others will provide a teacher where travellers are living. LEAs or the Citizens Advice Bureau have information about what is available in the local area.

Useful organisations

The Gypsy Council for Education and Welfare

The Council has contacts nationwide. It liaises with local authorities on behalf of its members about site provision which may affect adult education.

 **Contact:** *The Gypsy Council for Education and Welfare – 8 Hall Road, Aveley RM15 4HD. Tel: 01708 868986.*

Romanestan Publications

Produces relevant reports and books.

 **Contact:** *Romanestan Publications – 22 North End, Warley, Brentwood CM14 5LA. Tel: 01277 219491.*

Advisory Council for Education of Romany and Other Travellers (ACERT)

ACERT aims to promote equal access for travellers to all statutory and community services affecting education, health, safety and satisfactory living conditions of travellers' families. It produces an annual information pack which is available free of charge.

 **Contact:** *ACERT – Moot House, The Stowe, Harlow CM20 3AG. Tel: 01279 418666.*

Romani Rights Association

There are six regional bases in Somerset, Lincolnshire, Cambridgeshire, London, Kent and the Surrey/Hampshire border. The association visits sites, gives legal advice and takes occasional classes in adult literacy and Romani.

 **Contact:** *Romani Rights Association – Roman Bank, Walpole St Andrew P14 7HP. Tel: 01945 780326.*

The Romany Guild

The Romany Guild is an organisation run by travellers for travellers which is involved in welfare, education, planning and support work, as well as travellers' rights.

 **Contact:** *The Romany Guild – The Urban Farm, 50/56 Temple Mills Lane, London E15 2ER. Tel: 020 8555 7214.*

Further information

Rights for Travellers – £2 from the London Irish Women's Centre, 59 Church Street, Stoke Newington, London N16 0AR. Tel: 020 7249 7318.

32. Offenders and ex-offenders

This chapter covers:

- organisations which can help offenders and ex-offenders.

Just for the Record, an Employment Service publication, outlines how the Rehabilitation of Offenders Act affects jobseekers with a criminal record. Copies are obtainable from Jobcentres. There are also specialist voluntary organisations which offer advice and information.

NACRO
NACRO, the National Association for the Care and Resettlement of Offenders, has a number of New Careers Training centres in England and Wales which offer full-time adult and youth training in a wide range of vocational areas, and in basic skills such as literacy and numeracy. They can also offer employment advice.

NACRO's services are available to offenders and ex-offenders, whether or not they have been in prison, and to other disadvantaged people.

The Education and Training Awards Scheme offers financial assistance to ex-offenders for education or training. Anyone who has been convicted of a criminal offence and is within five years of their last custodial or non-custodial sentence is eligible. The scheme is not open to serving prisoners. The course must lead to a qualification recognised by a professional, educational or trade body, or be an Access or 'Return to Study' course.

 **Contact:** *NACRO Welfare Officer – 169 Clapham Road, London SW9 0PU. Tel: 020 7582 6500.*

SACRO (Safeguarding Communities – Reducing Offending)
SACRO aims to make communities safer by reducing offending, reducing conflict and influencing change in criminal justice and social policy. It provides a range of services throughout Scotland, including community mediation, supported accommodation and groupwork services.

 **Contact:** *SACRO's national office – 31 Palmerston Place, Edinburgh EH12 5AP. Tel: 0131 226 4222. Website: www.sacro.org.uk E-mail: info@sacro.org.uk*

Aberdeenshire/City of Aberdeen: SACRO – 18 Little Belmont Street, Aberdeen AB1 1JG. Tel: 01224 625560.

Clackmannanshire/Falkirk/Stirling: SACRO – 22 Meeks Road, Falkirk FK2 7ET. Tel: 01324 627824.

 **Contact:** *Edinburgh/Lothians: SACRO – Epworth Halls, Nicolson Square, Edinburgh EH8 9BX. Tel: 0131 622 7500.*

Fife: SACRO – 24 Hill Street, Kirkcaldy KY1 1HX. Tel: 01592 593100.

Glasgow: SACRO – 93 Hope Street, Glasgow G2 6LD. Tel: 0141 248 1763.

Highland: SACRO – The Old Schoolhouse, Culduthel Road, Inverness IV1 2AE. Tel: 01463 716325.

North/South Lanarkshire: SACRO – 11 Merry Street, Motherwell ML1 1JJ. Tel: 01698 230 433.

Orkney: SACRO – 4b Laing Place, Kirkwall KW15 1NW. Tel: 01856 875815.

NIACRO

NIACRO, the Northern Ireland Association for the Care and Resettlement of Offenders, is a charity providing services to prisoners, ex-offenders and their families. NIACRO also provides a range of training and employment opportunities under New Deal, Worktrack and European Union programmes targetting social inclusion. It works in partnership with Extern and the Probation Board for Northern Ireland to ensure quality service provision suited to the individual needs of the offender.

A National Lottery project, Lift Off, targets young people who, for whatever reason, do not participate in mainstream education and training programmes. In all the work, direct contact is made with employers to ensure equality of opportunity in recruitment and selection. NIACRO's training and employment programmes are provided across Northern Ireland, and details and locations may be obtained by contacting their HQ.

 **Contact:** *NIACRO – 169 Ormeau Road, Belfast BT7 1SQ. Tel: 028 9032 0157. E-mail: info.niacro@cinni.org*

Apex Charitable Trust Ltd

Apex Charitable Trust helps people with criminal records obtain jobs or self-employment by providing them with the skills they need in the labour market; it also works to break down the barriers to their employment, and increase employment opportunities in communities with high levels of crime and unemployment.

 **Contact:** *Apex Charitable Trust Ltd – Wingate Annexe, St Alphage House, 2 Fore Street, London EC2Y 5DA. Tel: 020 7638 5931. E-mail: apexho@globalnet.co.uk*

Section 4 The Gazetteer

The Gazetteer

To find out more about careers information, guidance and learning opportunities, use The Gazetteer as a list of contact points in your local area and elsewhere.

The Gazetteer is organised alphabetically by geographical area, based on counties and neighbouring unitary authorities in England and Wales, by Regional or Islands Councils in Scotland and by Library Boards in Northern Ireland.

Within each area, careers services, adult guidance services, TECs and other advisory organisations are always placed first, with colleges, training providers etc following, listed alphabetically.

There may be other providers of training and guidance operating in the area, or from further afield through distance or open learning or correspondence. Further information on these may be available in careers and adult guidance centres or public libraries.

Contents of The Gazetteer

England

Channel Islands

Isle of Man

Wales

Scotland

Northern Ireland

Bedfordshire and Luton

CfBT Bedfordshire Careers

Bedford Careers Centre, Eagle Court, Dame Alice Street, Bedford MK40 2SR. Tel: 01234 210000.

Dunstable Careers Centre, 21 West Street, Dunstable LU6 1SL. Tel: 01582 662949.

Luton Guidance Centre, Link House, 49 Alma Street, Luton LU1 2PL. Tel: 01582 728654. E-mail: athompson@cfbt.org.uk

Mid Beds Job Search & Guidance Service, 1a The Avenue, Flintwick MK45 1BP. Tel: 01525 715440.

Bedfordshire TEC, Woburn Court, 2 Railton Road, Woburn Road Industrial Estate, Kempston MK42 7PN. Tel: 01234 843100. Website: www.tec.co.uk/map/beds.html

Adult Education Service, Bedfordshire County Council, Education Department, County Hall, Cauldwell Street, Bedford MK42 9AP. Tel: 01234 363222.

Adult Education Service, Luton Borough Council, Education Department, Unity House, 111 Stuart Street, Luton LU1 5NP. Tel: 01582 548000.

Barnfield Technology Centre, Enterprise Way, Bramingham, Luton LU3 4BY. Tel: 01582 569500. Website: www.barnfield.ac.uk

Bedford College, Cauldwell Street, Bedford MK42 9AH. Tel: 01234 345151.

Cranfield University, Cranfield MK43 0AL. Tel: 01234 750111. Website: www.cranfield.ac.uk

De Montfort University Bedford, Lansdowne Road, Bedford MK40 2BZ. Tel: 01234 351966. Website: www.dmu.ac.uk

Dunstable College, Kingsway, Dunstable LU5 4HG. Tel: 01582 477776.

Institute of Sales and Marketing Management, National Westminster House, 31 Upper George Street, Luton LU1 2RD. Tel: 01582 411130.

Learning for Life Bedfordshire & Luton Ltd, 2 Railton Road, Woburn Road Industrial Estate, Kempston MK42 7PN. Tel: 01234 852216.

Silsoe College, (Cranfield University), Silsoe, Bedford MK45 4DT. Tel: 01525 863319. Website: www.silsoe.cranfield.ac.uk E-mail: recruitment@cranfield.ac.uk

University of Luton, Park Square, Luton LU1 3JU. Tel: 01582 34111. Website: www.luton.ac.uk E-mail: admissions@luton.ac.uk

Berkshire (includes Reading, Slough, West Berkshire, Wokingham, Royal Windsor and Maidenhead)

CfBT Thames Careers Guidance

Bracknell Careers Centre, Amber House, Market Street, Bracknell RG12 1JB. Tel: 01344 454151.

Maidenhead Careers Centre, 69 High Street, Maidenhead SL6 1JX. Tel: 01628 622481.

Newbury Careers Centre, 87 Northbrook Street, Newbury RG14 1AE. Tel: 01635 41722.

Reading Careers Centre, 16-18 Duke Street, Reading RG1 4RU. Tel: 0118 952 3800.

Slough Careers Centre, Connaught House, 46-48 High Street, Slough SL1 1EL. Tel: 01753 576136.

Windsor Careers Centre, East Berkshire College, Windsor Campus, Claremont Road, Windsor SL4 3AZ. Tel: 01753 576136.

Wokingham Careers Centre, 1st Floor, St Florian House, Milton Road, Wokingham RG40 1DB. Tel: 0118 978 6845.

Wokingham Adult Guidance Unit, St Florian House, Milton Road, Wokingham RG40 1DB. Tel: 0118 978 6845.

Thames Valley Enterprise, Pacific House, Imperial Way, Worton Grange, Reading RG2 0TF. Tel: 0118 921 4000. Website: www.tec.co.uk/map/tve.html

Berkshire College of Agriculture, Hall Place, Burchetts Green, Maidenhead SL6 6QR. Tel: 01628 824444. Website: www.berks-coll-ag.ac.uk E-mail: enquiries@bca.rmplc.co.uk

Berkshire College of Art and Design, Raymond Road, Maidenhead SL6 6DF. Tel: 01628 770769. Website: www.artec.org.uk E-mail: bcad@rmplc.ec.uk

Berkshire Education Department, Civic Centre, Reading RG1 7WA. Tel: 0118 939 0900.

Bracknell College, Church Road, Bracknell RG12 1DJ. Tel: 01344 420411. Website: www.bracknell.ac.uk E-mail: study@bracknell.ac.uk

College of Estate Management, Whiteknights, Reading RG6 6AW. Tel: 0118 986 1101. Website: www.cem.ac.uk E-mail: info@cem.ac.uk

East Berkshire College (Maidenhead, Windsor, Langley), Boyn Hill Avenue, Maidenhead SL6 8BY. Tel: 0800 923 0423. Website: www.eastberks.ac.uk

Newbury College, Oxford Road, Newbury RG14 1PQ. Tel: 01635 37000. Website: www.newbury-college.ac.uk E-mail: student-services@newbury-college.ac.uk

Reading College and School of Arts & Design, Crescent Road, Reading RG1 5RQ. Tel: 0118 967 5000. Website: www.reading-college.ac.uk E-mail: enquiries@reading-college.ac.uk

Thames Valley University, Slough Campus, Wellington Street, Slough SL1 1YG. Tel: 01753 534585. Website: www.tuv.ac.uk E-mail: learning-advice@tvu.ac.uk

University of Reading, Whiteknights, PO Box 217, Reading RG6 6AH. Tel: 0118 987 5123. Website: www.rdg.ac.uk E-mail: schools.liaison@rdg.ac.uk

Bristol, Bath and North East Somerset, North West Somerset and South Gloucestershire

Learning Partnership West

Guidance Shop, 14 Queen Square, Bath BAI 2HN. Tel: 01225 461501.

Guidance Shop, 4 Colston Avenue, Bristol BSI 4ST. Tel: 0117 987 3700.

Guidance Shop, 28 Gloucester Road North, Filton, Bristol BS7 0SJ. Tel: 0117 969 8101.

Guidance Shop, 5 The Kingsway, Kingswood, Bristol BS15 1BE. Tel: 0117 961 2760.

Guidance Shop, 45 Boulevard, Weston super Mare BS23 1PG. Tel: 01934 644443.

WESTEC, PO Box 164, St Lawrence House, 29-31 Broad Street, Bristol BS99 7HR. Tel: 0117 927 7116. Website: www.tec.co.uk/westec E-mail: @westec.co.uk

Bath and North East Somerset Council, Community Education Office, c/o Bath College, Avon Street, Bath BA1 1UP. Tel: 01225 312191.

Bath and Swindon College of Health Studies, Bath and Wessex House, Royal United Hospital, Combe Park, Bath BA1 3NG. Tel: 01225 824238.

Bath Spa University College, Newton Park, Newton St Loe, Bath BA2 9BN. Tel: 01225 875875. Website: www.bathspa.ac.uk E-mail: enquiries@bathspa.ac.uk

Bristol City Council Community Education, The Council House, College Green, Bristol BS1 5TR. Tel: 0117 922 2000.

Bristol Old Vic: Theatre School, 2 Downside Road, Clifton, Bristol BS8 2XF. Tel: 0117 973 3535.

City of Bath College, Avon Street, Bath BA1 1UP. Tel: 01225 312191. Website: www.citybathcoll.ac.uk E-mail: enquiries@mktcitybathcoll.ac.uk

City of Bristol College, Ashley Down, Bristol BS7 9BU. Tel: 0117 904 5000. Website: www.cityofbristol.ac.uk E-mail: cbc@sbristol.pcom.co.uk

City of Bristol College, The Hartcliffe Centre, Bishport Avenue, Hartcliffe, Bristol BS13 ORJ. Tel: 0117 963 9033. Website: www.cityofbristol.ac.uk

College of Care and Early Education, Broadlands Drive, Lawrence Weston, Bristol BS11 ONT. Tel: 0117 923 5706. E-mail: 'named person'@collegecareearlyed.ac.uk

Filton College, Filton Avenue, Filton, Bristol BS34 7AT. Tel: 0117 931 2121. Website: www.filton-college.ac.uk E-mail: admin@filton-college.ac.uk

North Somerset Council Education Department, Community Education Centre, Mizzymead Road, Nailsea, Bristol BS19 2HL. Tel: 01275 810659.

Norton-Radstock College, South Hill Park, Radstock, Bath BA3 3RW. Tel: 01761 433161. Website: www.nortcoll.ac.uk

Proteus Consultancy Ltd, Maggs House, 78 Queens Road, Clifton, Bristol BS8 1QX. Tel: 01202 431173. Website: www.proteus-net.co.uk E-mail: proteus@btinternet.com

Soundwell College, St Stephens Road, Kingswood, Bristol BS16 4RL. Tel: 0117 947 9270. Website: www.soundwell.ac.uk

South Gloucestershire Council Education Department, South Gloucestershire Offices, Bowling Hill, Chipping Sodbury, Bristol BS17 6JX. Tel: 01454 868686.

South West England Development Agency, 6th Floor, Gaunt's House, Denmark Street, Bristol BS1 5SD. Tel: 0117 922 0353. Website: www.soutwestengland.co.uk

Trinity College (Bristol), Stoke Hill, Stoke Bishop, Bristol BS9 1JP. Tel: 0117 968 2803. Website: www.trinity-bris.ac.uk E-mail: trinity-bris.ac.uk

University of Bath, Claverton Down, Bath BA2 7AY. Tel: 01225 323019. Website: www.bath.ac.uk

University of Bristol, Senate House, Tyndall Avenue, Bristol BS8 1TH. Tel: 0117 928 9000. Website: www.bristol.ac.uk E-mail: admissions@bristol.ac.uk

University of the West of England (Bristol), Frenchay Campus, Coldharbour Lane, Bristol BS16 1QY. Tel: 0117 965 6261. Website: www.uwe.ac.uk

West of England Management Centre, Engineers House, The Promenade, Clifton Down, Bristol BS8 3NB. Tel: 0117 973 1471. Website: www.eef.org.uk/western/ E-mail: eeswa@dail.pipex.com

Weston College, Knightstone Road, Weston super Mare BS23 2AL. Tel: 01934 411411. Website: www.weston.ac.uk

Buckinghamshire and Milton Keynes

Buckingham Careers Services

HQ, 662 North Row, Central Milton Keynes MK9 3AP. Tel: 01908 232808. Website: www.buckinghamcareers.co.uk E-mail: julia.valentinte@buckinghamcareers.co.uk

Aylesbury Careers Centre, Ground Floor, Walker House, George Street, Aylesbury HP20 2HU. Tel: 01296 397738. Website: www.buckinghamcareers.co.uk

High Wycombe Careers Centre, Wesley Court, Priory Road, High Wycombe HP13 6SE. Tel: 01494 551800. Website: www.buckinghamcareers.co.uk

Milton Keynes Careers Centre, 662 North Row, Central Milton Keynes MK9 3AP. Tel: 01908 232808. Website: www.buckinghamcareers.co.uk

Career Discovery, 70 Station Road, Amersham HP7 0BD. Tel: 01494 724615.

Development at Work, 130 Engain Drive, Shenley Church End, Milton Keynes MK5 6DH. Tel: 01908 506996. E-mail: bh@developmentatwork.com (services aimed at the executive market)

JMPS Ltd, 18 Temple Street, Aylesbury HP20 2RQ. Tel: 01296 393877. Website: www.jmps.co.uk E-mail: info@jmps.co.uk

Learning Link, Acorn House, 387 Midsummer Boulevard, Central Milton Keynes MK9 3HP. Tel: 0800 137080. Website: www.serif.org.uk E-mail: 113263.2715@compuserve.com

Thames Valley Enterprise, Pacific House, Imperial Way, Worton Grange, Reading RG2 0TF. Tel: 0118 921 4000. Website: www.tec.co.uk/map/tve.html

Amersham and Wycombe College, High Wycombe Campus, Spring Lane, Hackwell Heath HP10 9HE. Tel: 01494 735555. Website: www.amerwyc-coll.ac.uk

Aylesbury College, Oxford Road, Aylesbury HP21 8PD. Tel: 01296 588588. Website: www.aylesbury.ac.uk E-mail: studerv@aylesbury.ac.uk

Buckinghamshire College, Queen Alexandra Road, High Wycombe HP11 2ST. Tel: 01494 603030. Website: www.buckscol.ac.uk E-mail: cgrei101@buckscol.ac.uk

Chamber of Commerce, TEMPUS, 249 Midsummer Boulevard, Central Milton Keynes MK9 1EY. Tel: 01908 259000. Website: mk-chamber.co.uk E-mail: tempus@mk-chamber.co.uk

Education Department, Buckinghamshire County Council, County Hall, Walton Street, Aylesbury HP20 1UZ. Tel: 01296 395000.
Faculty of Health and Social Care, Park Square, Luton LU1 3JU. Tel: 01296 315578.

Milton Keynes College, Chaffron Way Centre, Woughton Campus West, Leadenhall, Milton Keynes MK6 5LP. Tel: 01908 684444. Website: www.mkcollege.co.uk

Missenden Abbey Management Centre, Great Missenden HP16 0BD. Tel: 01494 862904. Website: www.missendenabbey.ac.uk E-mail: enquiries@missendenabbey.ac.uk

National Film & TV School, Station Road, Beaconsfield HP9 1LG. Tel: 01494 671234. Website: www.thebiz.co.uk/natfilm.htm

SSVC, Chalfont Grove, Narcot Lane, Chalfont St Peters, Gerrards Cross SL9 8TN. Tel: 01494 874461/878388.

University of Buckingham, Hunter Street, Buckingham MK18 1EG. Tel: 01280 814080. Website: www.buckingham.ac.uk E-mail: admissions@buck.ac.uk

Cambridgeshire and Peterborough

Cambridge Careers Guidance Ltd

HQ, 7 The Meadow, Meadow Lane, St Ives PE17 4LG. Tel: 01480 463463.

Cambridge Careers Centre, 62 Burleigh Street, Cambridge CB1 1DN. Tel: 01223 362345.

Cambridge Careers Centre, Guidance Shop, Lion Yard Library, Cambridge CB3 3QD. Tel: 01223 311189.

Ely Careers Centre, 59 Market Street, Ely CB7 4LP. Tel: 01353 669099.

Huntingdon Careers Centre, Walden House, Market Hill, Huntingdon PE18 6NR. Tel: 01480 375827.

Peterborough Careers Centre, Cavell Court, Lincoln Road, Peterborough PE1 2RQ. Tel: 01733 311094.

Wisbech Careers Centre, 2 Stermyn Street, Wisbech PE13 1EQ. Tel: 01945 585128.

Business Link Central & Southern Cambridgeshire, The Business Centre, Station Road, Histon CB4 9LQ. Tel: 0345 882255. Website: www.tec.co.uk/map/cabstec.html

Greater Peterborough Training & Enterprise Council, Stuart House, City Road, Peterborough PEI 1QF. Tel: 01733 890808. Website: www.tec.co.uk/map/gptec.html

EEDA, East of England Development Agency, Compass House, Chivers Way, Histon, Cambridge CB4 9ZR. Tel: 01223 713900. Website: www.eeda.org.uk

Anglia Polytechnic University, East Road, Cambridge CB1 1PT. Tel: 01223 363271. Website: www.anglia.ac.uk E-mail: angliainfo@anglia.ac.uk

Cambridgeshire College of Agriculture and Horticulture, Landbeach Road, Milton, Cambridge CB4 6DB. Tel: 01223 860701.

Cambridge Regional College, Kings Hedges Road, Cambridge CB4 2QT. Tel: 01223 418200. Website: www.camre.ac.uk E-mail: enquiry@crc.tcom.co.uk

Education Department Cambridgeshire County Council, Shire Hall, Castle Court, Castle Street, Cambridge CB3 0AP. Tel: 01223 717111.

Homerton College, Hills Road, Cambridge CB2 2PH. Tel: 01223 507114. Website: www.homerton.cam.ac.uk E-mail: nt204@cam.ac.uk

Huntingdon Regional College, California Road, Huntingdon PE18 7BL. Tel: 01480 52346. Website: www.huntingdon.ac.uk E-mail: college@huntingdon@ac.uk

Isle College, Ramnoth Road, Wisbech PE13 0HY. Tel: 01945 582561. Website: www.isle.ac.uk

The Learning Centre, Central Library, Broadway, Peterborough PE1 1RX. Tel: 01733 897191. Website: www.learning-centre.demon.co.uk
E-mail: learning-centre@learning.centre.demon.co.uk

National Extension College, 18 Brooklands Avenue, Cambridge CB2 2HN. Tel: 01223 450200. Website: www.nec.ac.uk E-mail: info@nec.ac.uk

Peterborough Regional College, Park Crescent, Peterborough PE1 4DZ. Tel: 01733 767366. Website: www.peterborough.ac.uk E-mail: info@peterborough.ac.uk

University of Cambridge, The Old Schools, Trinity Lane, Cambridge CB2 1TN. Tel: 01223 337733. Website: www.cam.ac.uk

Cheshire, Warrington and Halton

Career Connections

Chester Careers Centre, 1st Floor, Goldsmith House, Hamilton Place, Chester CH1 1SE. Tel: 01244 606011.

Ellesmere Port Office, Coronation Road, Ellesmere Port L65 9AA. Tel: 0151 357 4544.

Cheshire Guidance Partnership

Head Office, No 2 The Stables, Gadbrook Park, Northwich CW9 7RG. Tel: 01606 305200. Website: www.careers-cgp.co.uk E-mail: info@careers-cgp.co.uk

Congleton Careers Centre, 35/37 Lawton Street, Congleton CW12 1RU. Tel: 01260 276116. Website: www.careers-cgp.co.uk E-mail: info@careers-cgp.co.uk

Crewe Careers Centre, 44/46 Victoria Street, Crewe CW1 2JE. Tel: 01273 251002. Website: www.careers-cgp.co.uk E-mail: info@careers-cgp.co.uk

Macclesfield Careers Centre, Chatham House, Churchill Way, Macclesfield SK11 6AY. Tel: 01625 424026. Website: www.careers-cgp.co.uk E-mail: info@careers-cgp.co.uk

Northwich Careers Centre, Brunner Court, 97 Witton Street, Northwich CW9 5DR. Tel: 01606 331515. Website: www.careers-cgp.co.uk E-mail: info@careers-cgp.co.uk

Runcorn Careers Centre, 23 High Street, Runcorn WA7 1AP. Tel: 01928 580220. Website: www.careers-cgp.co.uk E-mail: info@careers-cgp.co.uk

Warrington Careers Centre, 67/69 Sankey Street, Warrington WA1 1SL. Tel: 01925 416611. Website: www.careers-cgp.co.uk E-mail: info@careers-cgp.co.uk

Widnes Careers Centre, John Briggs House, Gerrard Street, Widnes WA8 6BE. Tel: 01928 704433. Website: www.careers-cgp.co.uk E-mail: info@careers-cgp.co.uk

Winsford Careers Centre, Wyvern House, The Drumber, Winsford CW7 1AU. Tel: 01606 815648. Website: www.careers-cgp.co.uk E-mail: info@careers-cgp.co.uk

North and Mid Cheshire TEC, Spencer House, Dewhurst Road, Birchwood, Warrington WA3 7PP. Tel: 01925 826515. Website: www.normidtec.co.uk E-mail: general@normidtec.co.uk

South and East Cheshire Training & Enterprise Council, PO Box 37, Dalton Way, Middlewich CW10 0HU. Tel: 01606 717009. Website: www.sectec.org.co.uk

Chester College of Higher Education, Parkgate Road, Chester CH1 4BJ. Tel: 01224 375444. Website: www.chester.ac.uk E-mail: b.reg@chester.ac.uk

Education Department, Cheshire County Council, County Hall, Chester CH1 1SQ. Tel: 01244 602351.

Halton College, Kingsway, Widnes, WA8 7QQ. Tel: 0151 423 1391. Website: www.haltoncollege.ac.uk E-mail: welcome.centre@haltoncollege.ac.uk

Macclesfield College, Park Lane, Macclesfield SK11 8LF. Tel: 01625 427744.

Mid-Cheshire College, Hartford Campus, Northwich CW8 1LJ. Tel: 01606 74444. Website: www.midchesh.u-net.com E-mail: admin@midchesh.u-net.com

North West England Development Agency, New Town House, Buttermarket Street, Warrington WA1 2LF. Tel: 01925 644654. Website: www.nwda.co.uk

Reaseheath College, Reaseheath, Nantwich CW5 6W. Tel: 01270 625131. Website: www.reaseheath.ac.uk E-mail: rheathl@reaseheath.ac.uk

South Cheshire College, Dane Bank Avenue, Crewe CW2 8AB. Tel: 01270 654654. Website: www.s-cheshire.ac.uk E-mail: info@s-cheshire.ac.uk

University College Chester, Parkgate Road, Chester CH1 4BJ. Tel: 01244 375444. Website: www.chester.ac.uk

University College Warrington, Padgate Campus, Crab Lane, Warrington WA2 0DB. Tel: 01925 494494. Website: www.ucw.warr.ac.uk E-mail: registry.he@warr.ac.uk

West Cheshire College, Eaton Road, Handbridge, Chester CH4 7ER. Tel: 01244 670561. Website: www.west-cheshire.ac.uk E-mail: r.munroe@west-cheshire.ac.uk

Cleveland Area (includes Middlesbrough, Stockton-on-Tees, Hartlepool, Redcar and Cleveland)

Future Steps Ltd

Hartlepool Careers Centre, 32 Victoria Road, Hartlepool TS26 8DD. Tel: 01429 275501. Website: www.futuresteps.co.uk E-mail: enquiries@futuresteps.co.uk

Middlesbrough Careers Centre, Fry Street, Middlesbrough TS1 1HD. Tel: 01642 240081. Website: www.futuresteps.co.uk E-mail: enquiries@futuresteps.co.uk

Redcar Careers Centre, 6-8 West Dyke Road, Redcar TS10 1DZ. Tel: 01642 490870. Website: www.futuresteps.co.uk E-mail: enquiries@futuresteps.co.uk

Stockton-on-Tees Careers Centre, 28 Silver Street, Stockton-on-Tees TS18 1SX. Tel: 01642 616031. Website: www.futuresteps.co.uk E-mail: enquiries@futuresteps.co.uk

Tees Valley TEC Ltd, Training & Enterprise House, 2 Queen's Square, Middlesbrough TS2 1AA. Tel: 01642 231023. Website: www.teesvalleytec.co.uk E-mail: info@teesvalleytec.ac.uk

Askham Bryan College, Avenue Place, Redcar Road, Guisborough TS14 6AX. Tel: 01287 633870.

Cleveland College of Art and Design, Administration Centre, Green Lane, Linthorpe, Middlesbrough TS5 7RJ. Tel: 01642 288888.

Education Department, Hartlepool Borough Council, Level 4, Civic Centre, Victoria Road, Hartlepool TS24 8AY. Tel: 01429 523756.

Education Department, Middlesbrough Borough Council, PO Box 191, 2nd Floor, Civic Centre, Middlesbrough TS1 2XS. Tel: 01642 818480.

Education Department, Redcar & Cleveland Borough Council, PO Box 83, Council Offices, Kirkleatham Street, Redcar TS10 1YA. Tel: 01642 444356.

Education Department, Stockton-on-Tees Borough Council, PO Box 228, Municipal Buildings, Church Road, Stockton-on-Tees TS18 1XE. Tel: 01642 393939. E-mail: sbradford@virginet.co.uk

Hartlepool College of Further Education, Stockton Street, Hartlepool TS25 7NT. Tel: 01429 295111. Website: www.hartlepoolfe.ac.uk E-mail: enquiries@hartlepoolfe.ac.uk

Middlesbrough College, Roman Road, Linthorpe, Middlesbrough TS5 5PJ. Tel: 01642 333333. Website: www.middlesbro.ac.uk

Redcar and Cleveland College, Corporation Road, Redcar TS10 1EZ. Tel: 01642 473132. Website: www.cleveland.ac.uk

Stockton and Billingham College of Further Education, The Causeway, Billingham TS23 2DB. Tel: 01642 552101.

Teesside Tertiary College, Douglas Street, Middlesbrough TS4 2JW. Tel: 01642 275000. Website: www.ttc.ac.uk E-mail: enquiries@ttc.uk

University College Stockton, University Boulevard, Thornaby, Stockton TS17 6BH. Tel: 01642 335300. Website: www.dur.ac.uk

University of Teesside, Middlesbrough TS1 3BA. Tel: 01642 218121. Website: www.tees.ac.uk

Cornwall

Cornwall and Devon Careers Ltd

Bodmin Careers Centre, 85 Fore Street, Bodmin PL31 2JB. Tel: 01208 77999. Website: www.careers-cd.org.uk

Penzance Careers Centre, 2 Alverton Street, Penzance TR18 2QW. Tel: 01736 362244. Website: www.careers-cd.org.uk

Pool Careers Centre, Carnon Building, Wilson Way, Pool, Redruth TR15 3RS. Tel: 01209 315171. Website: www.careers-cd.org.uk

Truro Careers Centre, Chiltern House, City Road, Truro TR1 2JL. Tel: 01872 277993. Website: www.careers-cd.org.uk

Link into Learning, Westhaul Park, Par Moor Road, St Austell PL25 3RF. Tel: 01726 816550. Website: www.linklearning.clara.net E-mail: janet@linklearning.clara.net

Devon and Cornwall Training & Enterprise Council, Foliot House, Brooklands, Budshead Road, Crown Hill, Plymouth PL6 5XIZ. Tel: 01752 767929. Website: www.thebiz.co.uk/devtec.htm E-mail: dctec@zynet.co.uk

Cambourne School of Mines, Pool, Redruth TR15 3SE. Tel: 01209 714866. Website: www.ex.ac.uk/csm E-mail: r.j.hancock@csm.ex.ac.uk

Cornwall College, Trevenson Road, Redruth TR15 3RD. Tel: 01209 611611. Website: www.cornwall.ac.uk

Devon Training for Skills, Block A, Ashleigh Way, Language Office Complex, Plympton, Plymouth PL7 7JX. Tel: 01752 343242. Website: www.devon-cc.gov.uk

Education Services, Cornwall County Council, County Hall, Truro TR1 3AY. Tel: 01872 322433.

Falmouth College of Arts, Woodlane, Falmouth TR11 4RA. Tel: 01326 211077. Website: www.falmouth.ac.uk E-mail: admissions@falmouth.ac.uk

Penwith College, St Clare Street, Penzance TR18 2SA. Tel: 01736 335000.

St Austell College, Trevarthian Road, St Austell PL25 4BU. Tel: 01726 67911. Website: www.stacoll.demon.co.uk E-mail: info@stacoll-demon.co.uk

Truro College, College Road, Truro TR1 3XX. Tel: 01872 264251. Website: www.truroolc.demon.co.uk E-mail: courses@truroolc.demon.co.uk

Cumbria

Cumbria Careers Ltd

Barrow Careers Centre, John Whinnerah Institute, Abbey Road, Barrow-in-Furness LA14 1XN. Tel: 01229 824052.

Carlisle Careers Centre, 28 Lowther Street, Carlisle CA3 8DH. Tel: 01228 596272.

Kendal Careers Centre, 124 Highgate, Kendal LA1 4HE. Tel: 01539 730045.
Maryport Careers Centre, 67 Wood Street, Maryport CA15 6LD. Tel: 01900 815928.
Penrith Careers Centre, 43 Middlegate, Penrith CA11 7XR. Tel: 01768 865296.
Ulverston Careers Centre, 6 Cross Street, Ulverston LA12 7LF. Tel: 01229 583466.
Whitehaven Careers Centre, 60-62 Lowther Street, Whitehaven CA28 7DS. Tel: 01946 695541.
Workington Careers Centre, 213 Vulcan's Lane, Workington CA14 2BT. Tel: 01900 604674.

Enterprise Cumbria Ltd, Venture House, Regents Court, Guard Street, Workington CA14 4EW. Tel: 01900 66991. Website: tec.co.uk/map/cumb.html

Carlisle College, Victoria Place, Carlisle CA1 1HS. Tel: 01228 819000. Website: www.carlisle.ac.uk E-mail: marketing@carlisle.ac.uk

Cumbria College of Art and Design, Brampton Road, Carlisle CA3 9AY. Tel: 01228 400300. Website: cumbriacad.ac.uk E-mail: q@cumbriacad.ac.uk

Education Department, Cumbria County Council, 5 Portland Square, Carlisle CA1 1PU. Tel: 01228 606060.

Furness College, Howard Street, Barrow-in-Furness LA14 1NB. Tel: 01229 825017. Website: www.furness.ac.uk E-mail: cours.enq@furness.ac.uk

Kendal College, Milnthorpe Road, Kendal LA9 5AY. Tel: 01539 724313. Website: www.kendal.ac.uk E-mail: enquiries@kendal.ac.uk

Newton Rigg College, Penrith CA11 0AH. Tel: 01768 863791. Website: www.newtonrigg.ac.uk E-mail: info@newtonrigg.ac.uk

West Cumbria College, Park Lane, Workington CA14 2RW. Tel: 01900 64331. Website: www.westcumbcoll.ac.uk E-mail: wcc@westcumbcoll.ac.uk

Derbyshire and Derby City

Derbyshire Careers Service Ltd

Alfreton Guidance & Learning Centre, 10 High Street, Alfreton DE55 7BN. Tel: 01773 521821. Website: www.derbyshire-careers.co.uk E-mail: central@derbyshire-careers.co.uk

Chesterfield Careers Centre, 61-63 Low Pavement, Chesterfield S40 1PB. Tel: 01246 201581. Website: www.derbyshire-careers.co.uk E-mail: central@derbyshire-careers.co.uk

Clowne Careers Centre, North Derbyshire Tertiary College, Rectory Road, Clowne, Chesterfield S43 4BQ. Tel: 01246 570790. Website: www.derbyshire-careers.co.uk E-mail: central@derbyshire-careers.co.uk

Derby Careers Centre, Curzon House, 8 Curzon Street, Derby DE1 1LL. Tel: 01332 200033. Website: www.derbyshire-careers.co.uk E-mail: central@derbyshire-careers.co.uk

Heanor Careers Centre, Jobcentre, Howitt Buildings, High Street, Heanor DE75 7EZ. Tel: 01773 723200. Website: www.derbyshire-careers.co.uk E-mail: central@derbyshire-careers.co.uk

Ilkeston Careers Centre, 81 Bath Street, Ilkeston DE7 8AP. Tel: 0115 930 2636. Website: www.derbyshire-careers.co.uk E-mail: central@derbyshire-careers.co.uk

Long Eaton Careers Centre, 36 Tamworth Road, Long Eaton, Nottingham NG10 1BD. Tel: 0115 973 2806. Website: www.derbyshire-careers.co.uk E-mail: central@derbyshire-careers.co.uk

Matlock Careers Centre, Crown Square, Matlock DE4 3AT. Tel: 01629 760403.
Website: www.derbyshire-careers.co.uk E-mail: central@derbyshire-careers.co.uk

Ripley Careers Centre, Market House, Market Place, Ripley DE5 3BR. Tel: 01773 745921.
Website: www.derbyshire-careers.co.uk E-mail: central@derbyshire-careers.co.uk

Shirebrook Careers Centre, 110 Market Street, Shirebrook NG20 8AD. Tel: 01623 742374.
Website: www.derbyshire-careers.co.uk E-mail: central@derbyshire-careers.co.uk

Swadlincote Centre for Guidance & Learning, Rinway, Swadlincote DE11 8JL.
Tel: 01283 817900. Website: www.derbyshire-careers.co.uk
E-mail: central@derbyshire-careers.co.uk

Lifetime Careers Stockport and High Peak

Buxton Careers Centre, 9 The Quadrant, Buxton SK17 6AW. Tel: 01298 22322.

Glossop Careers Centre, 84 High Street West, Glossop SK13 8BB. Tel: 01457 864641.

North Derbyshire Options Advice & Guidance Centre, 63 Low Pavement,
Chesterfield S40 1PB. Tel: 01246 200034.

North Derbyshire Training & Enterprise Council, Block C, St Mary's Court, St Mary's Gate,
Chesterfield S41 7TD. Tel: 01246 551158. Website: www.tec.co.uk/map/nderby.html

South Derbyshire Chamber of Commerce, Training & Enterprise, St Helen's Court,
St Helen's Street, Derby DE1 3GY. Tel: 01332 290550.
Website: www.tec.co.uk/map/sderby.html

Broomfield College, Broomfield, Ilkeston DE7 6DN. Tel: 01332 831345.
Website: www.broomfield.ac.uk

Chesterfield College, Infirmary Road, Chesterfield S41 7NG. Tel: 01246 500500.

Derby Tertiary College, London Road, Wilmorton, Derby DE2 8UG. Tel: 01332 757570.
Website: www.derby-college.ac.uk

East Midland College of Beauty & Massage Therapies, Halliday House, 2 Wilson Street
Derby DE1 1PG. Tel: 01332 205788. Website: www.emnet.co.uk/emc

Education Service, Derby City Council, Education Office, Middleton House, 27 St Mary's Gate,
Derby DE1 3NN. Tel: 01332 716957. E-mail: 100442.2641@compuserve.com

Education Department, Derbyshire County Council, County Hall, Matlock DE4 3AG.
Tel: 01629 580000.

High Peak College, Harpur Hill, Buxton SK17 9JZ. Tel: 01298 71100.
Website: www.highpeak.ac.uk E-mail: m.taylor@highpeak.ac.uk

Mackworth College, Derby, Prince Charles Avenue, Mackworth, Derby DE22 4LR.
Tel: 01332 519951.

North Derbyshire Tertiary College, Rectory Road, Clowne, Chesterfield S43 4BQ.
Tel: 01246 810332. Website: www.ndtc.ac.uk

South East Derbyshire College, Field Road, Ilkeston DE7 5RS. Tel: 0115 932 4212.
Website: www.sedc.co.uk E-mail: admissions@sedc.co.uk

University of Derby, Kedleston Road, Derby DE22 1GB. Tel: 01332 622222.
Website: www.derby.ac.uk E-mail: admissions@derby.ac.uk

Devon

Cornwall and Devon Careers Ltd

Barnstaple Careers Centre, 90/91 Boutport Street, Barnstaple EX31 1SX. Tel: 01271 378585. Website: www.careers-cd.org.uk

Exeter Careers Centre, Ist Floor, Queen's House, Little Queen's Street, Exeter EX4 31J. Tel: 01392 203603. Website: www.careers-cd.org.uk

Newton Abbot Careers Centre, Bridge House, Sherborne Road, Newton Abbot TQ12 2QX. Tel: 01626 367579. Website: www.careers-cd.org.uk

Plymouth Careers Centre, Ist Floor, 10 Derry's Cross, Plymouth PLI 2SH. Tel: 01752 207700. Website: www.careers-cd.org.uk

Torquay Careers Centre, 236 Union Street, Torquay TQ1 2QS. Tel: 01803 200202. Website: www.careers-cd.org.uk

Devon & Cornwall TEC, Foliot House, Brooklands, Bushead Road, Crown Hill, Plymouth PL6 5XR. Tel: 01752 767929. Website: www.thebiz.co.uk/devtec.htm E-mail: dectec@zynet.co.uk

Academy of Co-ordinated Training, Bedford House, 1 North Street, Tavistock PL19 0AN. Tel: 01822 616333.

Bicton College of Agriculture, East Budleigh, Budleigh Salterton EX9 7BY. Tel: 01395 562300. Website: www.eclipse.co.uk/bicton E-mail: bc7623@mail.eclipse.uk

College of St Mark and St John, Derriford Road, Plymouth PL6 8BH. Tel: 01752 636751. Website: www.marjohn.ac.uk E-mail: promotion@marjohn.ac.uk

Lifelong Learning, Devon County Council, Room 122, County Hall, Exeter EX2 4QG. Tel: 01392 382055. Website: www.devon-cc.gov.uk

Dartington College of Arts, Totnes TQ9 6EJ. Tel: 01803 862224. Website: www.dartington.ac.uk E-mail: registry@dartington.ac.uk

East Devon College, Bolham Road, Tiverton EX16 6SH. Tel: 01884 235200. Website: www.eastdevon.ac.uk E-mail: admissions@admin.eastdevon.ac.uk

Exeter College, Hele Road, Exeter EX4 4JS. Tel: 01392 205 222. Website: www.exe-coll.ac.uk E-mail: reception@exe-coll.ac.uk

Ivybridge Community College, Harford, Ivybridge PL21 0JA. Tel: 01752 896662.

Kingsbridge Community College, Tresillian, 112 Fore Street, Kingsbridge TQ7 1AW. Tel: 01548 853298.

Mid Teign Community Education, Adult Education Centre, Market Street, Newton Abbot TQ12 2RJ. Tel: 01626 354584.

NW Plymouth Community Education, Sir John Hunt Community College, Lancaster Gardens, Plymouth PL5 4AA. Tel: 01752 780589.

North Devon College, Old Sticklepath Hill, Barnstaple EX31 2BQ. Tel: 01271 345291.

Plymouth Adult Education, Plymstock School Campus, Church Road, Plymouth PL9 9AZ. Tel: 01752 406847.

Plymouth College of Art and Design, Tavistock Place, Plymouth PL4 8AT. Tel: 01752 203434. Website: www.pcad.plym.ac.uk E-mail: enquiries@pcad.plym.ac.uk

Plymouth College of Further Education, King's Road, Plymouth PL2 5QG. Tel: 01752 305300. Website: www.pcfe.plymouth.ac.uk E-mail: reception@pcfe.plymouth.ac.uk

South Devon College, Newton Road, Torquay TQ2 5BY. Tel: 01803 400700.
Website: www.s-devon.ac.uk E-mail: courses@s-devon.ac.uk

University of Exeter, Northcote House, The Queen's Drive, Exeter EX4 4QJ. Tel: 01392 263030.
Website: www.exeter.ac.uk E-mail: admissions@exeter.ac.uk

University of Plymouth, Drake Circus, Plymouth PL4 8AA. Tel: 01752 232232.
Website: www.plym.ac.uk E-mail: ncrocker@plymouth.ac.uk

Dorset, Poole and Bournemouth

Dorset Careers

HQ, Business Development Group, 3 Kingland Road, Poole BH15 1SH. Tel: 01202 677558.
Website: www.dorset-careers.co.uk E-mail: bdg@mail.dorset-careers.co.uk

Bournemouth Branch, 5-6 Lansdowne House, Christchurch Road, Bournemouth BH 1 3JP.
Tel: 01202 315331. Website: www.dorset-careers.co.uk
E-mail: bdg@mail.dorset-careers.co.uk

Blandford Branch, 7-8 Barnack Walk, Blandford DT11 7AL. Tel: 01258 454454.
Website: www.dorset-careers.co.uk E-mail: bdg@mail.dorset-careers.co.uk

Poole Branch, 3 Kingland Road, Poole BH15 1SH. Tel: 01202 677557.
Website: www.dorset-careers.co.uk E-mail: bdg@mail.dorset-careers.co.uk

Weymouth Branch, 29 St Thomas Street, Weymouth DT4 8EJ. Tel: 01305 782180.
Website: www.dorset-careers.co.uk E-mail: bdg@mail.dorset-careers.co.uk

Dorset Training & Enterprise Council, 25 Oxford Road, Bournemouth BH8 8EY.
Tel: 01202 299284. E-mail: dorset.tec@fornix.org.uk

Arts Institute at Bournemouth, Wallisdown Road, Poole BH12 5HH. Tel: 01202 533011.
Website: www.arts-inst-bournemouth.ac.uk E-mail: general@arts-inst-bournemouth.ac.uk

Bournemouth and Poole College of Further Education, Landsdowne Centre,
Landsdowne Road, Bournemouth BH1 1SE. Tel: 01202 205656.
Website: www.bournemouthandpoole-cfe.ac.uk

Bournemouth University, Fern Barrow, Poole, Dorset BH12 5BB. Tel: 01202 524111.
Website: www.bournemouth.ac.uk E-mail: prospectus@bournemouth.ac.uk

Education, Libraries and Arts Directorate, Dorset County Council, County Hall, Colliton Park,
Dorchester DT1 1XJ. Tel: 01305 251000.

Education Service, Poole Borough Council, Civic Centre, Poole BH15 2RU. Tel: 01202 633633.

Kingston Maurward College, Kingston Maurward, Dorchester DT2 8PY. Tel: 01305 264738.
Website: www.kmc.ac.uk E-mail: administration@kmc.ac.uk

Shaftesbury College, Wincombe Centre, Wincombe Business Park, Shaftesbury SP7 9QJ.
Tel: 01747 850237.

Weymouth College, Cranford Avenue, Weymouth DT4 7LQ. Tel: 01305 761100.
Website: www.weycoll.ac.uk E-mail: devunit@weycoll.ac.uk

Durham and Darlington

County Durham Careers Service

HQ/Graduate Connections, Aykley Heads House, Aykley Heads, Durham DH1 5TS. Tel: 0191 383 1777.

Bishop Auckland Careers Centre, 3a Market Place, Bishop Auckland DL14 7NJ. Tel: 01388 603468.

Chester le Street Careers Centre, Terriff House, Station Road, Chester le Street DH3 3HF. Tel: 0191 388 3019.

Consett Careers Centre, 5b Medomsley Road, Consett DH8 5HE. Tel: 01207 502795.

Darlington Careers Centre, Central House, Gladstone Street, Darlington DL3 6JX. Tel: 01325 346300.

Durham Careers Centre, 3rd Floor, Bridge House, North Road, Durham City DH1 4PW. Tel: 0191 384 9766.

Peterlee Careers Centre, Ridgemount House, Bede Way, Peterlee SR8 1EA. Tel: 0191 586 7551.

County Durham Training & Enterprise Council, Valley Street North, Darlington DL1 1TJ. Tel: 01325 351166. Website: www.enquiries@cdtec.co.uk E-mail: ask@cdtec.co.uk

Bishop Auckland College, Woodhouse Lane, Bishop Auckland DL14 6JZ. Tel: 01388 443000. Website: www.bacoll.ac.uk E-mail: enquiries@bacoll.ac.uk

Community Education, Education Departments, Durham County Council, County Hall, Durham DH1 5UJ. Tel: 0191 383 3258.

Darlington College of Technology, Cleveland Avenue, Darlington DL3 7BB. Tel: 01325 503030. Website: www.darlington.ac.uk

Derwentside College, Park Road, Consett DH8 5EE. Tel: 01207 585900. Website: www.derwentside.ac.uk

Durham College of Agriculture and Horticulture, Houghall, Durham DH1 3SG. Tel: 0191 386 1351. Website: www.houghall.ac.uk E-mail: david.bentley@virgin.net

East Durham Community College, Burnhope Way Centre, Burnhope Way, Peterlee SR8 1NU. Tel: 0191 518 2000. Website: www.eastdurham.ac.uk/ E-mail: enquiry@eastdurham.ac.uk

New College Durham, Framwellgate Moor Centre, Durham DH1 5ES. Tel: 0191 375 4000. Website: www.newdur.ac.uk E-mail: admissions@newdur.ac.uk

University of Durham, University Office, Old Shire Hall, Durham DH1 3HP. Tel: 0191 374 2000. Website: www.dur.ac.uk

Essex, Southend and Thurrock

Essex Careers & Business Partnership Ltd

HQ, Westergaard House, The Matchyns, London Road, Rivenhall CM8 3HA. Tel: 01376 391 300. Website: www.careersbp.co.uk

Basildon Careers Centre, The Basildon Centre, Basildon SS14 1EF. Tel: 01268 501300. Website: www.careersbp.co.uk

Braintree Careers Centre, 19 Bocking End, Braintree CM7 9AE. Tel: 01376 557400. Website: www.careersbp.co.uk

Brentwood Careers Centre, 98 High Street, Brentwood CM14 4AP. Tel: 01227 693300. Website: www.careersbp.co.uk

Burnham Careers Centre, Essex County Library, 103 Station Road, Burnham-on-Crouch CM0 8HQ. Tel: 01621 785666. Website: www.careersbp.co.uk

Canvey Careers Centre, 129 Furtherwick Road, Canvey Island SS8 7AL. Tel: 01268 683067. Website: www.careersbp.co.uk

Chelmsford Careers Centre, Chelmer Gate, 193-196 Moulsham Street, Chelmsford CM2 0LG. Tel: 01245 706806. Website: www.careersbp.co.uk

Clacton Careers Centre, 42 Old Road, Clacton-on-Sea C015 1HJ. Tel: 01255 254300. Website: www.careersbp.co.uk

Colchester Careers Centre, Manor House, 50 Manor Road, Colchester CO3 3LX. Tel: 01206 717100. Website: www.careersbp.co.uk

Epping Forest Careers Centre, Hetton House, Station Road, Loughton IG10 4NY. Tel: 020 8508 4110. Website: www.careersbp.co.uk

Grays Careers Centre, 5 Clarence Road, Grays, Essex RM17 6NE. Tel: 01375 362800. Website: www.careersbp.co.uk

Halstead Careers Centre, 3-4 Eastdene, Trinity Street, Halstead CM9 1JF. Tel: 01787 478408. Website: www.careersbp.co.uk

Harlow & Uttlesford Careers Centre, Watergarden Offices, College Square, The High, Harlow CM20 1AE. Tel: 01279 625300. Website: www.careersbp.co.uk

Harwich Careers Centre, Essex County Library, Upper Kingsway, Dovercourt, Harwich C012 3JT. Tel: 01255 503799. Website: www.careersbp.co.uk

Maldon Careers Centre, Essex County Library, Carmelite House, Whitehorse Lane, Maldon CM9 7FW. Tel: 01621 853552. Website: www.careersbp.co.uk

Rayleigh Careers Centre, Burley House, 15-17 High Street, Rayleigh SS6 7EW. Tel: 01268 749600. Website: www.careersbp.co.uk

Saffron Walden Careers Centre, Fairycroft, Audley Road, Saffron Walden CM11 3HD. Tel: 01799 522369. Website: www.careersbp.co.uk

South Woodham Ferrers Careers Centre, William de Ferrers Library, Trinity Square, South Woodham Ferrers, Chelmsford CM3 5JU. Tel: 01245 327159. Website: www.careersbp.co.uk

Southend Careers Centre, Rutland House, 90-92 Baxter Avenue, Southend-on-Sea SS2 6HZ. Tel: 01268 749600. Website: www.careersbp.co.uk

Witham Careers Centre, Witham Library, Newland Street, Witham CM8 2AQ. Tel: 01376 520776. Website: www.careersbp.co.uk

Essex Training & Enterprise Council, Centre for Lifetime Learning, Redwing House, Hedgerows Business Park, Colchester Road Chelmsford CM2 5PB. Tel: 01245 450123. Website: www.essex.tec.co.uk

Adult Community College, Grey Friars, High Street, Colchester CO1 1UG. Tel: 01206 542242.

Anglia Polytechnic University, Victoria Road South, Chelmsford CM1 1LL. Tel: 01245 493131. Website: www.anglia.ac.uk E-mail: angliainfo@anglia.ac.uk

Basildon College, Nethermayne, Basildon SS16 5NN. Tel: 01268 532015. Website: www.basildon.ac.uk/

Braintree College, Church Lane, Braintree CM7 5SN. Tel: 01376 321711. Website: www.braintree.ac.uk E-mail: mhansen@braintree.ac.uk

Chelmsford College, Moulsham Street, Chelmsford CM2 OJQ. Tel: 01245 265611.
Website: www.chelmcollege.u-net.com E-mail: info@chelmcollege.u-net.com

Colchester Institute, Sheepen Road, Colchester C03 3LL. Tel: 01206 718000.

Epping Forest College, Borders Lane, Loughton IG1O 3SA. Tel: 020 8502 8726.

Harlow College, Velizy Avenue, Town Centre, Harlow CM20 3LH. Tel: 01279 868000.

Learning Services Department, Essex County Council, PO Box 47, County Hall, Victoria Road South, Chelmsford CM1 1LD. Tel: 01245 492211.
Website: www.essex.gov.uk/educat/fs_02.htm

South East Essex College, Carnarvon Road, Southend-on-Sea SS2 6LS. Tel: 01702 220400.
Website: www.se-essex-college.ac.uk E-mail: marketing@se-essex-college.ac.uk

Thurrock College, Woodview, Grays RM16 2YR. Tel: 01375 391199.
Website: www.thurrock.ac.uk E-mail: admissions@thurrock.ac.uk

University of Essex, Wivenhoe Park, Colchester C04 3SQ. Tel: 01206 873666.
Website: www.essex.ac.uk E-mail: admin@essex.ac.uk

Writtle College, Chelmsford CM1 3RR. Tel: 01245 424200. Website: www.writtle.ac.uk
E-mail: postmaster@writtle.ac.uk

Gloucestershire (excluding South Gloucestershire – see Bristol entry)

Learning Partnership West

Cheltenham Careers Centre, 4 Imperial Square, Cheltenham GL50 1QB. Tel: 01242 250317.

Gloucester Careers Centre, 92-96 Westgate Street, Gloucester GLI 2PE. Tel: 01452 426900.

Stroud Careers Centre, 9 Lansdown, Stroud GL5 IBB. Tel: 01453 757133.

FOCUS Partnership (Gloucester), Blaisdon Hall, Blaisdon, Longhope GL7 0AQ.
Tel: 01452 830247.

Gloucestershire TEC, Conway House, 33-35 Worcester Street, Gloucester GL1 3AJ.
Tel: 01452 524488.

Bridgeway Associates Ltd, PO Box 16, Chipping Campden GL55 6ZB. Tel: 01386 8418407.
E-mail: 101705.3237@compuserve.com

Cheltenham & Gloucester College of Higher Education, PO Box 220, The Park, Cheltenham GL50 2QF. Tel: 01242 532700. Website: www.chelt.ac.uk E-mail: gthatcher@chelt.ac.uk

Cirencester College, Fosse Way Campus, Stroud Road, Cirencester GL7 IXA. Tel: 01285 640994.
Website: www.cirencester.ac.uk E-mail: adult.guidance@cirencester.ac.uk

Education Office, Gloucestershire County Council, Shire Hall, Westgate Street, Gloucester GL1 2TP. Tel: 01452 425400.

Gloucestershire College of Arts and Technology, Brunswick Campus, Brunswick Road, Gloucester GL1 1HU. Tel: 01452 426529.

Hartpury College, Hartpury House, Hartpury GL19 3BE. Tel: 01452 700283.

Royal Agricultural College, Stroud Road, Cirencester GL7 6JS. Tel: 01285 652531.
Website: www.royagcol.ac.uk E-mail: admissions@royagcol.ac.uk

The Royal Forest of Dean College, Five Acres Campus, Berry Hill, Coleford GL16 7JT.
Tel: 01594 833416.

Stroud College of Further Education, Stratford Road, Stroud GL5 4AH. Tel: 01453 763424.
Website: www.stroudj.demon.co.uk E-mail: guidance@stroudj.demon.co.uk

Hampshire, Southampton and Portsmouth

V T Southern Careers Ltd

HQ, 223 Southampton Road, Paulsgrove, Portsmouth PO6 4QA. Tel: 023 9235 4555. Website: www.vtis.com E-mail: vtsc.com

Aldershot Centre, Suite 3, Wesley Chambers, Queen's Road, Aldershot GU11 3JD. Tel: 01252 311411.

Andover Centre, Cricklade College, Charlton Road, Andover SP10 1EJ. Tel: 01264 323271.

Basingstoke Centre, Sun Alliance House, 37-41 Wote Street, Basingstoke RG21 1LU. Tel: 01256 467666.

Eastleigh Centre, 2nd Floor, Civic Offices, Leigh Road, Eastleigh SO50 9YN. Tel: 023 8064 1655.

Fareham Centre, 1st Floor, County Library Building, Osborn Road, Fareham PO16 7EW. Tel: 01329 232918.

Havant Centre, Civic Offices, Civic Centre Road, Havant PO9 2AX. Tel: 023 9248 4719.

Isle of Wight Centre, 29 High Street, Newport, Isle of Wight PO30 1SS. Tel: 01983 525060.

Portsmouth Centre, Chaucer House, 30 Isambard Brunel Road, Portsmouth PO1 2DR. Tel: 023 9275 6756.

Ringwood Centre, Ringwood & District Community Association, Greyfriars, 44 Christchurch Road, Ringwood BH24 1DW. Tel: 01425 473103.

Southampton Centre, 1 The Carronades, New Road, Southampton S014 OAA. Tel: 023 8023 5523.

Totton Centre, Totton College, Water Lane, Totton SO40 3ZX. Tel: 023 8087 1344.

Winchester Centre, 12-14 City Road, Winchester SO23 8SD. Tel: 01962 868411.

Hampshire Training & Enterprise Council Ltd, 25 Thackeray Mall, Fareham P016 OPQ. Tel: 01329 230099. Website: www.hampshiretec.co.uk

Alton College, Old Odiham Road, Alton GU34 2LX. Tel: 01420 88118. E-mail: altoncollege@campus.bt.com

Basingstoke College of Technology, Worthing Road, Basingstoke RG21 8TN. Tel: 01256 54141. Website: www.bcot.ac.uk

Brockenhurst College, Lyndhurst Road, Brockenhurst S042 7ZE. Tel: 01590 625555. Website: www.brock.ac.uk E-mail: enquiries@brock.ac.uk

Cricklade College, Charlton Road, Andover SP10 1EJ. Tel: 01264 363311. Website: www.cricklade.ac.uk E-mail: info@cricklade.ac.uk

Eastleigh College, Chestnut Avenue, Eastleigh S05 5BF. Tel: 023 8032 6326. Website: www.eastleigh.ac.uk E-mail: goplaces@eastleigh.ac.uk

Education Department (Adult Continuing Education), Hampshire County Council, The Castle, Winchester SO23 8UG. Tel: 01962 846452.

Fareham College, Bishopsfield Road, Fareham PO14 1NH. Tel: 01329 815200. Website: www.fareham.ac.uk E-mail: info@fareham.ac.uk

Farnborough College of Technology, Boundary Road, Farnborough GU14 6SB. Tel: 01252 515511. Website: www.farn-ct.ac.uk E-mail: infor@farn-ct.ac.uk

Havant College, New Road, Havant PO9 1QL. Tel: 023 9248 3856. Website: www.havant.ac.uk E-mail: enquiries@havant.ac.uk

Highbury College of Technology, Dovercourt Road, Highbury, Portsmouth PO6 2SA. Tel: 023 9238 3131. Website: www.highbury.ac.uk E-mail: info@highbury.ac.uk

King Alfred's University Sector College, Sparkford Road, Winchester S022 4NR. Tel: 01962 841515. Website: www.wkac.ac.uk

LSU College of Higher Education, The Avenue, Southampton S017 1BG. Tel: 023 8022 8761.

Portsmouth College of Art, Design and Further Education, Winston Churchill Avenue, Portsmouth PO1 2DJ. Tel: 023 9282 6435.

South Downs College, College Road, Waterlooville PO7 8AA. Tel: 023 9279 7979.

Southampton Institute, East Park Terrace, Southampton S014 OYN. Tel: 023 8031 9000. Website: www.solent.ac.uk

Southampton City College, St Mary Street, Southampton S014 1AR. Tel: 023 8057 7400. Website: www.southampton-city.ac.uk E-mail: information@southampton-city.ac.uk

Sparsholt College Hampshire, Sparsholt, Winchester S021 2NF. Tel: 01962 776441. Website: www.sparshot.ac.uk E-mail: enquiry@sparshot.ac.uk

Totton College, Water Lane, Totton SO40 3ZX. Tel: 023 8087 4874. Website: www.totton.ac.uk E-mail: info@totton.ac.uk

University of Portsmouth, University House, Winston Churchill Avenue, Portsmouth PO1 2UP. Tel: 023 92 8 76543. Website: www.port.ac.uk E-mail: admissions@port.ac.uk

University of Southampton New College, The Avenue, Southampton SO17 1BG. Tel: 023 8059 7261. Website: www.soton.ac.uk E-mail: vah@soton.ac.uk

University of Southampton, Highfield, Southampton S017 1BJ. Tel: 023 8059 5000. Website: www.soton.ac.uk

Winchester School of Art, Park Avenue, Winchester SO23 8DL. Tel: 01962 842500. Website: www.soton.ac.uk/~wsart/ E-mail: artsrec@soton.ac.uk

Hereford and Worcester

Hereford & Worcester Careers Service Ltd

HQ, County Buildings, St Mary's Street, Worcester WR1 1TW. Tel: 01905 765487. Website: www.worcester.gov.uk/careers

Bromsgrove Careers Centre, County Offices, Windsor Street, Bromsgrove B60 2BL. Tel: 01527 575855. Website: www.worcester.gov.uk/careers

Droitwich Careers Centre, Droitwich Job Centre, Clarendon House, 16 St Andrew's Street, Droitwich WR9 8DY. Tel: 01905 684590. Website: www.worcester.gov.uk/careers

Evesham Careers Centre, County Offices, Swan Lane, Evesham WR11 4TZ. Tel: 01386 42111. Website: www.worcester.gov.uk/careers

Hereford Careers Centre, 11 St Owen Street, Hereford HR1 2JB. Tel: 01432 269404. Website: www.worcester.gov.uk/careers

Kidderminster Careers Centre, Youth & Careers Centre Building, 2nd Floor, Bromsgrove Street, Kidderminster DY10 1PF. Tel: 01562 822511. Website: www.worcester.gov.uk/careers

Redditch Careers Centre, Canon Newton House, Evesham Walk, Kingfisher Centre, Redditch B97 4HA. Tel: 01527 66525. Website: www.worcester.gov.uk/careers

Worcester Careers Centre, 10-12 Farrier Street, Worcester WRI 3BH. Tel: 01905 765526. Website: www.worcester.gov.uk/careers

Chamber of Commerce, Training & Enterprise Herefordshire and Worcestershire, Hassell House, St Nicholas Street, Worcester WR1 1UW. Tel: 0800 104010.

Education Department, Herefordshire New Unitary Authority, PO Box 185, Blackfriars Street, Hereford HR4 9ZR. Tel: 01432 260900.

Evesham College, Cheltenham Road, Evesham WR11 6LP. Tel: 01386 41091.

Herefordshire College of Art & Design, Folly Lane, Hereford HR1 1LT. Tel: 01432 273359. Website: www.hereford-art-col.ac.uk E-mail: hcad@hereford-art-col.ac.uk

Herefordshire College of Technology, Folly Lane, Hereford HR1 1LT. Tel: 01432 352235. Website: www.hereford-tech.ac.uk E-mail: enquiries@hereford-tech.ac.uk

Hindlip College, Hindlip, Worcester WR3 8SS. Tel: 01386 552443. Website: www.pershore.ac.uk E-mail: academic-services@pershore.ac.uk

Holme Lacy College, Holme Lacy, Hereford HR2 6LL. Tel: 01432 870316. E-mail: holmelacycollege@xcompuserve.com

Kidderminster College, Hoo Road, Kidderminster DY10 1LX. Tel: 01562 820811. Website: www.kidderminster.ac.uk E-mail: admissions@kidderminster.ac.uk

North East Worcestershire College, Bromsgrove Campus, Blackwood Road, Bromsgrove B60 1PQ. Tel: 01527 570020. Website: www.ne-worcs.ac.uk E-mail: info@ne-worcs.ac.uk

Pershore College of Horticulture, Avonbank, Pershore WR10 3JP. Tel: 01386 552443. Website: www.pershore.ac.uk E-mail: academic-services@pershore.ac.uk

Royal National College for the Blind, College Road, Hereford HR1 1EB. Tel: 01432 265725. Website: www.rncb.ac.uk E-mail: md@rncb.ac.uk

University College Worcester, Henwick Grove, Worcester WR2 6AJ. Tel: 01905 855000. Website: www.worc.ac.uk

Worcester College of Technology, Deansway, Worcester WR1 2JF. Tel: 01905 725555.

Hertfordshire

Hertfordshire Careers Services Limited

HQ, New Barn Centre, Travellers Lane, Hatfield AL10 8XG. Tel: 01707 281401. Website: www.herts-careers.co.uk E-mail: info@herts-careers.co.uk

Cheshunt Careers Centre, 178 Crossbrook Street, Cheshunt EN8 8JY. Tel: 01992 621426. Website: www.herts-careers.co.uk E-mail: info@herts-careers.co.uk

Hatfield & Potters Bar Careers Centre, 19c Albans Road East, Hatfield, AL10 0NT. Tel: 01707 283900. Website: www.herts-careers.co.uk E-mail: info@herts-careers.co.uk

Hemel Hempstead Careers Centre, Marlowes, Hemel Hempstead HP1 1HQ. Tel: 01442 261511. Website: www.herts-careers.co.uk E-mail: info@herts-careers.co.uk

Letchworth Careers Centre, Goldsmith Centre, Broadway, Letchworth SG6 3GB. Tel: 01462 685123. Website: www.herts-careers.co.uk E-mail: info@herts-careers.co.uk

St. Albans & Borehamwood Careers Centre, Hertfordshire House, Civic Centre, St Albans AL1 3LZ. Tel: 01727 816944. Website: www.herts-careers.co.uk E-mail: info@herts-careers.co.uk

Stevenage Careers Centre, College Campus, Six Hills Way, Stevenage SG11 7LB. Tel: 01438 351582. Website: www.herts-careers.co.uk E-mail: info@herts-careers.co.uk

Ware & Bishops Stortford Careers Centre, Walton Road, Ware SG12 9PQ. Tel: 01920 466314. Website: www.herts-careers.co.uk E-mail: info@herts-careers.co.uk

Watford Careers Centre, 65 Queens Road, Watford WD1 2QN. Tel: 01923 231132. Website: www.herts-careers.co.uk E-mail: info@herts-careers.co.uk

Careers Concern, The White Cottage, Great Wymondley, Hitchin SG4 7ET. Tel: 01483 357143. Website: www.laflin.force9.co.uk E-mail: careersconcern@laflin.force4.co.uk

CareerSense, 4 Farriers Close, Codicote, Hitchin SG4 8DU. Tel: 01438 821469.

Hertfordshire Training & Enterprise Council, 45 Grosvenor Road, St Albans AL1 3AW. Tel: 01727 813600. Website: www.herts.tec.co.uk E-mail: info@herts.tec.co.uk

Education Department, Hertfordshire County Council, County Hall, Hertford SG13 8DF. Tel: 01992 555555.

Hertford Regional College, Broxbourne Centre,Turnford, Broxbourne EN10 6AE. Tel: 01992 466451. Website: www.hertreg.ac.uk

Institute of Sales & Marketing Management, Romeland House, Romelands Hill, St Albans AL3 4ET. Tel: 01727 812500. E-mail: sales@ismm.co.uk

North Hertfordshire College, Monkswood Way, Stevenage SG1 1LA. Tel: 01462 424242.

Oaklands College, St Albans City Campus, St Peter's Road, St Albans AL1 3RX. Tel: 01272 737080.

University of Hertfordshire, College Lane, Hatfield AL10 9AB. Tel: 01707 284000. Website: www.herts.ac.uk

West Herts College, Watford Campus, Hempstead Road, Watford WD1 3GZ. Tel: 01923 257500. Website: www.westherts.ac.uk E-mail: janw@westherts.ac.uk

Humberside Area (includes East Riding of Yorkshire, Kingston upon Hull and North Lincolnshire)

The Humberside Partnership

Beverley Career Development Centre, 3 Northbar Within, Beverley HU17 8AP. Tel: 01482 862741. Website: www.thumpship.co.uk E-mail: patmc@hcareers.karoo.co.uk

Bransholme Career Development Centre, 76 Goodhart Road, North Point Shopping Centre, Hull HU7 4EF. Tel: 01482 835780. Website: www.thumpship.co.uk E-mail: patmc@hcareers.karoo.co.uk

Bridlington Career Development Centre, 20 Blenheim Road, Bridlington YO16 4LD. Tel: 01262 678943. Website: www.thumpship.co.uk E-mail: patmc@hcareers.karoo.co.uk

Goole Career Development Centre, 71-73 Boothferry Road, Goole DN14 6BB. Tel: 01405 764558. Website: www.thumpship.co.uk E-mail: patmc@hcareers.karoo.co.uk

Grimsby Career Development Centre, Queen Street, Grimsby DN31 IJA. Tel: 01472 355303. Website: www.thumpship.co.uk E-mail: patmc@hcareers.karoo.co.uk

Hessle Career Development Centre, Southgate, Hessle HU13 0SN. Tel: 01482 647127. Website: www.thumpship.co.uk E-mail: patmc@hcareers.karoo.co.uk

Hull Career Development Centre, Queen Victoria House, Alfred Gelder Street, Hull HU1 2AY. Tel: 01482 223081. Website: www.thumpship.co.uk E-mail: patmc@hcareers.karoo.co.uk

Scunthorpe Career Development Centre, 60 Oswald Road, Scunthorpe DN15 7PQ. Tel: 01274 282200. Website: www.thumpship.co.uk E-mail: patmc@hcareers.karoo.co.uk

COTEC Training Services Ltd, Unit 1, Dalton Street, Hull HU8 8BB. Tel: 01482 581189.

Humberside TEC, The Maltings, Silvester Street, Hull HU1 3HL. Tel: 01482 22649.

Beverley College of Further Education, Gallows Lane, Beverley HU17 7DT. Tel: 01482 868362.

Bishop Burton College, Bishop Burton, Beverley HU17 8QG. Tel: 01964 553000. Website: www.bishopb-college.ac.uk E-mail: enquiries@bishopb-college.ac.uk

Directorate of Education and Personal Development, North Lincolnshire Council, Hewson House, PO Box 35, Station Road, Brigg DN20 8XJ. Tel: 01724 297240.

Education, Leisure & Libraries, East Riding of Yorkshire Council, Essex House, Manor Street, Hull HU13 9BA. Tel: 01482 613781.

East Yorkshire College, St Mary's Walk, Bridlington Y016 5W. Tel: 01262 672676.

Education Office, North East Lincolnshire Council, Eleanor Street, Grimsby DN32 9DU. Tel: 01472 313131.

Grimsby College, Nuns Corner, Grimsby DN34 5BQ. Tel: 01472 311222. Website: www.grimsby.ac.uk E-mail: info@net1.grimsby.ac.uk

Hull College, Queen's Gardens, Hull HU1 3DG. Tel: 01482 329943. Website: www.hull-college.ac.uk E-mail: khristosoliver@hull-college.ac.uk

Kingston upon Hull City Council, Learning Services, Essex House, Manor Street, Hull HU1 1YD. Tel: 01482 613161. Website: www.kuhcc.demon.co.uk E-mail: eduit@kuhcc.demon.co.uk

North Lindsey College, Kingsway, Scunthorpe DN17 1AJ. Tel: 01724 281111. Website: www.northlindsey.ac.uk E-mail: info@northlindsey.ac.uk

University of Hull, Hull HU6 7RX. Tel: 01482 346311. Website: www.hull.ac.uk

University of Humberside, Cottingham Road, Hull HU6 7RT. Tel: 01482 440550. Website: www.humber.ac.uk E-mail: marketing@humber.ac.uk

Isle of Wight

VT Southern Careers Ltd

Isle of Wight Centre, 29 High Street, Newport PO30 1SS. Tel: 01983 525060.

Wight Training & Enterprise, Mill Court, Furrlongs, Newport PO30 2AA. Tel: 01983 822818. Website: www.businesslinkiow.co.uk E-mail: panreception@whiteenterprise.co.uk

Thames Consultancy, PO Box 6, Yarmouth, Freshwater, Isle of Wight PO41 0YS. Tel: 01983 761321. Website: bridgeuk@aol.com

Adult Education Service, Isle of Wight Council, County Hall, Newport PO30 1UD. Tel: 01983 823490.

Isle of Wight College, Medina Way, Newport PO30 5TA. Tel: 01983 526631. Website: www.iwightc.ac.uk E-mail: gillp@iwightc.ac.uk

Kent, Gillingham, Rochester and Medway

Kent Careers Services

Ashford Careers Centre, 22a High Street, Ashford TN24 8TD. Tel: 01233 625516. Website: www.kentcareers.co.uk E-mail: info@kentcareers.co.uk

Canterbury Careers Centre, 40a-41 Dover Street, Canterbury CT1 3HQ. Tel: 01227 780890. Website: www.kentcareers.co.uk E-mail: info@kentcareers.co.uk

Chatham Careers Centre, 205-217 New Road, Chatham ME4 4QA. Tel: 01634 843646. Website: www.kentcareers.co.uk E-mail: info@kentcareers.co.uk

Folkestone Careers Centre, 14-18 Bouverie Place, Folkestone CT20 1AU. Tel: 01303 243974. Website: www.kentcareers.co.uk E-mail: info@kentcareers.co.uk

Gravesend Careers Centre, 8-9 Berkley Crescent, Gravesend DA12 2AF. Tel: 01474 358192. Website: www.kentcareers.co.uk E-mail: info@kentcareers.co.uk

Maidstone Careers Centre, Ground Floor, 35 Earl Street, Maidstone ME14 1LG. Tel: 01622 200700. Website: www.kentcareers.co.uk E-mail: info@kentcareers.co.uk

Margate Careers Centre, 3rd Floor, Mill Lane House, Margate CT9 1LB. Tel: 01843 220028. Website: www.kentcareers.co.uk E-mail: info@kentcareers.co.uk

Sittingbourne Careers Centre, 3rd Floor, Thames House, Sittingbourne ME10 4BJ. Tel: 01795 471282. Website: www.kentcareers.co.uk E-mail: info@kentcareers.co.uk

Tonbridge Careers Centre, 2nd Floor, River Walk, Tonbridge TN9 1DF. Tel: 01732 367710. Website: www.kentcareers.co.uk E-mail: info@kentcareers.co.uk

Learning & Business Link Co Ltd, 26 Kings Hill Avenue, Kings Hill, West Malling ME19 4AE. Tel: 01732 220000. Website: www.kenttec.demon.co.uk E-mail: inform@kenttec.demon.co.uk

Canterbury Christ Church College, North Holmes Road, Canterbury CT1 1QU. Tel: 01227 767700. Website: www.cant.ac.uk E-mail: admissions@cant.ac.uk

Canterbury College, New Dover Road, Canterbury CT1 3AJ. Tel: 01227 811111.

Education and Libraries, Kent County Council, Sessions House, County Hall, Maidstone ME14 2XQ. Tel: 01622 671411.

Hadlow College of Agriculture and Horticulture, Hadlow, Tonbridge TN11 0AL. Tel: 01732 850551. Website: www.hadlow.ac.uk E-mail: rwjb@hadlow.ac.uk

Kent County Council Adult Careers Guidance, Adult Careers Guidance, 85 High Street, Chatham ME4 4EE. Tel: 01634 819137.

Kent Institute of Art and Design, Oakwood Park, Maidstone ME16 8AG. Tel: 01622 757286. Website: www.kiad.ac.uk

Mid-Kent College of Higher and Further Education, Horsted, Maidstone Road, Chatham ME5 9UQ. Tel: 01634 830633. Website: www.midkent.ac.uk E-mail: courseinformation@midkent.ac.uk

North West Kent College, Miskin Road, Dartford DA1 2LU. Tel: 0800 074 1447. Website: www.nwkent.ac.uk

Orpington College of Further Education, The Walnuts, High Street, Orpington BR6 OTE. Tel: 01689 899700. E-mail: hx89@dial.pipex.com

South Kent College, The Grange, Shorncliffe Road, Folkestone CT20 2NA. Tel: 01303 850061. Website: www.southkent.ac.uk

Thanet College, Ramsgate Road, Broadstairs CT10 1PN. Tel: 01843 605040. Website: www.thanet.ac.uk E-mail: student_services@thanet.ac.uk

University of Kent at Canterbury, Canterbury CT2 7NZ. Tel: 01227 764000. Website: www.ukc.ac.uk E-mail: admissions@ukc.ac.uk

West Kent College, Brook Street, Tonbridge TN9 2PW. Tel: 01732 358101.

Wye College, University of London, Ashford TN25 5AH. Tel: 01233 812401. Website: www.wye.ac.uk E-mail: registry@wye.ac.uk

Lancashire and Blackburn

CareerLink (West Lancashire), Chorley House, Centurion Way, Leyland, Preston PR51TZ. Tel: 01772 642400.

East Lancashire Careers Service

Accrington Careers Centre, 10 St James' Street, Accrington BB5 1EL. Tel: 01254 393316 .

Blackburn Careers Centre, Unit 2, Duke Street, Blackburn BB2 1DH. Tel: 01254 609060.

Burnley Careers Centre, Top Floor, Britannic Building, Hargreaves Street, Burnley BB11 1DU. Tel: 01282 435219.

Clitheroe Careers Centre, 5 Swan Courtyard, Castle Street, Clitheroe BB7 2DQ. Tel: 01200 444799.

Colne Careers Centre, 16 Albert Road, Colne BB8 0AA. Tel: 01282 862138.

Darwen Careers Centre, 41 Railway Road, Darwen BB3 2RJ. Tel: 01254 707540.

Nelson Careers Centre, Arndale Centre, 4 Leeds Road, Nelson BB9 9SL. Tel: 01282 613067.

Rawtenstall Careers Centre, Unit 7, Valley Centre, Rawtenstall BB4 7QF. Tel: 01706 213014.

The BEST Centre, 83 Euston Road, Morecambe LA4 5JY. Tel: 01524 831721. Website: www.the-bestcentres-1.freeserve.co.uk E-mail: diane@the-bestcentres-1.freeserve.co.uk

Brook House Access Point, Brookhouse Business Centre, Whalley Range, Blackburn BB1 6BB. Tel: 01254 676796.

ELTEC, Red Rose Court, Clayton Business Park, Clayton le Moors, Accrington BB5 5JR. Tel: 01254 301333. Website: www.eltec.co.uk E-mail: marketing@eltec.ac.uk

LAWTEC, Caxton Road, Fulwood, Preston, PR2 9ZB. Tel: 01772 792111.

Accrington and Rossendale College, Sandy Lane, Accrington BB5 2AW. Tel: 01254 354036. Website: www.accross.ac.uk E-mail: info@accross.ac.uk

The Adult College, PO Box 603, White Cross Education Centre, Quarry Road, Lancaster LA1 3SE. Tel: 01524 60141. Website: www.adultcol.acl@ednet.lancs.ac.uk E-mail: info@adultcol.acl@ednet.lancs.ac.uk

Alston Hall College, Alston Lane, Longridge, Preston PR3 3BP. Tel: 01772 784661. Website: www.alstonhall.u-net.com

Blackburn College, Feilden Street, Blackburn BB2 1LH. Tel: 01254 292929. Website: www.blackburn.ac.uk

Blackpool and the Fylde College, Ashfield Road, Bispham, Blackpool FY2 0HB. Tel: 01253 352352. Website: www.blackpool.ac.uk E-mail: vc@blackpool.ac.uk

Burnley College, Shorey Bank, Ormerod Road, Burnley BB11 2RX. Tel: 01282 711345. Website: www.burnley.ac.uk

Edge Hill University College, St Helen's Road, Ormskirk L39 4QP. Tel: 01695 575171.

Education and Cultural Services Department, Lancashire County Council, PO Box 61, County Hall, Preston PR1 8RJ. Tel: 01772 254868.

Lancashire Enterprises plc, Enterprise House, 17 Ribblesdale Place, Preston PR1 3NA. Tel: 01772 203020.

Lancaster and Morecambe College, Morecambe Road, Lancaster LA1 2TY. Tel: 01524 66215. Website: www.lanmore.ac.uk E-mail: info@lanmore.ac.uk

Lancaster University, University House, Lancaster LA1 4YW. Tel: 01524 65201.
Website: www.lancs.ac.uk E-mail: ugadmissions@lancaster.ac.uk

Myerscough College, Myerscough Hall, Bilsborrow, Preston PR3 0RY. Tel: 01995 640611.
Website: www.myerscough.ac.uk

Nelson and Colne College, Scotland Road, Nelson BB9 7YT. Tel: 01282 440209.
Website: www.nelson.ac.uk E-mail: reception@nelson.ac.uk

Preston College, St Vincent's Road, Fulwood, Preston PR2 9UR. Tel: 01772 225000.
Website: www.preston-coll.ac.uk E-mail: reception@preston-coll.ac.uk

Runshaw College, Langdale Road, Leyland, Preston PR5 2DQ. Tel: 01772 622677.

St Martin's College, Bowerham Road, Lancaster LA1 3JD. Tel: 01524 384200.
Website: www.ucsm.ac.uk E-mail: admission@ucsm.ac.uk

Skelmersdale College, West Bank, Calder Building, Yewdale, Southway, Skelmersdale WN8 6JA.
Tel: 01695 52393. Website: www.skelmersdale.ac.uk
E-mail: student.services@skelmersdale.ac.uk

University of Central Lancashire, Preston PR1 2HE. Tel: 01772 201201.
Website: www.uclan.ac.uk E-mail: c.enquiries@uclan.ac.uk

University College of St Martin, Bowerham Road, Lancaster LA1 3JD. Tel: 01524 384384.
Website: www.ucsm.ac.uk

Leicestershire, Leicester City and Rutland

Leicestershire Careers and Guidance Services Ltd

Leicester Careers Centre, 1 Pocklingtons Walk, Leicester LE1 6BT. Tel: 0116 262 7254.
Website: www.leicester-careers.co.uk E-mail: leics@leicester-careers.co.uk

Coalville Careers Centre, 87 Belvoir Road, Coalville LE67 3PH. Tel: 01530 812231.
Website: www.leicester-careers.co.uk E-mail: coal@leicester-careers.co.uk

Hinckley Careers Centre, 51 Castle Street, Hinckley LE10 1DA. Tel: 01455 632719.
Website: www.leicester-careers.co.uk E-mail: hinck@leicester-careers.co.uk

Loughborough Careers Centre, 7 Fennel Street, Loughborough LE11 1UQ. Tel: 01509 214002.
Website: www.leicester-careers.co.uk E-mail: lough@leicester-careers.co.uk

Market Harborough Careers Centre, 2 St Mary's Road, Market Harborough LE16 7DU.
Tel: 01858 462309. Website: www.leicester-careers.co.uk
E-mail: mktharb@leicester-careers.co.uk

Melton Mowbray Careers Centre, Melton Mowbray College, Asfordby Road, Melton Mowbray
LE13 0HJ. Tel: 01664 69966. Website: www.leicester-careers.co.uk
E-mail: melton@leicester-careers.co.uk

Oakham Careers Centre, 8 Melton Road, Oakham LE15 6AY. Tel: 01572 756655.
Website: www.leicester-careers.co.uk E-mail: oakham@leicester-careers.co.uk

Leicestershire Training & Enterprise Council, Meridian East, Meridian Business Park,
Leicester LE3 2WZ. Tel: 0116 2651515.

Brooksby College, Brooksby, Melton Mowbray LE14 2LJ. Tel: 01664 434291.
Website: www.brooksby.ac.uk E-mail: library@brooksby.ac.uk

Charles Keene College, Painter Street, Leicester LE1 3WA. Tel: 0116 251 6037.
Website: www.ckeene.ac.uk E-mail: advice@ckeene.ac.uk

De Montfort University, The Gateway, Leicester LE1 9BH. Tel: 0116 255 1551.
Website: www.dmu.ac.uk

Education Department, Leicestershire County Council, Room 17, County Hall, Glenfield, Leicester LE3 8RF. Tel: 0116 265 6352.

International Co-operative College, Stanford Hall, Loughborough LE12 5QR.
Tel: 01509 852333.

Loughborough College, Radmoor, Loughborough LE11 3BT. Tel: 01509 215831.
Website: www.loucoll.ac.uk E-mail: loucoll@loucoll.ac.uk

Loughborough College of Art and Design, Epinal Way, Loughborough LE11 3GE.
Tel: 01509 261515.

Loughborough University, Loughborough LE11 3TU. Tel: 01509 222498.
Website: www.lboro.ac.uk E-mail: prospectus-enquiries@lboro.ac.uk

Melton Mowbray College, Asfordby Road, Melton Mowbray LE13 0HJ. Tel: 01664 567431.

North Warwickshire & Hinckley College, London Road, Hinkley LE10 1HQ. Tel: 024 7624 3084. Website: www.nwarks-hinckley.ac.uk E-mail: the.college@nwarks-hinckley.ac.uk

University of Leicester, University Road, Leicester LE1 7RH. Tel: 0116 252 20047.
Website: www.le.ac.uk E-mail: careers@le.ac.uk

Wigston College of Further Education, Station Road, Wigston Magna, Leicester LE8 2DW.
Tel: 0116 288 5051. Website: www.wigston-college.ac.uk
E-mail: barrie@wigston-college.ac.uk

Lincolnshire and North East Lincolnshire (excluding North Lincolnshire – see Humberside entry)

Lincolnshire Careers and Guidance Services Ltd

HQ, Witham house, Pelham Centre, Kesteven Street, Lincoln LN5 8HE. Tel: 01522 875000.
Website: www.lincolnshire.net/lcgs E-mail: careers@lincscg.co.uk

Boston Careers Centre, County Hall, Boston PE21 6LX. Tel: 01205 310010.
Website: www.lincolnshire.net/lcgs E-mail: boston@lincscg.co.uk

Gainsborough Careers Centre, 6 Church Street, Gainsborough DN21 2JH. Tel: 01427 612096.
Website: www.lincolnshire.net/lcgs E-mail: gainsborough@lincscg.co.uk

Grantham Careers Centre, St Peter's Hill, Grantham NG31 6PY. Tel: 01476 566379.
Website: www.lincolnshire.net/lcgs E-mail: grantham@lincscg.co.uk

Lincoln Careers Centre, Aquis House, Clasketgate, Lincoln LN2 1JZ. Tel: 01522 875455.
Website: www.lincolnshire.net/lcgs E-mail: lincoln@lincscg.co.uk

Louth Careers Centre, Eastfield House Annexe, Eastfield Road, Louth LN11 7AN.
Tel: 01507 600800. Website: www.lincolnshire.net/lcgs E-mail: louth@lincscg.co.uk

Skegness Careers Centre, 30 Roman Bank, Skegness PE25 2AL. Tel: 01754 762595.
Website: www.lincolnshire.net/lcgs E-mail: skegness@lincscg.co.uk

Sleaford Careers Centre, Council Offices, Eastgate, Sleaford NG34 7EB. Tel: 01529 414144.
Website: www.lincolnshire.net/lcgs E-mail: sleaford@lincscg.co.uk

Spalding Careers Centre, 1-2 Station Street, Spalding PE11 1EF. Tel: 01775 766151.
Website: www.lincolnshire.net/lcgs E-mail: spalding@lincscg.co.uk

Stamford Careers Centre, 12 Broad Street, Stamford PE9 1PG. Tel: 01780 762238.
Website: www.lincolnshire.net/lcgs E-mail: stamford@lincscg.co.uk

Greater Peterborough Chamber of Commerce, Training & Enterprise, Stuart House, City Road, Peterborough PE1 1QF. Tel: 01733 890808. Website: www.gpccte.co.uk E-mail: gpccte@gpccte.co.uk

Lincolnshire Training & Enterprise Council, Lincolnshire Careers & Guidance Services, Brayford House, Brayford Wharf North, Lincoln LN1 1XN. Tel: 01522 567765.

Boston College, Skirbeck Road, Boston PE21 6JF. Tel: 01205 365701. Website: www.boston.ac.uk E-mail: enquiry@boston.ac.uk

De Montfort University, Lincoln School of Agriculture & Horticulture, Caythorpe Court, Caythorpe, Grantham NG32 3EP. Tel: 01400 272521. Website: www.dmu.ac.uk

De Montfort University, Lincoln School of Applied Arts and Design, Chad Varah House, Wordsworth Street, Lincoln LN1 3BP. Tel: 01522 512912. Website: www.dmu.ac.uk

Education and Cultural Services Directorate, Lincolnshire County Council, County Offices, Newland, Lincoln LN1 1YQ. Tel: 01522 552222.

Grantham College, Stonebridge Road, Grantham NG31 9AP. Tel: 01476 400200. Website: www.grantham.ac.uk E-mail: enquiry@grantham.ac.uk

North Lincolnshire College, Lincoln Centre, Monks Road, Lincoln LN2 5HQ. Tel: 01522 876000. Website: www.nlincs-coll.ac.uk E-mail: n/c@nlincs-coll.ac.uk

Stamford College, Drift Road, Stamford PE9 1XA. Tel: 01780 764141.

London – Greater

Barking and Dagenham

Futures Careers Guidance

Careers Centre, Unit 7, Monteagle Court, 32-38 Wakering Road, Barking IG11 8TE. Tel: 020 8591 9999.

Careers Centre, Barking College, Dagenham Road, Rush Green, Romford RM7 0UX. Tel: 01708 753377. Website: www.futures-careers.co.uk

London East TEC, Cityside House, 40 Adler Street, London E1 1EE. Tel: 020 7377 1866.

Barking College, Dagenham Road, Romford RM7 0XU. Tel: 01708 766841. Website: www.barking-coll.ac.uk

Education Department, London Borough of Barking & Dagenham, Town Hall, Barking IG11 7LU. Tel: 020 8592 4500.

University of East London, Longbridge Road, Dagenham RM8 2AS. Tel: 020 8590 7000. Website: www.uel.ac.uk E-mail: g.brown@uel.ac.uk

Barnet

Prospect Careers Services, North Finchley Library, Ravensdale Avenue, London N12 9HP. Tel: 020 8446 5554.

Adult Guidance Service, 1st Floor, 31-33 Market Square, Edmonton Green, London N9 0TZ. Tel: 020 8350 4221.

Barnet Careers & Educational Guidance for Adults, North Finchley Library, Ravendale Avenue, London N12 9HP. Tel: 020 8446 5554.

North London Training & Enterprise Council, Dumayne House, 1 Fox Lane, Palmers Green, London N13 4AB. Tel: 020 8447 9422. Website: www.nltec.co.uk E-mail: post@nltec.co.uk

Barnet College, Wood Street, Barnet, London EN5 4AZ. Tel: 020 8440 6321. Website: www.barnet.ac.uk

Educational Services, London Borough of Barnet, Friern Barnet Lane, London N11 3DL. Tel: 020 8359 3029.

Hendon College, Corner Mead, Grahame Park Way, Colindale, London NW9 5RA. Tel: 020 8200 8300. Website: www.hendon.ac.uk

Jews' College, Schaller House, Albert Road, Hendon, London NW4 2SJ. Tel: 020 8203 6427. E-mail: jewscoll@clus1.ulcc.ac.uk

Oak Hill College, Chase Side, Southgate, London N14 4PS. Tel: 020 8449 0467. Website: www.oakhill.ac.uk

Bexley

Prospects Careers Services, Bexley Careers Centre, Bexley Civic Offices, Broadway, Bexleyheath DA6 7LB. Tel: 020 8303 7777.

CIRCA Ltd, 65 Tweedy Road, Bromley, Kent BR1 3NH. Tel: 020 8464 5639.

SOLOTEC, Lancaster House, 7 Elmfield Road, Bromley BR1 1LT. Tel: 020 8313 9232. Website: www.solotec.co.uk

Bexley College, Tower Road, Belvedere DA17 6JA. Tel: 01332 404000.

Directorate of Education and Leisure Services, Bexley Council, Hill View, Hill View Drive, Welling, Kent DA16 3RY. Tel: 020 8303 7777.

Rose Bruford College, Lamorbey Park, Burnt Oak Lane, Sidcup DA15 9DF. Tel: 020 8300 3024.

Brent

Lifetime Careers (Brent and Harrow)

Wembley Careers Centre, Ground Floor, York House, Empire Way, Wembley HA9 0PA. Tel: 020 8951 3703. Website: www.london.lifetime-careers.co.uk E-mail: enquiries@london.lifetime-careers.co.uk

Willesden Careers Centre, Room SF02, College of North West London, Dudden Hill Lane, Willesden, London NW10 1DG. Tel: 020 7451 5439.
Website: www.london.lifetime-careers.co.uk
E-mail: enquiries@london.lifetime-careers.co.uk

Brent Adult Guidance Service, 1 Moorland Gardens, Stonebridge, London NW10 8DY. Tel: 020 8961 3703.

North West London TEC, Kirkfield House, 118-120 Station Road, Harrow HA1 2RL. Tel: 020 8901 5000.

College of North West London, Dudden Hill Lane, Willesden, London NW10 1DG. Tel: 020 8208 5000.

Education, Arts and Libraries, London Borough of Brent, PO Box 1, Chesterfield House, 9 Park Lane, Wembley HA9 7RW. Tel: 020 8838 0808.

Hendon College, Corner Mead, Grahame Park, Colindale, London NW9 5RA. Tel: 020 8266 4090.
Website: www.hendon.ac.uk E-mail: info@hendon.ac.uk

Bromley

Prospects Careers Services, Bromley Careers Centre, 11a London Road, Bromley, Kent BR1 1BY. Tel: 020 8313 9500.

SOLOTEC, Lancaster House, 7 Elmfield Road, Bromley BR1 1LT. Tel: 020 8313 9232.
Website: www.solotec.co.uk

Bromley College of Further and Higher Education, Rookery Lane, Bromley Common BR2 8HE. Tel: 020 8295 7004.

Education Department, London Borough of Bromley, Civic Centre, Stodewell Close, Bromley BR1 3UH. Tel: 020 8464 3333.

Ravensbourne College of Design and Communication, Walden Road, Elmstead Woods, Chislehurst BR7 5SN. Tel: 020 8289 4900.

Croydon

Prospects Croydon Careers Centre, 112-114 High Street, Croydon CR0 1ND. Tel: 020 8401 0301.

SOLOTEC, Lancaster House, 7 Elmfield Road, Bromley BR1 1LT. Tel: 020 8313 9232.
Website: solotec.co.uk

InterFaces, 84 Alderton Road, Croydon CR0 6HJ. Tel: 020 8654 0808.
Website: www.interfaces.co.uk E-mail: info:interfaces.co.uk

Coulsdon College, Placehouse Lane, Old Coulsdon CR5 1YA. Tel: 01737 551176.
Website: www.coulsdon.ac.uk E-mail: gen.enquiries@coulsdon.ac.uk

Croydon College, Fairfields, Croydon, Surrey CR9 1DX. Tel: 020 8686 5700.

Education Department, London Borough of Croydon, Taberner House, Park Lane, Croydon CR9 1TP. Tel: 020 8686 4433.

John Ruskin College, Selsdon Park Road, South Croydon CR2 8JJ. Tel: 020 8651 1131.

Ealing

CfBT West London Careers

Ealing Careers Centre, Saunders House, 52-53 The Mall, Ealing, London W5 3TA. Tel: 020 8579 1633.

Southall Careers Centre, Southall Opportunities Centre, Town Hall, High Street, Southall UB1 3HA. Tel: 020 8814 3510.

West London TEC, Sovereign Court, 15-21 Staines Road, Hounslow TW3 3HA. Tel: 020 8577 1010.

Ealing Tertiary College, Acton Centre, Mill Hill Road, London W3 8UX. Tel: 0345 023 883. Website: www.ealingcoll.ac.uk

Education Department, London Borough of Ealing, Perceval House, 14-16 Uxbridge Road, Ealing, London W5 2HL. Tel: 020 8579 2424.

London College of Music & Media, Thames Valley University, St Mary's Road, London W5 5RF. Tel: 020 8231 2304.

Thames Valley University, Ealing Campus, St Mary's Road, London W5 5RF. Tel: 020 8579 5000. Website: www.tvu.ac.uk E-mail: learning.advice@tvu.ac.uk

Enfield

Adult Guidance Service, 1st Floor, 31-33 Market Square, Edmonton Green, London N9 0TZ. Tel: 020 8350 4221.

North London TEC, Dumayne House, 1 Fox Lane, Palmers Green, London N13 4AB. Tel: 020 8447 9422. Website: www.nltec.co.uk E-mail: post@nltec.co.uk

Capel Manor Horticultural and Environmental Centre, Bullsmoor Lane, Enfield EN1 4RQ. Tel: 020 8366 4442.

Education Group, London Borough of Enfield, Civic Centre, Silver Street, Enfield EN1 3XQ. Tel: 020 8379 3201.

Enfield College, 73 Hertford Road, Enfield EN3 5HA. Tel: 020 8372 7635.

Middlesex University School of Lifelong Learning, Trent Park, Bramley Road, London N14 4YZ. Tel: 020 8362 5000. Website: www.lle.mdx.ac.uk

Southgate College, High Street, London N14 6BS. Tel: 020 8886 6521.

Haringey

Haringey Adult Guidance Service, Central Library, 2nd Floor, High Road, London N22 6XD. Tel: 020 8829 9308.

North London TEC, Dumayne House, 1 Fox Lane, Palmers Green, London N13 4AB. Tel: 020 8447 9422. Website: www.nltec.co.uk E-mail: post@nltec.co.uk

Adult and Community Education Services, London Borough of Haringey, 48 Station Road, Wood Green, London N22 4TY. Tel: 020 8975 9700.

College of North East London, Tottenham Centre, High Road, London N15 4RU. Tel: 020 8802 3111.

Middlesex University, White Hart Lane, London N17 8HR. Tel: 020 8362 5000. Website: www.mdx.ac.uk E-mail: admissions@mdx.ac.uk

Harrow

Lifetime Careers (Brent and Harrow)

Harrow Careers Centre, Ground Floor, Hygeia House, 66 College Road, Harrow HA1 1BX. Tel: 020 8861 1531. Website: www.london.lifetime-careers.co.uk E-mail: enquiries@london.lifetime-careers.co.uk

North West London TEC, Kirkfield House, 118-120 Station Road, Harrow HA1 2RL. Tel: 020 8901 5000.

Education Department, London Borough of Harrow, PO Box 22, Civic Centre, Harrow, London HA1 2UW. Tel: 020 8424 1910.

Greenhill College, Lowlands Road, Harrow HA1 3AQ. Tel: 020 8869 8600.

Stanmore College, Elm Park, Stanmore HA7 4BQ. Tel: 020 8420 7700.

Weald College, Brookshill, Harrow Weald, HA3 6RR. Tel: 020 8420 8888. Website: www.weald.ac.uk E-mail: principal@weald.ac.uk

Havering

Futures Careers Guidance

Havering Careers Centre, Holgate Court, Western Road, Romford RM1 3JS. Tel: 020 8591 9999. Website: www.futures-careers.co.uk

London East TEC, Cityside House, 40 Adler Street, London E1 1EE. Tel: 020 7377 1866.

Directorate of Education and Community Services, London Borough of Havering, Broxhill Centre, Broxhill Road, Romford RM4 1XN. Tel: 01708 773790.

Havering College of F & HE, Ardleigh Green Road, Hornchurch RM11 2LL. Tel: 01708 462801. Website: www.havering-college.ac.uk

Hillingdon

CfBT West London Careers

Uxbridge Careers Centre, Terrace Offices, Civic Centre, Uxbridge UB8 1UW. Tel: 01895 257855.

LINK Educational Guidance Service, 1st Floor, Fountains Mill, 81 High Street, Uxbridge UB8 1JR. Tel: 01895 234729.

West London TEC, Sovereign Court, 15-21 Staines Road, Hounslow TW3 3HA. Tel: 020 8577 1010.

Adult and Continuing Education, London Borough of Hillingdon, Civic Centre, Uxbridge UB8 1UW. Tel: 01895 676690.

Brunel University, Uxbridge UB8 3PH. Tel: 01895 274000. Website: www.brunel.ac.uk E-mail: courses@brunel.ac.uk

London Bible College, Green Lane, Northwood HA6 2UW. Tel: 01923 826061.

Uxbridge College, Park Road, Uxbridge UB8 1NQ. Tel: 01895 853333. Website: www.uxbridge.ac.uk E-mail: enquiries@uxbridge.ac.uk

Hounslow

CfBT West London Careers

Hounslow Careers Centre, 6 Lampton Road, Hounslow TW3 1JL. Tel: 020 8577 5478.

Next Step, 7-9 Staines Road, Hounslow TW3 3HA. Tel: 0800 377388.

West London TEC, Sovereign Court, 15-21 Staines Road, Hounslow TW3 3HA. Tel: 020 8577 1010.

Brunel University College, 300 St Margaret's Road, Twickenham TW1 1PT. Tel: 020 8891 0121. Website: www.brunel.ac.uk

Educational Department, London Borough of Hounslow, Civic Centre, Lampton Road, Hounslow TW3 4DN. Tel: 020 8865 5303.

West Thames College, London Road, Isleworth TW7 4HS. Tel: 020 8568 0244.

Kingston upon Thames

Search

New Malden Centre, Ground Floor, CI Tower, Dukes Avenue, New Malden, Surrey KT3 4TD. Tel: 020 8410 4105. Website: www.careersite-search.org.uk E-mail: support@careersite-search.org.uk

AZTEC, Manorgate House, 2 Manorgate Road, Kingston upon Thames KT2 7AL. Tel: 0808 100 6050. Website: www.aztec.iip.co.uk

Hillcroft College, South Bank, Surbiton, Surrey KT6 6DF. Tel: 020 8399 2688. Website: www.hillcroft.ac.uk E-mail: enquiry@hillcroft.ac.uk

Kingston Adult Education Service, North Kingston Centre, Richmond Road, Kingston upon Thames KT2 5PE. Tel: 020 8547 6707. Website: www.rbk@kingston.gov.uk E-mail: adult.education@rbk.kingston.gov.uk

Kingston College, Kingston Hall Road, Kingston upon Thames KT1 2AQ. Tel: 020 8546 2151. Website: www.kingston-college.ac.uk E-mail: info@kingston-college.ac.uk

Kingston University, Cooper House, 40-46 Surbiton Road, Kingston upon Thames KT1 2HX. Tel: 020 8547 7053. Website: www.kingston.ac.uk E-mail: admissions-info@kingston.ac.uk

Merton

Search

Wimbledon Centre, Ground Floor, Tuition House, 27-37 St Georges Road, Wimbledon, London SW19 4DS. Tel: 020 8296 1060. Website: www.careersite-search.org.uk E-mail: support@careersite-search.org.uk

AZTEC, Manorgate House, 2 Manorgate Road, Kingston upon Thames KT2 7AL. Tel: 0808 100 6050. Website: www.aztec.iip.co.uk

Merton College, Morden Park, London Road, Morden, Surrey SM4 5QX. Tel: 020 8640 3001. Website: www.merton.ac.uk E-mail: info@merton.ac.uk

Merton Adult College, Whatley Avenue, London SW20 9NS. Tel: 020 8543 9292.

Wimbledon School of Art, Merton Hall Road, London SW19 3QA. Tel: 020 8408 5000. Website: www.wimbledon.ac.uk E-mail: art.wimbledon.ac.uk

Newham

Futures Careers Guidance

Careers Centre, Units 5 & 6, Broadway Chambers, 2 The Broadway, Stratford, London E15 4QP. Tel: 020 8227 1500. Website: www.futures-careers.co.uk

Education Department, London Borough of Newham, Education Offices, Broadway House, 322 High Street, London E15 1AJ. Tel: 020 8555 5552.

Newham College of FE, East Ham Campus, High Street South, London E6 4ER. Tel: 020 8257 4000.

Redbridge

Futures Careers Guidance

Careers Centre, Broadway Chambers, 1 Cranbrook Road, Ilford IG12 4DU. Tel: 020 8478 9098. Website: www.futures-careers.co.uk

London East TEC, Cityside House, 40 Alder Street, London E1 1EE. Tel: 020 7377 1866.

Education Department, London Borough of Redbridge, Floor 2, Lynton House, Ilford IG1 1NN. Tel: 020 8478 3020.

Redbridge College, Little Heath, Romford RM6 4XT. Tel: 020 8548 7402.

Richmond upon Thames

CfBT West London Careers

Twickenham Careers Centre, 1Ilex house, 94 Holly Road, Twickenham TW1 4HF. Tel: 020 8891 6162.

West LondonTEC, Sovereign Court, 15-21 Staines Road, Hounslow TW3 3HA. Tel: 020 8577 1010.

Education Department (Adult Education), London Borough of Richmond upon Thames, Regal House, London Road, Twickenham TW1 3QB. Tel: 020 8891 7500.

Richmond Adult & Community College, Clifden Road, Twickenham TW1 4LT. Tel: 020 8891 5907. Website: www.racc.org.uk E-mail: lisa@racc.org.uk

Richmond upon Thames College, Egerton Road, Twickenham TW2 7SJ. Tel: 020 8607 8000.

St Mary's College, Waldergrave Road, Twickenham, Middlesex TW1 4SX. Tel: 020 8240 4000. Website: www.smuc.ac.uk

Sutton

Prospects Careers Services, 2 Carshalton Road, Sutton SM1 4RA. Tel: 020 8642 6442.

SOLOTEC, Lancaster House, 7 Elmfield Road, Bromley BR1 1LT. Tel: 020 8313 9232. Website: www.solotec.co.uk

Carshalton College of Further Education, Nightingale Road, Carshalton SM5 2EJ. Tel: 020 8770 6890. Website: www.carshalton.ac.uk

Education Offices, London Borough of Sutton, The Grove, Carshalton, Surrey SM5 3AL. Tel: 020 8770 5000.

Sutton College of Liberal Arts, St Nicholas Way, Sutton, Surrey SM1 2EJ. Tel: 020 8770 6901.

Waltham Forest

Futures Careers Guidance

Careers Centre, 398a Hoe Street, Walthamstow, London E17 9AA. Tel: 020 8521 9020. Website: www.futures-careers.co.uk

Education & Occupational Advice Service for Adults, Adult Education Service (LBWF), Chestnut House, 398 Hoe Street, London E17 9AA. Tel: 020 8521 4311.

London East TEC, Cityside House, 40 Alder Street, London E1 1EE. Tel: 020 7377 1866.

Education Department, London Borough of Waltham Forest, Municipal Offices, High Road, Leyton, London E10 5QJ. Tel: 020 8527 5544.

Waltham Forest College, Forest Road, London E17 4JB. Tel: 020 8527 2311. Website: www.waltham.ac.uk E-mail: guidance@waltham.ac.uk

London – Inner

Camden

Capital Careers

Camden Centre, 78 Parkway London NW1 7AN. Tel: 020 7482 3996. Website: www.capital-careers.ltd.uk

FOCUS Central London, Centre Point, 103 New Oxford Street, London WC1A 1DR. Tel: 020 7896 8484. Website: ww.focus-central-london.co.uk E-mail: info@focus-central-london.co.uk

Architectural Association, School of Architecture, 34-36 Bedford Square, London WC1B 3ES. Tel: 020 7636 0974.

Birkbeck College, University of London, Malet Street, London WC1E 7HX. Tel: 020 7631 6000.

Central School of Speech and Drama, Embassy Theatre, 64 Eton Avenue, London NW3 3HY. Tel: 020 7722 8183.

Central St Martins College of Art & Design, Southampton Row, London WC1B 4AP. Tel: 020 7514 7000.

City Literary Institute, Stukeley Street, Drury Lane, London WC2B 5LJ. Tel: 020 7430 0543.

Education Department (Adult Education), Camden London Borough Council, Crowndale Centre, 218-220 Eversholt Street, London NW1 1BD. Tel: 020 7911 1525.

Institute of Education, University of London, 20 Bedford Way, London WC1H 0AL. Tel: 020 7580 1122.

Kingsway College, Regents Park Centre, Longford Street, London NW1 3HB. Tel: 020 7306 5700.

London Contemporary Dance School, The Place, 17 Duke's Road, London WC1H 9AB. Tel: 020 7387 0152.

Prince of Wales's Institute of Architecture, 14-15 Gloucester Gate, Regent's Park, London NW1 4HG. Tel: 020 7916 7380.

Royal Academy of Dramatic Art, 18 Chenies Street, London WC1E 7EX. Tel: 020 7636 7076.

Royal Free Hospital School of Medicine, University of London, Rowland Hill Street, London NW3 2PF. Tel: 020 7794 0500.

Royal Veterinary College, University of London, Royal College Street, London NW1 0TU. Tel: 020 7468 5000. Website: www.rvc.ac.uk

School of Oriental and African Studies, University of London, Thornhaugh Street, Russell Square, London WC1H 0GX. Tel: 020 7637 2388. Website: www.soas.ac.uk E-mail: study@soas.ac.uk

School of Pharmacy, University of London, 29-39 Brunswick Square, London WC1N 1AX. Tel: 020 7753 5800.

School of Slavonic and East European Studies, University of London, Senate House, Malet Street, London WC1E 7HU. Tel: 020 7862 8519. Website: www.ssees.ac.uk

Training Access Company, Unit 14, Eurolink Business Centre, 49 Effra Road, Brixton, London SW1 1BZ. Tel: 020 7924 9440.

University College London, Gower Street, London WC1E 6BT. Tel: 020 7387 7050.

Working Men's College, Crowndale Road, London NW1 1TR. Tel: 020 7387 2037.

City of London

FOCUS Central London, Centre Point, 103 New Oxford Street, London WC1A 1DR. Tel: 020 7896 8484. Website: www.focus-central-london.co.uk E-mail: info@focus-central-london.co.uk

Education Department, Corporation of London, PO Box 270, Guildhall, London EC2P 2EJ. Tel: 020 7332 1750.

London Development Partnership, 301 Central Market, Smithfield, London EC1A 9LY. Tel: 020 7248 5555.

Guildhall School of Drama and Music, Silk Street, Barbican, London EC2Y 8DT. Tel: 020 7628 2571.

London Guildhall University, 133 Whitechapel High Street, London E1 7QA. Tel: 020 7320 1000. Website: www.lgu.ac.uk E-mail: admiss@lgu.ac.uk

Greenwich

London South Bank Careers

Greenwich Centre, 47 Woolwich New Road, London SE18 6EW. Tel: 020 8355 5100. Website: www.lsbcareers.co.uk E-mail: careers@lsbcareers.co.uk

SOLOTEC, Lancaster House, 7 Elmfield Road, Bromley BR1 1LT. Tel: 020 8313 9232. Website: www.solotec.co.uk

Education Department, London Borough of Greenwich, Riverside House, Woolwich High Street, Woolwich, London SE18 6DF. Tel: 020 8312 5880.

University of Greenwich, Bexley Road, Eltham, London SE9 2PQ. Tel: 020 8331 8000. Website: www.gre.ac.uk

Woolwich College, Villas Road, Plumstead, London SE18 7PN. Tel: 020 8488 4800. Website: www.woolwich.ac.uk E-mail: info@woolwich.ac.uk

Hackney

FOCUS Central London, Centre Point, 103 New Oxford Street, London WC1A 1DR.
Tel: 020 7896 8484. Website: www.focus-central-london.co.uk
E-mail: info@focus-central-london.co.uk

Hackney Education Advice Service for Adults, 27b Dalston Lane, Hackney, London E8 3DF.
Tel: 020 7923 9020. E-mail: heas@hackney.gov.uk

Cordwainers College, 182 Mare Street, London E8 3RE. Tel: 020 8985 0273.
Website: www.cordwainers.ac.uk E-mail: enquiries@cordwainers.ac.uk

Directorate of Education and Leisure Services, London Borough of Hackney,
Edith Cavell Building, Enfield Road, London N1 5AZ. Tel: 020 8356 5000.

Hackney Community College, Shoreditch Campus, Falkirk Street, London N1 6HQ.
Tel: 020 7613 9000.

Hammersmith and Fulham

Capital Careers

Hammersmith and Fulham Centre, 181 King Street, London W6 9JU. Tel: 020 8741 2441.
Website: www.capital-careers.ltd.uk

FOCUS Central London, Centre Point, 103 New Oxford Street, London WC1A 1DR.
Tel: 020 7896 8484. Website: www.focus-central-london.co.uk
E-mail: info@focus-central-london.co.uk

Education & Training Advice for Adults (Hammersmith), Community & Learning Leisure
Service, Macbeth Street, Hammersmith, London W6 9JJ. Tel: 020 7741 8441.

Charing Cross and Westminster Medical School, University of London, Reynolds Building,
St Dunstan's Road, London W6 8RP. Tel: 020 8383 0000. Website: www.ic.ac.uk

Education Department, Hammersmith and Fulham London Borough Council, Macbeth Centre,
Macbeth Street, Hammersmith, London WC12 9JJ. Tel: 020 8846 9090.

Hammersmith and West London College, Giddon Road, Barons Court, London W14 9BL.
Tel: 020 8741 1688.

Holborn College, Greyhound Road, London W14 9RY. Tel: 020 7385 3377.

KLC School of Interior Design, KLC House, Springvale Terrace, London W14 0HE.
Tel: 020 7602 8592.

Islington

Enterprise Careers

Guidance Service for Adults, City and Islington College, Bunhill Row, London EC1Y 8LQ.
Tel: 020 7614 0210.

FOCUS Central London, Centre Point, 103 New Oxford Street, London WC1A 1DR. Tel: 020 7896 8484. Website: www.focus-central-london.co.uk E-mail: info@focus-central-london.co.uk

City and Islington College, The Marlborough Building, 383 Holloway Road, London N7 0RN. Tel: 020 7700 9333.

City University London, Northampton Square, London EC1V 0HB. Tel: 020 7477 8000. Website: www.city.ac.uk

Education Department, Islington London Borough Council, Laycock Street, London N1 1TH. Tel: 020 7457 5754.

St Mungos, c/o Bridge Training Centre, Bridge Close, London W10 6JW. Tel: 020 8960 6474.

University of North London, 166-220 Holloway Road, London N7 8DB. Tel: 020 7607 2789. Website: www.unl.ac.uk E-mail: admissions@unl.ac.uk

Kensington and Chelsea

Capital Careers

Kensington & Chelsea Centre, 273 Kensington High Street, London. Tel: 020 7938 5311. Website: www.capital-careers.ltd.uk

FOCUS Central London, Centre Point, 103 New Oxford Street, London WC1A 1DR. Tel: 020 7896 8484. Website: www.focus-central-london.co.uk E-mail: info@focus-central-london.co.uk

One Step, Campden Institute, 95 Lancaster Road, London W11 1QQ. Tel: 020 7221 4425.

Chelsea College of Art and Design, Manresa Road, London SW3 6LS. Tel: 020 7547 7751.

Community Languages Centres, St Judes Crypt, 24 Collingham Road, London SW5 0LX. Tel: 020 7370 2097.

Notting Dale Urban Studies Centre (IT courses for adults), 189 Freston Road, London W10 6TH. Tel: 020 8969 8942.

Education & Library Services, Royal Borough of Kensington and Chelsea, Town Hall, Horton Street, London W8 7NX. Tel: 020 7361 3334.

Heythrop College, University of London, Kensington Square, London W8 5HQ. Tel: 020 7795 6600. Website: www.heythrop.ac.uk E-mail: a.clarkson@heythrop.ac.uk

Kensington & Chelsea College, Wornington Road, London W10 5QQ. Tel: 020 7573 3600.

The London Academy of Music and Dramatic Art, Tower House, 226 Cromwell Road, London SW5 0SR. Tel: 020 7373 9883.

Lambeth

London South Bank Careers

Lambeth Centre, 1-5 Acre Lane, Brixton, London SW2 5TB. Tel: 020 8355 5200. Website: www.lsbcareers.co.uk E-mail: careers@lsbcareers.co.uk

FOCUS Central London, Centre Point, 103 New Oxford Street, London WC1A 1DR. Tel: 020 7896 8484. Website: www.focus-central-london.co.uk E-mail: info@focus-central-london.co.uk

Lambeth Adult Guidance, Lambeth Directions, 1-5 Acre Lane, Brixton, London SW2 5SD. Tel: 020 7926 3060.

The City and Guilds of London Art School, 124 Kennington Park Road, London SE1 4W. Tel: 020 7735 2306. Website: www.rmplc.co.uk/eduweb/sites/cgartsc/index.html. E-mail: cgartsc@rmplc.co.uk

Education Department, London Borough of Lambeth, 234-244 Stockwell Road, London SW9 9SP. Tel: 020 7926 1000.

King's College School of Medicine and Dentistry, King's College London, James Clerk Maxwell Building, 57 Waterloo Road, London SE1 8WA. Tel: 020 7872 3381. Website: www.kcl.ac.uk E-mail: ucas.enquiries@kcl.ac.uk

Lambeth Accord, 336 Brixton Road, London SW9 7AA. Tel: 020 7274 2299. E-mail: worklinkaccord@dial.pipx.com

Lambeth College, Clapham Centre, 45 Clapham Common South Side, London SW4 9BL. Tel: 020 7501 5010. Website: www.lambethcollege.ac.uk E-mail: admissions@lambethcollege.ac.uk

Marine Society College of the Sea, 202 Lambeth Road, London SE1 7JW. Tel: 020 7261 9535. Website: www.marine-society.org.uk

Morley College, 61 Westminster Bridge Road, London SE1 7HT. Tel: 020 7928 8501.

United Medical and Dental Schools of Guy's and St Thomas's Hopitals, Lambeth Palace Road, London SE1 7EH. Tel: 020 7922 8013.

Lewisham

London South Bank Careers

Lewisham Centre, 2nd Floor, Romer House, 132 Lewisham High Street, London SE13 6JJ. Tel: 020 8355 5050. Website: www.lsbcareers.co.uk E-mail: careers@lsbcareers.co.uk

SOLOTEC, Lancaster House, 7 Elmfield Road, Bromley BR1 1LT. Tel: 020 8313 9232. Website: www.solotec.co.uk

Community Education Lewisham, Mornington Centre, Stanley Street, Deptford, London SE8 4BL. Tel: 020 8691 5959.

Goldsmiths College, University of London, New Cross, London SE14 6NW. Tel: 020 7919 7171. Website: www.goldsmiths.ac.uk E-mail: admissions@gold.ac.uk

Laban Centre for Movement and Dance, Laurie Grove, New Cross, London SE14 6NH. Tel: 020 8692 4070. Website: www.laban.co.uk E-mail: info@laban.co.uk

Lewisham College, Lewisham Way, London SE4 1UT. Tel: 020 8692 0353. Website: www.lewisham.ac.uk/college/ E-mail: info@lewisham.ac.uk

Southwark

London South Bank Careers

Southwark Centre, 128 Rye Lane, Peckham, London SE15 4SB. Tel: 020 8355 5150. Website: www.isbcareers.co.uk E-mail: careers@isbcareers.co.uk

FOCUS Central London, Centre Point, 103 New Oxford Street, London WC1A 1DR. Tel: 020 7896 8484. Website: www.focus-central-london.co.uk E-mail: info@focus-central-london.ac.uk

Southwark Education & Training and Advice for Adults, Thomas Calton Centre, Alpha Street, London SE15 4NX. Tel: 020 7639 6818.

Camberwell College of Arts, Peckham Road, London SE5 8UF. Tel: 020 7514 6300.

London College of Printing and Distributive Trades, Elephant and Castle, London SE1 6SB. Tel: 020 7514 6562. Website: www.lcpdt.inst.ac.uk E-mail: k.depling@lcpdt.inst.ac.uk

South Bank University, Borough Road, London SE1 0AA. Tel: 020 7928 8989. Website: www.sbu.ac.uk E-mail: enrol@sbu.ac.uk

Southwark College, The Cut, London SE1 8LE. Tel: 020 7815 1500. Website: www.southwark.ac.uk

Southwark Education and Leisure Services Department, Southwark London Borough Council, 1 Bradenharm Close, London SE17 2QA. Tel: 020 7525 5050.

Tower Hamlets

Futures Careers

Tower Hamlets Centre, 35 Bow Road, London E3 2AD. Tel: 020 8983 3535. Website: www.futures-careers.co.uk

Education Department, Tower Hamlets London Borough Council, 5 Clove Crescent, London E14 2BG. Tel: 020 7364 5000.

Queen Mary and Westfield College, University of London, London E1 4NS. Tel: 020 7975 5555. Website: www.qmw.ac.uk/

St Bartholomew's and Royal London Hospital School of Medicine and Dentistry, Turner Street, London E1 2AD. Tel: 020 7377 7611. Website: www.qmw.ac.uk E-mail: admissions@qmw.ac.uk

Tower Hamlets College, Poplar Centre, Poplar High Street, London E14 0AF. Tel: 020 7538 5888.

Wandsworth

Search

Battersea Centre, 17 Falcon Road, Battersea London SW11 2PJ. Tel: 020 7326 8700. Website: www.careersite-search.org.uk E-mail: support@careersite-search.org.uk

AZTEC, Manorgate House, 2 Manorgate Road, Kingston upon Thames KT2 7AL. Tel: 0808 100 6050. Website: www.aztec.iip.co.uk

Academy of Live and Recorded Arts, The Royal Victoria Patriotic Building, Trinity Road, Wandsworth, London SW18 3SX. Tel: 020 8870 6475. Website: www.alra.demon.co.uk E-mail: patsy@alra.demon.co.uk

Education Department, Wandsworth London Borough Council, Town Hall, Wandsworth High Street, London SW18 2PU. Tel: 020 8871 7891.

Roehampton Institute London, Senate House, Roehampton, London SW15 5PU. Tel: 020 8392 3000. Website: www.roehampton.ac.uk E-mail: admissions@roehampton.ac.uk

St George's Hospital Medical School, University of London, Cranmer Terrace, Tooting, London SW17 0RE. Tel: 020 8672 9944.

South Thames College, Wandsworth High Street, Wandsworth SW18 2PP. Tel: 020 8918 7777. Website: www.south-thames.ac.uk E-mail: studentservices@south-thames.ac.uk

Westminster College, Battersea Park Road, London SW11 4JR. Tel: 020 7556 8000. Website: www.westminster-cfe.ac.uk E-mail: admissions@westminster-cfe.ac.uk

Westminster

Capital Careers

Westminster Careers Centre, 3-4 Picton Place, London W1M 5DP. Tel: 020 7487 4504. Website: www.capital-careers.ltd.uk

FOCUS Central London, Centre Point, 103 New Oxford Street, London WC1A 1DR. Tel: 020 7896 8484. Website: www.focus-central-london.co.uk E-mail: info@focus-central-london.co.uk

British School of Osteopathy, 275 Borough High Street, London SE1 1JE. Tel: 020 7402 0222. Website: www.bso.ac.uk

City of Westminster College, 25 Paddington Green, London W2 1NB. Tel: 020 7723 8826.

Courtauld Institute of Art, Somerset House, North Block, Strand, London WC2R 0RN. Tel: 020 7873 2649. Website: www.kcl.ac.uk/inst/courtauld/int.htm

Education and Leisure Department, Westminster City Council, Westminster City Hall, PO Box 240, Victoria Street, London SW1E 6QP. Tel: 020 7641 6000.

European Business School, Regent's College, Inner Circle, Regent's Park, London NW1 4NS. Tel: 020 7487 7400.

Imperial College of Science, Technology & Medicine, London SW7 2AZ. Tel: 020 7589 5111. Website: www.ic.ac.uk E-mail: admissions@ic.ac.uk

King's College London, Strand, London WC2R 2LS. Tel: 020 7836 5454. Website: www.kcl.ac.uk

London Business School, Sussex Place, Regent's Park, London NW1 4SA. Tel: 020 7262 5050.

London College of Fashion, 20 John Prince's Street, London W1M 0BJ. Tel: 020 7514 7400.

London School of Economics and Political Science, Houghton Street, London WC2A 2AE. Tel: 020 7405 7686.

Royal Academy Schools, Piccadilly, London W1V 0DS. Tel: 020 7439 7438.

Royal Academy of Music, Marylebone Road, London NW1 5HT. Tel: 020 7873 7373.

Royal College of Art, Kensington Gore, London SW7 2EU. Tel: 020 7590 4101. Website: www.rca.ac.uk E-mail: c.frayling@rca.ac.uk

Royal College of Music, Prince Consort Road, London SW7 2BS. Tel: 020 7589 3643.

St Mary's Hospital Medical School, Norfolk Place, Paddington, London W2 1PG.
Tel: 020 7723 1252. Website: www.ic.ac.uk E-mail: admissions@ic.ac.uk

Trinity College of Music, Mandeville Place, London W1M 6AG. Tel: 020 8935 5773.
Website: www.tcm.ac.uk E-mail: mray@tcm.ac.uk

University of Westminster, 309 Regent Street, London W1R 8AL. Tel: 020 7911 5000.
Website: www.wmin.ac.uk

Manchester – Greater

Bolton

Lifetime Careers (Bolton, Bury and Rochdale)

Bolton Careers Centre, Chatsworth House, Bold Street, Bolton BL1 1LS. Tel: 01204 840789.
Website: www.lifetime-careers.co.uk

Bolton & Bury Chamber, Clive House, Clive Street, Bolton BL1 1ET. Tel: 01204 397350.

Bolton College, The Guidance Centre, Manchester Road, Bolton BL2 1ER. Tel: 01204 531411.

Bolton Community Education Service, Clarence Street Centre, Clarence Street, Bolton BL1 2ET.
Tel: 01204 525500.

Bolton Institute of Higher Education, Deane Road, Bolton BL3 5AB. Tel: 01204 528851.

Bolton Metro EPDU, The Quest Centre, Brownlow Way, Bolton BL1 2UB. Tel: 01204 396668.

Bury

Lifetime Careers (Bolton, Bury and Rochdale)

Bury Careers Centre, 13-15 Broad Street, Bury BL9 0DA. Tel: 0161 763 5884.

Bolton & Bury Chamber, Clive House, Clive Street, Bolton BL1 1ET. Tel: 01204 397350.

Bury College, Market Street, Bury BL9 0BG. Tel: 0161 280 8205.

Bury Lifelong Learning, Athenaeum House, Market Street, Bury BL9 0BN. Tel: 0161 253 5000.

Manchester

Careers Partnership Ltd

Harpurhey Careers Office, Harpurhey District Centre, Manchester M9 4DH. Tel: 0161 205 1644.

Longsight Careers Office, 1 Stanley Grove, Longsight, Manchester M12 4AA.
Tel: 0161 248 7684.

West Didsbury Careers Office, 141 Barlow Moor Road, West Didsbury, Manchester M20 8PQ.
Tel: 0161 445 0136.

Wythenshawe Careers Office, Alpha House, Rowlands Way, Wythenshawe, Manchester M22 5RG. Tel: 0161 437 4288.

Manchester Training & Enterprise Council Ltd, Lee House, 90 Great Bridgewater Street, Manchester M1 5JW. Tel: 0161 236 7222. Website: www.manchester-tec.co.uk

City College Manchester, Barlow Moor Road, West Didsbury, Manchester M20 2PQ. Tel: 0161 957 1500. Website: www.manchester-city-coll.ac.uk

Fielden Cegos Ltd, The Towers, Towers Business Park, Wilmslow Road, Didsbury, Manchester M20 2FZ. Tel: 0161 445 2426. Website: www.fielden-house.co.uk E-mail: customerservicce@fielden-cegos.co.uk

Manchester Council Education Department, Plymouth Grove Centre, Hathergate Road, Longsight, Manchester M13 0BY. Tel: 0161 273 4736.

Manchester Business School, Booth Street West, Manchester M15 6PB. Tel: 0161 275 6311. Website: www.mbs.ac.uk

Manchester College of Arts and Technology, City Centre Campus, Lower Hardman Street, Manchester. Tel: 0161 953 5995. Website: www.mancat.ac.uk E-mail: jom.whitham@mancat.ac.uk

Manchester Metropolitan University, All Saints Building, All Saints, Manchester M15 6BH. Tel: 0161 247 2000. Website: www.mmu.ac.uk E-mail: enquiries@mmu.ac.uk

Open College, St Paul's, 781 Wilmslow Road, Didsbury, Manchester M20 2RW. Tel: 0161 434 0007. Website: www.thebiz.co.uk/opencoll.htm

Royal Northern College of Music, 124 Oxford Road, Manchester M13 9RD. Tel: 0161 907 5200. Website: www.rncm.ac.uk E-mail: info@rncm.ac.uk

University of Manchester, Oxford Road, Manchester M13 9PL. Tel: 0161 275 2000. Website: www.man.ac.uk

University of Manchester Institute of Science and Technology, PO Box 88, Sackville Street, Manchester M60 1QD. Tel: 0161 236 3311. Website: www.umist.ac.uk E-mail: webmaster@umist.ac.uk

Oldham

Oldham Careers Service Partnership

Adult Guidance Unit, Brunswick House, Brunswick Square, Union Street, Oldham OL1 1DE. Tel: 0161 911 4296.

Oldham Chamber of Commerce, Training & Enterprise, Adult Guidance Network, Meridian Centre, King's Street, Oldham OL8 1EZ. Tel: 0161 620 0006.

Oldham College, Rochdale Road, Oldham OL9 6AA. Tel: 0161 624 5214. Website: www.oldham.ac.uk E-mail: info@oldham.ac.uk

Youth & Community Education Services (Education & Leisure Services), Oldham Metropolitan Borough Council, Civic Centre, PO Box 40, West Street, Oldham OL1 1XJ. Tel: 0161 911 3000.

Rochdale

Lifetime Careers (Bolton, Bury and Rochdale)

Heywood Careers Centre, 7 Church Place, Hartley Street, Heywood OL10 1LS. Tel: 01706 622770. Website: www.lifetime-careers.co.uk E-mail: lifetime@zen.co.uk

Middleton Careers Centre, Unit F10a, 1st Floor, Arndale Centre, Middleton M24 4EL. Tel: 0161 643 3125. Website: www.lifetime-careers.co.uk E-mail: lifetime@zen.co.uk

Rochdale Careers Centre, Unit 2, Bus Station Complex, Smith Street, Rochdale OL16 1YG. Tel: 01706 759515. Website: www.lifetime-careers.co.uk E-mail: lifetime@zen.co.uk

Rochdale Borough Chamber of Commerce, Training & Enterprise (Pathways), St James Place, 160-162 Yorkshire Street, Rochdale OL16 2DL. Tel: 01706 644909. Website: www.rbccte.co.uk E-mail: info@rbccte.co.uk

Education Department, Rochdale Metropolitan Borough Council, PO Box 70, Municipal Offices, Smith Street, Rochdale OL16 1YD. Tel: 01706 647474.

Hopwood Hall College, Middleton Campus, Rochdale Road, Middleton, Manchester M24 6XH. Tel: 0161 643 7560. E-mail: dowda@rmplc.co.uk

Salford

Careers Partnership

Salford Careers Centre, The Coach House, 25 Bolton Road, Pendleton, Salford M6 7HL. Tel: 0161 743 0163.

Salford Education & Training Advice Service (SETAS), Salford Opportunities Centre, 2 Paddington Close, Pendleton, Salford M6 5PL. Tel: 0161 745 7233.

Manchester Training & Enterprise Council, Lee House, 90 Great Bridgewater Street, Manchester M1 5JW. Tel: 0161 236 7222. Website: www.manchester-tec.co.uk

Education & Leisure Directorate, Salford City Council, Chapel Street, Salford M3 5LT. Tel: 0161 837 1740.

Salford College, Worsley Campus, Walkden Road, Worsley, Manchester M28 7QD. Tel: 0161 211 5101. Website: www.salford-col.ac.uk E-mail: centad@salford.ac.uk

Salford University, Salford, Greater Manchester M5 4WT. Tel: 0161 295 5000. Website: www.salford.ac.uk

Stockport

Lifetime Careers Stockport & High Peak

Careers Centre, Strathblane House, Ashfield Road, Cheadle SK8 1BB. Tel: 0161 282 2220. Website: www.lifetime-careers.co.uk

Stockport & High Peak Training & Enterprise Council, The Pathfinder Centre, Regal House, Duke Street, Stockport SK1 3AB. Tel: 0161 476 7400.

Stockport College of Further and Higher Education, Wellington Road South, Stockport SK1 3UQ. Tel: 0161 958 3100.

Education Division, Stockport Metropolitan Borough Council, Town Hall, Piccadilly, Stockport SK1 3XE. Tel: 0161 474 3812.

Tameside

Careers Partnership

Ashton Careers Office, 82 Old Street, Ashton Under Lyne OL6 7JT. Tel: 0161 330 1528.

Tameside Education Advice Service for Adults, Tameside College of Technology, Beaufort Road, Ashton under Lyne, Greater Manchester OL6 6NX. Tel: 0161 908 6600.

Manchester Training & Enterprise Council Ltd, Lee House, 90 Great Bridgewater Street, Manchester M1 5JW. Tel: 0161 236 7222. Website: www.manchester-tec.co.uk

Education Department, Tameside Metropolitan Borough Council, Council Offices, Wellington Road, Ashton under Lyne OL6 6DL. Tel: 0161 330 8355. Website: www.edu.tameside.gov.uk E-mail: catherinemoseley@edu.tameside.gov.uk

Tameside College of Technology, Beaufort Road, Ashton under Lyne OL6 6NX. Tel: 0161 908 6600. Website: www.tamesidecollege.ac.uk E-mail: info@tamesidecollege.ac.uk

Trafford

Careers Partnership Ltd

Stretford Careers Office, 4th Floor, Arndale House, Chester Road, Stretford, Manchester M32 9XY. Tel: 0161 864 1977.

Manchester Training & Enterprise Council Ltd, Lee House, 90 Great Bridgewater Street, Manchester M1 5JW. Tel: 0161 236 7222. Website: www.manchester-tec.co.uk

Education Department, Trafford Metropolitan Borough Council, PO Box 19, Town Hall, Tatton Road, Sale M33 7YR. Tel: 0161 912 1212.

North Trafford College of Futher Education, Talbot Road, Stretford, Manchester M32 0XH. Tel: 0161 886 7000. Website: www.northtraford.ac.uk E-mail: admissions@northtrafford,.ac.uk

South Trafford College, Manchester Road, West Timperley, Altrincham WA14 5PQ. Tel: 0161 952 4699. Website: www.stcoll.ac.uk

Wigan

Education Business Partnership (Wigan) Ltd

Leigh Careers and Jobsearch Centre, The Leigh Investment Centre, Bradshawgate, Leigh WN7 4NP. Tel: 01942 705800.

Wigan Careers and Jobsearch Centre, London House, Standish Gate, Wigan WN1 1XP. Tel: 01942 733378.

Higher Folds Guidance Shop, Heart of the Community, Higher Folds Enterprise Centre, 118-120 Coronation Drive, Leigh WN7 2YZ. Tel: 01942 703303.

Ince Guidance Shop, Ince Library, Smithy Green, Wigan WN2 2AT. Tel: 01942 492989.

Marsh Green Guidance Shop, Marsh Green Library, Harrow Road, Marsh Road, Wigan WN5 4QL. Tel: 01942 221881.

Wigan Borough Partnership – Guidance Directorate, Wigan Investment Centre, Waterside Drive, Wigan WN3 5BA. Tel: 01942 705705.

Education Department, Wigan Metropolitan Borough Council, Gateway House, Standishgate, Wigan WN1 1AE. Tel: 01942 828892.

Wigan and Leigh College, PO Box 53, Parson's Walk, Wigan WN1 1RS. Tel: 01942 761600. Website: www.wigan-leigh.ac.uk E-mail: admissions@wigan-leigh.ac.uk

Merseyside

Knowsley

Careerdecisions Ltd

Huyton Careers Centre, 12-14 Lansdowne Way, Huyton L36 9Y17. Tel: 0151 949 5700.

Kirkby Careers Centre, 142 Cherryfield Drive, Kirkby L32 8RX. Tel: 0151 545 5400.

The Careers Centre, Knowsley Community College (Roby Site), Rupert Road, Roby, Huyton L36 9TD. Tel: 0151 477 5792.

Merseyside TEC, Tithebarn House, Tithebarn Street, Liverpool L2 2NZ. Tel: 0151 236 0026. Website: www.merstec.u-net.com E-mail: info@merstec.u-net.com

Education Department, Knowsley Metropolitan Borough Council, Huyton Hey Road, Huyton L36 5YH. Tel: 0151 489 6000.

Knowsley Community College, Rupert Road, Roby, Huyton L36 9TD. Tel: 0151 477 5700.

Liverpool

Careerdecisions Ltd

HQ, 2nd Floor, Minster House, Paradise Street, Liverpool L1 3EU. Tel: 0151 709 0550. Website: www.careerdecisions.co.uk E-mail: mickf@career.u-net.com

Liverpool City Careers Centre, 2nd Floor, Merseyside House, 9 South John Street, Liverpool L1 8BN. Tel: 0151 709 5400.

Liverpool East Careers Centre, Liverpool Community College, Broadgreen Road, Old Swan, Liverpool L13 5SQ. Tel: 0151 228 2285.

Liverpool North Careers Centre, Townsend Avenue, Norris Green, Liverpool L11 5AG. Tel: 0151 270 2246.

Liverpool South Careers Centre, 1st Floor, Belmont House, Hunts Cross Shopping Centre, Speke Hall Road, Liverpool L25 9GB. Tel: 0151 336 9400.

City of Liverpool Adult Guidance Service, Roscommon Centre, Roscommon Street, Liverpool L5 3NE. Tel: 0151 233 1600.

CENTEC, Business Centre, East Lancashire Road, Liverpool L10 5BE. Tel: 0151 525 1954.

Merseyside TEC, 4th Floor, Tithebarn House, Tithebarn Street, Liverpool L2 2NZ. Tel: 0151 236 0026. Website: www.merstec.u-net.com E-mail: info@merstec.u-net.com

City of Liverpool Community College, Old Swan, Broadgreen Road, Liverpool L13 5SQ. Tel: 0151 252 1515.

Education Directorate, Liverpool City Council, 14 Sir Thomas Street, Liverpool L1 6BJ. Tel: 0151 225 2822.

Liverpool Hope University, Hope Park, Liverpool L16 9JD. Tel: 0151 291 3000. Website: www.hope.ac.uk

Liverpool John Moores University, Roscoe Court, 4 Rodney Street, Liverpool L1 2TZ. Tel: 0151 231 5090. Website: cwis.livjm.ac.uk E-mail: recruitment@livjm.ac.uk

University of Liverpool, Abercromby Square, Liverpool L69 3BX. Tel: 0151 794 2000. Website: www.liv.ac.uk E-mail: rayder:liverpool.ac.uk

Sefton

Careerdecisions Ltd

Bootle-Crosby Careers Centre, 1st Floor, Daniel House, Stanley Road, Bootle L20 3RG. Tel: 0151 955 6300.

Southport Careers Centre, The Duke's House, Mornington Road, Southport PR9 0TS. Tel: 01704 504509.

Merseyside TEC, 4th Floor, Tithebarn House, Tithebarn Street, Liverpool L2 2NZ. Tel: 0151 236 0026. Website: www.merstec.u-net.com E-mail: info@merstec.u-net.com

Education Department, Sefton Metropolitan Borough Council, Town Hall, Oriel Road, Bootle L20 7AE. Tel: 0151 934 3236.

Hugh Baird College of Technology, Balliol Road, Bootle, Liverpool L20 7EW. Tel: 0151 934 4441. Website: www.hughbaird.uk.com

Southport College, Mornington Road, Southport PR9 0TT. Tel: 01704 500606. Website: www.southport.mernet.org.uk E-mail: southport@southport.mernet.org.uk

St Helens

St Helens Career Services Ltd, Smithkline Beecham Building, Water Street, St Helens WA10 1QQ. Tel: 01744 633500. Website: www.merseyworld.com/sthelens-careers E-mail: options@sthelenscareers.prestel.co.uk

St Helens Chamber of Commerce, Training & Enterprise, 7 Waterside Court Technology Campus, St Helens WA9 1UB. Tel: 01744 742000.

Community Education Department, St Helens Metropolitan Borough Council, The Rivington Centre, Rivington Road, St Helens WA10 4ND. Tel: 01744 455464. E-mail: facet.sthelens@cableinet.co.uk

St Helens College, Brook Street, St Helens WA10 1PZ. Tel: 01744 733766.

Wirral

Career Connections

Head Office, Conway Buildings, Conway Street, Birkenhead L41 6DJ. Tel: 0151 666 4508.

Bebington Careers Centre, 41/43 Bebington Road, New Ferry L62 5BE. Tel: 0151 645 5586.

Birkenhead Careers Centre, Conway Buildings, Conway Street, Birkenhead L41 6DJ. Tel: 0151 666 4385.

Ellesmere Port Careers Centre, Coronation Road, Ellesmere Port. Tel: 0151 357 4544.

Wallasey Careers Centre, Liscard Municipal Buildings, 52 Seaview Road, Wallasey L45 4FY. Tel: 0151 638 5625.

West Kirby Careers Centre, 1st Floor, West Kirby Concourse, Grange Road, West Kirby L48 4HX. Tel: 0151 625 2716.

CEWTEC, Egerton House, 2 Tower Road, Birkenhead L41 1FN. Tel: 0151 650 0555. Website: www.cewtec.co.uk

Education Offices, Metropolitan Borough of Wirral, Hamilton Building, Conway Street, Birkenhead L41 4FD. Tel: 0151 666 2121.

Wirral Metropolitan College, IBMC Europa Boulevard, Conway Park, Birkenhead L41 4NT. Tel: 0151 551 7000. Website: www.wmc.ac.uk E-mail: clasi@wmc.ac.uk

Norfolk

Norfolk Careers Services Ltd

Dereham Careers Centre, 1a Aldiss Court, High Street, Dereham, Norfolk NR19 1DU. Tel: 01362 694939. Website: www.norfolk-careers.co.uk E-mail: duc@norfolk-careers.co.uk

Great Yarmouth Careers Centre, 4 Church Plain, Great Yarmouth, Norfolk NR30 1PL. Tel: 01493 856723. Website: www.norfolk-careers.co.uk E-mail: duc@norfolk-careers.co.uk

King's Lynn Careers Centre, 5-9 Chapel Street, King's Lynn, Norfolk PE30 1EG. Tel: 01553 666500. Website: www.norfolk-careers.co.uk E-mail: duc@norfolk-careers.co.uk

North Walsham Careers Centre, 1a St Nicholas Court, North Walsham, Norfolk NR28 9BY. Tel: 01692 408200. Website: www.norfolk-careers.co.uk E-mail: duc@norfolk-careers.co.uk

Norwich Careers Centre, 83-87 Pottergate, Norwich, Norfolk NR2 1DZ. Tel: 01603 215300. Website: www.norfolk-careers.co.uk E-mail: duc@norfolk-careers.co.uk

Thetford Careers Centre, 2 Well Street, Thetford, Norfolk IP24 2BL. Tel: 01842 855800. Website: www.norfolk-careers.co.uk E-mail: duc@norfolk-careers.co.uk

Norfolk & Waveney Enterprise Partnership, St Andrew's House, St Andrew Street, Norwich NR2 4TP. Tel: 01603 763812.

City College Norwich, Ipswich Road, Norwich NR2 2LS. Tel: 01603 773311. Website: www.ccn.ac.uk E-mail: info@ccn.ac.uk

The College of West Anglia, Tennyson Avenue, King's Lynn, Norfolk PE30 2QW. Tel: 01553 761144. Website: www.norcat.ac.uk E-mail: enqiries@norcat.ac.uk

Easton College, Easton, Norwich NR9 5DX. Tel: 01603 742105.

Education Department, Norfolk County Council, County Hall, Martineau Lane, Norwich NR1 2DL. Tel: 01603 222146.

Great Yarmouth College, Southtown, Great Yarmouth NR31 0ED. Tel: 01493 655261. Website: www.gtyarmouthcoll.ac.uk

Norwich School of Art and Design, St George Street, Norwich NR3 1BB. Tel: 01603 611393. Website: www.nsad.ac.uk E-mail: info@nsad>ac.uk

University of East Anglia, Norwich NR4 7TJ. Tel: 01603 456161. Website: www.uea.ac.uk/

Northamptonshire

Career Path (Northamptonshire) Ltd

Brackley Careers Centre, 33 High Street, Brackley NN13 5DW. Tel: 01280 704659.

Corby Careers Centre, 2nd Floor, Chisolm House, The Links, 9 Queen's Square, Corby NN17 1PD. Tel: 01536 202917.

Daventry Careers Centre, Badby Road, West Daventry NN11 4UP. Tel: 01327 705831.

Kettering Careers Centre, St Mary's Road, Kettering NN15 7AH. Tel: 01536 513862.

Northampton Careers Centre, The Adult Guidance Unit, 30 Billing Road, Northampton NN1 5DQ. Tel: 01604 234762.

Rushden Careers Centre, 1st Floor, The Rushden Centre, Newton Road, Rushden NN10 0PT. Tel: 01933 353553.

Wellingborough Careers Centre, 12 Church Street, Wellingborough NN8 4PA. Tel: 01933 222626.

Northamptonshire Adult Guidance, Russell House, Rickyard Road, Northampton NN3 3QZ. Tel: 01604 410236.

Northamptonshire Chamber, Royal Pavilion, Summerhouse Road, Moulton Park, Northampton NN3 6BJ. Tel: 01604 671200.

Adult Education Service, Northamptonshire County Council, Education and Libraries, PO Box 149, County Hall, Guildhall Road, Northampton NN1 1AU. Tel: 01604 236236.

Daventry Tertiary College, Badby Road West, Daventry, Northamptonshire NN11 4HJ. Tel: 01327 300232. Website: www.davcoll.ac.uk E-mail: ir5@davcoll.ac.uk

Knuston Hall Residential College, Irchester, Northants. Tel: 01933 312104. Website: www.knustonhall.org.uk

Moulton College, Moulton, Northampton NN3 7RR. Tel: 01604 491131. Website: www.moulton.ac.uk E-mail: enquiries@moulton.ac.uk

Nene College of Higher Education, Boughton Green Road, Northampton NN2 7AL. Tel: 01604 735500. Website: www.nen.ac.uk

Northampton College, Booth Lane, Northampton NN3 3RF. Tel: 01604 734030.

Northamptonshire Uplands Adult Education, Montsaye School, Greening Road, Rothwell, Kettering NN14 6BB. Tel: 01536 712623.

Tresham Institute of Further and Higher Education, St Mary's Road, Kettering, Northamptonshire NN15 7BS. Tel: 01527 410252. Website: www.idiom.co.uk/schools/tresham.htm

Universtiy College Northampton, Park Campus, Boughton Green Road, Northampton NN2 7AL. Tel: 01604 735500. Website: www.northampton.ac.uk E-mail: admissions@northampton.ac.uk

Northumberland

Northumberland Guidance Co Ltd

Alnwick Careers Centre, Bongate Within, Alnwick NE66 1TD. Tel: 01665 603726. Website: www.ngcl.co.uk E-mail: enquiries@ngcl.co.uk

Ashington Careers Centre, 88-90 Station Road, Ashington NE63 8RN. Tel: 01670 816511. Website: www.ngcl.co.uk E-mail: enquiries@ngcl.co.uk

Blyth Careers Centre, 7 Sextant House, Freehold Street, Blyth NE24 2BA. Tel: 01670 361361. Website: www.ngcl.co.uk E-mail: enquiries@ngcl.co.uk

Hexham Careers Centre, 16 Market Street, Hexham NE46 3NU. Tel: 01434 604044. Website: www.ngcl.co.uk E-mail: enquiries@ngcl.co.uk

Careers Action for Adults, Ashington Careers Centre, 88-90 Station Road, Ashington NE63 8RN. Tel: 01670 816511. Website: www.ngcl.co.uk E-mail: enquiries@ngcl.co.uk

Information Station, 4 Laburnham Terrace, Ashington NE66 0XX. Tel: 01670 520510

Northumberland Training & Enterprise Council, 2 Craster Court, Manor Walks, Cramlington NE23 6XX. Tel: 01670 713303.

Adult & Community Education, Northumberland County Council, Education Department, County Hall, Morpeth NE61 2EF. Tel: 01670 533000.

Kirkley Hall College, Ponteland, Newcastle upon Tyne NE20 0AQ. Tel: 01661 860808.

Northumberland College, College Road, Ashington NE63 9RG. Tel: 01670 841200. Website: www.northland.ac.uk E-mail: info@northland.ac.uk

Nottinghamshire and City of Nottingham

GuideLine Career Services Ltd

Head Office, Heathcote Buildings, Heathcote Street, Nottingham NG1 3AA. Tel: 0115 912 6611. Website: www.guideline-careers.co.uk E-mail: enquiries@guideline-careers.co.uk

Eastwood Careers Centre, 158 Nottingham Road, Eastwood, Nottingham NG16 3GG. Tel: 01773 713449.

Hucknall Careers Centre, MB House, Woodstock Street, Hucknall, Nottingham NG15 7SN. Tel: 0115 840 2067.

Mansfield Careers Centre, 30-32 Regent Street, Mansfield NG18 1SS. Tel: 01623 632000.

Newark Careers Centre, 27 Lombard Street, Newark NG24 1XG. Tel: 01636 702084.

Nottingham Careers Centre, 24-32 Carlton Street, Hockley, Nottingham NG1 1NN. Tel: 0115 948 4484.

Retford Careers Centre, County Council Office, Chancery Lane, Retford DN22 6DG. Tel: 01777 710701.

Worksop Careers Centre, Ryton Street, Worksop S80 2AY. Tel: 01909 473165.

East Midlands Development Agency, 2/4 Weekday Cross, Nottingham NG1 2GB. Tel: 0115 952 7870. Website: www.emda.org.uk

Greater Nottingham TEC, Castle Marina Park, Marina Road, Nottingham NG7 1TN. Tel: 0115 941 3313.

North Nottinghamshire TEC, Edwinstowe House, Centre for Business Excellence, Edwinstowe, North Nottinghamshire NG21 9PR. Tel: 0800 591067. Website: www.north-notts.co.uk/nntec

Adult Community Education, Nottinghamshire County Council, County Hall, West Bridgford NG2 7QP. Tel: 0115 982 3823.

Brackenhurst College, Brackenhurst, Southwell NG25 0QF. Tel: 01636 817000.

Broxtowe College of Further Education, High Road, Chilwell, Beeston NG9 4AH. Tel: 0115 917 5252.

Education Department, Nottingham City Council, Sandfield Centre, Sandfield Road, Menton, Nottingham NG7 1QH. Tel: 0115 915 0706.

New College Nottingham (Arnold & Carlton), Digby Avenue, Mapperley, Nottingham NG3 6DR. Tel: 0115 952 0052.

New College Nottingham (Basford Hall), Stockhill Lane, Basford, Nottingham NG6 0NB. Tel: 0115 916 2001. Website: www.basford.demon.c.o.uk New College Nottingham (Clarendon), Pelham Avenue, Mansfield Road, Nottingham NG5 1AL. Tel: 0115 960 7201. Website: www.clarendon.ac.uk E-mail: enquiries@clarendon.ac.uk

Newark & Sherwood College, Friary Road, Newark NG24 1PB. Tel: 01636 680680. Website: www.newark.ac.uk

North Nottinghamshire College, Carlton Road, Worksop S81 7HP. Tel: 01909 473561. Website: www.nnotts-col.ac.uk E-mail: contact@nnotts-col.ac.uk

Nottingham Community College, Carlton Road, Nottingham NG3 2NR. Tel: 0115 910 1455.

Nottingham Trent University, Burton Street, Nottingham NG1 4BU. Tel: 0115 941 8418. Website: www.ntu.ac.uk/ E-mail: marketing@ntu.ac.uk

People's College of Tertiary Education, Maid Marian Way, Nottingham NG1 6AB. Tel: 0115 912 3444. Website: www.peoples.ac.uk

South Nottinghamshire College, Greythorn Drive, West Bridgford, Nottingham NG2 7GA. Tel: 0115 914 6400.

South Notts Training Agency, Cawley House, 96 Cliff Road, Nottingham NG1 1GD. Tel: 0115 958 7257.

University of Nottingham, University Park, Nottingham NG7 2RD. Tel: 0115 951 5151. Website: www.nottingham.ac.uk

West Nottingham College, Chesterfield Road South, Mansfield NG19 7BB. Tel: 01623 627191.

Oxfordshire

CfBT Thames Careers Guidance

HQ, Abingdon Office, Publishing House, 62 Stert Street, Abingdon OX14 3UQ. Tel: 01235 520430.

Banbury Careers Centre, 2 Broughton Road, Banbury OX16 9PZ. Tel: 01295 256224.

Didcot Careers Centre, 197 The Broadway, Didcot OX11 8RU. Tel: 01235 813115.

Oxford Careers Centre, 104 Gloucester Green, Oxford OX1 2RH. Tel: 01865 790716.

New Start Adult Guidance Service, Cherwell, East Street Centre, East Street, Grimsbury, Banbury OX16 7LJ. Tel: 01295 265160.

New Start Adult Guidance Service, Oxford City, East Oxford Education Complex, Union Street, Oxford OX4 1JR. Tel: 01865 798081.

New Start Adult Guidance Service, Vale and South, Community Education Office, Carswell School Annexe, Conduit Road, Abingdon OX14 1DB. Tel: 01235 537677.

New Start Adult Guidance Service, West, Burford Community Centre, Cheltenham Road, Burford OX18 4PL. Tel: 01367 253446.

Heart of England TEC Learning Link, 60 St Aldates, Oxford OX1 1ST. Tel: 01865 200466.

Heart of England Training & Enterprise Council (Oxfordshire), 26-27 The Quandrant, Abingdon Science Park, Barton Lane, Abingdon OX14 3YS. Tel: 01235 553240.

Abingdon College, North Court Road, Abingdon OX14 1NN. Tel: 01235 555585.

Education Department, Oxfordshire County Council, Macclesfield House, New Road, Oxford OX1 1NA. Tel: 01865 792422.

North Oxfordshire College and School of Art, Broughton Road, Banbury OX16 9QA. Tel: 01295 252221.

Oxford Brookes University, Headington Hill Hall, Headington, Oxford OX3 0BP. Tel: 01865 241111. Website: www.brookes.ac.uk

Oxford College of Further Education, Oxpens Road, Oxford OX1 1SA. Tel: 01865 245871. Website: www.oxfe.ac.uk E-mail: carolbishop@oxfe.ac.uk

Plater College, Pullens Lane, Oxford OX3 ODT. Tel: 01864 740500. Website: www.plater.ac.uk E-mail: reception@plater.ac.uk

Ruskin College, Walton Street, Oxford OX1 2HE. Tel: 01865 554331. Website: www.ruskin.ac.uk

Rycotewood College, Priest End, Thame OX9 2AF. Tel: 01844 212501. Website: www.oxfe.ac.uk E-mail: enquiries_rycote.@oxfe.ac.uk

University of Oxford, University Offices, Wellington Square, Oxford OX1 2JD. Tel: 01865 270000. Website: www.ox.ac.uk

West Oxfordshire College, Holloway Road, Witney OX8 7EE. Tel: 01993 703464. Website: www.oxfe.ac.uk E-mail: enquiries_woc@oxfe.ac.uk

Westminster College, Oxford OX2 9AT. Tel: 01865 247644. Website: www.ox-west.ac.uk E-mail: marketing@ox-west.ac.uk

Shropshire, Telford and Wrekin

Shropshire Careers Service Ltd

Business Development and Support Services, 7 Anstice Square, Madeley, Telford TF7 5BD. Tel: 01952 582439. Website: www.shropcareers.org.uk E-mail: enquiry@shropcareers.org.uk

Bridgnorth Branch, Bridgnorth College, Stourbridge Road, Bridgnorth WV15 6AL. Tel: 01746 765001.

Ludlow Branch, 20 Castle Street, Ludlow SY8 1AT. Tel: 01584 873725.

Madeley Branch, 7 Anstice Square, Madeley, Telford TF7 5BD. Tel: 01952 684289.

Market Drayton Branch, 11 High Street, Market Drayton TF9 1PY. Tel: 01630 654138.

Oswestry Branch, 32 Upper Brook Street, Oswestry SY1 2TB. Tel: 01691 659111.

Shrewsbury Branch, 1st Floor, Victoria House, Victoria Quay, Shrewsbury SY1 1HH. Tel: 01743 231464.

Wellington Branch, 4 Landau Court, Tan Bank, Wellington, Telford TF1 1HE. Tel: 01952 643070.

Shropshire Chamber of Commerce, Training & Enterprise, Trevithick House, Stafford Park 4, Telford TF3 3BA. Tel: 0345 543210. Website: www.tec.co.uk/map/shrop.html

Adult & Community Education, Shropshire County Council Education Department, The Shirehall, Abbey Foregate, Shrewsbury SY2 6ND. Tel: 01743 255943.

Harper Adams University College, Edgmond, Newport, Shropshire TF10 8NB. Tel: 01952 815324. Website: www.hauc.ac.uk E-mail: enquiry@hauc.ac.uk

North Shropshire College, College Road, Oswestry SY11 2SA. Tel: 01691 688000. Website: www.n-shropshire.ac.uk E-mail: enquiries@n-shropshire.ac.uk

Shrewsbury College of Arts and Technology, London Road, Shrewsbury SY2 6PR. Tel: 01743 342342. Website: www.s-cat.ac.uk E-mail: prospects@s-cat.ac.uk

Telford College of Arts and Technology, Haybridge Road, Wellington, Telford TF1 2NP. Tel: 01952 642200. Website: www.tcat.ac.uk E-mail: webboss@tcat.ac.uk

Telford & Wrekin Education and Training Service, Civic Offices, PO Box 213, Telford Town Centre TF3 4LL. Tel: 01952 202058.

Walford College, Baschurch, Shrewsbury SY4 2HL. Tel: 01939 26200. Website: www.walford-college.ac.uk E-mail: info@walford-college.ac.uk

Somerset (excluding North East and North West Somerset – see Bristol entry)

Somerset Careers Services Ltd

HQ, Crescent House, The Mount, Taunton TA1 3TT. Tel: 01823 321212.

Bridgwater Careers Office, 4-6 East Quay, Bridgwater TA6 5AZ. Tel: 01278 423788.

Frome Careers Office, Northover House, North Parade, Frome BA11 1AU. Tel: 01373 465302.

Street Careers Office, 6 Leigh Road, Street BA16 0HA. Tel: 01458 443051.

Taunton Careers Office, Crescent House, The Mount, Taunton TA1 3TT. Tel: 01823 321212.

Yeovil Careers Office, 40-42 Hendford, Yeovil BA20 1UW. Tel: 01935 427511.

Opportunity Shop, 3 Mendip House, High Street, Taunton TA1 2SX. Tel: 01823 321165.

Somerset Community Education, Learning Advice Centre, 72 South Street, Yeovil BA20 1QF. Tel: 01935 410810.

Somerset TEC, East Reach House, East Reach, Taunton TA1 3EN. Tel: 01823 321188.

Bridgwater College, Bath Road, Bridgwater TA6 4PZ. Tel: 01278 441234.
Website: www.bridgwater.ac.uk E-mail: inbox@bridgwater.ac.uk

Cannington College, Cannington, Bridgwater TA5 2LS. Tel: 01278 655000.
Website: www.cannington.ac.uk E-mail: admin@cannington.ac.uk

Education Department, Somerset County Council, County Hall, Taunton TA1 4DY.
Tel: 01823 355455.

Richard Huish College, South Road, Taunton TA1 3DZ. Tel: 01823 270171.
Website: www.richuish.ac.uk E-mail: petera@staffp.richuish.ac.uk

Somerset College of Arts and Technology, Wellington Road, Taunton TA1 5AX.
Tel: 01823 366311.

Strode College, Church Road, Street BA16 0AB. Tel: 01458 844400.

Yeovil College, Mudford Road, Yeovil BA21 4DR. Tel: 01935 423921. E-mail: oayeovil@rmplc.co.uk

Staffordshire and Stoke-on-Trent

3 S Strategies Ltd

Head Office, Foregate House, 70 Foregate Street, Stafford ST16 2PX. Tel: 01785 355700.
Website: www.staffscareers.co.uk E-mail: info@staffscareers.co.uk

Burton Careers Centre, The Rotunda, 131a High Street, Burton upon Trent DE14 1LN.
Tel: 01283 239400.

Cannock Careers Centre, Balfour House, 84 High Green, Cannock WS11 1BE.
Tel: 01543 510270.

Hanley Careers Centre, 46-58 Pall Mall, Hanley, Stoke-on-Trent ST1 1EE. Tel: 01782 295300.

Lichfield Careers Centre, Old Library Building, Bird Street, Lichfield WS13 6PN.
Tel: 01543 510683.

Newcastle Careers Centre, Hassell Street, Newcastle under Lyme ST5 1AR. Tel: 01782 297383.

Rugeley Careers Centre, Council Offices, Anson Street, Rugeley WS15 2BA. Tel: 01889 256190.

Stafford Careers Centre, 6 Market Street, Stafford ST16 2JZ. Tel: 01785 356656.

Tamworth Careers Centre, 56a Albert Road, Tamworth B79 7JN. Tel: 01827 475580.

Staffordshire Training & Enterprise Council, Festival Way, Festival Park, Stoke-on-Trent
ST1 5TQ. Tel: 01782 202733.

Burton upon Trent College, Lichfield Street, Burton upon Trent DE14 3RL. Tel: 01283 545401.

Cannock Chase Technical College, The Green, Cannock WS11 1UE. Tel: 01543 462200.

Education Department, Staffordshire County Council, Tipping Street, Stafford ST16 2DH.
Tel: 01785 223121.

Keele University, Staffordshire ST5 5BG. Tel: 01782 584005. Website: www.keele.ac.uk
E-mail: aaa30@keele.ac.uk

Leek College of Further Education & School of Art, Stockwell Street, Leek ST13 6DP.
Tel: 01538 398866.

Newcastle under Lyme College, Liverpool Road, Newcastle under Lyme ST5 2DF.
Tel: 01782 254265. Website: www.ncl-u-lyme.ac.uk E-mail: mary.bradshaw@ncl-u-lyme.ac.uk

Rodbaston College, Rodbaston, Penkridge ST19 5PH. Tel: 01785 712209.
E-mail: ralph@rodagri.demon.co.uk

Stafford College, Earl Street, Stafford ST16 2QR. Tel: 01785 223800. E-mail: 71134.4202@compuserve.com

Staffordshire University, College Road, Stoke-on-Trent ST4 2DE. Tel: 01782 294000. Website: www.staffordshire.ac.uk

Stoke-on-Trent College, Stoke Road, Shelton, Stoke-on-Trent ST4 2DG. Tel: 01782 208208.

Tamworth College, Croft Street, Upper Gungate, Tamworth B79 8AE. Tel: 01827 310202. Website: www.tamworth.ac.uk E-mail: enquiries:tamworth.ac.uk

Suffolk

Suffolk Careers Ltd

Western Area Office, 43 St Andrew's Street South, Bury St Edmunds 1PB 3PH. Tel: 01284 768493. Website: www.suffolkcareers.co.uk

Southern Area Office, St Helen's Court, St Helen's Street, Ipswich IP4 2JZ. Tel: 01473 581449. Website: www.suffolkcareers.co.uk

Norfolk & Waveney TEC, St Andrew's House, St Andrew's Street, Norwich NR2 4TP. Tel: 01603 763812.

Suffolk TEC, 2nd Floor, Crown House, Crown Street, Ipswich IP1 3HS. Tel: 01473 296000. Website: www.suffolktec.co.uk

Education Offices, Suffolk County Council, St Andrew House, County Hall, Ipswich IP4 1LJ. Tel: 01473 583000.

Lowestoft College, St Peters Street, Lowestoft NR32 2NB. Tel: 01502 583521. Website: www.westoft.ac.uk E-mail: info@westoft.ac.uk

Otley College, Otley, Ipswich IP6 9EY. Tel: 01473 785543. Website: www.otleycollege.ac.uk E-mail: mail@otleycollege.ac.uk

West Suffolk College, Out Risbygate, Bury St Edmunds IP33 3RL. Tel: 01284 716354. Website: www.westsuffolk.ac.uk E-mail: info@westsuffolk.ac.uk

Surrey

Surrey Careers Services

Camberley Careers Centre, Portesbery Road, Camberley GU15 3SZ. Tel: 01276 27172.

Epsom Careers Centre, 83 East Street, Epsom KT17 1DN. Tel: 01372 722291.

Guildford Careers Centre, Finance House, Park Street, Guildford GU1 4XB. Tel: 01483 576121.

Redhill Careers Centre, 1st Floor, 3 London Road, Redhill RH1 1LY. Tel: 01737 773801.

Staines Careers Centre, Fairacre House, Fairfield Avenue, Staines TW18 4AB. Tel: 01784 455082.

Woking Careers Centre, 'Lismore', 9c Heathside Road, Woking GU22 7EU. Tel: 01483 760041.

Surrey Training & Enterprise Council, Technology House, 48-54 Goldsworth Road, Woking GU21 1LE. Tel: 01483 728190. Website: www.surreytec.ac.uk

South East of England Development Agency, SEEDA House, Cross Lanes, Guildford, Surrey GU1 1YA. Tel: 01483 484 226. Website: www.seeda.co.uk

Brooklands College, Heath Road, Weybridge KT13 8TT. Tel: 01932 853300. Website: www.brooklands.ac.uk

East Surrey College, Claremont Road, Gatton Point North, Redhill RH1 2JX. Tel: 01737 772611. Website: www.esc.org.uk

Education Department (Adult & Continuing Education), Surrey County Council, Penrhyn Road, Kingston upon Thames KT1 2DJ. Tel: 020 8541 9567. Website: www.surreycc-gov.uk

Guildford College of Further and Higher Education, Stoke Park, Guildford GU1 1EZ. Tel: 01483 448585. Website: www.guildford.ac.uk E-mail: info@guildford.ac.uk

Guildford School of Acting, Milmead Terrace, Guildford GU2 5AT. Tel: 01483 560701. Website: gsa.drama.ac.uk E-mail: enquiries@gsa.drama.ac.uk

Merrist Wood College, Worplesdon, Guildford GU3 3PE. Tel: 01483 884000. Website: www.merristwood.ac.uk E-mail: info@merristwood.ac.uk

NESCOT – Epsom's College of Further and Higher Education, Reigate Road, Ewell KT17 3DS. Tel: 020 8394 1731.

Royal Holloway, University of London, Egham, Surrey TW20 0EX. Tel: 01784 434455. Website: www.rhbnc.ac.uk E-mail: liaison-office:rhbnc.ac.uk

Royal Military Academy Sandhurst, Camberley GU15 4PQ. Tel: 01276 63344.

The Surrey Institute of Art and Design, Falkner Road, Farnham GU9 7DS. Tel: 01252 722441. Website: www.surrart.ac.uk E-mail: registry@surrart.ac.uk

University of Surrey, Guildford, Surrey GU2 5XH. Tel: 01483 300800. Website: www.surrey.ac.uk E-mail: information@surrey.ac.uk

Sussex – East, and Brighton and Hove

Sussex Careers Services

Brighton and Hove Careers & Information Centre, Frederick House, 42 Frederick Place, Brighton BN1 1AT. Tel: 01273 827400. Website: www.sussexcareers.co.uk E-mail: infounit@sussexcareers.co.uk

Eastbourne Careers Centre, 22-24 Gildredge Road, Eastbourne BN21 4SA. Tel: 01323 745500. Website: www.sussexcareers.co.uk E-mail: infounit@sussexcareers.co.uk

Hastings Careers Centre, 1st Floor, Queensbury House, Havelock Road, Hastings TN34 1BP. Tel: 01424 425780. Website: www.sussexcareers.co.uk E-mail: infounit@sussexcareers.co.uk

Lewes Careers Centre, Lewes Tertiary College, Mountfield Road, Lewes BN7 2XH. Tel: 01273 473141. Website: www.sussexcareers.co.uk E-mail: infounit@sussexcareers.co.uk

Portslade Careers Centre, Portslade Community College, Chalky Road, Portslade BN41 2WS. Tel: 01273 411751. Website: www.sussexcareers.co.uk E-mail: infounit@sussexcareers.co.uk

Sussex Enterprise, Greenacre Court, Station Road, Burgess Hill RH15 9DF. Tel: 01444 259259. Website: www.sussexenterprise.co.uk E-mail: marketing@sussexenterprise.co.uk

Brighton College, Pelham Street, Brighton BN1 4FA. Tel: 01273 667788. Website: www.bricoltech.ac.uk E-mail: info@bricoltech.ac.uk

Community & Continuing Education, Educational Services, Brighton & Hove Council, PO Box 2503, Kings House, Grand Avenue, Hove BN3 2SU. Tel: 01273 293609. Website: www.brighton-hove.gov.uk E-mail: aidan.pettitt@brighton-hove.gov.uk

Eastbourne College of Arts & Technology, Cross Levels Way, Eastbourne BN21 2UF. Tel: 01323 644711. Website: www.ecat.ac.uk E-mail: ecat@ecat.ac.uk

Education Department (Community Education), East Sussex County Council, PO Box 4, County Hall, St. Anne's Crescent, Lewes BN7 1SG. Tel: 01273 481000.

Hastings College of Arts and Technology, Archery Road, St Leonards-on-Sea TN38 0HX. Tel: 01424 442222.

Lewes Tertiary College, Mountfield Road, Lewes BN7 2XH. Tel: 01273 483188. Website: www.lewescollege.ac.uk E-mail: info@lewes.college.ac.uk

Plumpton College, Ditchling Road, Plumpton, Lewes BN7 3AE. Tel: 01273 890454. Website: www.plumpton.ac.uk E-mail: staff@plumpton.ac.uk

University of Brighton, Mithras House, Lewes Road, Moulsecoomb, Brighton BN2 4AT. Tel: 01273 600900. Website: www.brighton.ac.uk/. E-mail: admissions@brighton.ac.uk

University of Sussex, Falmer, Brighton BN1 9RH. Tel: 01273 678416. Website: www.sussex.ac.uk E-mail: admissions@sussex.ac.uk

Sussex – West

VTWS Careers Ltd

Bognor Regis Careers Centre, 18a Sudley Road, Bognor Regis PO21 1EU. Tel: 01243 860277. Website: www.vtis.com/vtws E-mail: info@vtis.com

Chichester Careers Centre, 1 The Chambers, Chapel Street, Chichester PO19 1DL. Tel: 01243 771666. Website: www.vtis.com/vtws E-mail: info@vtis.com

Crawley Careers Centre, Gresham House, Station Road, Crawley RH10 1EZ. Tel: 01293 528374. Website: www.vtis.com/vtws E-mail: info@vtis.com

East Grinstead Careers Centre, Library Building, 32 West Street, East Grinstead RH19 4SR. Tel: 01342 321564. Website: www.vtis.com/vtws E-mail: info@vtis.com

Haywards Heath Careers Centre, 135 South Road, Haywards Heath RH16 4LY. Tel: 01444 450262. Website: www.vtis.com/vtws E-mail: info@vtis.com

Horsham Careers Centre, Marlborough House, 50 East Street, Horsham RH12 1HN. Tel: 01403 261465. Website: www.vtis.com/vtws E-mail: info@vtis.com

Worthing Careers Centre, Revenue Chambers, Chapel Road, Worthing BN11 1SG. Tel: 01903 205612. Website: www.vtis.com/vtws E-mail: info@vtis.com

Sussex Enterprise, Greenacre Court, Station Road, Burgess Hill RH15 9DF. Tel: 01444 259259. Website: www.sussexenterprise.co.uk E-mail: marketing@sussexenterprise.co.uk

Adult & Community Education, West Sussex County Council, County Hall, West Street, Chichester PO19 1RF. Tel: 01243 777100. Website: www.westsussex.gov.uk E-mail: colin/holliday@westsussex.gov.uk

Brinsbury College, North Heath, Pulborough RH20 1DL. Tel: 01798 877400. Website: www.brinsbury.ac.uk E-mail: principal@brinsbury.ac.uk

Chichester College of Arts, Science and Technology, Westgate Fields, Chichester PO19 1SB. Tel: 01243 786321. Website: www.chichester.ac.uk E-mail: info@chichester.ac.uk

Crawley College, College Road, Crawley RH10 1NR. Tel: 01293 442200. E-mail: crawcol@rmplc.co.uk

Northbrook College, Littlehampton Road, Goring-by-Sea, Worthing BN12 6NU. Tel: 01903 606060. Website: www.nbcol.ac.uk E-mail: enquiries@nbcol.ac.uk

University College Chichester, College Lane, Chichester PO19 4PE. Tel: 01243 816000. Website: www.chihe.ac.uk E-mail: admissions@chihe.ac.uk

Tyne and Wear area

Gateshead

Tyneside Careers

Gateshead Centre, Interchange Centre, West Street, Gateshead NE8 1BH. Tel: 0191 490 1717. Website: www.tynesidecareers.co.uk E-mail: helpline@tynesidecareers.co.uk

Youth Information Shop, Unit 1/16, 45 Garden Walk, Metro Centre, Gateshead NE11 9DX. Tel: 0191 490 1999. Website: www.tynesidecareers.co.uk E-mail: helpline@tynesidecareers.co.uk

Tyneside Training & Enterprise Council, Moongate House, 5th Avenue Business Park, Team Valley Trading Estate, Gateshead NE11 0BF. Tel: 0191 491 6000. Website: www.tynesidetec.co.uk E-mail: olivia.grant@tynesidetec.co.uk

Education Department, Gateshead Metropolitan Borough Council, Civic Centre, Regent Street, Gateshead NE8 1HH. Tel: 0191 477 1011.

Gateshead College, Durham Road, Gateshead NE9 5BN. Tel: 0191 490 0300. Website: www.gateshead.ac.uk

Newcastle Upon Tyne

Tyneside Careers

Newcastle Careers Centre, 2 Eldon Court, Perry Street, Newcastle upon Tyne. Tel: 0191 491 1717. Website: www.tynesidecareers.co.uk E-mail: helpline@tynesidecareers.co.uk

Tyneside Training & Enterprise Council, Moongate House, 5th Avenue Business Park, Team Valley Trading Estate, Gateshead NE11 0BF. Tel: 0191 491 6000. Website: www.tynesidetec.co.uk E-mail: olivia.grant@tynesidetec.co.uk

Continuing Education, Newcastle County Council, Civic Centre, Barras Bridge, Newcastle upon Tyne NE1 8PU. Tel: 0191 232 8520 Ext 5332. Website: www.newcastle.gov.uk E-mail: julie.hickin@newcastle.gov.uk

One North East, Great North House, Sandyford Road, Newcastle NE1 8ND. Tel: 0191 261 0026. Website: www.onenortheast.co.uk

Newcastle College, Rye Hill Campus, Scotswood Road, Newcastle upon Tyne NE4 5BR. Tel: 0191 200 4000. Website: www.ncl-coll.ac.uk E-mail: enquiries@ncl-coll.ac.uk

University of Newcastle upon Tyne, Newcastle upon Tyne NE1 7RU. Tel: 0191 222 6000. Website: www.ncl.ac.uk E-mail: admissions-enquiries@ncl.ac.uk

University of Northumbria at Newcastle, Ellison Place, Newcastle upon Tyne NE1 8ST. Tel: 0191 232 6002. Website: www.unn.ac.uk E-mail: admissions@unn.ac.uk

North Tyneside

Tyneside Careers

North Shields Centre, 1-4 Russell Street, North Shields NE29 0BJ. Tel: 0191 490 1717. Website: www.tynesidecareers.co.uk E-mail: helpline@tynesidecareers.co.uk

Wallsend Centre, 205 Park Road, Wallsend NE28 7NL. Tel: 0191 490 1717. Website: www.tynesidecareers.co.uk E-mail: helpline@tynesidecareers.co.uk

Tyneside Training & Enterprise Council, Moongate House, 5th Avenue Business Park, Team Valley Trading Estate, Gateshead NE11 0BF. Tel: 0191 491 6000. Website: www.tynesidetec.co.uk E-mail: olivia.grant@tynesidetec.co.uk

Adult Education Service, North Tyneside Council, Stephenson Centre, Citadel East, Killingworth NE12 6UQ. Tel: 0191 200 8329.

North Tyneside College, Embleton Avenue, Wallsend NE28 9NJ. Tel: 0191 229 5000. Website: www.ntyneside.ac.uk

South Tyneside

Tyneside Careers

South Shields Centre, Central Library Building, Prince George Square, South Shields NE33 2PE. Tel: 0191 490 1717. Website: www.tynesidecareers.co.uk E-mail: helpline@tynesidecareers.co.uk

South Shields Centre, Stanhope Complex, Gresford Street, South Shields NE33 4SZ. Tel: 0191 456 3932. Website: www.tynesidecareers.co.uk E-mail: helpline@tynesidecareers.co.uk

Tyneside Training & Enterprise Council, Moongate House, 5th Avenue Business Park, Team Valley Trading Estate, Gateshead NE11 0BF. Tel: 0191 491 6000. Website: www.tynesidetec.co.uk E-mail: olivia.grant@tynesidetec.co.uk

Education Offices, South Tyneside Metropolitan Borough Council, Stanhope Complex, Greford Street, South Shields NE33 4SZ. Tel: 0191 455 2444.

South Tyneside College, St George's Avenue, South Shields NE34 6ET. Tel: 0191 427 3500. Website: www.stc.ac.uk E-mail: tlc@stc.ac.uk

Sunderland

Pathways Adult Guidance Centre, 1st Floor, City Library and Arts Centre Building, 30-32 Fawcett Street, Sunderland SR1 1RE. Tel: 0191 553 7444.

Sunderland City Training & Enterprise Council, Sunderland Business & Innovation Centre, Sunderland Enterprise Park, Sunderland SR5 2TA. Tel: 0191 516 6000. Website: www.sunderland.tec.org.uk

City of Sunderland College, Bede Centre, Durham Road, Sunderland SR3 4AH. Tel: 0191 511 6000.

Education & Community Services, City of Sunderland, PO Box 101, Civic Centre, Sunderland SR2 7DN. Tel: 0191 553 1000.

University of Sunderland, Langham Tower, Ryhope Road, Sunderland SR2 7EE. Tel: 0191 515 2000. Website: www.sunderland.ac.uk E-mail: student-helpline@sunderland.ac.uk

Warwickshire

Warwickshire Careers Service Ltd

HQ, 10 Northgate Street, Warwick CV34 4SR. Tel: 01926 401300. E-mail: warwickshire.careers@dial/pipex.com

Atherstone Careers Office, Long Street, Atherstone CV9 1AX. Tel: 01827 712482.

Leamington Spa Careers Office, 2 Euston Square, Leamington Spa CV32 4ND. Tel: 01926 334241.

Nuneaton Careers Office, King Edward Road, Nuneaton CV11 4BB. Tel: 024 7634 7677.

Rugby Careers Office, Newton Hall, Lower Hillmorton Road, Rugby CV21 3TU. Tel: 01788 541333.

Stratford upon Avon Careers Office, The Willows, Alcester Road, Stratford upon Avon CV37 9QP. Tel: 01789 266841.

Warwick Careers Office, 10 Northgate Street, Warwick CV34 4SR. Tel: 01926 401300.

Coventry & Warwickshire Chamber of Commerce, Training & Enterprise, Oak Tree Court, Harry Weston Road, Coventry CV3 2UN. Tel: 024 7665 4321. Website: www.cwcci.co.uk

Education Department, Warwickshire County Council, 22 Northgate Street, Warwick CV34 4SP. Tel: 01926 410410.

North Warwickshire & Hinckley College, Hinckley Road, Nuneaton CV11 6BH. Tel: 024 7624 3000. Website: www.nwarks-hinckley.ac.uk E-mail: the.college@nwarks-hinckley.ac.uk

Rugby College of FE, Lower Hillmorton Road, Rugby CV21 3QS. Tel: 01788 338800. Website: www.rugbycoll.ac.uk E-mail: info@rugbycoll.ac.uk

Stratford-upon-Avon College, The Willows North, Alcester Road, Stratford upon Avon CV37 9QR. Tel: 01789 266245. Website: www.stratford-upon-avon.co.uk/college E-mail: college@strat.avon.ac.uk

Warwickshire College, Royal Leamington Spa and Moreton Morrell, Warwick New Road, Leamington Spa CV32 5JE. Tel: 01926 318000. Website: www.warkscol.ac.uk E-mail: enquiries@warwickshirecol.ac.uk

West Midlands area

Birmingham

Careers and Education Business Partnership

City Centre Office, 100 Broad Street, City Centre, Birmingham B15 1AE. Tel: 0121 248 8004/5.

Handsworth Centre, 11 Soho Road, Handsworth, Birmingham B21 9SN. Tel: 0121 554 9973.

Selly Oak Centre, 778 Bristol Road, Selly Oak, Birmingham B29 6NA. Tel: 0121 248 8150.

Sutton Coldfield Centre, Lichfield Road, Sutton Coldfield, Birmingham B74 2NP. Tel: 0121 355 1021.

Yardley Centre, Church Road, Yardley, Birmingham B25 8UX. Tel: 0121 248 8200.

Advantage West Midlands, 2 Priestley Wharf, Aston Science Park, Holt Street, Birmingham B7 4BZ. Tel: 0121 380 3500. Website: www.wmda.org.uk

Birmingham & Solihull Training & Enterprise Council, Chaplin Court, 80 Hurst Street, Birmingham B5 4TS. Tel: 0121 622 4419. Website: www.bstec.broadnet.co.uk E-mail: customerservices@bstec.broadnet.co.uk

Aston University, Aston Triangle, Aston, Birmingham B4 7ET. Tel: 0121 359 3611. Website: www.aston.ac.uk E-mail: prospectus@aston.ac.uk

Birmingham College of Food, Tourism and Creative Studies, Summer Row, City Centre, Birmingham B3 1JB. Tel: 0121 604 1000. Website: www.bcftcs.ac.uk E-mail: marketing@bcftcs.ac.uk

Birmingham Conservatoire, Paradise Place, Birmingham B3 3HG. Tel: 0121 331 5901. Website: www.uce.ac.uk E-mail: claire.britcliffe@uce.ac.uk

BOLDU Ltd, St Georges House, 40-49 Price Street, Birmingham B4 6LA. Tel: 0121 359 6628. Website: www.boldu.co.uk

Bournville College of Further Education, Bristol Road South, Northfield, Birmingham B31 2AJ. Tel: 0121 476 9898. Website: www.bournville.ac.uk E-mail: info@bournville.ac.uk

East Birmingham College, Garretts Green Lane, Garretts Green, Birmingham B33 0TS. Tel: 0121 743 4471. Website: www.ebham.ac.uk E-mail: sknottonbelt@ebham.ac.uk

Education Department, Birmingham City Council, Margaret Street, Birmingham B3 3BU. Tel: 0121 303 2872.

Fircroft College, 1018 Bristol Road, Selly Oak, Birmingham B29 6LH. Tel: 0121 472 0116. Website: www.sellyoak.ac.uk E-mail: j.wilcox.fircroft@sellyoak.ac.uk

Handsworth College, The Council House, Soho Road, Birmingham B21 9DL. Tel: 0121 256 1111. Website: www.handsworth.ac.uk E-mail: info@handsworth.ac.uk

Matthew Boulton College of Further and Higher Education, Sherlock Street, Sparkbrook, Birmingham B5 7DB. Tel: 0121 446 4545. Website: www.matthew-boulton.ac.uk E-mail: ask@matthew-boulton.ac.uk

Newman College of Higher Education, Genners Lane, Bartley Green, Birmingham B32 3NT. Tel: 0121 476 1181. Website: www.newman.ac.uk

North Birmingham College, Aldridge Road, Great Barr, Birmingham B44 8NE. Tel: 0121 360 3543. Website: www.northbham.ac.uk E-mail: enquire@northbham.ac.uk

Selly Oak College, Bristol Road, Selly Oak, Birmingham B29 6LQ. Tel: 0121 472 4231. Website: www.sellyoak.ac.uk

South Birmingham College, Cole Bank Road, Hall Green, Birmingham B28 8ES. Tel: 0121 694 5000. Website: www.sbirmc.ac.uk

Sutton Coldfield College of Further Education, Lichfield Road, Sutton Coldfield, Birmingham B74 2NW. Tel: 0121 355 5671.

University of Birmingham, Edgbaston, Birmingham B15 2TT. Tel: 0121 414 3344. Website: www.bham.ac.uk E-mail: postmaster@bham.ac.uk

University of Central England in Birmingham, Perry Barr, Birmingham B42 2SU. Tel: 0121 331 5000. Website: www.uce.ac.uk E-mail: prospectus@uce.ac.uk

Westhill College, Weoley Park Road, Selly Oak, Birmingham B29 6LL. Tel: 0121 472 7245. Website: www.westhill.ac.uk

Coventry

Quality Careers Services Ltd, Casselden House, Greyfriars Lane, Coventry CV1 2GZ. Tel: 024 7683 1714.

Employment & Advice Centre, Hillfields, 12 Victoria Street, Coventry CV1 5LZ. Tel: 024 7655 0564.

Coventry & Warwickshire Chamber of Commerce, Training & Enterprise, Oak Tree Court, Harry Weston Road, Coventry CV3 2UN. Tel: 024 7665 4321. Website: www.cwcci.co.uk

City of Coventry Education Department, Council Offices, Earl Street, Coventry CV1 5RS. Tel: 024 7683 3333.

Coventry Technical College, Butts, Coventry CV1 3GD. Tel: 024 7652 6700. Website: www.covcollege.ac.uk

Coventry University, Priory Street, Coventry CV1 5FB. Tel: 024 7688 7688. Website: www.coventry.ac.uk E-mail: suadvice@coventry.ac.uk

Henley College, Henley Road, Bell Green, Coventry CV2 1ED. Tel: 024 7662 6300. Website: www.henley-cov.ac.uk E-mail: enquiries@henley-cov.ac.uk

Hereward College, Bramston Crescent, Tile Hill Lane, Coventry CV4 9SU. Tel: 024 7646 1231. Website: www.hereward.demon.co.uk

Tile Hill College of Further Education, Tile Hill Lane, Coventry CV4 9SU. Tel: 024 7646 4500. Website: www.tilehill.ac.uk E-mail: info@tilehill.ac.uk

University of Warwick, Coventry CV4 7AL. Tel: 024 7652 3523. Website: www.warwick.ac.uk

Dudley

Prospects Careers Services (Black Country)

Dudley Careers Centre, 10 Wolverhampton Street, Dudley DY1 1DA. Tel: 01384 242414.

Stourbridge Careers Centre, Stourbridge College, Church Street Centre, Church Street, Stourbridge DY8 1LY. Tel: 01384 397281.

Dudley Training & Enterprise Council, Dudley Court South, Waterfront East, Brierley Hill, Dudley DY5 1XN. Tel: 01384 485000.

Halesowen Outreach, Halesowen Library, Queensway Mall, The Cornbow, Halesowen B63 4AJ. Tel: 0121 503 0300.

Community & Lifelong Learning Unit, 8 Parsens Street, Dudley DY2 1JJ. Tel: 01384 815181.

Dudley College of Technology, The Broadway, Dudley DY1 4AS. Tel: 01384 455433. Website: www.dudleycol.ac.uk E-mail: student.services@dudleycol.ac.uk

Halesowen College, Whittingham Road, Halesowen B63 3NA. Tel: 0121 550 1451. E-mail: halesowen@dial.pipex.com

Stourbridge College, Hagley Road, Oldswinford, Stourbridge DY8 1QU. Tel: 01384 344344. Website: www.stourbridge.ac.uk E-mail: info@stourbridge.ac.uk

Sandwell

Prospects Careers Services (Black Country)

Smethwick Careers Centre, Crocketts Lane, Smethwick, Warley, Sandwell B66 3BS. Tel: 0121 558 2901.

West Bromwich Careers Centre, 155-157 High Street, Princess Parade, West Bromwich B70 7QX. Tel: 0121 525 5161.

Sandwell Training & Enterprise Council, 1st Floor, Black Country House, Rounds Green Road, Oldbury B69 2DG. Tel: 0121 543 4452.

Tipton Opportunities Shop, High Street, Prince's End, Tipton DY4 9JE. Tel: 0121 557 5302.

Department of Education & Community Services, Sandwell Metropolitan Borough Council, PO Box 41, Shaftesbury House, 102 High Street, West Bromwich B70 9LT. Tel: 0121 569 8409.

Sandwell College of Further and Higher Education, Woden Road South, Wednesbury WS10 0PE. Tel: 0121 556 6000.

Solihull

Central Careers

Chemsley Wood Centre, 289 Bosworth Drive, Chemsley Wood B37 5DP. Tel: 0121 770 1861.

Solihull Careers Centre, Orchard House, Council House, Solihull B91 3BN. Tel: 0121 704 6711.

Birmingham & Solihull Training & Enterprise Council, Chaplin Court, 80 Hurst Street, Birmingham B5 4TS. Tel: 0121 622 4419. Website: www.bstec.broadnet.co.uk E-mail:customerservices@bstec.broadnet.co.uk

Solihull College, Blossomfield Road, Solihull B91 1SB. Tel: 0121 678 7000.

Walsall

Prospects Careers Services (Black Country)

Walsall Careers Centre, 30 Station Street, Walsall WS2 9JZ. Tel: 01922 636333.

Willenhall Careers Centre, 2 Walsall Street, Willenhall WV13 2EX. Tel: 01902 366281.

Access to Opportunity Shop, Walsall TEC, Ground Floor, Norwich Union House, 17 Lichfield Street, Walsall WS1 1TU. Tel: 0800 626827.

Walsall TEC, 5th Floor, Townsend House, Townsend Square, Walsall WS1 1NS. Tel: 01922 424242.

Education Department, Walsall Metropolitan Borough Council, Civic Centre, Darwell Street, Walsall WS1 1DQ. Tel: 01922 650000.

Walsall Link Courses Information Service, Brownhills Activities Centre, Chester Road, North Brownhills, Walsall WS8 7JW. Tel: 01543 370703.

Walsall College of Arts & Technology, St Paul's Street, Walsall WS1 1XN. Tel: 01922 657000. Website: www.walcat.ac.uk E-mail: 1.beverley@walcat.ac.uk

Wolverhampton

Prospects Careers Services (Black Country)

Bilston Careers Centre, 30 Church Street, Bilston WV14 0AH. Tel: 01902 408811.

Wolverhampton Careers Centre, 118-119 Salop Street, Wolverhampton WV3 0RX. Tel: 01902 773040.

Wolverhampton GATE, 11 Clarence Street, Wolverhampton WV1 4JL. Tel: 01902 558111.

Wolverhampton Chamber, Enterprise House, Pendeford Business Park, Wobaston Road, Wolverhampton WV9 5HA. Tel: 01902 445500.

Wolverhampton Adult Education Service, Old Hall Street, Wolverhampton WV1 3AU. Tel: 01902 558180. Website: www.old-hallstreet.org.uk

University of Wolverhampton, Wulfruna Street, Wolverhampton WV1 1SB. Tel: 01902 321000. Website: www.wlv.ac.uk E-mail: enquiries@wlv.ac.uk

Wulfrun College, Paget Road, Wolverhampton WV6 0DU. Tel: 01902 317700. Website: www.wulfrun.ac.uk E-mail: info@wulfrun.ac.uk

Wiltshire and Swindon

Lifetime Careers Wiltshire

HQ, 7 Ascot Court, White Horse Business Park, Trowbridge BA14 0XA. Tel: 01225 716000. Website: www.wiltshire.lifetime-careers.co.uk E-mail: enquiries@wiltshire.lifetime-careers.co.uk

Careers Centre, 1 Wicker Hill, Trowbridge BA14 8JS. Tel: 01225 716450.

Careers Centre, Avon Reach, Monkton Hill, Chippenham SN15 1EE. Tel: 01249 449900.

Careers Centre, 65 Milford Street, Salisbury SP1 2BP. Tel: 01722 424400.

Careers Centre, 4 Temple Chambers, Temple Street, Swindon SN1 1SQ. Tel: 01793 549200.

Chippenham College, Cocklebury Road, Chippenham SN15 3QD. Tel: 01249 464644. Website: www.chipcoll.ac.uk E-mail: chipcol@rmplc.ac.uk

Education Department, Wiltshire County Council, County Hall, Trowbridge BA 14 8JB. Tel: 01225 713000.

Lackham College, Lacock, Chippenham SN15 2NY. Tel: 01249 466800. E-mail: lackham@rmplc.co.uk

New College, Helston Road, Park North, Swindon SN3 2LA. Tel: 01793 611470. Website: www.newcollege.co.uk E-mail: admissions@newcollege.co.uk

Royal Military College of Science, Cranfield University, Shrivenham, Swindon SN6 8LA. Tel: 01793 782551. Website: www.rmcs.cranfield.ac.uk E-mail: prospectus@rmcs.cranfield.ac.uk

Salisbury College, Southampton Road, Salisbury SP1 2LW. Tel: 01722 344344. Website: www.salcol.com E-mail: enquiries@salcol.com

Swindon College, Regent Circus, Swindon SN1 1PT. Tel: 01793 491591. Website: www.swindon-college.ac.uk/

Swindon Borough Council, Department of Education, Sanford House, Sanford Street, Swindon SN1 1QH. Tel: 01793 463069.

Trowbridge College, College Road, Trowbridge BA14 0ES. Tel: 01225 766241. Website: www.trowcoll.ac.uk E-mail: info@trowcoll.ac.uk

Wiltshire and Swindon Training & Enterprise Council, The Bora Building, Westlea Campus, Westlea Down, Swindon. Tel: 01793 501500.

Yorkshire – North, and City of York

Guidance Enterprise Group

HQ, Guidance House, York Road, Thirsk YO7 3BT. Tel: 01845 526699. Website: www.guidance-enterprise.co.uk E-mail: info@guidance-enterprise.co.uk

Harrogate Careers Centre, 15-17 Station Bridge, Harrogate HG1 1SP. Tel: 01423 871722. Website: www.guidance-enterprise.co.uk E-mail: info@guidance-enterprise.co.uk

Northallerton Careers Centre, 159-160 High Street, Northallerton DL7 8JZ. Tel: 01609 773537. Website: www.guidance-enterprise.co.uk E-mail: info@guidance-enterprise.co.uk

Scarborough Careers Centre, Pavilion House, Westborough, Scarborough YO11 1UY. Tel: 01723 373009. Website: www.guidance-enterprise.co.uk E-mail: info@guidance-enterprise.co.uk

Selby Careers Centre, 2 Abbey Yard, Selby YO8 4PS. Tel: 01757 703538. Website: www.guidance-enterprise.co.uk E-mail: info@guidance-enterprise.co.uk

Skipton Careers Centre, Navigation House, Belmont Bridge, Skipton BD23 1RL. Tel: 01756 792948. Website: www.guidance-enterprise.co.uk E-mail: info@guidance-enterprise.co.uk

York Careers Centre, Merchant House, 11a Piccadilly, York YO1 9WB. Tel: 01904 656655. Website: www.guidance-enterprise.co.uk E-mail: info@guidance-enterprise.co.uk

Acomb Advice Centre, 7 Odsal House, Front Street, Acomb, York YO2 3BL. Tel: 01904 786394.

New Options, 23 Finkle Street, Selby YO8 4DT. Tel: 01757 706996.

North Yorkshire TEC, TEC House, 7 Pioneer Business Park, Amy Johnson Way, Clifton Moorgate, York YO30 4TN. Tel: 01904 691939. Website: www.nyorks-tec.co.uk

North Yorkshire TAP/Learning Helpline, Bedale Hall, North End, Bedale DL8 1AA. Tel: 01677 425900. Website: www.nytap.demon.co.uk E-mail: om@nytap.demon.co.uk

Askham Bryan College, Askham Bryan, York YO2 3PR. Tel: 01904 772277. Website: www.askham-bryan.ac.uk E-mail: mktg@askham-bryan.ac.uk

Education Department, North Yorkshire County Council, County Hall, Northallerton DL7 8AE. Tel: 01609 780780.

Craven College, High Street, Skipton BD23 1JY. Tel: 01756 791411. Website: www.craven-college.ac.uk E-mail: enquiries@craven-college.ac.uk

Educational Services Department, City of York Council, PO Box 404, 10-12 George Hudson Street, York YO1 6ZG. Tel: 01904 613161.

Harrogate College, Hornbeam Park, Harrogate HG2 8QT. Tel: 01423 879466. Website: www.harrogate.ac.uk

Selby College, Abbot's Road, Selby YO8 8AT. Tel: 01757 211000. E-mail: selby.college@rmplc.co.uk

University of Ripon & York, York Campus, Lord Mayor's Walk, York YO13 7EX. Tel: 01904 656771. Website: www.ucrysj.ac.uk

University College Scarborough, Filey Road, Scarborough YO11 3AZ. Tel: 01723 362392. Website: www.ucscarb.ac.uk E-mail: external@ucscarb.ac.uk

University of York, Heslington, York YO10 5DD. Tel: 01904 430000. Website: www.york.ac.uk/ E-mail: admissions@york.ac.uk

York College of Further and Higher Education, Tadcaster Road, Dringhouses, York YO24 1UA. Tel: 01904 770200.

Yorkshire Coast College, Lady Edith's Drive, Scarborough YO12 5RN. Tel: 01723 372105. Website: www.ycoastco.ac.uk E-mail: r.wood@ycoastco.ac.uk

Yorkshire – South

Barnsley

Lifetime Careers Barnsley, Doncaster & Rotherham

HQ, Learning Information Services, Mexborough Business Centre, College Road, Mexborough S64 9JP. Tel: 0800 374 820.

Barnsley Careers Centre, 12-14 Midland Street, Barnsley S70 1SE. Tel: 01226 205686.

Barnsley & Doncaster Training & Enterprise Council, The Conference Centre, Eldon Street, Barnsley S70 2JL. Tel: 01226 248088.

Barnsley College, Old Mill Lane Site, Church Street, Barnsley S70 2AX. Tel: 01226 730191. Website: www.barnsley.ac.uk E-mail: admissions@barnsley.ac.uk

Education Department, Barnsley Metropolitan Borough Council, Bereslai Close, Barnsley S70 2HS. Tel: 01226 770770.

Doncaster

Lifetime Careers Barnsley, Doncaster & Rotherham
Doncaster Careers Centre, 3-4 Kingsway House, Hallgate, Doncaster DN1 3NX. Tel: 01302 366065.

Mexborough Careers Centre, 26-28 Main Street, Mexborough S64 9DW. Tel: 01709 578337.

Barnsley & Doncaster Training & Enterprise Council, The Conference Centre, Eldon Street, Barnsley S70 2JL. Tel: 01226 248088.

Directorate of Education, Doncaster Metropolitan Borough Council, PO Box 266, The Council House, College Road, Doncaster DN1 3AD. Tel: 01302 737222.

Doncaster College, Waterdale, Doncaster DN1 3EX. Tel: 01302 553553.

Rotherham

Lifetime Careers Barnsley, Doncaster & Rotherham Ltd
Rotherham Careers Centre, 14 High Street, Rotherham S60 1PP. Tel: 01709 821184.

Starting Point Adult Guidance for Careers, Eastwood Lane, Rotherham S65 1EG. Tel: 01709 835277.

Rotherham Chamber of Commerce, Training & Enterprise, Moorgate House, Moorgate Road, Rotherham S60 2EN. Tel: 01709 830511.

Dearne Valley College, Manvers Park, Wath upon Dearne, Rotherham S63 6PX. Tel: 01709 513333.

Education Office, Rotherham Metropolitan Borough Council, Norfolk House, Walker Place, Rotherham S60 1QT. Tel: 01709 382121.

Rother Valley College, Doe Quarry Lane, Dinnington, Sheffield S31 7NH. Tel: 01909 550550.

Rotherham College of Arts and Technology, Eastwood Lane, Rotherham S65 1EG. Tel: 01709 722777.

Thomas Rotherham College, Moorgate Road, Rotherham S60 2BE. Tel: 01709 828606.

Sheffield

Sheffield Careers Guidance Services, AEEU House, Furnival Gate, Sheffield S1 3SL. Tel: 0114 201 2800.

Careers Service for Adults, 42 Union Street, Sheffield S1 2JP. Tel: 0114 201 2770.

Sheffield Training & Enterprise Council, St Mary's Court, 55 St Mary's Road, Sheffield S2 4AQ. Tel: 0114 270 1991. Website: www.sheffieldtec.co.uk

Education Department, Sheffield Metropolitan City Council, Leopold Street, Sheffield S1 1RJ. Tel: 0114 273 5659.

Rother Valley College, Doe Quarry Lane, Dinnington, Sheffield S31 2NF. Tel: 01909 550550. Website: www.rothervalley.ac.uk E-mail: student.services@rothervalley.ac.uk

Sheffield College, PO Box 345, Sheffield S2 2YY. Tel: 0114 260 3603. Website: www.sheffcol.ac.uk E-mail: mail@sheffcol.ac.uk

Sheffield Hallam University, City Campus, Howard Street, Sheffield S1 1WB. Tel: 0114 225 5555. Website: www.shu.ac.uk E-mail: liaison@shu.ac.uk

University of Sheffield, Sheffield S10 2TN. Tel: 0114 222 2000. Website: www.shef.ac.uk/~admit/ E-mail: ug.admissions@sheffield.ac.uk

Yorkshire – West

Bradford

Careers Bradford Ltd

Adult Guidance Services, 3rd Floor, Midland House, 14 Cheapside, Bradford BD1 4JA. Tel: 01274 829430. Website: www.careersb.bradtec.co.uk E-mail: info@careersb.bradtec.co.uk

Bradford Careers Office, 3rd Floor, Midland House, 14 Cheapside, Bradford BD1 4JA. Tel: 01274 829400. Website: www.careersb.bradtec.co.uk E-mail: info@careersb.bradtec.co.uk

Keighley Careers Office, 3 Bow Street, Keighley BD21 3PB. Tel: 01535 210262. Website: www.careersb.bradtec.co.uk E-mail: info@careersb.bradtec.co.uk

Education Advice Service for Adults (EASA), 15 Petergate, Bradford BD1 1DR. Tel: 01274 753658. Website: www.eas9.legend.yorks.com/ E-mail: eas9@legend.co.uk

Bradford & District Training & Enterprise Council, Mercury House, 4 Manchester Road, Bradford BD5 0QL. Tel: 01274 751333. Website: www.bradtec.co.uk

Bowling Community College, The Centre, Flockton Road, East Bowling, Bradford BD4 7RH. Tel: 01274 773310.

Bradford & Ilkley Community College, Great Horton Road, Bradford, BD7 1AY. Tel: 01274 753042. Website: www.bilk.ac.uk E-mail: student.service@bilk.ac.uk

City Training Services, 29/41 Chapel Street, Little Germany, Bradford BD1 5BY. Tel: 01274 728316.

Keighley College, Cavendish Street, Keighley BD21 3DF. Tel: 01535 618555. Website: www.keighley.ac.uk E-mail: guidance@keighley.ac.uk

Shipley College, Exhibition Road, Shipley BD18 3JW. Tel: 01274 757222. Website: www.shipley.ac.uk

University of Bradford, Bradford BD7 1DP. Tel: 01274 232323. Website: www.brad.ac.uk E-mail: ug-admissions@bradford.ac.uk

Calderdale

Calderdale & Kirklees Careers Service Partnership

HQ, 78 John Williams Street, Huddersfield HD1 1EH. Tel: 01484 226700.

Halifax Careers Centre, 16 Alexandra Street, Halifax HX1 1BS. Tel: 01422 342106.

Calderdale & Kirklees Training & Enterprise Council, Park View House, Woodvale Office Park, Woodvale Road, Brighouse HD6 4AB. Tel: 01480 4400770. Website: www.cktec.co.uk

Calderdale Metropolitan Borough Council, Education Department, PO Box 33, Northgate House, Northgate, Halifax HX1 1UN. Tel: 01422 357257. Website: www.nthgate.demon.co.uk E-mail: ces@nthgate.demon.co.uk

Calderdale College, Francis Street, Halifax HX1 3UZ. Tel: 01422 357357. Website: www.calderdale.ac.uk

Kirklees

Calderdale & Kirklees Careers Service Partnership

Huddersfield Careers Centre, Upperhead Row, Huddersfield HD1 2JS. Tel: 01484 226800

Dewsbury Library and Careers Centre, Theperail Park, Railway Street, Dewsbury WF1 8EQ. Tel: 01924 324200.

Calderdale & Kirklees Training & Enterprise Council, Park View House, Woodvale Office Park, Woodvale Road, Brighouse HD6 4AB. Tel: 01480 4400770. Website: www.cktec.co.uk

Dewsbury College, Halifax Road, Dewsbury WF13 2SA. Tel: 01924 436221. Website: www.dewsbury.ac.uk E-mail: info@dewsbury.ac.uk

Education Service (Adult Education) Kirklees Council, Oldgate House, 2 Oldgate, Huddersfield HD1 6QW. Tel: 01484 225242. E-mail: gavin.tonkin@geoz.poptel.org.uk

Huddersfield Technical College, New North Road, Huddersfield HD1 5NN. Tel: 01484 536521. Website: www.huddcoll.ac.uk E-mail: info@huddcoll.ac.uk

University of Huddersfield, Queensgate, Huddersfield HD1 3DH. Tel: 01484 422288. Website: www.hud.ac.uk E-mail: prospectus@hud.ac.uk

Leeds

Leeds Careers Guidance

HQ, No 1, Eastgate, Leeds LS2 7YP. Tel: 0113 225 9000 /0808 100 8081. E-mail: lcghq@aol.com

Morley Careers Centre, Morley Town Hall, Queen Street, Morley LS27 9DY. Tel: 0113 247 7111.

Jobs and Training Information Service, 2 Great George Street, Leeds LS2 8BA. Tel: 0113 247 6937.

Leeds Training & Enterprise Council, Belgrave Hall, Belgrave Street, Leeds LS2 8DD. Tel: 0113 234 7666. Website: www.leedstec.co.uk E-mail: tecinfo@leedstec.co.uk

Joseph Priestley College, Peel Street, Morley LS27 8QE. Tel: 0113 253 5050. Website: www.joseph-priestley.ac.uk E-mail: helpline@joseph-priestley.ac.uk

Leeds College of Music, 3 Quarry Hill, Leeds LS2 7PD. Tel: 0113 222 3400.

Leeds City Council, Department of Community Benefits & Rights, Further Education, Civic Hall Annexe, Leeds LS1 1UR. Tel: 0113 247 4709.

Leeds College of Art & Design, Jacob Kramer Building, Blenheim Walk, Leeds LS2 9AQ. Tel: 0113 202 8000. Website: www.leeds_art.ac.uk E-mail: info@leeds_art.ac.uk

Leeds College of Building, North Street, Leeds LS2 7QT. Tel: 0113 222 6000.

Leeds College of Technology, Cookridge Street, Leeds LS2 8BL. Tel: 0113 243 0381.

Leeds Metropolitan University, Calverley Street, Leeds LS1 3HE. Tel: 0113 283 3113. Website: www.lmu.ac.uk E-mail: course-enquiries@lmu.ac.uk

Northern School of Contemporary Dance, 98 Chapeltown Road, Leeds LS7 4BH. Tel: 0113 219 3000. Website: www.nscd.ac.uk

Park Lane College, Park Lane, Leeds LS3 1AA. Tel: 0113 216 2000. Website: www.parklanecoll.ac.uk

Thomas Danby College, Roundhay Road, Leeds LS7 3BG. Tel: 0113 249 4912. Website: www.thomasdanby.ac.uk E-mail: info@thomasdanby.ac.uk

Trinity & All Saints University College, Brownberrie Lane, Horsforth, Leeds LS18 5HD. Tel: 0113 283 7100. Website: www.tasc.ac.uk

University of Leeds, Leeds LS2 WT. Tel: 0113 243 1751. Website: www.leeds.ac.uk

Yorkshire Forward, Westgate House, 100 Wellington Street, Leeds LS1 4LT. Tel: 0113 242 6268. Website: www.yorkshireforward.com

Wakefield

Wakefield District Guidance Services

Wakefield Careers Centre, 24 Wood Street, Wakefield WF1 2ED. Tel: 01924 302640.

Castleford Careers Centre, 21-23 Sagar Street, Castleford WF10 1AG. Tel: 01977 552824.

Pontefract Careers Centre, 9 Market Place, Pontefract WF8 1AG. Tel: 01977 690600.

Hemsworth Careers Centre, Becca House, Market Street, Hemsworth WF9 4JY. Tel: 01977 722260.

Five Towns Resource Centre, Welbeck Street, Castleford WF10 1DR. Tel: 01977 519625.

Prospect Corner Career Development Centre, 9 Market Place, Pontefract WF8 1AG. Tel: 01977 602292.

Wakefield Training & Enterprise Council, Grove Hall, 60 College Grove Road, Wakefield WF1 3RN. Tel: 01924 299907.

Westfield Resource & Enterprise Centre, Westfield Lane, South Eimsall, Pontefract WF9 2PU. Tel: 01977 645477.

Bretton Hall, West Bretton, Wakefield WF4 4LG. Tel: 01924 830261. Website: www.bretton.ac.uk E-mail: bretton@bretton.ac.uk

Education Department (Adult Education), Wakefield Metropolitan District Council, Manygates Education Centre, Manygates Lane, Wakefield WF2 7DQ. Tel: 01924 300900.

Wakefield College, Margaret Street, Wakefield WF1 2DH. Tel: 01924 789789. Website: www.wakcoll.ac.uk

Channel Islands

Guernsey

Guernsey Careers Service, Education Department, Grange Road, St Peter Port GY1 1RQ. Tel: 01481 710821. Website: www.gcs.gov.gg E-mail: sitemaster@gcs.gov.gg

Education Department, States of Guernsey Education Council, Grange Road, St Peter Port GY1 1RQ. Tel: 01481 710821.

Guernsey College of Further Education, Routes des Coutanchez, St Peter Port GY1 2TT. Tel: 01481 727121.

Jersey

Jersey Careers Service, Education Department, PO Box 142, St Saviour JE4 8QJ. Tel: 01534 509351.

States of Jersey Education Department, PO Box 142, Jersey JE4 8QJ. Tel: 01534 509500.

Highlands College, PO Box 1000, St Saviour, Jersey JE4 9QA. Tel: 01534 608608.

Isle of Man

Careers Centre, 14 Hill Street, Douglas, Isle of Man IM2 1EF. Tel: 01624 685128. E-mail: careers@gov.im

Education Department, Murray House, Mount Havelock, Douglas IM1 2SG. Tel: 01624 685820.

Isle of Man College, Homefield Road, Douglas. Tel: 01624 648200.

Wales

Dyfed area

Carmarthenshire, Ceredigion and Pembrokeshire

Cwmni Gyrfaoedd Dyfed Careers Company, Head Office, Pensarn, Carmarthen SA13 2BT. Tel: 01267 228400.

West Wales TEC, Orchard House, Orchard Street, Swansea SA1 5DJ. Tel: 01792 354000. Website: www.westwales.tec.org.uk E-mail: mailbox@westwales.tec.org.uk

Carmarthenshire College of Technology and Art, Graig Campus, Sandy Road, Llanelli SA15 4DN. Tel: 01554 748000. Website: www.ccta.ac.uk E-mail: admissions@ccta.ac.uk

Coleg Ceredigion/Ceredigion College of Further Education, Llanbadarn Campus, Llanbadarn Fawr, Aberystwyth, Ceredigion SY23 3BP. Tel: 01970 624511. Website: www.ceredigion.ac.uk E-mail: prospectus@ceredigion.ac.uk

Education Department, Carmarthenshire County Council, Pibwrlwyd, Carmarthen SA31 2NH. Tel: 01267 224501. Website: www.satproj.org.uk E-mail: carmsleahq@satproj.org.uk

Education Department, Ceredigion County Council, County Offices, Marine Terrace, Aberystwyth SY33 2DE. Tel: 01970 617911.

Education Department, Pembrokeshire County Council, County Hall, Haverfordwest, Pembs SA61 1TP. Tel: 01437 764551. Website: www.pembrokeshire.gov.uk E-mail: rhidian.smith@pembrokeshire.gov.uk

Pembrokeshire College, Haverfordwest, Pembrokeshire SA61 1SZ. Tel: 01437 765247. Website: www.pembrokeshire.ac.uk E-mail: info@pembrokeshire.ac.uk

Trinity College, Carmarthen SA31 3EP. Tel: 01267 676767. Website: www.trinity-cm.ac.uk E-mail: registry@trinity-cm.ac.uk

University of Wales, Lampeter SA48 7ED. Tel: 01570 423530. Website: www.lampeter.ac.uk E-mail: recruit@lampeter.ac.uk

University of Wales, Old College, King Street, Aberystwyth SY23 2AX. Tel: 01970 622021. Website: www.aber.ac.uk E-mail: admissions@aber.ac.uk

Welsh Institute of Rural Studies, University of Wales Aberystwyth, Llanbadarn Campus, Aberystwyth, Ceredigion SY23 3AL. Tel: 01970 624471. Website: www.wirs.aber.ac.uk/ E-mail: wirs@aber.ac.uk

Flintshire, Wrexham and Denbighshire

Careers Plus – Gyrfau A Mwy

Head Office, 2nd Floor, St David's Building, Daniel Owen Square, Earl Road, Mold, Flintshire CH7 1DD. Tel: 01352 750456. Website: www.careersplus.co.uk E-mail: admin@careersplus.co.uk

Careers Shop – Mold Area, Unit 1 , Daniel Owen Square, Earl Road, Mold, Flintshire CH7 1DD. Tel: 01352 755798. Website: www.careersplus.co.uk E-mail: admin@careersplus.co.uk

Careers Shop – Deeside Area, 85-87 Chester Road West, Shotton, Deeside CH5 1BZ. Tel: 01244 813316. Website: www.careersplus.co.uk E-mail: admin@careersplus.co.uk

Careers Shop – Wrexham Area, 36-39 Chester Street, Wrexham LL13 8AH. Tel: 01978 266802. Website: www.careersplus.co.uk E-mail: admin@careersplus.co.uk

CELTEC, Wynnstay Building, Hightown Barracks, Kingsmill Road, Wrexham LL13 8BH. Tel: 01978 290049. Website: www.celtec.co.uk E-mail: celtec@celtec.co.uk

Deeside College/Coleg Glannau Dyfrdwy, Kelsterton Road, Connah's Quay, Deeside CH5 4BR. Tel: 01244 831531. Website: www.deeside.ac.uk E-mail: enquiries@deeside.ac.uk

Denbighshire County Council, c/o County Hall, Mold CH7 6GR. Tel: 01824 706700. Website: www.denbighshire.gov.uk

Department of Education & Leisure Services, Wrexham County Borough Council, Roxburgh House, Hill Street, Wrexham LL11 1SN. Tel: 01978 297400.

Directorate of Education, Culture & Information,

Education Department, Conwy County Borough Council, Government Buildings, Dinerth Road, Colwyn Bay, North Wales LL28 4UL. Tel: 01492 575031.

Llysfasi College, Ruthin, Denbighshire LL15 2LB. Tel: 01978 790263. Website: www.llysfasi.ac.uk E-mail: admin@llysfasi.ac.uk

North East Wales Institute of HE, Plas Coch, Mold Road, Wrexham LL11 2AW. Tel: 01978 290666. Website: www.newi.ac.uk

Welsh College of Horticulture, Northop, Mold CH7 6AA. Tel: 01352 841000. Website: www.wcoh.ac.uk

Yale College, Grove Park Road, Wrexham LL12 7AA. Tel: 01978 311794. Website: www.yale.ac.uk E-mail: admissions@yale.ac.uk

Gwent area

Newport, Monmouthshire, Torfaen and Blaenau Gwent

Gwent Careers

Head Office, Ty Glyn, Albion Road, Pontypool NP4 6GE. Tel: 01495 756666. Website: www.gwent-careers.org.uk E-mail: gcareers@globalnet.co.uk

Newport Careers Office, 16 Charles Street, Newport NP9 1JU. Tel: 01633 265203. Website: www.gwent-careers.org.uk E-mail: ncareers@globalnet.co.uk

Pontypool Careers Office, Town Bridge, Park Road, Pontypool NP4 6JE. Tel: 01494 750015. Website: www.gwent-careers.org.uk E-mail: pcareers@globalnet.co.uk

Adult Prospects, Newport & Gwent Enterprise, Enterprise Way, Newport NQ9 2AQ. Tel: 01633 254041. Website: www.netwales.co.uk

Gwent TEC, Glyndwr House, Cleppa Park, Newport, Gwent NP1 9BA. Tel: 01633 817777. Website: www.tec.co.uk/map/gwent/html

Arrow Training Associates Ltd, Training Centre, School Hill Trading Estate, Chepstow NP6 5PH. Tel: 01291 626322.

Community Education, Leisure & Libraries, Caerphilly Road, Ystard Mynach CF82 7ES. Tel: 01443 864868. Website: www.caerphilly.gov.uk

Education Department, Blaenau Gwent County Borough Council, Victoria House, Victoria Business Park, Ebbw Vale NP3 6ER. Tel: 01495 355434.

Education Department, Monmouth, County Hall, Cwmbran NP44 2XH. Tel: 01633 644487. Website: www.monmouthshire.gov.uk E-mail: davidyoung@monmouthshire.gov.uk

Education Department, Newport County Borough Council, Civic Centre, Newport NP4 4UR. Tel: 01633 232431.

Gwent Tertiary College, Usk Campus, The Rhadye, Usk NP5 1XJ. Tel: 01495 333333. Website: www.gwent-tertiary.ac.uk

Torfaen Adult & Continuing Education, County Hall, Cwmbran, Torfaen NP44 2XH. Tel: 01633 648155. Website: www.torfaen.gov.uk E-mail: margaret.slater@torfaen.gov.uk

University of Wales College, Carleon Campus, PO Box 179, Newport NP18 3YH. Tel: 01633 432432. Website: www.newport.ac.uk E-mail: uic@newport.ac.uk

Gwynedd area

Conwy, Gwynedd and Isle of Anglesey

The Careers Company – Y Cwmni Gyrfa

Head Office, 5 Stryd Castell, Caenarfon, Gwynedd LL55 1SE. Tel: 01286 679199. Website: www.careers-yrfa.org.uk E-mail: post@careers-gyrfa.org.uk

Bangor Careers Centre, Llys Gwynedd, Ffordd Gwynedd, Bangor LL57 1DT. Tel: 01248 364682. Website: www.careers-yrfa.org.uk E-mail: post@careers-gyrfa.org.uk

Caernarfon Careers Centre, 5 Stryd y Castell, Caernarfon LL55 1SE. Tel: 01286 679221. Website: www.careers-yrfa.org.uk E-mail: post@careers-gyrfa.org.uk

Holyhead Careers Centre, Sgwar y Farchnad, Caergybi, Ynys Mon LL65 1UF. Tel: 01407 762177. Website: www.careers-yrfa.org.uk E-mail: post@careers-gyrfa.org.uk

Llandudno Careers Centre, 25 Stryd y Capel, Llandudno LL30 2SY. Tel: 01492 871900. Website: www.careers-yrfa.org.uk E-mail: post@careers-gyrfa.org.uk

Porthmadog Careers Centre, 10 Heol y Wyddfa, Porthmadog LL49 9HT. Tel: 01766 514501. Website: www.careers-yrfa.org.uk E-mail: post@careers-gyrfa.org.uk

Rhyl Careers Centre, Station Buildings, Ffordd Bodfor, Rhyl LL18 1AT. Tel: . Website: www.careers-yrfa.org.uk E-mail: post@careers-gyrfa.org.uk

CELTEC, Unit 6, St Asaph Business Park, St Asaph, Denbighshire LL17 0LJ. Tel: 01745 538500. Website: www.celtec.co.uk E-mail: celtec@celtec.co.uk

Coleg Harlech, Harlech, Gwynedd, LL46 2PU. Tel: 01766 780363. Website: www.harlech.ac.uk/ E-mail: harlech.ac.uk

Coleg Llandrillo, Rhos-on-Sea, Colwyn Bay, Clwyd LL28 4HZ. Tel: 01492 546666. Website: www.llandrillo.ac.uk E-mail: admissions@llandrillo.ac.uk

Coleg Meirion-Dwyfor, Fford Ty'n Coed, Dolgellau, Gwynedd LL40 2SW. Tel: 01341 422827.

Coleg Menai, Ffordd Ffriddoed, Bangor LL40 2SW. Tel: 01248 370125.

Department of Education & Culture, Gwynedd Council, County Offices, Shirehall Street, Caernarfon L55 1SH. Tel: 01286 672255. Website: www.cyngor-gwynedd.gov.uk E-mail: plw@cyngor-gwynedd.gov.uk

University of Wales, Bangor, Gwynedd LL57 2DG. Tel: 01248 351151. Website: www.bangor.ac.uk E-mail: admissions@bangor.ac.uk

Mid Glamorgan area

Bridgend, Caerphilly, Merthyr Tydfil and Rhondda Cynon Taff

Mid Glamorgan Careers Ltd

Aberdare Careers Centre, 3-4 High Street, Aberdare CF44 7AA. Tel: 01685 875795.

Bridgend Careers Centre, 1st Floor, Derwen House, Court Road, Bridgend CF13 1BN. Tel: 01656 653600.

Caerphilly Careers Centre, The Twyn, Caerphilly CF37 1JL. Tel: 029 2085 2505.

Merthyr Tydfil Careers Centre, 27 Lower High Street, Merthr Tydfil CF47 8DP. Tel: 01685 723421.

Pontyridd Careers Centre, Upper Church Street, Pontypridd CF37 2UF. Tel: 01443 486741.

Tonypandy Careers Centre, 232 Court Street, Tonypandy CF40 2BR. Tel: 01443 432555.

Mid Glamorgan TEC, Unit 17-20 Centre Court, Main Avenue, Treforest Industrial Estate, Pontypridd, Mid Glamorgan CF37 5YL. Tel: 01443 841594. Website: www.thebiz.co.uk/mglam.htm

Aberdare College of Further Education, Cwmdare Road, Aberdare CF44 8ST. Tel: 01685 887500. Website: www.aberdare.ac.uk

Bridgend College, Cowbridge Road, Bridgend CF31 3DF. Tel: 01656 766588. Website: www.bridgend.ac.uk E-mail: enquiries@bridgend.ac.uk

Directorate of Education & Leisure, Caerphilly County Borough Council, Council Offices, Caerphilly Road, Ystad Mynach, Mengoed CF82 7EP. Tel: 01443 864948.

Education Department, Bridgend County Borough Council, Sunnyside, Bridgend CF13 4AR. Tel: 01656 642200.

Education Department, Rhondda, Cyon, Taff County Borough Council, The Education Centre, Grawen Street, Porth CF39 0BU. Tel: 01443 687666.

Merthyr Tydfil College, Ynysfach, Merthyr Tydfil CF48 1AR. Tel: 01685 726000. Website: www.merthyr.ac.uk E-mail: college@merthyr.ac.uk

Merthyr Tydfil County Borough Council Education Directorate, Ty Keir Hardie, Riverside Court, Avenue De Clichy, Merthyr Tydfil CF47 8XD. Tel: 01685 724600. E-mail: merthyrlea@btconnet.com

Pencoed College, Pencoed, Bridgend CF35 5LG. Tel: 01656 860202. Website: www.pencoed.ac.uk

Pontypridd College, Ynys Terrace, Rhydyfelin, Pontypridd CF37 5RN. Tel: 01443 662800. Website: www.pontypridd.ac.uk

Rhondda College, Llynpia, Tonypandy, Rhondda Cynon, Taff CF40 2TQ. Tel: 01443 662800. Website: www.pontypridd.ac.uk

University of Glamorgan, Pontypridd CF37 1DL. Tel: 01443 480480. Website: www.glam.ac.uk/home.html

Ystrad Mynach College, Twyn Road, Ystrad Mynach, Hengoed CF82 7XR. Tel: 01443 816888.

Powys area

Powys Careers Guidance Service

Head Office and Careers Information Centre, The Lindens, Spa Road, Llandrindod Wells, Powys LD1 5EY. Tel: 01597 825898. Website: www.careers.powys.gov.uk E-mail: careers@powys.gov.uk

Careers Information Centre, The Old College, Station Road, Newton, Powys SY16 1BE. Tel: 01686 626959. Website: www.careers.powys.gov.uk E-mail: careers@powys.gov.uk

Careers Information Centre, Ground Floor, 48 Free Street, Brecon LD3 7BN. Tel: 01874 624619. Website: www.careers.powys.gov.uk E-mail: careers@powys.gov.uk

Powys TEC, 1st Floor, St Davids House, Newton, Powys SY16 1RB. Tel: 01686 622494. Website: www.tec.co.uk/map/powys.html

Coleg Powys, Llanidloes Road, Newton, Powys SY16 4HU. Tel: 01686 622722. Website: www.coleg-powys.ac.uk E-mail: enquiries@coleg-powys.ac.uk

Powys LEA, County Hall, Llandrindod, Powys LD1 5LG. Tel: 01597 826422. E-mail: education@powys.gov.uk

South Glamorgan area

Cardiff City and Vale of Glamorgan

CareerPaths (Cardiff & Vale) Ltd

Cardiff Careers Office, 53 Charles Street, Cardiff CF10 4GD. Tel: 01221 255700.

Barry Careers Office, 100 Holton Road, Barry CF63 4RN. Tel: 01446 701177. Website: www.careerpaths.org.uk E-mail: info@careerpaths.org.uk

South Glamorgan Training & Enterprise Council, 3-7 Drakes Walk, Waterfront 2000, Atlantic Wharf, Cardiff CF1 5AN. Tel: 029 2026 1000. Website: www.thebiz.co.uk/sglamtec.htm

Barry College, Colcot Road, Barry CF6 8YJ. Tel: 01446 743520. Website: www.barry.ac.uk E-mail: enquiries@barry.ac.uk

Cardiff Tertiary College, Trowbridge Road, Rumney, Cardiff CF3 8XZ. Tel: 029 2025 0250.

Cardiff University, Cardiff, PO Box 494, Cardiff CF1 3Y1. Tel: 029 2087 4404.
Website: www.cf.ac.uk E-mail: admissions@cf.ac.uk

Education Department, Cardiff City Council, County Hall, Atlantic Wharf, Cardiff CF10 4UW.
Tel: 029 2087 2902.

Education & Library Services, Vale of Glamorgan, Civic Offices, Holton Road, Barry CF63 4RU.
Tel: 01446 700111.

University of Wales College of Medicine, Heath Park, Cardiff CF4 4XN. Tel: 029 2074 2027.
Website: www.uwcm.ac.uk E-mail: uwcmadmissions@cf.ac.uk

University of Wales Institute, Cardiff, Western Avenue, Cardiff CF5 2SG. Tel: 029 2050 6070.
Website: www.uwic.ac.uk E-mail: uwicinfo@uwic.ac.uk

Welsh College of Music and Drama, Castle Grounds, Cathays Park, Cardiff CF1 3ER.
Tel: 029 2034 2854. Website: www.wcmd.ac.uk E-mail: drama.admissions@wcmd.ac.uk
music.admissions@wcmd.ac.uk

West Glamorgan area

Neath, Port Talbot and Swansea

The Careers Business Company

HQ, The Gateway Centre, City & County of Swansea Training Centre, Beaufort Road, Morriston,
Swansea SA6 8EZ. Tel: 01792 704807.

Swansea Careers Centre, 69 The Kingsway, Swansea. Tel: 01792 644444.

Port Talbot Careers Centre, 56 Station Road, Port Talbot. Tel: 01639 871933.

Neath Careers Centre, 7 Angle Place, Neath. Tel: 01639 636391.

Gorseinon Careers Centre, Unit 2a Cross Street, Gorseinon. Tel: 01792 897333.

West Wales TEC, Orchard House, Orchard Street, Swansea SA1 5DJ. Tel: 01792 354000.
Website: www.westwales.tec.org.uk E-mail: mailbox@westwales.tec.org.uk

Afan College, Margam, Port Talbot SA13 2AL. Tel: 01639 882107. Website: www.afan.ac.uk

County of Swansea, Community & Outdoor Residential Education Service, Dan y Coed House,
West Cross, Swansea. Tel: 01792 401548.

Education, Leisure & Lifelong Learning Department, Neath & Port Talbot County Borough,
Aberowan House, Port Talbot SA13 1PJ. Tel: 01639 763539.

Gorseinon College, Belgrave Road, Gorseinon SA4 2RF. Tel: 01792 890700.
Website: www.gorseinon.ac.uk

Neath College, Dwr-y-Felin Road, Neath SA10 7RF. Tel: 01639 634271.
Website: www.neath.ac.uk E-mail: enquiries@neath.ac.uk

Swansea College, Tycoch, Swansea SA2 9EB. Tel: 01792 284000. Website: www.swancoll.ac.uk

Swansea Institute of Higher Education, Mount Pleasant, Swansea SA1 6ED.
Tel: 01792 481000. Website: www.sihe.ac.uk E-mail: enquiry@sihe.ac.uk

University of Wales Swansea, Singleton Park, Swansea SA2 8PP. Tel: 01792 295111.
Website: www.swansea.ac.uk E-mail: admissions@swansea.ac.uk

Scotland

Argyll and Bute

Argyll and Bute Careers Partnership Ltd

Campbeltown Area Careers Office, Hazelburn Business Park, Milknowe, Campbeltown PA28 6HA. Tel: 01586 552795/553334.

Dunoon Area Careers Office, 4 Argyll Street, Dunoon PA23 7HJ. Tel: 01369 705816.

Lochilphead Careers Office, Dalriada House, Lochnell Street, Lochgilphead PA31 8RA. Tel: 01546 602725.

Oban Area Careers Office, 23 Stevenson Street, Oban PA34 5NA. Tel: 01631 564697.

Islay Careers Office, Kilarrow House, Bowmore, Isle of Islay PA43. Tel: 01496 810545.

Rothesay Careers Office, Bute Business Centre, 81 Victoria Street, Rothesay, Isle of Bute PA20 OAP. Tel: 01700 503600.

Rutherglen/Cambuslang Careers Office, 380 King Street, Rutherglen G73 1DQ. Tel: 0141 613 5211. E-mail: cambslangco@enterprise.net

Argyll and The Islands Enterprise, The Enterprise Centre, Kilmory Industrial Estate, Lochgilphead PA31 8SH. Tel: 01546 602281. Website: www.hie.co.uk/aie/aie.html

Education Offices, Argyll and Bute Council, Argyll House, Alexander Parade, Dunoon PA23 8AJ. Tel: 01369 704000. Website: www.com-edu-argyllho.demon.co.uk E-mail: jimmccrossan@com-edu-argyllho.demon.co.uk

Borders area

Scottish Borders Careers

Head Office, Waukrigg Mill, Duke Street, Galashiels TD1 1QD. Tel: 01896 754884. Website: dialspace.dial.pipex.com/town/way/gkh31 E-mail: gkh31@dial.pipex.com

Pathways Adult Guidance Service, Galashiels Area Office, Langlee Complex, Marigold Drive, Galashiels TD1 2LP. Tel: 01896 755110. E-mail: educ555@aol.com

Scottish Borders Enterprise, Bridge Street, Galashiels TD1 1SW. Tel: 01896 758991. Website: www.thebiz.co.uk/bordent.htm

Borders College, Thorniedean House, Melrose Road, Galashiels TD1 2AF. Tel: 01896 756440. Website: www.ceg.org.uk/guidnet/data/colleges/borders.htm

Education Department, Scottish Borders Council, Council Headquarters, Newton St Boswells, Melrose TD6 0SA. Tel: 01835 825090.

Heriot-Watt University Scottish Borders Campus, Netherdale, Galashiels, Selkirkshire TD1 3HF. Tel: 01896 753351. Website: www.hw.ac.uk

Central Region area

Clackmannanshire, Falkirk and Stirling

Careers Central Ltd

Alloa Careers Office, 39-43 Bank Street, Alloa FK10 1HP. Tel: 01259 215214.
E-mail: careers@careers-central.sol.co.uk

Falkirk Careers Office, 1a Bank Street, Falkirk FK1 1NB. Tel: 01324 620311.
E-mail: careers@careers-central.sol.co.uk

Grangemouth Careers Office, 15 La Porte Precinct, Grangemouth FK3 8AZ. Tel: 01324 472397.
E-mail: careers@careers-central.sol.co.uk

Stirling Careers Office, 6 Viewfield Place, Stirling FK8 1NQ. Tel: 01786 462036.
E-mail: careers@careers-central.sol.co.uk

Adult Learning Information and Guidance Service (ALIGS), Careers Central Ltd, Head Office, Enterprise House, Springkerse Business Park, Stirling FK7 7UF. Tel: 01786 446150.
E-mail: careers@careers-central.sol.co.uk

Forth Valley Enterprise, Laurel House, Laurelhill Business Park, Stirling FK7 9JQ.
Tel: 01786 451919. Website: www.forthvalley.co.uk

Clackmannan College of Further Education, Branshill Road, Alloa FK10 3BT.
Tel: 01259 215121. Website: www.scet.org.uk/educ/online/colleges/clackman.asp

Education & Community Services Headquarters, The Clackmannanshire Council, Room 28, Lime Tree House, Alloa FK10 1EX. Tel: 01259 450000.

Education Service, Falkirk Council, McLaren House, Marchmont Avenue, Polmont, Falkirk FK2 0NZ. Tel: 01324 506600.

Education Service, Stirling Council, Viewforth, Stirling FK8 2ET. Tel: 01786 442650.

Falkirk College of Further and Higher Education, Grangemouth Road, Falkirk FK2 9AD.
Tel: 01324 403000. Website: www.flkcol.demon.co.uk
E-mail: 101544.3517@compuserve.com

University of Stirling, Stirling FK9 4LA. Tel: 01786 467046. Website: www.stirling.ac.uk
E-mail: s-c-liasion@stirling.ac.uk

Dumfries and Galloway

Dumfries and Galloway Careers Service

Annan Careers Office, Ednam Street, Annan DG12 6EF. Tel: 01461 204916.

Castle Douglas Careers Office, 4 Market Street, Castle Douglas DG7 1BE. Tel: 01556 504827.

Dumfries Careers Centre, Loreburn Centre, High Street, Dumfries DE1 2BD. Tel: 01387 272510.

Lockerbie Careers Office, Council Offices, Dryfe Road, Lockerbie DG11 2AP. Tel: 01576 205066.

Newton Stewart Careers Office, Penninghame Centre, Auchendoon Road, Newton Stewart DG8 6HD. Tel: 01671 402692.

Stranraer Careers Office, Barony College, off Lewis Street, Stranraer DG9 7AL.
Tel: 01776 889793.

Dumfries and Galloway Enterprise, Solway House, Dumfries Enterprise Park, Tinwald Downs Road, Heathall, Dumfries DG1 3SJ. Tel: 01387 245000. Website: www.dge.co.uk

Barony College, Parkgate, Dumfries DG1 3NE. Tel: 01387 860251. Website: www.scet.org.uk/educ/online/colleges/barony.asp.

Dumfries and Galloway College, Heathhall, Dumfries DG1 3QZ. Tel: 01387 261261. Website: www.scet.org.uk/educ/online/colleges/d&g.asp.

Education Offices, Dumfries and Galloway Council, Education Offices, Dumfries and Galloway Council, 30 Edinburgh Road, Dumfries DG1 1NW. Tel: 01387 260427.

East Ayrshire

Ayrshire Careers Partnership Ltd

Cumnock Careers Office, Unit 21, Glaisnock Business Centre, Townhead Street, Cumnock. Tel: 01290 423422.

Dalmellington Careers Office, 8 High Street, Dalmellington KA6 7QM. Tel: 01292 551191.

Irvine Careers Office, 36-38 Bank Street, Irvine KA12 0LP. Tel: 01294 272421.

Kilmarnock Careers Office, 2 The Cross, Kilmarnock KA1 1LR. Tel: 01563 527165.

East Ayrshire Enterprise Initiative, 65 King Street, Kilmarnock. Tel: 01563 544554.

Enterprise Ayrshire, 17-19 Hill Street, Kilmarnock, KA3 1HA. Tel: 01563 26623. Website: www.thebiz.co.uk/ayrshent.htm

Kilmarnock College, Holehouse Road, Kilmarnock KA3 7AT. Tel: 01563 523501. Website: www.kilmarnock.ac.uk E-mail: enquiries@kilmarnock.ac.uk

East Ayrshire Council, Council Headquarters, London Road, Kilmarnock KA3 7BU. Tel: 01563 576000. Website: www.east-ayrshire.gov.uk E-mail: education@east-ayrshire.gov.uk

East Dunbartonshire

Dunbartonshire and Lomond Careers Service

Clydebank Careers Office, West Thormson Street, Clydebank G81 3AE. Tel: 0141 952 1454. E-mail: careers@dlcsp.org.uk

Dumbartonshire Enterprise Co, Spectrum House, Clydebank Business Park, Clydebank G81 2DR. Tel: 0141 951 2121.

Clydebank College, Kilbowie Road, Clydebank G81 2AA. Tel: 0141 952 7771. Website: www.clydebank.ac.uk

East Dunbartonshire Council, Boclair House, 100 Milngavie Road, Bearsden, Glasgow G61 2TQ. Tel: 0141 578 8000.

East Renfrewshire

Renfrewshire Careers Partnership Ltd

Barrhead Area Careers Office, 7 Bank Street, Barrhead G78 2RA. Tel: 0141 881 2886.

East Renfrewshire Council, Council Headquarters, Eastwood Park, Rouken Glen Road, East Renfrewshire G46 6UG. Tel: 0141 577 3000. Website: www.eastrenfrewshire.gov.uk E-mail: mathisonm@eastrenfrewshire.gov.uk

Fife

Fife Careers Ltd

Cowdenbeath Careers Centre, 320 High Street, Cowdenbeath KY4 9NT. Tel: 01383 313141.

Cupar Careers Centre, Carslogie Road, Cupar KY15 4HY. Tel: 01334 412240.

Dunfermline Careers Centre, 1 Douglas Street, Dunfermline KY12 7EB. Tel: 01383 312200.

Glenrothes Careers Centre, Albany House, Glenrothes KY7 5NZ. Tel: 01593 415188.

Kirkcaldy Careers Centre, Carlyle House, Kirkcaldy KY1 1DB. Tel: 01592 412380.

Leven Careers Centre, 57 High Street, Leven KY8 4NE. Tel: 01333 592580.

Fife Adult Guidance Network Project, Community Service, Fife Council, Fife House, North Street, Glenrothes KY7 5LT. Tel: 01592 416240.

Fife Enterprise Ltd, Kingdon House, Saltie Centre, Glenrothes, Fife KY6 2AQ. Tel: 01592 623000. Website: www.thebiz.co.uk/fifent.htm

Education Department, Fife Council, Fife House, North Street, Glenrothes KY7 5LT. Tel: 01592 414141.

Elmwood College, Cupar, Fife KY15 4JB. Tel: 01334 658800. Website: www.elmwood.ac.uk E-mail: contact@elmwood.ac.uk

Fife College of Further and Higher Education, St Brycedale Avenue, Kirkcaldy, Fife KY1 1EX. Tel: 01592 286591. Website: www.fife.ac.uk E-mail: enquiries@fife.ac.uk

Glenrothes College, Station Road, Glenrothes KY6 2RA. Tel: 01592 772233. Website: www.scet.org.uk/educ/online/colleges/glen.asp

Lauder College, Halbeath, Dumfermline, Fife KY11 5DY. Tel: 01383 845000.

University of St Andrews, Old Union Buildings, North Street, St Andrews, Fife KY16 9AJ. Tel: 01334 476161.

Glasgow City

Glasgow Careers Service

Anniesland Careers Centre, 52 Hatfield Drive, Glasgow G12 0YE. Tel: 0141 339 6845. Website: www.glasgow-careers.co.uk

Barmulloch Careers Centre, 182 Rye Road, Glasgow G21 3JX. Tel: 0141 558 5625. Website: www.glasgow-careers.co.uk

Cardonald Careers Centre, 1829 Paisley Road West, Glasgow G52 3SS. Tel: 0141 810 4416. Website: www.glasgow-careers.co.uk

Drumchapel Careers Centre, The Open Gate Learning Centre, 44 Hecla Square, Drumchapel G15 8NH. Tel: 0141 949 4883. Website: www.glasgow-careers.co.uk

Easterhouse Careers Office, John Wheatley College, 1200 Westerhouse Road, Glasgow G34 9JW. Tel: 0141 771 7602. Website: www.glasgow-careers.co.uk

Maryhill Careers Office, 910-914 Maryhill Road, Glasgow G20 7TA. Tel: 0141 946 6441. Website: www.glasgow-careers.co.uk

Parkhead Careers Office, 135 Westmuir Street, Glasow G31 5EX. Tel: 0141 554 6662. Website: www.glasgow-careers.co.uk

Queens Park Careers Office, 465 Victoria Road, Glasgow G42 8RL. Tel: 0141 423 8632. Website: www.glasgow-careers.co.uk

Soutside Careers Office, Glenspean Centre, 29 Mamore Street, Glasgow G43 2YX. Tel: 0141 636 0637. Website: www.glasgow-careers.co.uk

Glasgow Adult Guidance Network, Partners in Learning Centre, The Adelphi, 12 Commercial Road, Glasgow G54 0PQ. Tel: 0141 429 8180.

Glasgow Development Agency, Atrium Court, 50 Waterloo Street, Glasgow G2 6HQ. Tel: 0141 204 1111.

Anniesland College, Hatfield Drive, Glasgow G12 0YE. Tel: 0141 357 3969. Website: www.anniesland.ac.uk E-mail: a.reception@anniesland.ac.uk

Cambuslang College, 85 Hamilton Road, Cambuslang, Glasgow G72 7NY. Tel: 0141 641 6600. Website: www.south-lanarkshire-college.ac.uk

Cardonald College, 690 Mosspark Drive, Glasgow G52 3AY. Tel: 0141 272 3333. Website: www.cardonald.ac.uk E-mail: enquiries@cardonald.ac.uk

Central College of Commerce, 300 Cathedral Street, Glasgow G1 2TA. Tel: 0141 552 3941. Website: www.centralcollege.ac.uk

Community Education Service, Glasgow City Council, Nye Bevan House, 20 India Street, Glasgow G2 4PF. Tel: 0141 287 6748. Website: www.dialspace.dial.pipex.com/town/plaza/pp04

Cumbernauld College, Tryst Road, Town Centre, Cumbernauld, Glasgow G67 1HU. Tel: 01236 731811. Website: www.cumbernauld.ac.uk E-mail: cumbernauld_college@cumbernauld.ac.uk

Glasgow Caledonian University, City Campus, Cowcaddens Road, Glasgow G4 0BA. Tel: 0141 331 3000. Website: www.glasgow-caledonian.ac.uk

Glasgow College of Building and Printing, 60 North Hanover Street, Glasgow G1 2BP. Tel: 0141 332 9969.

Glasgow College of Food Technology, 230 Cathedral Street, Glasgow G1 2TG. Tel: 0141 552 3751. Website: www.gtn.org.uk

Glasgow College of Nautical Studies, 21 Thistle Street, Glasgow G5 9XB. Tel: 0141 565 2500. Website: www.glasgow-nautical.ac.uk E-mail: enquiries@glasgow-nautical.ac.uk

Glasgow School of Art, 167 Renfrew Street, Glasgow G3 6RQ. Tel: 0141 353 4500. Website: www.gsa.ac.uk

John Wheatley College, 1346 Shettleston Road, Glasgow G32 9AT. Tel: 0141 778 2426. Website: www.jwheatley.ac.uk E-mail: admissions@jwheatley.ac.uk

Langside College, 50 Prospecthill Road, Glasgow G42 9LB. Tel: 0141 649 4991.

North Glasgow College, Springburn Campus, 110 Flemington Street, Glasgow G21 4BX. Tel: 0141 558 9001.

Royal Scottish Academy of Music and Drama, 100 Renfrew Street, Glasgow G2 3DB. Tel: 0141 332 4101 ext 90. Website: www.rsamd.ac.uk E-mail: registry@rsamd.ac.uk

Stow College, 43 Shamrock Street, Glasgow G4 9LD. Tel: 0141 332 1786.

University of Glasgow, Glasgow G12 8QQ. Tel: 0141 339 8855. Website: www.gla.ac.uk

University of Strathclyde, 16 Richmond Street, Glasgow G1 1XQ. Tel: 0141 552 4400. Website: www.strath.ac.uk

Grampian area

City of Aberdeen, Aberdeenshire and Moray

Grampian Careers

HQ, 377 Union Street, Aberdeen AB11 6BT. Tel: 01224 285200. E-mail: gc@g.careers.org.uk

Elgin Careers Office, 11 North Guildry Street, Elgin IV30 1JR. Tel: 01343 548884.

Inverurie Careers Office, Unit 6, Garioch Centre, Constitution Street, Inverurie AB51 4SQ. Tel: 01467 623623.

Peterhead Careers Office, 16 Prince Street, Peterhead AB4 6PL. Tel: 01779 479345.

Grampian Enterprise Ltd, 27 Albyn Place, Aberdeen AB1 1YL. Tel: 01224 211500. Website: www.thebiz.co.uk/grampent.htm

Moray, Badenoch and Strathspey Enterprise, Elgin Business Centre, Maisondieu Road, Elgin, Inverness IV30 1RH. Tel: 01343 550567. Website: www.thebiz.co.uk/morayent.htm

STEPahead (Grampian Enterprise), 381 Union Street, Aberdeen AB1 2BX. Tel: 01224 310300. Website: www.stepahead.org. E-mail: diannepirie@stepahead.org

Aberdeen College, Gallowgate, Aberdeen AB9 1DN. Tel: 01224 612000. Website: www.abcol.ac.uk E-mail: enquiry@abcol.ac.uk

Banff and Buchan College of Further Education, Henderson Road, Fraserburgh, Aberdeenshire AB43 9GA. Tel: 01346 586100. Website: www.banff-buchan.ac.uk E-mail: csi.bbc.fe@banff-buchan.ac.uk

Aberdeenshire Council, Education & Recreation, Woodhill House Annexe, Western Road, Aberdeen AB16 5GJ. Tel: 01224 664630. Website: www.wiredshire.org.uk E-mail: mstewart.er@aberdeenshire.gov.uk

Education Department, City of Aberdeen Council, Summerhill Education Centre, Stronsay Drive, Aberdeen AB15 6JA. Tel: 01224 208626. E-mail: 101660.3557@compuserve.com

Education Department, Moray Council, Council Buildings, High Street, Elgin, Moray IV30 1BX. Tel: 01343 563097.

Moray College, Moray St, Elgin, Moray IV30 1JJ. Tel: 01343 554321. Website: www.moray.ac.uk

Northern College of Education, Aberdeen Campus, Hilton Place, Aberdeen AB24 4FA. Tel: 01224 283500. Website: www.norcol.ac.uk

Robert Gordon University, Schoolhill, Aberdeen AB10 1FR. Tel: 01224 262000. Website: www.rgu.ac.uk/. E-mail: i.centre@rgu.ac.uk

SAC: The National College for Food, Land & Environmental Studies, Craibstone Estate, Bucksburn, Aberdeen AB21 9YA. Tel: 01224 711000. Website: www.sac.ac.uk E-mail: etsu@au.sac.ac.uk

University Of Aberdeen, King's College, Aberdeen AB24 3FX. Tel: 01224 272090. Website: www.abdn.ac.uk E-mail: srs@admin.abdn.ac.uk

Highland

Highland Careers Services Ltd

HQ, Fodderty Way, Dingwall Business Park, Dingwall IV15 9XB. Tel: 01349 864914. Website: www.highlandcs.demon.co.uk

Highland Adult Guidance Network, Highland Careers Service, 4th Floor, River House, Young Street, Inverness IV3 5BQ. Tel: 01436 252118. Website: www.highlandcs.demon.co.uk

Caithness and Sutherland Enterprise, 2 Princess Street, Thurso KW14 7BQ. Tel: 01847 66115. Website: www.thebiz.co.uk/caithent.htm

Inverness and Nairn Enterprise, 13b Harbour Road, Longman Industrial Estate, Inverness IV1 1SY. Tel: 01463 713504.

Education Department, Highland Council, Glenurquhart Road, Inverness IV3 5NX. Tel: 01463 702000.

Inverness College, 3 Longman Road, Inverness IV1 1SA. Tel: 01463 236681.

Lochaber Ltd, St Mary's House, Gordon Square, Fort William, PH33 6DY. Tel: 01397 702160 or 704326.

Moray Badenoch & Strathspay Enterprise, Elgin Business Centre, Maisondieu Road, Elgin IV30 1RH. Tel: 01343 550567.

Ross & Cromarty Enterprise, 69-71 High Street, Invergordon IV18 0AA. Tel: 01349 853666.

Sabhal Mor Ostaig, Teangue, Sleat, Isle of Skye IV44 8RQ. Tel: 01471 844373.

Skye and Lochalsh Enterprise, King's House, The Green, Portree, Isle of Skye IV51 9BS. Tel: 01478 612841.

Thurso College, Ormlie Road, Thurso KW14 7EE. Tel: 01847 896161.

Inverclyde

Renfrewshire Careers Partnership Ltd

Greenock Area Careers Office, 105 Dalrymple Street, Greenock PA15 2HU. Tel: 01475 721271.

Inverclyde Council, Community Support Services, High Holm Avenue, Port Glasgow PA14 5JN. Tel: 01475 745227.

James Watt College of Further and Higher Education, Finnart Campus, Finnart Street, Greenock PA16 8HF. Tel: 01475 724433. Website: www.jameswatt.ac.uk

Islands – Orkney, Shetland & Western Isles

Orkney Opportunities Centre, 2 Albert Street, Kirkwall, Orkney KW15 1HP. Tel: 01856 872460. E-mail: opportunities.centre@orkney.com

Shetland Careers Service, Careers Office, Toll Clock Centre, 26 North Road, Lerwick ZE1 ODE. Tel: 01595 695791.

The Western Isles Careers Service, 30 Francis Street, Stornoway HS1 2ND. Tel: 01851 701333. Website: www.hebrides.com/org/careers E-mail: careers.westisle@btinternet.com

The Western Isles Careers Service, Lionacleit Education Centre, Benbecula HS7 5PJ. Tel: 01870 603345. E-mail: careers.benbecula@btinternet.com

The Western Isles Careers Service, Adult Guidance Centre, Town Hall, South Beach Street, Stornoway HS1 2BE. Tel: 01851 705200. E-mail: aguid.westilse@btinternet.com

Orkney Enterprise Ltd, 14 Queen Street, Kirkwall, Orkney Island, KW15 1JE. Tel: 01856 874638.

Shetland Enterprise Company Ltd, Toll Clock Shopping Centre, 26 North Road, Lerwick, Shetland ZE1 0DE. Tel: 01595 693177. Website: www.bis.uk com/bis/hi/shetlnd.htm E-mail: shetland.enterprise@zetnet.co.uk

Western Isles Enterprise, lomairt nian Eilean Siar, 3 Harbour View, Cramwell Street Quay, Stornoway HS1 2DF. Tel: 01851 703703. Website: www.hie.co.uk

Education and Community Services Department, Shetland Islands Council, Hayfield House, Hayfield Lane, Lerwick, Shetland ZE1 0QD. Tel: 01595 744000.

Education & Leisure Services Department, Western Isles Council Offices, Sandwick Road, Stornoway PA87 2BW. Tel: 01851 703773.

Education & Recreation Services Department, Orkney Islands Council Offices, School Place, Kirkwall KW15 1NY. Tel: 01856 873535.

Lews Castle College, Stornoway, Isle of Lewis HS2 0XR. Tel: 01851 703311. Website: www.lews.uhi.ac.uk E-mail: admin_office/lcc@fc.uhi.ac.uk

North Atlantic Fisheries College, Port Arthur, Scalloway, Shetland Isles ZE1 0UN. Tel: 01595 880328. Website: www.nafc.ac.uk E-mail: admin@nafc.ac.uk

Orkney College, Kirkwall, Orkney KW15 1LX. Tel: 01856 872839. Website: www.uhi.ac.uk/orkney E-mail: isla_scott@fc.uhi.ac.uk

Shetland College of Further Education, Gremista, Lerwick, Shetland ZE1 0PX. Tel: 01595 695514.

Lothian area

City of Edinburgh, East Lothian, Midlothian and West Lothian

Career Development Edinburgh and Lothians

HQ, 17 Logie Mill, Edinburgh EH7 4HG. Tel: 0131 556 7384. Website: www.cdel.co.uk E-mail: cdel@btinternet.com

Adult Guidance Service, Cairncross House, 25 Union Street, Edinburgh EH1 3LR. Tel: 0131 556 8440. Learning Line – 0131 556 8770.

Bathgate Career Development Centre, 25 North Bridge Street, Bathgate EH48 4PJ. Tel: 01506 630529.

Dalkeith Career Development Centre, 20 Croft Street, Dalkeith EH21 7PQ. Tel: 0131 663 7287.

Edinburgh East Career Development Centre, Cairncross House, 25 Union Street, Edinburgh EH1 3LR. Tel: 0131 556 7384.

Edinburgh West Career Development Centre, Atholl House, 2 Canning Street, Edinburgh EH3 8EG. Tel: 0131 228 7520.

Livingston Career Development Centre, Pentland House, Almondvale South, Livingston EH54 6NG. Tel: 01506 434249.

Musselburgh Career Development Centre, Adam Ferguson House, Station Road, Musselburgh EH21 7PQ. Tel: 0131 665 3120.

Craigmillar Adult Learning Advice Centre, 656 Niddrie Mains Terrace, Edinburgh EH16 4NX. Tel: 0131 661 8482.

Edinburgh Compact and Impact, 5 Murrayburn Drive, Edinburgh EH14 2SU. Tel: 0131 442 4450.

Training Access Points (TAP), 8 St Mary's Street, Edinburgh EH1 1SU. Tel: 0131 557 5822.

Lothian Education Business Partnership, Atholl House, 2 Canning Street, Edinburgh EH3 8EG. Tel: 0131 228 7537.

Department of Education & Community Services, East Lothian Council, Council Building, Haddington EH41 3HA. Tel: 01620 827631. Website: www.eastlothian.gov.uk

Edinburgh College of Art, Lauriston Place, Edinburgh EH3 9DF. Tel: 0131 221 6000. Website: www.ecs.ac.uk

Edinburgh's Telford College, Crewe Toll, Edinburgh EH4 2NZ. Tel: 0131 332 2491. Website: www.ed-coll.ac.uk E-mail: mail@ed-coll.ac.uk

Education Department, City of Edinburgh Council, Wellington Court, 10 Waterloo Place, Edinburgh EH1 3EG. Tel: 0131 469 3000. Website: www.hq.educ.edin.go.uk/

Education Division, Midlothian Council, 8 Lothian Road, Dalkeith, Midlothian EH23 4PE. Tel: 0131 270 7500.

Education Services, West Lothian Council, Lindsay House, South Bridge Street, Bathgate, EH48 1TS. Tel: 01506 776000.

Heriot-Watt University, Edinburgh EH14 4AS. Tel: 0131 449 5111. Website: www.hw.ac.uk

Jewel & Esk Valley College, Newbattle Road, Dalkeith EH22 3AE. Tel: 0131 660 1010. Website: www.jevc.ac.uk E-mail: info@jevc.ac.uk

Lothian and Edinburgh Enterprise Ltd, Apex House, 99 Haymarket Terrace, Edinburgh EH12 5HD. Tel: 0131 313 4000. Website: www.leel.co.uk E-mail: info@leel.co.uk

Moray House Institute of Education, Holyrood Campus, Holyrood Road, Edinburgh EH8 8AQ. Tel: 0131 556 8455. Website: www.hw.ac.uk

Napier University Edinburgh, Craiglockhart Campus, 219 Colinton Road, Edinburgh EH14 1DJ. Tel: 0131 444 2266.

Oatridge Agricultural College, Ecclesmachan, Broxburn EH52 6NH. Tel: 01506 854387. E-mail: oatridge_agricultural_collegeedu@msn.com

Queen Margaret University College, Edinburgh EH12 8TS. Tel: 0131 317 3000. Website: www.qmuc.ac.uk E-mail: admissions@qmuc.ac.uk

Stevenson College, Bankhead Avenue, Edinburgh EH11 4DE. Tel: 0131 535 4600. Website: www.stevenson.ac.uk E-mail: info@stevenson.ac.uk

University of Edinburgh, Old College, South Bridge, Edinburgh EH8 9YL. Tel: 0131 650 1000. Website: www.ed.ac.uk

Wester Hailes Education Centre, 5 Murrayburn Drive, Edinburgh EH14 2SU. Tel: 0131 442 2201.

West Lothian College, Marjoribanks Street, Bathgate EH48 1QJ. Tel: 01506 634300. Website: west-lothian.ac.uk E-mail: enquire@west-lothian.ac.uk

North Ayrshire

Ayrshire Careers Partnership Ltd

Ardrossan Careers Office, 66-80 Glasgow Street, Ardrossan KA22 8EH. Tel: 01294 468134.

Kilwinning Careers Office, Claremount Crescent, Kilwinning KA13 7HF. Tel: 01294 558295.

Adult Guidance Unit, 36-38 Bank Street, Irvine KA12 0LP. Tel: 01294 274318.

Education Department, North Ayrshire Council, Cunningham House, Irvine KA12 8EE. Tel: 01294 324400. E-mail: adv@naceducation.prestel.aco.uk

North Lanarkshire

Lanarkshire Careers Partnership Ltd

Airdrie Careers Office, Albert Primary School, 31 North Biggar Road, Airdrie ML6 6EJ. Tel: 01236 762623. E-mail: airdrieco@enterprise.net

Bellshill Careers Office, Main Street, Bellshill ML4 1AR. Tel: 01698 746985. E-mail: bellshillco@enterprise.net

Coatbridge Careers Office, Community Centre, 2 Corsewall, Coatbridge ML5 1QQ. Tel: 01236 424471. E-mail: coatbridgeco@enterprise.net

Cumbernauld Careers Centre, Muirfield Centre, Brown Road, Seafar, Cumbernauld G67 1AA. Tel: 01236 720889. E-mail: cumbernauldco@enterprise.net

Motherwell Careers Office, 303 Brandon Street, Motherwell ML1 1RS. Tel: 01698 254555. E-mail: motherwellcareers@enterprise.net

Wishaw Careers Office, 232 Main Street, Wishaw ML2 7ND. Tel: 01698 355329. E-mail: wishawcareers@enterprise.net

Lanarkshire Development Agency, New Lanarkshire House, Strathclyde Business Park, Bellshill ML4 3AD. Tel: 01698 745454. Website: www.adapt.ecotec.co.uk E-mail: adapt.ecotec.co.uk

Coatbridge College, Kildonan Street, Coatbridge ML5 3LS. Tel: 01236 436000. Website: www.coatbridge.ac.uk E-mail: admissions@coatbridge.ac.uk

Cumbernauld College, Tryst Road, Town Centre, Cumbernauld G67 1HU, Tel; 01236 731811. Website: cumbernauld.ac.uk E-mail: cumbernauld.college@cumbernauld.ac.uk

North Lanarkshire Council, Education Department, Municipal Buildings, Kildonan Street, Coatbridge ML5 3BT. Tel: 01236 812222,

Motherwell College, Dalzell Drive, Motherwell ML1 2DD. Tel: 01698 232323.
Website: www.motherwell.co.uk E-mail: mcol@motherwell.co.uk

Renfrewshire

Renfrewshire Careers Partnership Ltd

Johnstone Area Careers Office, 12 Laighcartside Street, Johnstone PA5 8BY.
Tel: 01505 326758/328869.

Paisley Area Careers Office, Abbey House, 8a Seedhill Road, Paisley PA1 1JS.
Tel: 0141 842 5777.

Renfrewshire Enterprise, 25-29 Causeyside Street, Paisley PA1 1UG. Tel: 0141 848 0101.
Website: www.renfent.co.uk

Education and Leisure Services Renfrewshire Council, South Building, Cotton Street, Paisley PA1 1LE. Tel: 0141 842 5663. Website: www.renfrewshire.gov.uk

Paisley Partnership Regeneration Company, 10 Falcon Crescent, Ferguslie Park, Paisley PA3 1NS. Tel: 0141 887 7707. Website: www.paisley-partnership.co.uk

Reid Kerr College, Renfrew Road, Paisley PA3 4DR. Tel: 0141 889 4225.
Website: www.scet.org.uk/educ/online/colleges/reidker.asp.

University of Paisley, High Street, Paisley PA1 2BE. Tel: 0141 848 3000.
Website: www.paisley.ac.uk

South Ayrshire

Ayrshire Careers Partnership

HQ, County Buildings, Wellington Square, Ayr KA7 1DR. Tel: 01292 612236.

Ayr Careers Office, 28 Boswell Park, Ayr KA7 1QF. Tel: 01292 281421.

Ayr College, Dam Park, Ayr KA8 0EU. Tel: 01292 265184. Website: www.ayrcoll.ac.uk
E-mail: webmaster@ayrcoll.ac.uk

Access North Ayr, Russell Street Building, Limonds Wynd, Ayr. Tel: 01292 610524.
Website: www.accessna.u-net.com E-mail: post@access.u-net.com

Education Services South Ayrshire Council, County Buildings, Wellington Square, Ayr KA7 1DS. Tel: 01292 612236.

The Scottish Agricultural College, Auchincruive, Ayr KA6 5HW. Tel: 01292 520331.
Website: www.sac.ac.uk

South Lanarkshire

Lanarkshire Careers Partnership Ltd

East Kilbride Careers Office, St Bride's High School, Platthorn Drive, East Kilbride G74 1NL.
Tel: 01355 225478. E-mail: eastkilbrideco@enterprise.net

Hamilton Careers Office, 23 Windmill Road,Saffronhall, Hamilton ML3 6LX. Tel: 01698 337475. E-mail: hamiltonco@enterprise.net

Lanark Careers Office, Lanark Grammar, Albany Drive, Lanark ML11 9AQ. Tel: 01555 662248. E-mail: lanarkco@enterprise.net

Lanarkshire Careers HQ, 23 Windmill Road, Saffronhall, Hamilton ML3 6LX. Tel: 01698 337474. E-mail: lanarkshirecareers@lanarkhq.enterprise-plc.com

Larkhall Careers Office, 3-7 Raploch Street, Larkhall ML9 1AE. Tel: 01698 881446. E-mail: larkhallco@enterprise.net

Bell College of Technology, Almada Street, Hamilton ML3 0JB. Tel: 01698 283100. Website: intsvrl.bell.ac.uk

Education Services South Lanarkshire Council, Council Offices, Almada Street, Hamilton ML3 0AA. Tel: 01698 454379.

Tayside area

Tayside Careers Ltd

Arbroath Careers Centre, Bellevue House, Springfield Terrace, Arbroath DD11 1EL. Tel: 01241 870441.

Dundee Careers Centre, Argyll House, Marketgait, Dundee DD1 1QP. Tel: 01382 435126.

Perth Careers Centre, Highland House, St Catherine's Road, Perth PH1 5RY. Tel: 01738 637639.

Information Services Unit, Argyll House, Marketgait, Dundee DD1 1QP. Tel: 01382 435163.

Network for Adult Guidance, 95-99 Douglas Street, Dundee DD1 5AT. Tel: 01382 226678.

New Directions, 88 Commercial Street, Dundee DD1 2AP. Tel: 01382 206116.

Scottish Enterprise Tayside, Enterprise House, North Lindsay Street, Dundee DD1 1HT. Tel: 01382 223100.

Angus College, Keptie Road, Arbroath DD11 3EA. Tel: 01241 432600. Website: www.scet.org.uk/educ/online/colleges/angus.asp

Dundee College, Old Glamis Road, Dundee DD3 8LE. Tel: 01382 834834.

Dundee City Council – Neighbourhood Resources and Development, Mitchell Street Centre, Mitchell Street, Dundee DD2 2LJ. Tel: 01382 435809.

Education Department Angus Council, County Building, Market Street, Forfar DD8 3WE. Tel: 01307 461460.

Education Department Dundee Council, Crichton Street, Dundee DDI 3RJ. Tel: 01382 223 2810.

Education Services, Perth and Kinross Council, Blackfriars, Perth PH1 5LU. Tel: 01738 476200. Website: www.pkc.gov.uk

Northern College of Education, Dundee Campus, Gardyne Road, Dundee DD5 1NY. Tel: 01382 464900. Website: www.norcol.ac.uk

Perth College, Creiff Road, Perth PH1 2NX. Tel: 01738 632020. Website: www.perth.fc.uhi.ac.uk E-mail: admissions@perth.fc.uhi.ac.uk

University of Abertay Dundee, Bell Street, Dundee DD1 1HG. Tel: 01382 308080. Website: www.abertay-dundee.ac.uk

University of Dundee, Nethergate, Dundee DD1 4HN. Tel: 01382 344160.
Website: www.dundee.ac.uk E-mail: srs@dundee.ac.uk

West Dunbartonshire

Dunbartonshire and Lomond Careers Service

Dumbarton Careers Office, 2 McLean Place, Dumbarton G82 1PY. Tel: 01389 761421.
E-mail: careers@dlcsp.org.uk

Kirkintilloch Careers Office, Whitegates, Lenzie Road, Kirkintilloch G66 3BL. Tel: 0141 776 3998.
E-mail: careers@dlcsp.org.uk

Dunbartonshire Enterprise, Spectium House, Clydebank Business Park, Clydebank, G81 2DR.
Tel: 0141 951 2121. Website: www.dunent.co.uk E-mail: de@scotnet.co.uk

Education & Leisure Services, West Dunbartonshire Council, Regional Offices, Garshake Road, Dumbarton G82 3PU. Tel: 01389 737309.

Northen Ireland

Belfast

Education & Library Board, 40 Academy Street, Belfast BT1 2NQ. Tel: 028 9056 4000.

Educational Guidance Service for Adults, 2nd Floor, Glendinning House, 6 Murray Street, Belfast BT1 6DN. Tel: 028 9024 4274. Website: www.egsa.dnet.co.uk
E-mail: info@egsa.dnet.co.uk

Training & Employment Agency Head Office, Adelaide House, 39-49 Adelaide Street, Belfast BT2 8FD. Tel: 028 9025 7777.

Training & Employment Agency Belfast Office, Gloucester House, 57-63 Chichester Street, Belfast BT1 4RA. Tel: 028 9025 2222.

Training & Employment Agency Falls Road, 43-45 Falls Road, Belfast BT12 4PD.
Tel: 028 9025 1346.

Training & Employment Agency Shankhill Road, 178-180 Shankhill Road, Belfast BT13 2BH.
Tel: 028 9033 0063.

Belfast Institute of Further and Higher Education, Ground Floor, Park House, 87-91 Great Victoria Street, Belfast BT2 7AG. Tel: 028 9026 5265.

Crescent Arts Centre, 2-4 University Road, Belfast BT7 1NH. Tel: 028 9025 2338.

Dundonald Flexible Learning Centre, 7 Ballyregan Road, Dundonald, Belfast BT16 0HY.
Tel: 028 9048 2804.

East Belfast Open Learning Centre, 3 Castlereagh Street, Belfast BT5 4NE.
Tel: 028 9087 3300.

Carryduff Open Learning Centre, Carryduff Library, Church Road, Carryduff, Belfast BT8 3DT. Tel: 028 9081 3568.

North Belfast Open Learning Centre, 1st Floor, Capitol House, 393/395 Antrim Road, Belfast BT15 2QZ. Tel: 020 9087 3500.

Old Museum Arts Centre, 7 College Square North, Belfast BT1 6AR. Tel: 028 9023 3332.

Open Universtiy, 40 University Road, Belfast BT7 1SU. Tel: 028 9024 5025.

The Queen's University of Belfast, University Road, Belfast BT7 1NN. Tel: 028 9024 5133. Website: www.qub.ac.uk E-mail: admissions@qub.ac.uk

St Mary's University College, 191 Falls Road, Belfast BT12 6FE. Tel: 028 9032 7678.

Stranmillis University College, Stranmillis Road, Belfast BT9 5DY. Tel: 028 9038 1271.

Ulster People's College, 30 Adelaide Park, Belfast BT9 6FY. Tel: 028 9066 5161.

University of Ulster, Belfast Campus, York Street, Belfast BT15 1ED. Tel: 028 9032 8515.

Workers' Educational Association, 1 Fitzwilliam Street, Belfast BT9 6AW. Tel: 028 9032 9718.

Workers' Educational Association, 11 Stranmillis Road, Belfast BT9 5AF. Tel: 028 9068 7710.

North-Eastern

Education & Library Board, County Hall, 182 Galgorm Road, Ballymena, Co Antrim BT42 1HN. Tel: 028 2565 3333.

Training & Employment Agency Antrim Office, 25-27 Church Street, Antrim BT41 4BE. Tel: 028 9446 2834.

Training & Employment Agency Bellymena Office, 35-39 Bridge Street, Ballymena BT43 5EL. Tel: 028 254 1135.

Training & Employment Agency Ballymoney Office, 32 Main Street, Ballymoney BT53 6AL. Tel: 028 276 2565.

Training & Employment Agency Carrickfergus Office, 20 West Street, Carrickfergus BT38 7AR. Tel: 028 9335 1449.

Training & Employment Agency Coleraine Office, 41 Church Street, Coleraine BT52 1AW. Tel: 028 7051 211.

Training & Employment Agency Larne Office, 75 Main Street, Larne BT40 1HH. Tel: 028 2827 3371.

Training & Employment Agency Magherafelt Office, 28 Queen Street, Magherafelt BT45 6AB. Tel: 028 7933 804.

Training & Employment Agency Newtownabbey Office, 41 Church Road, Glenmount Road, Newtonabbey BT36 7UX. Tel: 028 9054 8111.

Ballyearl Arts and Leisure Centre, 585 Doagh Road, Newtownabbey BT36 8RZ. Tel: 028 9084 8287.

Causeway Institute of Further & Higher Education, 2 Coleraine Road, Ballymoney BT53 6BP. Tel: 028 2766 2258.

Causeway Institute of Further & Higher Education, Union Street, Coleraine BT52 1QA. Tel: 028 7054 717.

Clotworthy Arts Centre, Antrim Castle Gardens, Randlestown, Antrim BT41 4LH. Tel: 028 9442 8000.

East Antrim Institute of Further & Higher Education, 32-34 Pound Street, Larne BT40 1SQ. Tel: 028 2827 2268.

East Antrim Institute of Further & Higher Education, 400 Shore Road, Newtonabbey BT37 9RS. Tel: 028 9085 5000.

Flowerfield Arts Centre, 185 Coleraine Road, Portstewart BT55 7HU. Tel: 028 2783 3959.

Moyle Enterprise Centre/Open Learning, 61 Leyland Road, Ballycastle BT54 6EZ. Tel: 028 2076 3737.

Moyola Open Learning Centre, Moyola Technology Unit, Moyola Industrial Estate, Moyola Road, Castledawson, Magherafelt BT45 8HN. Tel: 028 7946 9484.

North East Institute of Further & Higher Education, Fountain Street, Antrim BT41 4AL. Tel: 028 9446 3916.

North East Institute of Further & Higher Education, Farm Lodge Avenue, Ballymena BT43 7DJ. Tel: 028 2565 2871.

North East Institute of Further & Higher Education, Moneymore Road, Magherafelt BT45 6AE. Tel: 028 7932 462.

The Rural College, Derrynoid Road, Draperstown BT45 7DW. Tel: 028 7929 100.

University of Ulster, Coleraine Campus, Cromore Road, Coleraine BT52 1SA. Tel: 028 7044 141.

University of Ulster, Jordantown Campus, Shore Road, Newtownabbey, Co Antrim BT37 0QB. Tel: 028 9036 5131.

Workers' Educational Association, 10 Broadway Avenue, Ballymena BT43 7AA. Tel: 028 2565 5685.

South-Eastern

Education & Library Board, Grahamsbridge Road, Dundonald, Belfast BT16 0HS. Tel: 028 9056 6200.

Training & Employment Agency Ballynahinch Office, 20 High Street, Ballynahinch BT24 8AB. Tel: 028 9756 2986.

Training & Employment Agency Bangor Agency, 65 High Street, Bangor BT20 5BE. Tel: 028 9127 9999.

Training & Employment Agency Downpatrick Office, Rathkeltair House, Market Street, Downpatrick BT30 6LZ. Tel: 028 4461 8023.

Training & Employment Agency Lisburn Office, 71 Bow Street, Lisburn BT28 1BJ. Tel: 028 9262 3300.

Training & Employment Agency Newcastle Office, 113 Main Street, Newcastle BT33 0AE. Tel: 028 4372 5001.

Training & Employment Agency Newtownards Office, 9 Conway Square, Newtownards BT23 4DA. Tel: 028 4281 8653.

Ards Art Centre, Town Hall, Conway Street, Newtownards BT23 4DB. Tel: 028 4281 0803.

Castlereagh College of Further Education, Montgomery Road, Belfast BT6 9JD. Tel: 028 9079 7144.

Comber Open Learning Centre, 36 Castle Street, Comber BT23 5DY. Tel: 028 9187 2049.

Down Civic Arts Centre, 2-6 Irish Street, Downpatrick BT30 6BN. Tel: 028 4461 5283.

East Down Institute of Further & Higher Education, Market Street, Downpatrick BT30 6ND. Tel: 028 4461 5815.

East Down Institute of Further & Higher Education, Donard Street, Newcastle BT33 0AP. Tel: 028 4372 2451.

Harmony Hill Arts Centre, Clonmore House, 54 Harmony Hill, Lisburn BT27 4ES. Tel: 028 9267 8219.

Lisburn Institute of Further and Higher Education, Castle Street, Lisburn BT27 4SU. Tel: 028 9267 7225.

North Down and Ards Institute of Further & Higher Education, Castle Park Road, Bangor BT20 4TF. Tel: 028 9127 1254.

North Down and Ards Institute of Further & Higher Education, Newtownards Centre, Victoria Avenue, Newtownards BT23 3ED. Tel: 028 9181 2116.

Southern

Education & Library Board, 3 Charlemont Place, Armagh BT61 9AZ. Tel: 028 3751 2200.

Training & Employment Agency Armagh Office, Ulster Gazette, Shopping Centre, 56 Scotch Street, Armagh BT61 7PU. Tel: 028 3752 3322.

Training & Employment Agency Banbridge Office, 50 Newry Street, Banbridge BT32 3HA. Tel: 028 4062 149.

Training & Employment Agency Cookstown Office, 17 Oldtown Street, Cookstown BT80 8EE. Tel: 028 7966 950.

Training & Employment Agency Dungannon Office, 5 Thomas St Centre, Dungannon BT70 1HW. Tel: 028 8772 2525.

Training & Employment Agency Kilkeel Office, Newry Street, Kilkeel BT34 4DN. Tel: 028 4362 873.

Training & Employment Agency Lurgan Office, 10a High Street, Lurgan BT66 8AW. Tel: 028 3834 4325.

Training & Employment Agency Newry Office, 5-13 Marcus Street, Newry BT34 1ET. Tel: 028 3061 222.

Training & Employment Agency Portadown Office, 27A Magowan Buildings, West Street, Portadown BT62 3PN. Tel: 028 3839 6266.

Armagh College of Further Education, Lonsdale Street, Armagh BT61 7HN. Tel: 028 3752 2205.

Brownlow Community Learning Centre, Tullygally Primary School, 20 Meadowbrook, Craigavon BT65 5AA. Tel: 028 3834 4543.

Coalisland Training Services, 51 Dungannon Road, Coalisland, Co Tyrone BT71 4HP. Tel: 028 8774 8512.

East Tyrone College of Further Education, Loy Street, Cookstown BT80 8PZ. Tel: 028 8676 2620.

East Tyrone College of Further Education, Circular Road, Dungannon BT71 6BQ. Tel: 028 8772 2323.

Newry Arts Centre, 1a Bank Parade, Newry BT55 6HD. Tel: 028 3026 6232.

Newry College of Further Education, Patrick Street, Newry BT35 8DW. Tel: 028 3026 1071.

The Queen's University at Armagh, 39 Abbey Street, Armagh, Co Armagh BT61 7EB. Tel: 028 3751 0678.

Upper Bann Institute of Further & Higher Education, Castlewellan Road, Banbridge BT32 4AY. Tel: 028 4066 2582.

Upper Bann Institute of Further & Higher Education, Kitchen Hill, Lurgan BT66 6AZ. Tel: 028 3832 6135.

Upper Bann Institute of Further & Higher Education, 26 Lurgan Road, Portadown BT63 4BH. Tel: 028 3833 7111.

Workers' Educational Association, 1st Floor, Ballybot House, 28 Cornmarket, Newry BT35 8BG. Tel: 028 3036 9947.

Western

Education & Library Board, Campsie House, 1 Hospital Road, Omagh, Co Tyrone BT79 0AW. Tel: 028 8241 1411.

Training & Employment Agency, Enniskillen Office, Paget Square, Enniskillen BT74 7HS. Tel: 028 6632 3511.

Training & Employment Agency Limavady Office, 43a Market Street, Limavady BT49 0AB. Tel: 028 7776 5967.

Training & Employment Agency Londonderry Office, 5 Waterloo Place, Londonderry BT48 6BT. Tel: 028 7127 3700.

Training & Employment Agency Londonderry Office, 75 Duke Street, Londonderry BT47 1FP. Tel: 028 7131 9107.

Training & Employment Agency Omagh Office, 10 High Street, Omagh BT78 1BQ. Tel: 028 8224 4921.

Training & Employment Agency Strabane Office, 23 Upper Main Street, Strabane BT28 8AS. Tel: 028 7138 2332.

Eden Place Arts Centre, Rossville Street, Londonderry BT48 6LB. Tel: 028 7126 3418.

Fermanagh College of Further Education, Fairview, 1 Dublin Road, Enniskillen BT74 6AD. Tel: 028 6632 2431.

Limavady College of Further Education, Main Street, Limavady BT49 0EX. Tel: 028 7776 2334.

North West Institute of Further & Higher Education, Strand Road, Londonderry BT48 7BY. Tel: 028 7138 2317.

North West Institute of Further & Higher Education, Derry Road, Strabane BT82 8DX. Tel: 028 7139 2317.

Omagh College of Further Education, Mountjoy Road, Omagh BT79 7AH. Tel: 028 8224 5433.

University of Ulster, Magee Campus, Magee College, Northland Road, Londonderry BT48 7JL. Tel: 028 7137 1371.

Workers' Educational Association, 11b Clarendon Street, Londonderry BT48 7EP. Tel: 028 7136 9947.

Workers' Educational Association, 23 Market Street, Enniskillen BT74 7DS. Tel: 028 6665 5685.

Publishers' names and addresses

Careers and Occupational Information Centre (COIC)
PO Box 298A, Thames Ditton, Surrey KT7 0ZS
Tel: 020 8957 5030
Fax: 020 8957 5012
Website: www.dfee.gov.uk/cid/coic/coichome.htm
E-mail: coic@dataforce.co.uk

CSU
Prospects House, Booth Street East, Manchester M13 9EP
Tel: 0161 277 5271
Fax: 0161 277 5220

Central Bureau
10 Spring Gardens, London SE1A 2BN
Tel: 020 7389 4004
Fax: 020 7389 4426
Website: www.britcoun.org/cbeve/
E-mail: info@centralbureau.org.uk

Hobsons
The Client Services Department, Biblios Publishers' Distribution Services Ltd, Star Road, Partridge Green, West Sussex RH13 8LD
Tel: 01403 710851
Fax: 01403 711143
Website: www.hobsons.co.uk

How To Books Ltd
Customer Services Department, Plymbridge Distributors Ltd, Plymbridge House, Estover Road, Plymouth PL6 7PZ
Tel: 01752 202301
Fax: 01752 202331
Website: www.howtobooks.co.uk
E-mail: orders@plymbridge.com

Kogan Page Ltd
120 Pentonville Road, London N1 9JN
Tel: 020 7278 0433
Fax: 020 7837 6348
Website: www.kogan-page.co.uk
E-mail: kpinfo@kogan-page.co.uk

Lifetime Careers Publishing
7 Ascot Court, White Horse Business Park, Trowbridge BA14 0XA
Tel: 01225 716023
Fax: 01225 716025
Website: www.wiltshire.lifetime-careers.co.uk
E-mail: sales@wiltshire.lifetime-careers.co.uk

Trotman Publishing
2 The Green, Richmond, Surrey TW9 1PL
Tel: 0870 900 2665
Fax: 020 8486 1161
Website: www.trotmanpublishing.co.uk

Vacation Work Publications
9 Park End Street, Oxford OX1 1HJ
Tel: 01865 241978
Fax: 01865 790886
Website: www.vacationwork.co.uk
E-mail: david@vacationwork.co.uk

Index of organisations

Index of contents

D

E

F

W